Silence

DIARMAID MacCULLOCH

Silence

A Christian History

VIKING

VIKING
Published by the Penguin Group
Penguin Group (USA) Inc., 375 Hudson Street,
New York, New York 10014, USA

USA | Canada / UK | Ireland | Australia | New Zealand | India | South Africa | China
Penguin Books Ltd, Registered Offices: 80 Strand, London WC2R 0RL, England
For more information about the Penguin Group visit penguin.com
Copyright © Diarmaid MacCulloch, 2013

All rights reserved. No part of this book may be reproduced, scanned, or distributed in
any printed or electronic form without permission. Please do not participate in or
encourage piracy of copyrighted materials in violation of the author's rights. Purchase
only authorized editions.

First published in Great Britain by Allen Lane, an imprint of Penguin Books Ltd.

ISBN 9780670025565

Printed in the United States of America

1   3   5   7   9   10   8   6   4   2

For Sameer Patel

Contents

PART THREE

Silence through Three Reformations

PART FOUR

Reaching behind Noise in Christian History

Preface and Acknowledgements

I would like to thank the Trustees of the Gifford Lectures for their initial invitation to me in 2006 to give the lectures from which this book has sprung, and for their enthusiastic acceptance of my temerity in departing from their initial suggestion as to a topic for the lectures. Their hospitality in Edinburgh, one of my favourites among the world's great cities, home to my paternal family in my youth, was much appreciated, together with the hospitality of friends who enlivened my stay during the lectures, and stimulation from the audiences who enriched the sessions with their questions and comments. I am also very grateful to the Institute of Advanced Studies at the University of Edinburgh for generously giving me an Honorary Fellowship and a study for the duration of my visit, and to the Royal Society of Edinburgh for affording me the chance of a further evening in which to engage with those interested in talking further.

In previous books, I have relegated dates of births and deaths of people mentioned in the text to the index. Here I have felt it necessary to include them in the main text, since very frequently my narrative jumps around history at some speed, and it may be helpful for some to have a sense of where they are being taken chronologically. Similarly, as in my *History of Christianity*, I give readers a short cut at many points by referring them back to the pages in the book where they may find a fuller explanation of what is under discussion. I apologize to those for whom it interferes with the flow of the text. Some readers may object to my frequent footnoting of my own work. I was determined to keep this book at a readable length, unlike some among my previous oeuvre, the better to reflect the texture of the lectures from which it has sprung. Self-reference is a way of saving the detailed recapitulation of arguments I have already made elsewhere, and, perhaps more importantly, avoiding needless repetition of source citations. All biblical quotations are taken from the Ecumenical Edition Revised Standard Version of the Bible (New York, 1973), including the Apocrypha/Deuterocanonical books, unless otherwise stated. I use the Hebrew and Protestant numbering of the Psalms.

As usual, in creating a book from the lectures, I have much benefited from the warm support and encouragement of my indulgent and generous publisher Stuart Proffitt and my energizing literary agent Felicity Bryan. Both Stuart and Joy de Menil, my American editor, have immeasurably improved the text by their candid scrutiny and discriminating feel for what I should have said if I had but realized it, and once more, Sam Baddeley has also brought his sure instinct for language and his sub-editing skills to the book, to excellent effect. Professor Christopher Rowland performed a great service by his reading of the resulting text and providing friendly but searching criticism. Thanks go to a mighty host for sharing their knowledge and for their generous suggestions on reading and topics on which to reflect: principal among them are Sam Baddeley, Matthew Bemand-Qureshi, Kenneth Carveley, Anna Chrysostomides, Simon Cuff, Jane Dawson, James Dunn, Mark Edwards, Philip Endean SJ, Massimo Firpo, Derek Jay, Christopher Jones, Colum Kenny, Nick King SJ, Anik Laferrière, Philip Lindholm, Jolyon Mitchell, Maggie Ross, Chris Rowland, Elizabeth Koepping, Guy Stroumsa and Ronald Trueman. Dr Hudson Davis most generously made his doctoral dissertation available to me at short notice. To those friends and colleagues I will add one now alas dead: Robert Runcie, 102nd Archbishop of Canterbury. At a time when my feelings towards institutional Christianity were not very positive, he gave me an example of cheerful, practical spirituality, rueful self-knowledge and sheer *joie de vivre* which all leaders in the Church would do well to ponder. His friendship was one of the most important, enlightening and enjoyable that I have known.

The most important person to thank is Sameer, who had to put up with my selfish absorption in writing this book, and who provided tireless loving encouragement in my frequent moments of despair at the task.

Diarmaid MacCulloch
Octave of the Feast of Saint Enurchus, 2012

Introduction:
The Witness of Holmes's Dog

My favourite dog in detective fiction is the dog that did not bark in the night-time, thus affording Sherlock Holmes the vital clue for solving Sir Arthur Conan Doyle's little mystery 'Silver Blaze'. The dog who guarded the stable of the racehorse Silver Blaze did not bark, because '[o]bviously the midnight visitor was someone whom the dog knew well'; it was in fact the racehorse's trainer, intent on villainy.[1] I am also fond of another dog, probably a deliberate *hommage* to Holmes, created by G. K. Chesterton in his Father Brown story 'The Oracle of the Dog'. The supposed oracle in question was the anguished howl of a dog who had swum out to sea to retrieve a walking stick, apparently at the exact time that the murder had taken place. Father Brown cheerily debunked the illusion that the dog had supernatural knowledge: the dog howled because it was cheated of its natural presuppositions about the walking stick. The object was in reality a sword stick, the murder weapon, and so it had sunk beneath the waves and could not be retrieved as a dog would expect of a stick. And the illusion that the howl coincided with the time of death was in fact a human contrivance.

The two tales come to the same conclusion. Conan Doyle reminds us that often one of the most significant scraps of evidence to illuminate a particular historical question is what is *not* actually done or said. Chesterton's premise might seem the reverse of Holmes's, since what is important is what the dog did, not what it did not do, but it is really the same: as he spells it out, 'A dog is a devil of a ritualist. He is as particular about the precise routine of a game as a child about the precise repetition of a fairy-tale.'[2] Chesterton's insight is as much about human anthropology as canine psychology. Like dogs, we are pattern-making animals. The historian's main task is to dig down to find these patterns, to reconstruct the crystalline structures in the actions and the pronouncements of people and to explain their meaning, as far as fragile and pattern-making human beings are capable of doing so. Only when we know the patterns well can we point out what is missing; what should be there, but is not.

Silence, then, is a vital part of what is missing in history, a necessary tool to help us make sense of the written and visual evidence that we possess. The novelist Margaret Atwood has observed that 'two and two doesn't necessarily get you the truth. Two and two equals a voice outside the window ... The living bird is not its labelled bones.' Silence is a major part of that flesh in which the bones of positive historical evidence need clothing.[3] An example of a silence which has always fascinated me, from my first historical specialization in the sixteenth century, is the almost total absence of the Christian name Mark in late medieval and Tudor England, when the names of two of his fellow-Evangelists are common, and another, John, is overwhelmingly present. The one obvious exception which proves the rule, Anne Boleyn's unfortunate musician Mark Smeaton, might explain later Tudor silence by discrediting the name because he was executed for treasonous adultery with the queen, but does not account for what went before. This is one silence, apparently trivial, yet surely significant, for which so far I have found no good explanation. If we were to solve it, we might learn something new about the fifteenth and sixteenth centuries.

The dogs of Holmes and Father Brown also tell us why history is such a subversive discipline, and why all its enquiries have a potentially transforming effect on the present: comfortable expectations are disrupted when we realize that the dog is not an oracle, but just a dog. Chesterton drew a breezily theistic moral from his story, which appears to be one of the main sources of the commonly repeated but apocryphal remark attributed to him that when people stop believing in God, they don't believe in nothing, they believe in anything. His version in 'The Oracle of the Dog' was, 'It's the first effect of not believing in God that you lose your common sense and can't see things as they are.'[4] Whether or not we find Chesterton's homespun Thomism congenial, the method of Holmes and Father Brown is that of the critical historian, which naturally includes the historian of religion.

It embodies a call to refocus, to see things as they are. Both the dog's silence in the night-time, and the dog's howl of bewilderment, are the clues which we really need.

There is a very considerable literature now on silence in religion; what might make this book different? I approach the subject out of a life spent in teaching and researching history, but also spent in fruitful encounters with Christian Churches and Christian lives. Religious patterns are among the most traceable and universally occurring in the fabric of human societies, and they have been at the centre of my life's business. All through my historical career, I have been keenly aware of the importance of silence in human affairs, for a good biographical reason: from an early age, I was conscious of being gay, and that proved to be a great blessing for a young historian. In the Britain of half a century ago, gay teenagers were keenly aware of what could not be said; of when to be silent and of how to convey messages in other ways. In much of the rest of the world, depressingly, those skills are still necessary. I was lucky to be able to face up to this challenge early on, was able to live life as I wished, and have enjoyed life much more as a result, but this life-experience has left me alert to the ambiguities and multiple meanings of texts, and to the ambiguities and multiple meanings in the behaviour of people around me. I have become attuned to listening to silence and to finding within it the keys to understanding many situations, far beyond anything to do with sexuality. Particularly in the still half-hidden structures of gay sociability, there are all sorts of means of disclosure and concealment, ways of encoding meaning and subverting the mainstream assumptions of society. As a gay child and teenager, I also effortlessly developed the historian's other essential quality, a sense of distance: an observer status in the rituals constructed for a heterosexual society in a world which in reality was not quite like that. I did not need the jargon of post-modernism to teach me elementary survival strategies in this world of mirrors, just what Chesterton would have called common sense.

It will be apparent that the first sort of silence I encountered in my life was primarily an absence, exactly the sort of absence with which Doyle and Chesterton dealt: that of humans failing to make public or explicit the full range of patterns around which they were thinking and leading their lives. I shall be considering such absences of noise in

3

the later part of this book, and also what happens when silence ends; the recent history of sexuality has been one of the most dramatic examples of such phenomena. Inflexible pattern-makers get very angry when their patterns are under threat, or when others offer new patterns, or when it is pointed out that there are parts of the pattern missing; that is why so much conservative religion in the modern world seems so deeply and perpetually cross.

My own first experience thus predisposed me to deal with silence in religion primarily as evasion and wilful avoidance of truths. Yet experience has also taught me to recognize and enjoy the much more pleasing and edifying truth that silence may be positive as well as negative. Even at the most mundane level of human life, there are white lies, and there are things not said because it is kinder not to say them. But there is much more than that, and the book begins with different and arguably much more positive silences. The Christian faith is based on the assertion that there is more to an understanding of silence than simply the interaction of humans with humans, or even of the interaction of humans with societies or landscapes around them. Whether or not one accepts the assumptions of theism (belief in a God), it belittles and impoverishes human experience not to treat seriously the Christian assertion of divinity, and it is the duty of any historian of religion to explore the working out of faith in the past with appropriate sympathy and understanding. Some will see that silences lie at the centre of religious experience, and will wish to affirm that they have had a profound and unfolding effect on the history of Christianity.

As I explore those silences which may be more than mere absence, I am painfully aware that a Gifford Lecturer more than a hundred years ago, William James, magisterially pre-empted me in this, in delivering the first version of one of his most important and influential books, *Varieties of Religious Experience*.[5] It has been daunting, first in the Gifford Lectures and now in this book, to follow in the wake of a writer who bequeathed us one of the foundational attempts to describe the nature of mysticism. Parts One to Three of this book nevertheless trace the theme through nearly three millennia of monotheism up to the beginning of the eighteenth century, as silence dances through the history not merely of Christianity, but of the religious ideas that fed into its first flourishing in the life and death of Jesus.

For silences are by no means the exclusive property of the Christian faith. Judaism, one of Christianity's two matrices, began a lively conversation about silence. Some silences were imported into Judaism and Christian belief from elsewhere – a very great deal from the Greek culture which provides Christianity's other main parent, or perhaps from even further afield. Some may still be in the course of discovery. All these varied discussions of silence may have a problematic relationship to the discourse from which the Christian faith is constructed, in which one foundation strand, based on the Gospel of John, gives Jesus the Christ the name 'Word', or rather calls him by the Greek word which means so much more than simply 'word'. *Logos* is the whole act of speech, or the structured thought behind the speech, and from there its meanings spill outwards into conversation, narrative, musing, meaning, reason, report, rumour, even pretence.

How does silence relate to the Christ who is *Logos*? The series of Gifford Lectures from which this book sprang was of course an incarnation of that problem. No doubt many of those at my lectures savoured the incongruity of their lecturer talking for six hours about silence, but I thought that the Principal and University might feel that their money had been ill-spent if I simply stood there mute for the allotted time and collected my fee and travel-expenses. It is hardly a new problem: we have been arguing vociferously about how to talk about silence, from the first efforts of Christian theologians in the second century to create a distinctively Christian 'negative theology', through to Theodor Adorno's critique of Ludwig Wittgenstein's famous remark about what to do with that about which we cannot speak.[6] One of the aims of this book is to explore this 'negative theology'. It is a technical term of art for theologians, whose connotations are far from negative, unlike the pejorative sense of that word now commonly used in everyday conversation. Instead, 'negative theology' promises a fruitful road into divinity, based on a tradition stretching all the way back to Greek philosophy and some of the strands within the Hebrew Scriptures. We shall be meeting that tradition a great deal.

What follows can only be a sketch, or the starting of a number of hares. And it is in the nature of the starting of hares that the hares are thereby in grave danger of death. Any critical historian of Christianity is in the same peril. Arnaldo Momigliano (1908–87), a great historian of antiquity, who as one of his admiring students observed 'refused to distinguish between scholarship and life', commented with a mixture of ruefulness and zest about the specially combative nature of expounding the history of religion: 'Other historians can be satisfied with simply retelling the past. The chances that they will be challenged are few. The historian of the Church knows that at any point he will be challenged. The questions with which he deals are controversial. And the controversy is never one of pure dogma or of pure fact – the two are interrelated.'[7]

As my probing progresses, critics will observe that it becomes biased towards the history of the Western Church of the Latin Rite and its successors in Protestantism and post-Reformation Roman Catholicism. There is rich material in that history, but I am acutely aware that it is a distorted sample of Christian experience, and that more might be said about Orthodox Christianity as well as the non-Chalcedonian Churches which for several centuries seemed to be the future in Christian development. Previously I have done my best, both on the printed page and on camera, to introduce a perspective on the Christian past which gives a proper place to these Eastern stories. So I feel rueful about my omissions now, but I can do no more than point out the problem before someone else does. In particular, one distortion of a more balanced Christian history (particularly a history of Christian silence) is provided by the accident that the Western Latin Christian tradition has been in a position of worldly power for more of its history than any other branch of Christianity. Those who have a particular reverence for the Church in communion with the Holy See will no doubt feel that I have been unduly hard on it. If they do, my regrets are not very fulsome. As we know from many walks of life, the powerful often have a lot to hide, and they strive to regulate the right to silence.

Power is often sustained by distortions of truth or reality, particularly when power takes the form of claiming a monopoly on truth. It is hardly surprising, then, that Christianity's most lasting and powerful monarchy, the papacy, has gathered to itself more silences of shame and distortion of the truth than other sources of authority in the Christian tradition. Yet Protestants should not be complacent; in their days of power, they have had a good deal to answer for as well. The ending of many of Christianity's less than admirable silences is the result of the Western Churches' loss of inappropriate worldly power, as the long Constantinian era appears to have come to its end. The powerful are likewise inclined to monopolize noise: so, for instance, Churches in positions of power have announced their dominant presence by the ringing of bells, and when Churches have been deprived of power, as by the Ottomans or the Bolsheviks, the bells have been silenced.[8] We have had to strain very hard to listen to some of the voices of the powerless throughout the Christian story; and among the histories of the powerless, I number the last thousand years of non-Chalcedonian Christian history, about which, alas, I go on to say little. From the stories of power, Christianity may learn a lesson. Strident proclamation has many dangers, and silence has its own eloquence. Sometimes, as we shall see, the gap between them can be bridged by laughter.

I opened by recalling two stories from the classic age of murder mysteries, and will be pleased if the reader treats this book as a detective story. In the best traditions of that genre, it seeks to see a pattern behind apparent chaos: to draw together matters which at first sight seem completely unrelated to each other, still less directly relevant to a quest for silence. It leaves a trail of clues whose importance may not be immediately obvious, but which will, I hope, fall into place as we stand in the drawing room at the end of the tale, like Hercule Poirot, to look back on its tangles and draw out their meaning. In the early stages of the quest, particularly as we seek silence in the pages of the Bible, the picture may not seem wholly in focus; but I trust that the reader will enjoy the later reappearance of these early scenes: how Hannah's encounter with a priest at Shiloh fired imaginations more than two millennia later, or what lessons for modern Christians about silence can be drawn from another dialogue, between the ultimate antagonists, Christ and Satan, over forty days in the Wilderness.

It is also of the essence of the satisfying detective story that it is linear, moving forward as events happen. In some respects I have occasionally breached the conventions of the genre, pointing forward to some future recurrence or expansion of a particular theme, but one important observance of the rule may initially cause puzzlement: I give the collection of books which Christians know as the Old

Testament a name which most of them will not recognize, *Tanakh*. This word Tanakh is a symbolic acronym, apparently coined in medieval Judaism, and formed from the three initial Hebrew letters of the three category-names of books which traditional Jewish scholarship has regarded it as containing: Law, Prophets and Writings. It has the advantage of suggesting the variety of the contents of these books, but there is something more important for our purposes: it avoids imposing on an independent body of literature the theologically loaded later Christian title of 'Old Testament'. We need to appreciate its contents on its own terms, free of the meanings found in it by the sect of first-century Judaism which, in the light of the life and death of Jesus, became Christianity.

Readers who reach as far as my remarks on the contribution made by Paul of Tarsus to this story will note that the early Christian communities which he founded or encouraged were not the best settings in which to encounter silence. It is only fair to point out that in one of the most famous passages of his letters to his protégés at Corinth, Paul makes a statement which could be regarded as the wash behind the painting in this book. While writing to Christians at Corinth, Paul succinctly presents a polarity which exists in all religious expression: that between words and being – and conspicuously not that between words and action:

> If I speak in the tongues of men and of angels, but have not love, I am
> a noisy gong or a clanging cymbal. And if I have prophetic powers, and
> understand all mysteries and all knowledge, and if I have all faith, so as
> to remove mountains, but have not love, I am nothing. If I give away all
> I have, and if I deliver my body to be burned, but have not love, I gain
> nothing.[9]

In Christian terms, though (startlingly) with no overt Christian reference, Paul presents his Corinthian friends with the subject of their common faith: the condemned Christ. The Christ of Paul's faith is helpless in agony on the Cross, yet for Paul and for those who follow the Christian way, the crucified one is more powerful in his silent suffering than any power of this world or even of the next. In the pages which follow, we meet some of those who over twenty centuries have reached out towards the same vision.

PART ONE

The Bible

I

Silence in Christian Prehistory: The Tanakh

ISRAEL AND THE CELEBRATION OF NOISE

As we embark on our voyage through silence, we must necessarily begin with the Bible: not a book but a plurality of books, as its names in Greek, Latin and even Anglo-Saxon proclaim. The Greek *Biblia* is in the plural, and Latin and later scholarly Anglo-Saxons made direct borrowing from the classical Latin word for 'library' when they called the bound volume which we call a Bible first a *bibliotheca* and then a *biblioðece*. It is a pity that other languages and modern Western usage have forgotten this earlier realism of the Western Church about its canonical sacred literature. What it reminds us is that there are many voices to be heard within the Bible.

Within the library, the earliest books, or the earliest layers within them, speak to the later; layer by layer, a conversation expands and is enriched. Three centuries of Enlightenment have sought to excavate these layers, and we cannot ignore the results of this triumph of Western scholarly patience: that excavation is part of the task we must set ourselves now. But since first the Hebrew Scriptures and then the Christian were fenced in by the idea of a closed canon, we have another perspective to deal with: the view from any one particular age which saw the canon as a seamless web, as a ready-prepared package of texts containing a common, timeless voice, rather than a fairly random chronological assembly of book acquisitions. A reader of the Bible with such an outlook (and that includes most Christians throughout the two millennia of Christian history) seizes on the voices he or she encounters, without caring much as to when the various

texts and books entered the library. Such a Christian goes on to fashion out of the voices a new conversation to fit the times. We have no
right to sneer at this process or declare it inauthentic, because Christianity is always beginning such fresh discussions.[1]

In the title of my previous book, I expressed my conviction that one
cannot understand Christianity without investigating its thousand
years of prehistory; so the story of silence in Christianity is a matter
of not two but three thousand years.[2] Consequently I shall spend
much time on the Tanakh, the Hebrew Scriptures which Christians
have renamed the Old Testament. The Tanakh is itself a collection
whose boundaries took centuries to establish; some of the earliest
parts of it to be recognized as authoritative – the first five books (Genesis to Deuteronomy, known otherwise as the Pentateuch) – probably
took their present form in the fourth century BCE, while the same process was not complete for other books, such as the largely second-century
texts now collected under the name of the Book of Daniel, until the
first century BCE.[3] What becomes apparent from a careful reading of
this hugely varied corpus of texts is the surprising degree of reserve or
even hostility apparent throughout its books towards the cluster of
ideas around silence. Alexander Cruden, that grimly indefatigable
one-man biblical search-engine of the eighteenth century, already perceived this when he prefaced his collection of usages of the word
'silence' with the observation that among other things, it 'does not
only signify the ordinary silence, or refraining from speaking; but also
in the stile of the Hebrews . . . an entire ruin or destruction, for a total
subjection . . . for death and the grave'.[4]

Cruden could point to such passages as Jeremiah 8.14, which links
silence to doom and destruction for the people of Judah. His reading
Bible was the King James Bible (KJB), which uses the word 'silence'
where the Revised Standard Version makes other interpretations: 'Why
do we sit still? Gather together, let us go into the fortified cities and
perish [KJB 'let us be silent'] there; for the Lord our God has doomed
us to perish [KJB 'hath put us to silence'], and has given us poisoned
water to drink, because we have sinned against the Lord.'[5] One of the
darkest examples is from Amos, one of the first prophets to have left
us a substantial bundle of pronouncements, writing on the fate await-
ing the Northern Kingdom of Israel in the eighth century BCE: 'Then

the Lord said to me, "The end has come upon my people Israel; I will never again pass by them. The songs of the temple shall become wailings in that day," says the Lord God; "the dead bodies shall be many; in every place they shall be cast out in silence."[6] This is a picture of a massacre too horrific even for the noise of mourning. Yahweh in different mood can bring the same silence on the enemies of his people: Isaiah 15.1, more or less repeated in Jeremiah 48, describes how various prominent settlements in Moab are 'laid waste' (or 'brought to silence', as the KJB has it). In the sixth century BCE, Babylon is seen by the second prophet gathered in the Book of Isaiah ('deutero-Isaiah') as about to suffer the same fate: 'Sit in silence, and go into darkness, O daughter of the Chaldeans; for you shall no more be called the mistress of kingdoms.'[7]

Repeatedly, the Tanakh links the silence and darkness of defeat in war to the ultimate human defeat in death and the darkness of the grave. Psalm 31 urges Yahweh to 'let [the wicked] go dumbfounded to Sheol [i.e. the silent pit of death or underworld]', and it pursues the theme of silencing the wicked with the verb *'ālam*, 'to be put to silence' or 'to be made dumb': 'Let the lying lips be dumb'.[8] Around this idea of dumbness or mute defeat, the people of Yahweh created a cluster of pejorative meanings, some maliciously gleeful, some agonized and despairing. They perceived that dumbness frequently equated with powerlessness, and so neither friend nor foe would prosper if they were dumb. There was much fun to be had at the expense of the visual representations of other (false) gods in human shape; the people of Israel sang in Yahweh's temple, picturing such images, classically in Psalm 115: 'Their idols are silver and gold, the work of men's hands. They have mouths, but do not speak; eyes, but do not see ... Those who make them are like them; so are all who trust in them.'[9] The idols make no sense as objects of worship, because they lack even the senses which ordinary humans possess. Their worshippers might be regarded as less than fully human, because they wilfully turn away from the right use of their God-given faculties. A certain sort of Protestant Christian would find this a very congenial theme later, as we shall see (below, p. 130).

Like Psalm 31, Psalm 115 creates a close association between dumb idols and death and the grave; only a few verses after taunting the statues, it reminds the singer that the dead are no better than idols, for '[t]he dead do not praise the Lord, nor do any that go down into silence'. The immediate contrast is with the joy of the singers in the Temple: 'But we will bless the Lord from this time forth and for evermore. Praise the Lord!'[10] The first Isaiah paints an ecstatic picture of the coming of Yahweh into Jerusalem in glory, which will prompt his people to become the opposite of the useless idols of the heathen (and the opposite of the heathen themselves), for they will use all their human senses and faculties in the vocal and physical praise of the one true God. Then 'the eyes of the blind shall be opened, and the ears of the deaf unstopped; then shall the lame man leap like a hart, and the tongue of the dumb sing for joy.'[11] Israelites who rejected dumb idols in the form of men might be thought to have got beyond the idea that the gods had ears like human beings, and so would appreciate a physical sound for divine praises, but it was hard to escape the general assumption in the ancient world that worship had to be vocal. Yahweh still demanded praise that could be heard. Besides, there was a good moral case to be made for vocal prayer, in terms of the good of the whole community. For many in the ancient world, there was every reason to distrust those who indulged in silent prayer: what had they got to hide, and what undesirable outcomes were they seeking?[12]

Thus a prevailing theme in the Tanakh is the goodness of cultic noise properly directed. Israel's public worship of God, certainly in its greatest cult-centre the Jerusalem Temple, was generally extremely noisy. How could it be otherwise, when particularly at the height of the Temple's fame in the Herodian period, on the eve of its destruction, countless thousands converged on it for high festivals from all over the Middle East? In Psalm 30, an unusually personal song of passionate mood-swings, the singer pleads with Yahweh for help and rejoices when it comes. He even tries a spot of emotional blackmail on the Deity, suggesting that the singer's death will result in the end of Yahweh's praises on earth:

> . . . to the LORD I made supplication:
> 'What profit is there in my death,
>   if I go down to the Pit?
> Will the dust praise thee?
>   Will it tell of thy faithfulness?'[13]

If dumb idols were bad, and dumb worshippers were bad because they did not sing divine praises, how much more culpable were dumb prophets? The whole point of a prophet was to be a mouthpiece of Yahweh, carrying urgent messages for his people, as is clear in the Greek word *prophēteia*: the gift of interpreting the will of the gods. That meant that the prophet had to roar like a lion on behalf of God (Amos 1.2), or sound like a trumpet (Isa. 58.1), and the classic condemnation of those who did not is to be found in that same prophet (or group of prophets) who saw himself as a trumpeter, the third prophet in the Book of Isaiah: 'His watchmen are blind, they are all without knowledge; they are all dumb dogs, they cannot bark' (Isa. 56.10).

In certain circumstances, Yahweh would punish his people by depriving them of the tough love represented by the prophet's voice. Such was the fate of Ezekiel, when Yahweh made his tongue cleave to the roof of his mouth, apparently for seven and a half years (Ezek. 3.25–6). The text of the Book of Ezekiel is manifestly in a state of some corruption, which has often been used to explain the puzzling fact that it describes the prophet continuing to perform prophetic actions and deliver divine oracles to the people during his years of enforced dumbness. But corruption of the text is always a rather desperate last throw for biblical or literary commentators, and in this case it is probably an unnecessary suggestion. It is possible to interpret the text as saying that God suspends Ezekiel's ability to be a mediator or arbitrator ('to be to them an *'îš môkîaḥ*', Ezek. 3.26): no longer can he put the people's case to God, but that does not stop him delivering God's judgements to them. He has become a communicator in one direction only, whereas before he communicated both ways, and that situation lasts until the prophet hears the news of the final fall of Jerusalem (Ezek. 24.26 and 33.22).[14]

It may also be a surprise to modern eyes how little the books of the Tanakh align the meanings of words for 'peace' or 'rest' with the concept of silence. One of the most frequently quoted, and one of the most familiar today even to non-Hebrew speakers, is 'Shalom'. It is a word with many shades of meaning, implying completeness, wholeness or prosperity before meaning peace. Other cognate Hebrew words have the same implication of a state of general prosperity and quiet everyday activity. It is this happy condition of peace in other settled peoples which attracts the jealous and destructive attention of the Children of Israel as they establish themselves in the land which the Lord has given them: massacre and conquest follow.[15] The message of Deuteronomy is that it is only when Israel has reached its promised land, when it has come 'to the rest [*hammeanūḥâ*] and to the inheritance which the Lord your God gives you', that the proper cult of the Temple begins. Peace and rest are associated with busy, regulated activity, especially liturgical activity.[16] This is echoed with sustained sarcasm in a vision of the first Isaiah, who sees 'the whole earth . . . at rest and quiet; they break forth into singing', which marks the beginning of an extraordinary mock-triumphal procession to welcome the entrance of the defeated King of Babylon into Sheol, an exultant mirror-image of the triumphs of Yahweh.[17] In such circumstances, 'peace' is as far from silence as the innocent chorus of happy villagers in the opening number of a traditional pantomime, before the villain enters.

A GOD WHO SPEAKS

Above all, Yahweh himself is a communicator, who in normal and desirable circumstances expresses himself in noise, usually emphatic noise. His act of creation, described in two different ways in the Book of Genesis, is intimately linked with the idea of speech. This is less thoroughgoing in the earlier account (now placed second in Genesis), in which God only starts speaking when he has created a man. God's first words to the man are orders as to what he can and cannot do, but straight away he also involves his man in the act of creation through speech, bringing his beasts and birds to the man 'to see what he would call them'.[18] The later account of creation is now called the 'Priestly' account since it is a layer of the text associated with authors in the Jerusalem Temple; it now forms the opening passage of Genesis. Immediately it links speech to the divine work ('And God said, "Let there be light"'); in this, it is surely aware of some contemporary Egyptian accounts of creation, which also envisaged the use of words to bring the earth into being.[19]

From the moment that God moves to end the formlessness and void state of the earth, day by day over six days, he repeatedly commands form into existence by speech, following on from 'Let there be light'; and then, at his first creation of sentient life, he adds words of blessing to the words of command.[20] The Priestly account adds that at the culmination of its seven-day structure, 'on the seventh day God finished his work which he had done, and he rested on the seventh day from all his work which he had done'. This day of rest received his blessing, like all the other days of activity, so it was a vital part of the creative process rather than simply an end of it.[21] Later commentators on Genesis were to make a great deal more out of this thought, as we shall see.

After his work of creation, God remained a God of words and communications with his people: like rulers on earth, he was a judge, a pronouncer of commands and admonishments. There is a particularly vivid picture of this at the end of 1 Kings, where the prophet Micaiah ben Imlah discomfits King Ahab with his vision of God sitting enthroned in glory, 'and all the host of heaven standing beside him on his right hand and on his left . . . and one said one thing, and another said another': that is, the heavenly court was full of a babble of voices such as King Ahab would be familiar with at his own court.[22] The Tanakh boasts several similar pictures from the period of the Israelite monarchies: God sits enthroned, his courtiers being either the lesser gods or spirits or seraphim: the royal court is alive with noise both ceremonial and political.[23]

Not only does God frequently appear amid a great deal of cosmic noise – thunder or fire, for instance[24] – but the point of his appearance is invariably to convey some message to his people: he needs a voice. Sometimes an emissary bears the message, as one would expect of a great king, but in the earlier examples of these encounters there is remarkably little difference between emissary and Deity. The Book of Numbers, for instance, contains one of the Tanakh's most engaging anecdotes of dumbness overcome for the Lord's purposes in wondrous fashion: Balaam's ass indignantly answers back against her master's mistreatment, pointing out that there is an angel of the Lord with a drawn sword barring the way forward. The voice of the angel to Balaam then elides very easily into the words of Yahweh.[25]

The most famous apparent counter-example of what might be a theophany of quietness is in Elijah's vision of God: a key moment for Israelite history, when Elijah's experience echoes that of Moses on Mount Sinai. After gale, earthquake and fire, Elijah hears what the King James Bible calls 'a still small voice', behind which phrase lies a Hebrew 'voice of thin silence' or 'sound of a light whisper' (*qôl demāmâ dāqâ*).[26] Some modern commentators raise the alarming possibility that this famous phrase could originally have had an entirely contrary meaning, as 'thunderous or crushing and roaring sound', which would make the vision a logical progression of drama rather than a deliberate anticlimax in this appearance of God.[27] Yet even if we keep the traditional reading, which has so fired the imagination of readers over more than two millennia, at least as early as those who created the first Greek translations of the Hebrew text, God's 'light whisper' is still obstinately if quietly loquacious.

Conversely, throughout the Tanakh the silence of God provokes a chorus of protest, expostulation and anguished supplication, expressing not merely a sense that it is a just judgement, but on occasion that it is an inexplicable affliction of the innocent. This was nothing new; the same motif can be found in Mesopotamian texts long pre-dating those in the Tanakh, maybe as early as around 2000 BCE.[28] God's silence was to be associated with the nation's many disasters, and a reaction was embedded in the liturgy of the Temple in the Psalms: no fewer than twelve of the 150 Psalms employ the phrase 'hide the face' in relation to God, and it is generally part of a lament from God's worshippers, who cannot understand why they are thus deprived.[29] Psalm 22 is the most obvious, not least because Jesus felt it to have a very personal significance as he was struck down by the Roman and Jewish authorities: 'My God, my God, why hast thou forsaken me? . . . O my God, I cry by day, but thou dost not answer; and by night, but find no rest.' This is not a picture of what Christians would later call a hidden God, *Deus absconditus*: this is a God who (for reasons best known to himself) has apparently taken a grim policy decision to withdraw his presence from his people, in the manner of a great power closing down its embassy to a foreign nation on the eve of war. In several of the prophets, this silence has a much more specific explanation: it is the expression of God's angry judgement. The prophet Micah, speaking as the kingdom of Judah faced the dizzyingly more powerful Assyrian Empire in the late eighth century BCE, pitilessly spells it out after he has made a lurid comparison of the rulers of Jerusalem to cannibals: 'Then they will cry to the Lord, but he will not answer them; he will hide his face from them at that time, because they have made their deeds evil.'[30]

'BE STILL BEFORE THE LORD'

On the basis of this admittedly lightning tour of the Tanakh, I would argue that the majority view among its various writers is that silence is not often a quality to be sought, dwelt on in meditation or commended. Yet amid so many scriptural voices, that is not going to be the whole story. First, the noisy worship of the Temple was perfectly capable of being hospitable to silence. From the outset, descriptions of its threefold division between antechamber, sanctuary and Holy of Holies show how the crowds might be kept physically at bay from the most sacred place. So the Tanakh does contain traces of the positive use of silence in worship in the Temple. It would be only natural to find this as one aspect of the public reverence of God, since the same was true in everyday society. Subjects fell silent in the presence of their rulers, and even the powerful were attentive to someone recognized as having something worthwhile to say. Job in his affliction looked wistfully back to the days when he was ranked among the great and the good:

> When I prepared my seat in the square, the young men saw me and withdrew, and the aged rose and stood; the princes refrained from talking, and laid their hand on their mouth; the voice of the nobles was hushed, and their tongue cleaved to the roof of their mouth ... Men listened to me, and waited, and kept silence for my counsel. After I spoke they did not speak again, and my word dropped upon them.[31]

So the crowds in the Temple would have found it unsurprising that on occasion they were expected to conform to social expectations, and keep silence before Yahweh.

The creators of the Hebrew Scriptures could look back to plenty of precedent for the transference of this reverence from rulers to gods, in older Mesopotamian sources such as the Epic of Gilgamesh or the *Enūma Eliš*. It was natural for societies to attribute much more to the power of the deity, far greater than that of any human authority. This power might strike the observer dumb with fear, as it does in the Exodus story's song of Moses, which pictures the hostile peoples of the earth 'as still as a stone' with terror as Yahweh passes by with his people, safe across the Red Sea.[32] The priests of the Temple were capable of turning this visceral fear into a controlled silence through the liturgy. Psalm 37, a poem which has obvious overtones of the Tanakh's 'Wisdom' tradition, that class of sacred literature which became important for the Israelites in expounding the shape of an orderly and tidy society, exhorts the worshipper to 'be still before the Lord, and wait patiently for him'.[33] Habakkuk, a prophet probably writing not long before the Babylonians captured and destroyed Jerusalem at the end of the sixth century BCE, interestingly contrasts the well-worn Israelite theme of dumb idols and the noisy worship done to them with the silence which should do proper honour to Yahweh. Indeed, the silence should be observed, not just in Israel, but in the whole world. This is a tiny early example of the insight of later prophets, and later of Christians, that the God of Israel had a universal jurisdiction:

> What profit is an idol when its maker has shaped it, a metal image, a teacher of lies? For the workman trusts in his own creation when he makes dumb idols! Woe to him who says to a wooden thing, Awake; to a dumb stone, Arise! Can this give revelation? Behold, it is overlaid with gold and silver, and there is no breath at all in it. But the Lord is in his holy temple; let all the earth keep silence before him.[34]

Significant in this connection is the charming story at the beginning of 1 Samuel about his mother Hannah, so long in despair at her childlessness. Praying in tears to God in the shrine of Shiloh, she was observed by Eli the priest, who was not pleased at what he took to be her irreverence: 'Hannah was speaking in her heart; only her lips moved, and her voice was not heard; therefore Eli took her to be a drunken woman. And Eli said to her, "How long will you be drunken? Put away your wine from you." But Hannah answered, "No, my lord,

I am a woman sorely troubled; I have drunk neither wine nor strong drink, but I have been pouring out my soul before the Lord."' Eli, impressed, sent her away with a blessing and the hope that Yahweh would answer her prayers, which of course he did, giving her a child, and Israel one of its greatest prophets.[35]

The point here seems to be that silent prayer to the Lord was a controversial and debatable custom: it could well be considered unnatural, and the story may have arisen as a conscious effort to justify it – particularly in view of the fact that the priest who had made this mistake about Hannah's honest piety had not served the true Temple in Jerusalem, but the now-discredited shrine in Shiloh. This story eventually proved crucial in making respectable the practice of silent prayer in both Judaism and Christianity, but the struggle was to be long and hard, as we shall see (below, pp. 63–4).[36]

One psalm significantly develops this theme of worshipful silence to give it a correspondence in the cosmos to silent worship on earth: Psalm 19. Those familiar with the Christian choral repertoire will not realize how exceptional it is among the Psalms, because they will frequently have sung lustily the setting of its opening verses made by Franz Josef Haydn (1732–1809) for his oratorio *The Creation*: still the most popular section of that whole work. 'The Heavens are telling the Glory of God' is a rumbustious chorus, in which Haydn significantly stops short of setting the end of the extraordinary diminuendo which closes down the psalm's opening proclamation, merely providing a glimpse of it in an unaccompanied vocal quartet, before he returns to one of the most operatically jolly of all his finales. Haydn was clearly exercised by the psalm-text's turn to wordlessness in the praise and knowledge of God, so uncharacteristic of the Psalms in general, and needed to play it down at this point in his work. The passage is remarkable for the number of variants on the idea of speech which it crams into a short space:

> Day to day pours forth speech,
>   and night to night declares knowledge.
> There is no speech, nor are there words;
>   their voice is not heard;
> Yet their voice goes out through all the earth,
>   and their words to the end of the world.

This is a glimpse of a cosmic worship of Yahweh beyond human speech: another claim to universal jurisdiction. It was to fire the imaginations of later writers, who imported many other silences into the Tanakh's visions of creation, and it was a help in completing the sense of correspondence between human reverence and the reverence of all creation. Yet it should be noted that even this psalm in its closing words (v. 14) cannot resist balancing silent contemplation of the divine with the speech of human worshippers:

> Let the words of my mouth and the meditation of my heart
>> be acceptable in thy sight,
> O Lord, my rock and my redeemer.

THE SUFFERING SERVANT

Another voice from the Tanakh was in the long term equally transformative of the status of silence in that offshoot of Judaism which became Christianity. It is what might be termed a 'minority report' on silence, from the second prophet included in the Book of Isaiah ('deutero-Isaiah'), who was writing just after Cyrus King of Persia had allowed the Babylonian exiles to return to Jerusalem and rebuild the Temple.[37] In the midst of the pronouncements which have come to be known as the Songs of the Suffering Servant, deutero-Isaiah says of this man of peace: 'He was oppressed, and he was afflicted, yet he opened not his mouth; like a lamb that is led to the slaughter, and like a sheep that before its shearers is dumb.'[38] This text of Isaiah is very close to a description by the earlier prophet Jeremiah of his own sufferings: 'But I was like a gentle lamb led to the slaughter. I did not know it was against me they devised schemes.' The commentator Klaus Baltzer points out the one feature of Isaiah's song which is unprecedented: 'the only unusual thing about the Servant's behaviour is his silence.'[39]

Although Jeremiah had inspired deutero-Isaiah's passage and perhaps the whole Suffering Servant motif, it is the later prophet who has then added the thought about dumbness.[40] A near echo of it is the opening of one of the most remarkable and individual of the Psalms,

39, where the singer recalls a state of dumb distress before addressing prayer and praise to God: 'I said, "I will guard my ways, that I may not sin with my tongue; I will bridle my mouth, so long as the wicked are in my presence." I was dumb and silent, I held my peace to no avail; my distress grew worse, my heart became hot within me.' The singer then emphasizes that words have only come to him through God's mercy, and he rehearses his patient submission to God which is so reminiscent of that of the Servant: 'I am dumb, I do not open my mouth; for it is thou who hast done it.'[41]

When the singer of Psalm 39 does open his mouth, he speaks of the brevity of human life and how it fades into nothingness. His tone of resignation comes close to the wintry smile at human folly that we encounter in the book of that most disconcerting of teachers, Ecclesiastes or Qoheleth, where the theme of God's silence has become a criticism of the capacity of 'Wisdom' literature (the tradition in which Qoheleth stands) to say anything ultimately useful or meaningful about God. Christianity, not a religion to appreciate anticlimax, has never found it easy to deal with that fading-away from the busy sounds of human life and the chatter of human knowledge which emerges at the end of Qoheleth's text, with its bleak picture of humanity sinking into old age in a series of elegant metaphors for the failing of physical faculties: 'in the day when the keepers of the house tremble, and the strong men are bent, and the grinders cease because they are few, and those that look through the windows are dimmed, and the doors on the street are shut; when the sound of the grinding is low . . .' All that can follow is death – expressed in more metaphors: 'the silver cord is snapped, or the golden bowl is broken, or the pitcher is broken at the fountain, or the wheel broken at the cistern.' Then 'all is vanity . . . the end of the matter; all has been heard'.[42]

The second Isaiah, who was writing in much the same era as Qoheleth, after the return of exiles from Babylon to Israel, draws a different, more positive message from silence. The returned people of Israel were doing their best to restore the ravaged Temple, painfully recovering from the trauma of defeat, destruction and exile, and debating how this experience might relate to Yahweh's purposes. They found in the second prophet's poetry an image of silence which not only reflected their own terrible experience, but looked forward in hope and restoration. Over the next centuries, successive generations first applied this message to their continuing sufferings as a community; then some began to see the silent Suffering Servant as an individual, perhaps the anointed one or Messiah who would save Israel. That was to prove an image of crucial importance for Christian self-identity; and dumbness was to be a vital part of that, as we shall see (below, pp. 33–5).[43]

SILENCE, PLATO AND THE CREATOR-GOD

The role of silence in Jewish tradition steadily expanded, as the boundaries of what were to be considered particularly authoritative or 'canonical' sacred books gradually became fixed into the Tanakh, a process which, as we have observed, was probably completed in the first century BCE. Alongside that development, there built up, from the late third century BCE to the first century CE, another literature which was a conscious meditation on or enrichment of this canonical corpus. A great number of these texts survive, many of which take on the guise of much older figures found in the Tanakh, to emphasize their own authority as revealing God's purposes and message in new ways. Hence their group description as 'apocalyptic', from the Greek *apokalypto*, 'unveil' or 'reveal'. They have often been discussed by Christians under the loaded title of 'Inter-Testamental literature', works falling between what Christians call the Old and New Testaments – clearly not a term which has any meaning within the Jewish tradition.[44]

The background to this literature was not merely Judaism's continuing conversation with its own troubled past as pictured in the Tanakh, but a new dialogue with an outside culture, in this case Greek, mediated by Hellenistic monarchs who had been generals in Alexander the Great's armies, and their successors. Over a century, from the late fourth century BCE, these new rulers turned Alexander's vast but fleeting conquests into great empires in the Seleucid Middle East and Ptolemaic Egypt; they battled for control of the Jewish heartland on their common frontier. Some of the cultural conversation between Judaism and Hellenism became extremely violent, as when, in the second century BCE, the boastful Seleucid king Antiochos IV Epiphanes tried forcefully to impose Greek values on his Jewish subjects, and instead provoked a successful rebellion against Seleucid rule and the establishment of the Jewish Hasmonaean kingdom.

The lure of Greek philosophy and intellectual inquiry was nevertheless too strong for consistent intellectual resistance on the part of the Jews. Not only did the Alexandrian Jewish community feel it essential to translate the Hebrew Scriptures into Greek, the great translation known as the Septuagint, but Jewish intellectuals sifted through a mass of Greek terminology in order to make sense of their tradition in Hellenistic forms. Much of the process remains obscure, and the era on the eve of the birth of Jesus is particularly difficult to understand, despite various manuscript discoveries of the last hundred years. The problem is not confined to Judaism; as one historian of silence in the Greek philosophical tradition ruefully remarks, '[t]he last century before Christ conceals many mysteries from the intellectual historian.'[45]

Many of the apocalyptic books are far more hospitable than the Tanakh itself to a positive notion of silence. Within them, the contours of Jewish religion can be seen changing and diversifying, and new themes emerge. Judaism in the three centuries before the Common Era was extremely diverse, not least because it was becoming dispersed way beyond its homeland, out through the eastern Mediterranean and the Middle East. One significant new development amid the diversity can be perceived in Jewish sacred literature of the period: a view of God as much more withdrawn from his world than had once been common in Israelite thought. Perhaps this conclusion was natural, given the baffling nature of Yahweh's interaction with his people, constantly providing new disasters to endure and new tyrannies (such as that of Antiochos Epiphanes) for Israel to overcome. In any event, it was encouraged by Judaism's increasing dialogue with Greek culture, which culminated in the work of the great Jewish scholar Philo of Alexandria (20 BCE–50 CE), an older contemporary of Jesus. Plato (424/3–348/7 BCE) had influenced various strands of Greek thought to conceive of one supreme, and very remote, divine being, beyond and above the traditional Greek pantheon, and beyond being itself. Echoing through the mind of any Hellenistic Jew with a claim to education, let alone in the writings of Philo, would be some of Plato's classic observations: in the *Republic* he said that 'the good itself is not essence but still transcends essence in dignity and surpassing power', and in the *Timaeus*, that 'to discover the Maker and Father of this Universe were a task indeed; and having discovered Him, to declare Him unto all men were a thing impossible'.[46]

This last observation resonated with a central devotional concern of Israel's religion in the restored Temple of Jerusalem. It seems to have been in the period after the restoration in the late sixth century BCE that the sacred name Yahweh, represented in scriptural texts by its four Hebrew letters (*Yodh, He, Waw, He,* known as the *Tetragrammaton* in Greek), ceased to be pronounced in speech and became a written word only, alluded to in the spoken word through a great number of circumlocutions, not merely in Hebrew, but later also in the related Middle Eastern languages called Aramaic, and in Jewish use of Greek. The Temple was now commonly regarded as the dwelling-place not so much of God, but of his name; this idea can already be found in the books of the Tanakh composed before the fall of Jerusalem, in the period of so-called 'Deuteronomistic' reform promoted from the reign of King Josiah of Judah (649–609 BCE), which concentrated Jewish cultic practice on the Temple. Alexandrian Greeks in particular emphasized the distance which most Jews ought to feel from the pronunciation of the divine name. Its successor in the Septuagint was the Greek word *Kyrios*, 'Lord', used in an absolute way, not as a descriptor for some other divine name such as Zeus. As Philo meditated and commented on the Hebrew Scriptures, the God of Israel was for him, in Guy Stroumsa's words, 'almost nameless'.[47]

So for thoughtful Jews, particularly those living in a Hellenistic environment, God dwelt more constantly in the highest heaven, and it was more likely than in earlier centuries that his messengers, angels or spirits, would be employed to bring his commands to humanity, speaking in their own voices. Any human encounter with him on the part of the apocalyptic writers was liable to involve a journey through an increasingly complicated and multi-compartmentalized heavenly court. By the first century BCE, when the Hasmonaean monarchy was decaying, God's household was very commonly as much as sevenfold in structure, appropriate to the perception that his royal throne was even more remote than those of the Hellenistic pharaohs or Seleucids. Much later apocalyptic literature, in the era contemporary with the first Christians, dispensed with any possibility of human journeys into heaven. In a text probably composed about the time of the final fall of Jerusalem in 70 CE, 2 Esdras 8.21 is frank in its view of the remoteness of God, 'whose throne is beyond measure, and whose glory is beyond comprehension'.

Where once the silence of God had been a matter for misery and loud complaint, now it was seen as just the way things were.[48] For even if God were silent, he still disclosed himself to his creation. So did the 'ultimate God' proposed by Plato. Philo happily took up another frequent Greek usage in the Septuagint, *logos*, to conceive of a first-born *Logos*, a Word, Reason or Discourse who was the Beginning and the Name of God, and who was to be perceived throughout the Tanakh. This was the form in which God disclosed himself, and Philo could see it as uniting God's inherent sovereignty and goodness in a form which (significantly for Christians reading him) could be seen in terms of threeness: 'while God is indeed one, His highest and chiefest powers are two, even goodness and sovereignty. Through His goodness He begat all that is, through His sovereignty He rules what He has begotten. And in the midst between the two there is a third which unites them, Reason [*logos*], for it is through reason that God is both ruler and good.'[49]

Philo would not have been ignorant of Plato's discussion of 'the good', or how much *Logos* resembled the 'World-Soul' in Plato's *Timaeus*, the first intelligence created to suffuse the world and make it intelligible, 'sufficing unto itself as acquaintance and friend. And because of all this He generated it to be a blessed God.'[50] Yet for a Jew, a concentration on *Logos* also reflected the way in which the sacred name Yahweh was no longer pronounced in Jewish religious life (or if it was, only in the specially privileged setting of the Temple). This new emphasis on 'Word' was a fruitful theme taken up by Christians after Philo, particularly through the Evangelist John, just as they also seized on the word *Kyrios* to describe their Messiah, Jesus. Philo was setting a wider new direction in philosophy. For him, silence had as much to convey about the sacred as did speech; each had its own virtue. Reason might recognize that, in some circumstances where it would be possible to speak, that moment was nevertheless not appropriate.[51]

The two creation stories of Genesis 1–2 positively invited creative rethinking on the part of their readers, as Jewish commentators strove to draw out their contrasting messages and enrich their brevity. There was an understandable interest in the Priestly account of God resting on the seventh day, which the original story itself clearly intended as an aetiology of the Sabbath rest, and as an emphasis on the primeval holiness of this distinctive institution of the Jewish people. The implication of the account was, as we have seen, that the seventh day was more than a withdrawal: it continued in some sense the work of creation. Moreover, the keeping of the Sabbath on earth, which was an exclusive privilege of the Jews, mirrored its observance in heaven: so says the Jewish Book of Jubilees, probably written at the end of the third century BCE: 'all the angels of the presence and all the angels of holiness, these two great classes – he has commanded us to keep the sabbath with him in heaven and on earth . . . Them alone [the Jews] on earth did he allow to eat and drink and keep sabbath on it.'[52]

Silence had not appeared explicitly in either of the two original creation accounts, which contrariwise had so emphasized speech, but now the idea of silence in creation began to make its appearance in apocalyptic literature. Consider 2 Esdras 6.39, written two centuries or so after Jubilees, and not improbably contemporary with Philo's discussions of silence. It elaborates on the primeval darkness and formlessness (*tōhūwabōhū*) before creation to add a new element to the description: 'the Spirit was hovering, and darkness and silence embraced everything.' If one read the Priestly account of creation with this significant extension of its text in mind, then there was a pleasing correspondence in the act of creation: it began in formless silence as the Spirit hovered, but on the Sabbath, it ended in the restful silence of a world fully formed and structured, a silence which Psalm 19 might be said to describe, as the heavens told the glory of God without the aid of words or speech. Small wonder that such a satisfactory symmetry seized the imagination of both Jews and early Christians in the first century CE. There could be no greater symbol of holiness than the Sabbath: and so the concept of the holiness of silence, which had been such a minority voice in the Tanakh, was greatly reinforced in these later texts.

Out of this pairing of primeval and Sabbath silences, and their pairing in both earth and heaven, a potent idea was arising amid the flux of Jewish religious thought around the start of the Common Era. One passage in 2 Esdras describes the conversation between the prophet Ezra and God's angel.[53] The angel in this instance sounds very much as though it is the direct mouthpiece of God, and she or he turns to what will happen after the Messiah has come:

> After these years [my son *in some versions*] the Messiah shall die, and all who draw human breath. And the world shall be turned back to primeval silence for seven days, as it was at the first beginnings; so that no one shall be left. And after seven days the world, which is not yet awake, shall be roused, and that which is corruptible shall perish. And the earth shall give up those who are asleep in it, and the dust those who dwell silently in it; and the chambers shall give up the souls which have been committed to them. And the Most High shall be revealed upon the seat of judgment . . .

In this extended picture of the last things, the end of time is a recapitulation of creation: the universe returns to its original silence, but then in the end, after the seventh day of this revisiting of the first age, all silences come at last to an end. In this scheme, silence has become a period of transition on the way to God's final judgement. This passage in 2 Esdras is by no means the only text of this period to reveal a fascination with the return to primeval silence, as we shall see.[54] Some of these have remained apocryphal to all present-day religious traditions, but not all of them. Some proclaimed the fulfilment of this Messianic hope, and were destined to form a new canon alongside the Tanakh for a newly constructed universal religion. They will lead us on the adventure out of Judaism which took its name from the Messiah-figure portrayed in that text of 2 Esdras: the Christian faith.

2

The Earliest Christian Silences:
The New Testament

JESUS: ENDING SILENCE

A second canonical collection of Middle Eastern sacred writings, named by Christians the New Testament, comes freighted with many questions about its interpretation, the most urgent of which is its relation to the earlier canonical collection, the Tanakh. Christians have struggled to answer this question since their faith was born, and in the last three centuries, Western Christians have greatly complicated the problem. Enlightenment biblical criticism, an heroic intellectual and spiritual exercise initiated in Christian Europe in the seventeenth century, added two further questions: first, what use did Jesus himself make of the Hebrew Scriptures which shaped his world, knowing as he did the effects of at least two centuries of Greek translation and apocalyptic reflection beyond its canonical text? Second, can we distinguish within the New Testament between Jesus's own reflections and the meditations of the earliest Christian communities?

The sacred books of Judaism signified something new to the first Christians; in the light of the life and teaching of Jesus, Christian interpretation increasingly ricocheted away from the interpretations of the Tanakh which Jesus himself would have known. The poet John Hollander articulates the issue well from a Jewish-American perspective, making the distinction between 'the Hebrew Bible' with which he grew up and 'the strange and powerful tendentious reading of it called the Old Testament'.[1] Frank Kermode builds on Hollander's insight to sum up the first Christian views of their inheritance: '[a] whole literature, produced over many centuries and forming the basis of a highly developed religion and culture, is now said to have value only insofar as it complies with the fore-understanding of later interpreters.'[2]

One of the earliest Christian texts, Paul's Epistle to the Romans, spells out this new understanding of the ancient corpus very clearly. Paul glorifies the God 'who is able to strengthen you according to my gospel and the preaching of Jesus Christ, according to the revelation of the mystery which was kept secret [*sesigēmenou*] for long ages but is now disclosed and through the prophetic writings is made known to all nations, according to the command of the eternal God, to bring about the obedience of faith . . .'[3] That phrase 'was kept secret' here is literally 'having been kept silent'. Thus in Paul's eyes, the ending of secrecy or silence is at the heart of understanding the Gospel he proclaims; the message which he is preaching is the unveiling of truths which had previously been locked up in the Tanakh, hidden from its uninstructed readers. By the mid-second century, Christians were beginning to apply to the new writings the same words 'Scripture' and 'Bible' which they used for the Tanakh.[4] But that only reinforced their distinctive view of the Tanakh's purpose and destiny. The so-called 'Nicene' Creed, which reached its present form in the late fourth century and is still in regular liturgical use throughout the Christian world, speaks of Jesus's resurrection on the third day 'according to the Scriptures', by which it means the Old and not the New Testament.[5] Built into Christian understanding of the function of the New Testament, therefore, is the notion that it exists to put an end to a great silence.

The letters of the Apostle Paul are notable for their lack of concern with Jesus's biography, or even apparently with what he thought and said, so amid the very few Christian texts which we still possess from the first century, we need to move forward from Paul a few decades, to the last years of the first century CE, before we find any surviving quasi-biographical accounts. These are the four Gospels, a genre of literature with remarkably little precedent in either Judaic or Greek sources, the earliest of which, Mark, is especially strange and individual.[6] The Evangelists provide their individual syntheses of earlier traditions, in a systematic attempt to make theological sense of the short earthly life of Jesus and his even briefer public ministry. Luke and Matthew or their continuators add their own contrasting sets of traditions about his birth and infancy; in Luke's birth narratives, Paul's theme of an end to the Tanakh's silence is turned into a story. The central character could not be more resonant for the purpose, for he is a priest of the Jerusalem Temple, Zechariah, whose name just happens to be the same as that of one of the last prophets in the Tanakh.

Zechariah, by now an old man, is visited by the angel Gabriel, who tells him that his aged wife Elizabeth will bear a son. He expresses scepticism: the Christian reader is expected to draw the conclusion that this is the reaction one would expect of a priest of the old dispensation, and forthwith Zechariah is rewarded by being struck dumb. His silence continues until he consents to an unexpected and unprecedented name, John, for his newborn son: as the priest names the boy, 'immediately his mouth was opened and his tongue loosed, and he spoke, blessing God'.[7] By now, the angel Gabriel has performed a second task: announcing to Mary, the young woman betrothed to Joseph, that she will bear the Son of God. So the prelude to the birth of Jesus involves a classic expression of dumbness turned to praise and prophecy which would be familiar to any attentive Jewish reader of the Tanakh, but the theme is doing new work for a new dispensation as well as discrediting the old one. First, the story neatly ties the subsequent ministry of John the Baptist into a place subordinate to the ministry and life of Jesus; clearly a prominent concern of the first followers of Jesus was to make sure that people did not get that relationship the wrong way round. More importantly, the tale turns the work of prophecy in the Tanakh towards the nascent Christian community's view of what God intended his ancient prophets to do: proclaim Jesus as the Christ or Messiah, now finally arrived on earth. Origen, Christianity's first great biblical commentator, saw that point nearly two centuries later: in a homily devoted to this passage from Luke, he links Zechariah to the prophets of old, and says with satisfaction: 'for us Christ does not remain silent, but for the Jews he keeps silence to this day.'[8]

JESUS: EMBRACING SILENCE

Behind the narratives and editorial opinions of the Gospel writers lurks the first interpreter of Jesus's life, Jesus himself. We have to do our best to glimpse through the four evangelical spotlights what we can of Jesus's own adaptation of the Tanakh's spectrum of views on silence. The best place to begin looking for clues is at the end of his ministry. Embedded within the Gospels are accounts of Jesus's arrest, trial and death; these are among the earliest layers, probably products of community recital. Even though they are already patently stylized and overlaid with interpretation, what seems apparent in these confrontations with Jewish and Roman authority is that Jesus used silence in a deliberate, self-conscious way to convey certain messages about himself.[9]

All four Passion narratives echo to the Psalms of lament, which speak in distress about the silence of God, and which are now applied to the circumstances of Jesus's impending death on the Cross. It is Psalm 22's cry of dereliction, 'My God, my God, why hast thou forsaken me?', which Mark and Matthew record as the last words of Jesus. Luke substitutes 'Father, into thy hands I commit my spirit!', which may sound at first more like a statement of calm resignation, but informed readers will know is a quotation of Psalm 31, in which the note of urgent appeal to God to listen and to act is even more insistent than in Psalm 22.[10] Psalm 69 also sounds like a tocsin in the background of the crisis; its verse 'for my thirst they gave me vinegar to drink' has become an event in Jesus's ordeal on the Cross in all four Gospels.[11] What is noticeable is that these Psalms of lament are present in the Passion narratives of all four Gospels, John's Gospel included, even though John does not often share the exegetical concerns of the three 'Synoptic Gospels' Matthew, Mark and Luke. That is a good indicator that Jesus himself had reached out to these ancient scriptural resources before his followers went to work on his biography.[12]

All these uses of the Psalms represent one of the darkly negative aspects of silence stressed in the Tanakh, the silence of God – but what is striking about the story of the Passion is its turn to what I have previously called the Tanakh's 'minority report' on silence. In Jesus's trials, the three Synoptic Gospels repeatedly portray him as silent at key moments in his questioning by the authorities. The likelihood that this is a basic layer in the narrative is again increased by the fact that one of these moments of silence also occurs in John's Gospel, a passage without exact parallel in the Synoptics.[13] It is all the more striking that John should record Jesus as delaying an answer to Pontius Pilate's questioning, because John's portrait of Jesus lays very little stress on his silence. That is hardly surprising, since the theme of John's interpretation of Jesus throughout his Gospel from its majestic hymn-like opening is his identification with *logos*, word, discourse. The Jesus of John spends most of the Gospel discussing himself.[14]

Another story of the trial is also shared by all four Evangelists: the Apostle Peter's panic-stricken denial to bystanders that he knows Jesus. Luke's version has an individual feature: after Peter has three times denied that he knows the man on trial, not only does the cock crow, as it does in all four Gospels, but Luke adds that 'the Lord turned and looked at Peter'.[15] It is that look which sends the Apostle into the depths of bitter recollection and penitence. If this is an editorial insertion – and it certainly corresponds to a particular interest in Jesus's silence which is noticeable in Luke's Gospel – it is still a significant addition to the range of silences in the Christian story. It is one of the most eloquent quiet stares in human history.[16]

The references behind Jesus's repeated refusals to answer the representatives of worldly power are at least twofold: first, to that strangest and most personal of psalms, Psalm 39, where the singer is dumb before God and then speaks with him in meditation on the brevity of human life (above, pp. 22–3). Beyond that, the controlling image is the patient silence of the Suffering Servant in deutero-Isaiah's text at chapter 53: 'He was oppressed, and he was afflicted, yet he opened not his mouth; like a lamb that is led to the slaughter, and like a sheep that before its shearers is dumb.'[17] If Jesus himself appropriated the Tanakh in this way, his followers fully appreciated the significance of the identification he had made between himself and the Suffering Servant. The Acts of the Apostles uses a version of Isaiah 53 as the centrepiece in its exemplary story of how an exotic visitor was converted to Christ on the way to Jerusalem; the passage, Acts 8.30–35, is the first account in that book of such a conversion beyond the Jews and the Samaritans. The treasurer of the Ethiopian queen is reading the passage from Isaiah and looking for guidance on it at the moment of his encounter on the road with the deacon Philip. When Judaism regrouped after the destruction of Jerusalem in 70 CE, it redefined its identity more narrowly in reaction to the disaster of losing the Temple, and eventually also in reaction to the growth of Christianity. Jewish consciousness of this Christian use of the Isaiah passage on dumbness must explain why Isaiah 52–53.12 did not form part of the public liturgical readings from the Prophets known as the Haphtaroth, even though the passages immediately before and after it were among those used, and even though Isaiah forms about half of extant Jewish lectionaries down to the end of the medieval period.[18] It is small wonder that following the precedent of Jerome's biblical commentary, the Book of Isaiah has often been referred to as 'the fifth Gospel' for Christians; this passage is at the heart of that insight.

Let us now move backwards towards the accounts of Jesus's public ministry before his Passion. Christianity's spectacular later turn to ascetic, eremetical and monastic life has encouraged a search for precedents in the life of Jesus. One prime inspiration was to be his agonized solitary prayer in the Garden of Gethsemane just before his arrest – once more its 'bedrock' status in the Gospels is indicated by the fact that it is present in all four. It has to be said that the agony in the garden has to be read against the grain if it is to fulfil its task for asceticism. The fact that Jesus's ordeal was solitary is not presented in the Synoptic Gospels as something that he had sought: to various degrees they stress his reproach to his disciples for not praying alongside him. That is part of the interesting untidiness and unexpectedness of the story. It is undeniable that all four versions hinge on a Jesus who addresses God and gets no reply.[19] That presents strong echoes of the Crucifixion theme of the appeal to a silent God in Psalm 22, but the story also has a cross-current of reference to the silent Suffering Servant of Isaiah 53, which Jerome exploited in the fourth century in his commentary on Matthew's Gospel. Jerome did his best to explain away the indecorous emotion of Jesus's agony in the garden, but he nevertheless first pioneered the application of the resonant term 'Man of

Sorrows' (*vir dolorum*) from Isaiah, in order to apply it to Jesus in Gethsemane.[20]

From the beginning, it is clear that Jerome was not alone in his worries. The Christian communities who produced different versions of the story of Gethsemane in the Gospels found it difficult to make a satisfactory version of the narrative, and introduced their own variants in the description as they struggled with it. In all three Synoptic Gospels, Jesus seems to be showing doubt, fear and even an anxiety to avoid what he knew was coming. Nowhere else do the Gospels come so close to an attempt to describe the inner feelings of the Saviour. Christians were to find that their early polemical opponents – Celsus, Porphyry, Julian the Apostate – were very ready to seize on this picture which seemed so far from the heroism that might have been expected of divinity, and John's brief version of the episode, consistent with his portrait of an assured divine Christ-*Logos*, has Jesus specifically rejecting the idea of an appeal to the Father to 'save me from this hour'.[21] However much actual Christian martyrs might have found the contemplation of their Saviour's agony and sense of abandonment comforting, early martyrologies generally did not find it a very convenient theme for their portraits of stoic defiance.

Another motif of Jesus's ministry seems unlikely to have been invented: the various accounts of his retreat to mountains and wilderness places.[22] This has also been a major theme on which ascetics have fruitfully dwelt over the centuries, but the original thrust of it was rather different in the text of the four Gospels. Like the establishment of the Twelve as the inner ring of Jesus's disciples, it represented a major appropriation of the identity of Israel; Jesus was re-enacting Moses' ascent of Mount Sinai (Exod. 24.1–2, 12–18), or recapitulating that ascent by Elijah when he met God as a still small voice (1 Kings 19.12). The Evangelists much enriched this pre-existing theme of the remaking of Israel which Jesus had created for himself. Thus once Jesus has descended from the mountain, he begins to construct the new people of God to correspond to the old Israel; he gives his own new teaching in amplification of the Law of Moses in a 'Sermon' (which Matthew places on the Mount and Luke on the Plain), while Luke precedes his version of this discourse by using that moment of descent to portray the calling of the Twelve.[23]

The obvious passage on which ascetics could later seize was the story shared by the three Synoptic writers of Jesus's Temptation. It is very succinct in Mark, who simply presents the reader with four statements: the Spirit drove Jesus into the Wilderness; he was there forty days, tempted by Satan; he was with the wild beasts; and the angels ministered to him. Mark's story is so brief that he must have expected his hearers to be familiar with it: if it is rooted in a real event, and there is no good reason to suppose that it is not, then once more Jesus was identifying himself in re-enacting Israel's forty years led by Moses in the wilderness. Matthew and Luke much expand Mark's cryptic account. They interrupt Jesus's forty-day silence with dialogue – but it is an inner dialogue, for this is a verbal contest with Satan, presenting very specific threefold moral and theological temptations which the Son of Man must overcome.[24] Matthew and Luke depict Jesus stopping the dialogue becoming a conversation, by simply turning each of his replies to Satan into a quotation from the Tanakh which brooks no answer. Thus when Satan (in Matthew's version) suggests 'If you are the Son of God, command these stones to become loaves of bread', Jesus retorts: 'It is written, "Man shall not live by bread alone, but by every word that proceeds from the mouth of God".'[25] Satan wishes to chatter: Jesus deflects the attempt. This is 'a battle with thoughts'.[26] Fourth-century solitaries and contemplatives found it easy to recognize this in what they did themselves as they turned away from words external and internal, by killing such chatter with crisp scriptural quotation. We shall return to their practice later (below, Ch. 3).

THE GOSPELS INTERPRET JESUS

All these various strands of the Synoptic Gospels suggest that there is some reason cautiously to agree with F. W. Faber (1814–63) when he talked with orotund Victorian piety of the 'silence-loving Heart of our ever-blessed Saviour'.[27] Nevertheless, we are now moving from the effort to glimpse the core of what Jesus said and did towards the interpretations which the Gospel writers put on the stories they inherited. At the beginning of their presentation of Jesus's public ministry, they cast their gaze forward through the Temptations in the Wilderness towards the Crucifixion; they show their audience what the Chosen One is and what he is not, and they emphasize that when the powers of this world crucified the Lord, they were doing the work of the evil power which is in the cosmos. It is also clear that some interpretations by the Evangelists pull away from any theme of silence which Jesus might have expressed, as one or two examples will show.

First, it is worth taking care to see the implications of a verb which Matthew uses significantly frequently in his Gospel, and not just in his version of the Temptations in the Wilderness: 'withdraw', *anachōreo*. We need to avoid reading backwards from the fact that, three centuries or more later, this word was to be appropriated as a technical description for a new category of solitariness in the Christian life, an anchorite – one who withdraws from the world. During its travels towards that usage, the verb *anachōreo* had been used in the Classical world with a slightly different implication: for withdrawal from public life, or a personal meditative withdrawal into one's inner resources. During the growing oppressiveness of imperial taxation in the third century CE, it became a term for Egyptians who took advantage of the closeness of the desert to flee the taxman. That radical act of tax-dodging was undoubtedly connected to the development of Christian monasticism in Egypt (below, pp. 69–71), and it probably encouraged the reapplication of the word to that new phenomenon in Church life. And so the verb as used in Matthew's text became newly charged with meaning for those who had embarked on a monastic vocation, a meaning which, in terms of the Evangelist's use of it in the first century CE, was anachronistic. Such spiritual withdrawal is not the primary meaning in Matthew. The verb is used in a simpler way to suggest strategic withdrawal, *reculer pour mieux sauter*, as Mary and Joseph did in their flight first to Egypt and then Galilee to escape Herod and Archelaus (Matt. 2.14, 22), or, later, as Jesus did to begin new stages in his mission.[28] What is noticeable is that Matthew hardly connects his use of this verb with Jesus's solitariness; in particular, not with his Temptation.

A second theme worth exploring is a cluster of very individual features in Mark (the earliest of the three Synoptic Gospel writers), which were modified or dropped when Matthew and Luke came to adapt Mark's material. The Jesus of Mark repeatedly, but not apparently consistently, commands silence on his disciples and on those who witness or experience his miracles. His disciples, equally without apparent consistency, misunderstand who he is and the significance of his message, even though the chief disciples among them are the symbolic Twelve, chosen for Jesus's eschatological purposes to represent the twelve tribes of Israel. More than a century ago these problems in Mark's Gospel were crystallized by Wilhelm Wrede in the title of his book which analysed it: the *Messianic Secret*.[29] Mark's motif of secrecy here could not be an authentic part of Jesus's biography, because there is no historical logic to it; it must be a set of symbolic references addressed to Mark's readers, whom Mark was fully making privy to what the secret of the Son of God actually was. It is a characteristic of Mark's Gospel that he knows his audience so well that he can make them do some of the work themselves: for instance, he does not bother to explain to his audience the meaning of the arresting but at first sight mysterious phrase 'the abomination of desolation', merely remarking 'Let him that readeth understand.'[30]

How, then, might these well-informed readers understand a picture of disciples who have been chosen by the Messiah yet still fail to penetrate what is often plainly said to them? A veritable theological industry has been based on this question, yet for a reader with a historical turn of mind many of the answers offered seem to avoid the straightforward deduction that Mark's pejorative presentation must be polemical. Jesus's disciples are undeniably his disciples, but they are presented as failing miserably as Apostles in his lifetime. What could Mark's motive be for this unheroic presentation? We know about the tensions between on the one hand the first Church in Jerusalem, led by relatives of Jesus (including his brother), and on the other, the Churches in which Paul of Tarsus had become a prominent teacher. It has been one of the clichés of Western biblical criticism since the days of Ferdinand Christian Baur nearly two centuries ago to see this clash as lying behind the text of the New Testament. The power of clichés normally lies in the fact that they are true.

The Jerusalem Church, it is clear, remained much closer to its parent Judaism than those increasingly Gentile Churches. This latter grouping revered the ministry and then the memory of Paul, who suffered the handicap of never having met the Lord in his public ministry, unlike his contemporaries in the Jerusalem leadership; Paul was very self-conscious in asserting his own very different claim to authority as an Apostle of Jesus Christ within the developing Christian movement.[31] In Mark's Gospel, the narrative does not just belittle the first disciples. Mark 'calls attention to the fact that Jesus's family had no understanding of him and no little hostility towards him' and he makes little of the identification of Jesus as Son of David.[32] For this Evangelist, genealogy or immediate contact with the Lord are not strong criteria for authority: 'Who are my mother and my brothers? . . . Whoever does the will of God is my brother, and sister, and mother.'[33] Hence Mark's picture of the disciples of Christ in his ministry: although they are imperfect disciples and they misunderstand so much, including Jesus's command of silence, undeniably they are still the original disciples.

Mark's deployment of silence and secrecy appears to extend into that greatest Christian silence of all, the Resurrection, a mystery which might be described in more senses than one as the vanishing point of the classical Christian message – for it is the silence at the heart of Christian literature. Nowhere in the New Testament is there a description of the Resurrection: it was beyond the capacity or the intention of the writers to describe it, and all they offered their readers were descriptions of the effects of the Resurrection on believing humanity, or indeed (in the Book of Revelation) of its effects on the cosmos. The New Testament is thus a literature with a blank at its centre, whereof it cannot speak; yet this blank is also its obsessive focus.[34] The silence about the Resurrection is doubled in Mark's Gospel, which ends with an extraordinary syntactical suddenness in the words 'for they were afraid' – 'ephobounto gar'.[35] There is only one other known example of an ancient Greek text culminating in the word gar (and it dates from two centuries after Mark wrote), although there are other examples of sentences with such an ending, including amid the books of the Bible. The use is always emphatic and abrupt: the effect might be likened in English to ending 'for they were afraid, you see', with nothing to follow it.[36]

Mark has no appearance of Jesus after he has been laid in the grave, just an empty tomb and a group of women terrified by their encounter with an angel. And why are these women who had known Jesus intimately so astonished at a resurrection which he had already publicly predicted three times? A Gospel which opened with a ringing proclamation that it was the story of the Son of God ends with this bizarre anticlimax. Small wonder that the Gospel was early supplied with a conclusion, the present text of Mark 16.9–20, which was more satisfactory and upbeat but clearly secondary in date, and little surprise that many modern scholars have speculated that a leaf of a codex or the end of a scroll of the original text went missing very early.

Frank Kermode has provided a sensitive reading of this apparently botched ending of Mark which is open to the possibility that it represents a choice of art rather than artlessness. Mark, he suggests, intentionally ends with 'the least forceful word' he could possibly find and with what Kermode rightly calls a 'stupid silence'. As the women flee, ringing in their ears is the angel's command: 'go, tell his disciples and Peter that he is going before you to Galilee; there you will see him, as he told you.' Mark tells us that in their terror the women do not obey; they remain silent, and the disciples do not hear the good news of the Resurrection from them. But the readers of Mark's community know what the good news is; they can supply it for themselves. Fancifully, one might envisage a recital of Mark's Gospel to these first readers, in which the final declamation of '*ephobounto gar*' is followed by a little pause of shock, followed by wild cheering and applause. What Mark seeks to affirm to the Christians with whom he identifies is that the people best placed to hear the good news missed it, both the women acknowledged to have found the empty tomb and the first disciples. By contrast, his own community has heard and understood it.[37]

PAUL'S NOISY CHRISTIANS

We have necessarily started with the Gospels in our quest to understand the place of silence in the ministry of Jesus, because they are the first documents to reveal much about his life. The Gospels in their present form post-date the very first finished Christian writings, the corpus of authentic letters (or Epistles) of Paul of Tarsus. These letters date from the decades immediately after the death of Jesus, but they are remarkably uninformative about what he did during his public missions. The constant problem with understanding any aspect of the development of Christian communities in their first century and a half is the void left by the vanished sources: a different sort of Christian silence, which means that much of the noise from the beginnings of Christianity is lost for ever. The problem is not as great as the extraordinary shortage of documentary context which surrounds the Qur'an and the first years of Islam; nevertheless one scholarly calculation is that around 85 per cent of the texts which we positively know to have once existed in the first 150 years of Christianity's life are now lost, to say nothing of texts from that period of whose existence we have never heard.[38] This silence has been reinforced for the Christian Church by the formation of a 'canon' of Scripture – texts which could be agreed to embody the word of God – and equally by the subtraction of disfavoured texts. Especially before 100 CE, it is overwhelmingly to the contents of canonical literature to which we are forced to turn: and so after the Gospels, to Paul, and the glimpses of early Christian life that he affords us.

Immediately obvious in Paul's letters is a concern for community-building in exciting but difficult circumstances: to appropriate J. B. Phillips's neat title for his translation of the Pauline corpus, they are 'letters to young Churches'.[39] Reading what Paul has to say to them, we get a glimpse of communities which include a significant proportion of worshippers whose background was outside Judaism, although many of them had previous experience of or sympathy for synagogue worship as *theosebeis* ('God-fearers') before they joined the followers of Christ.[40] Their worship is noisy with songs and psalms, a mark of the high-temperature spirituality which marks their meetings.[41] They also have that propensity to quarrelsomeness and self-assertion which is never far from a roomful of enthusiasts, and they are prone to proclaim their new faith in ways which may divide rather than build up the congregation. These include what have been called since the nineteenth century 'glossolalia', proclamations in an unknown tongue.

In a warning in his first letter to the Corinthians, Paul has regard to all these realities. He returns to that favourite motif of the Tanakh, the dumbness of idols, but he combines it with a recurrent theme in his letters: unrestrained prophecy is dangerous for the Churches. Such utterance may be the voice of a spirit who is as deceptive as a voiceless idol, for not every form of spirit-possession comes from the true God:

'You know that when you were heathen, you were led astray to dumb idols, however you may have been moved. Therefore I want you to understand that no one speaking by the Spirit of God ever says "Jesus be cursed!" and no one can say "Jesus is Lord" except by the Holy Spirit.'[42] This is only one of a series of pronouncements which illustrate Paul's suspicion of the lack of regulation in prophecy, let alone in the gift of tongues. I have already drawn attention (above, p. 8) to his words in 1 Corinthians 13, where he solemnly reminds the congregation in Corinth that neither prophecy nor (even more surprisingly) good deeds have any value without love. 'Do not *despise* prophesying, but *test* everything', is his carefully balanced precept to the Christians of Thessalonika.[43] And with that in mind, in the course of a discussion which represents the most sustained picture which has survived of worship in Pauline Church communities, he gives the Corinthians some nuanced pastoral advice which he intends to be heard and observed even by those who might have some useful prophecy to proclaim through the medium of glossolalia:

> If any speak in a tongue, let there be only two or at most three, and each in turn; and let one interpret. But if there is no one to interpret, let each of them keep silence in church and speak to himself and to God. Let two or three prophets speak, and let the others weigh what is said. If a revelation is made to another sitting by, let the first be silent. For you can prophesy one by one, so that all may learn and all be encouraged; and the spirits of prophets are subject to prophets. For God is not a God of confusion but of peace.[44]

This is remarkable. In ancient Israel, none but the enemies of God, or on occasions God himself (as in the case of Ezekiel), had tried to silence true prophets. Now Paul makes his command to silence prophecy a necessary aspect of community harmony. It is particularly significant that it is immediately followed by a straight prohibition on half the congregation speaking at all: with exceptional emphasis, Paul insists that 'as in all the churches of the saints, the women should keep silence in the churches'. The forcefulness of his assertion is a sure sign that, in many congregations, the situation was precisely the contrary. Early copyists occasionally moved this fragment of categorical prohibition elsewhere, probably because they were baffled by the clear discrepancy that, earlier in the same Epistle, Paul allows women to pray or prophesy as long as their heads are covered, but the position of the blanket ban in the text after the general regulation of glossolalia seems a logical train of thought.[45] The contradiction with the earlier material may reflect the origins of 1 Corinthians as more than one Pauline letter; texts composed on different occasions in reference to different situations may have subsequently been stitched together.

Running through such calls for restraint in Paul's Epistles is a concern for the reputation of the infant Christian communities in the eyes of outsiders: that preoccupation is echoed by those who expressed their admiration for Paul by writing in his name, such as the writers of letters to Timothy and Titus. This theme is quite foreign to the Tanakh, whose authors sought no justification for God's chosen people in terms of esteem in the eyes of Gentiles; fear of Israel, perhaps, on occasion, but not esteem. By contrast with the ancient Israelites, Paul worries about the external effect of glossolalia, even though he makes no attempt to deny their validity. He manipulates a prophecy of Isaiah for a rather forced justification of his perception that those who encounter speaking in tongues without any understanding of what is going on will only ridicule the Gospel message: an insight which some might consider to have considerable modern resonance.[46] As he says bluntly after quoting Isaiah: 'If, therefore, the whole church assembles and all speak in tongues, and outsiders or unbelievers enter, will they not say that you are mad?'[47]

This is one instance of a more general self-consciousness in the first-century Christian communities that comes across in the Epistles and the Acts of the Apostles. By and large, whenever the New Testament talks of peace, it addresses that theme to the life of its tiny communities of believers, whereas the Tanakh associated the idea either with the fate of whole peoples and polities (above, pp. 15–16), or, at the other extreme, with the personal repose of an individual within the people of Israel. The New Testament authors in general do not envisage or aspire to their communities achieving the same degree of political worldly power as the Israel of David and Solomon: given their status as subjects of the Roman Empire, in which there were increasingly dangerous political tensions between Jews and the imperial authorities, they would have been suicidally crazy to do so, quite apart from the fact that they were confidently expecting the Last Days to arrive, and all questions of human power were soon to be irrelevant. The only writer among them to call Christ a king uninhibitedly and without qualification is that very idiosyncratic New Testament author John the Divine, in the Book of Revelation. Mostly, early Christians appear extremely anxious to shrug off Roman suspicions that their founder had been a dangerous revolutionary with kingly pretensions.[48]

One might in unsympathetic mood call Paul's preoccupations with controlling glossolalia and disciplining prophecy symptoms of a new Christian quest for respectability in the Roman Empire: a strategy strengthened in the sub-Pauline letters. For instance, 1 Timothy urges 'that supplications, prayers, intercessions and thanksgivings be made for all men, for kings and all who are in high positions, that we may lead a quiet and peaceable life, godly and respectful [more accurately translated, 'a peaceful life in godliness and dignity'] in every way'.[49] The author of a letter attributed to the Apostle Peter has a similar thought: 'Be subject for the Lord's sake to every human institution, whether it be to the emperor as supreme, or to governors as sent by him to punish those who do wrong and to praise those who do right. For it is God's will that by doing right you should put to silence the ignorance of foolish men.' A little further on the author comes to yet another exhortation to women to express outward and inner quietness: 'Let not yours be the outward adorning with braiding of hair, decoration of gold, and wearing of fine clothing, but let it be the hidden person of the heart with the imperishable jewel of a gentle and quiet spirit, which in God's sight is very precious.'[50]

What might a peaceful life be meant to look like? Paul earlier commented on it in a way which would leave little room for contemplation: 'But we exhort you, brethren ... to aspire to live quietly, to mind your own affairs, and to work with your hands, as we charged you.'[51] The writer of 2 Thessalonians (maybe Paul or maybe not) says bossily, 'We hear that some of you are living in idleness [or disorderliness], mere busybodies, not doing any work. Now such persons we command and exhort in the Lord Jesus Christ to do their work in quietness and to earn their own living. Brethren, do not be weary in well-doing.'[52] Being disorderly is equated here with not doing any work. Back in the Bethany that Jesus had known, Martha rather than Mary would have applauded this sentiment.

It is easier to warm to Paul's concern for the internal peace and harmony of his frequently strife-ridden communities; so he pleads with his Thessalonians, 'Be at peace among yourselves.'[53] His preoccupation was shared by contemporary Christians who in other ways took a very different theological line from him, and whose views are represented in the Epistle of James: 'the harvest of righteousness is sown in peace by those who make peace. What causes wars, and what causes fighting among you? Is it not your passions that are at war in your members?'[54] Paul enlarges on this theme when he lays out for the Galatians the contrast between despicable and praiseworthy behaviour: 'Now the works of the flesh are plain: fornication, impurity, licentiousness, idolatry, sorcery, enmity, strife, jealousy, anger, selfishness, dissension, party spirit, envy, drunkenness, carousing, and the like ... But the fruit of the Spirit is love, joy, peace, patience, kindness, goodness, faithfulness, gentleness, self-control; against such there is no law.'[55] It may be worth remarking that Paul's list of vices sounds a good deal noisier than his list of virtues. And his argument is beautifully expressed to the Philippians in an exhortation which swells into a triumphant prediction of what the reward will be for this community expecting the imminent end of all earthly troubles: 'Rejoice in the Lord always; again I will say, Rejoice. Let all men know your forbearance. The Lord is at hand. Have no anxiety about anything, but in everything by prayer and supplication with thanksgiving let your requests be made known to God. And the peace of God, which passes all understanding, will keep your hearts and your minds in Christ Jesus.'[56]

George Beasley-Murray's comment on this passage is arresting: 'the peace of God, like a soldier, stands sentinel over the heart.'[57] This is perhaps the nearest that Paul of Tarsus comes to associating the concept of peace with a cosmic condition, rather than with his constant concern for the outward and inward domestic calm of his communities. It calls to mind that text of 2 Esdras which we have already encountered, probably post-dating Paul by a few decades, which similarly refers with an awed sense of inadequacy to God himself, 'whose throne is beyond measure, and whose glory is beyond comprehension'.[58] But Paul, at least in his surviving writings, explicitly turns away from writing the sort of apocalyptic text with which he would have been perfectly familiar, and which he was certainly qualified to write. He points out to the Corinthians that he himself had been transported into the third heaven. That was exactly the sort of journey through a multi-chambered heaven which apocalypticists had been describing for at least a century before, but Paul abruptly tells his audience that it is not lawful to disclose such things. That remark would much excite later Christian commentators, though it was never completely to end Christian efforts to do what Paul would not. Dante and Cardinal Newman were two who did not follow Paul's example, though they were careful to cast the journeys as poetic fictions.[59]

'ABOUT HALF AN HOUR'

The New Testament's final writer, John the Divine, by contrast had no hesitation in writing an apocalypse. In exile on Patmos, John witnesses the Four Horsemen of the Apocalypse doing their worst; then the din of praise goes up, and the Lamb which is Christ opens a series of seals on the scroll. 'When the Lamb opened the seventh seal, there was silence in heaven' – but the sentence has not ended, as John adds, with engaging banality – 'for about half an hour'.[60] Not half an hour: about half an hour. That is a puzzling phrase. Through its imprecision, it is in danger of undercutting the solemnity of this pause in the procession of end-time events, and imprecision is never a desirable quality in allegory or typology. There is a refreshing honesty in Nigel Turner's contribution to *Peake's Commentary*: 'No satisfactory explanation of the length is possible.'[61] That assessment of John's sudden vagueness can hardly be bettered, but it does not excuse an effort to explain the place of the silence in his unfolding Revelation.

John's witness of silence forms only part of the tribulations of the Last Days, and it is in no sense a culmination of them. It shuts down the first of three sets of seven events. The breaking open of the seals and the silence are followed (with interruptions) by seven soundings of trumpets, and the pouring-out of seven bowls; each of these sets of seven betokens some fresh disaster before the end of all tribulations.[62]

The approximate half-hour of silence is the only silence we are told of, as the events of Revelation unfold. Otherwise John's account is a crescendo of noise in the classic style of a theophany in the Tanakh: first catastrophic, then triumphant. Once all the tribulations and judgements of the wicked are past, there is no hint that the final triumph of the enthroned Lamb in a heavenly Jerusalem is anything but a round of perpetual worship: a greater, more glorious and more permanent version of the earthly Temple, whose ruins were by then no more than a miserable spectacle in a devastated provincial city. So the importance of the silence is not overriding, and it is not the goal of the tribulations in John's vision. Nevertheless, the image would have had a rich cluster of overtones and echoes for readers living at a time when there was still no great chasm between Christianity and Judaism. Both were recovering from the trauma of Christian expulsion from the Temple and the Temple's subsequent destruction in 70 CE.

One strand in the skein may therefore be the product of reflection on the now-vanished round of worship in the Jerusalem Temple: much of the structure of chapters 1–8 of Revelation, of which this silence is the culmination, can be seen as following the sequence of the daily arrangement of animal sacrifice in Jerusalem. Moreover, it is tempting to link the half-hour's place in the vision to a tradition, preserved in the Talmud, that in the fifth heaven, angels sing praises by night, but are silent by day so that Israel's praises may be heard. Plausibility for this interpretation is provided by what happens next in Revelation 8: an angel stands at the altar with incense 'to mingle with the prayers of all the saints'.[63]

Another picture of silence is provided in the Wisdom of Solomon, an apocryphal text which may well be from the same time as John the Divine's revelation. It includes an extended meditation on Israel's tribulations in Egypt at the time of Moses. The Wisdom of Solomon makes silence the trigger for God's vengeance on the Egyptians in his destruction of their first-born: 'while gentle silence enveloped all things, and night in its swift course was now half gone, thy all-powerful word leaped from heaven, from the royal throne, into the midst of the land that was doomed.' We might snatch gratefully at this mention of half a night, parallel to the approximate half-hour in Revelation 8, and take pleasure in the symmetry that, in both accounts, this turning point is likewise only part-way through the clash between Israel and Egypt, between righteousness and unrighteousness.[64]

Yet the most compelling context for the silence after the opening of seven seals is to be found by returning to the theme which ended our journey through the Tanakh: meditation on primeval silence and on a cosmic seventh day which Judaism had crafted out of its meditation on the opening story of creation in Genesis. One strong hint for this is the self-identification of him who sits on the throne: 'I am the Alpha and the Omega, the beginning and the end.' (Rev. 21.6) We have seen how the consideration of 'beginning and end' had steadily expanded, through from the Book of Jubilees in the second century BCE to texts more or less contemporary with Revelation, such as 2 Esdras, the pseudonymous apocalypse known as 2 Baruch or the work which masquerades as the work of Philo of Alexandria, the *Biblical Antiquities*. In all these texts, the unformed world before creation was silent. This silence was then repeated in the silence of the Sabbath at the end of creation. So it is hardly a surprise that silence will come again at the end of time.[65]

Such was the belief to be found in texts which show no Christian consciousness. First-century Christians added their confident belief that their Lord was imminently to return in the Last Days: so Sabbath silence can be glimpsed in Christian literature which post-dates the Book of Revelation. It is now connected to the Word, *Logos*, which John the Evangelist saw in the beginning of all things. John in the opening hymn of his Gospel took the unprecedented step of identifying this Word with a human being, Jesus the Messiah, or Christ.[66] John's association of ideas can be heard echoed in the letter of Ignatios or Ignatius, Bishop in Antioch, writing to the Christians of Magnesia about the same time that John was writing. Ignatius's reference to silence is all the more significant because it is a quite casual reference in the course of a different train of argument about persecution: 'For the most godly prophets lived in accordance with Christ Jesus. This is why they were persecuted, being inspired as they were by his grace in order that those who are disobedient might be fully convinced that there is one God who revealed himself through Jesus Christ his Son, who is his Word that came forth from silence . . .'[67] When writing to the Christians of Ephesus, Ignatius amplified the same thought, portraying the entire life of Christ as wrapped by God in silence:

> the virginity of Mary and her giving birth were hidden from the ruler of this age, as was also the death of the Lord – three mysteries to be loudly proclaimed, yet which were accomplished in the silence of God. How, then, were they revealed to the ages? A star shone forth in heaven brighter than all the stars; its light was indescribable and its strangeness caused amazement.[68]

In fact, in playing on this theme, Ignatius was returning us and his first readers to the gleeful assertion made by Paul of Tarsus in Romans 16 (above, p. 51): that God long deliberately hid the truth about Jesus to be found in the text of the Tanakh. Now the real story concealed from generations of the Jewish people had been revealed to Christian congregations like those who received the letters of the Bishop in Antioch.

Ignatius, writing at the turn of the first and second centuries, represented the last Christian generation which still swam in the same sea of memory and literary reference as Judaism, a religion which was itself at that time being painfully reformulated by the circle of Johanan ben Zakkai in Jamnia. The branches of what were now becoming two distinct world faiths found themselves at a moment of decision, which forced them to craft new identities to meet fresh situations of defeated expectations and potential despair. The Temple was gone: its loss was a trauma common to both Jews and Christians. For Christians, there was worse, for the Lord Jesus had not returned in glory, as they had confidently expected. The resulting changes, as we are about to discover, are already perceptible in other aspects of the letters of Ignatius. In exploring the next millennium and more, we shall encounter attitudes to the silences of the sacred which became radically different from the records either of the ministry of Jesus Christ, or of the new religious communities which Paul of Tarsus had shaped in the first century.

PART TWO

The Triumph of Monastic Silence

3

Forming and Breaking a Church:
100–451 CE

IGNATIUS, BISHOPS AND THE GREAT DISAPPOINTMENT

Using the traditional Christian terminology of Old and New Testaments for Judaeo-Christian sacred Scripture, it is apparent that there is a chronological hiatus between them: a period which some conservative Christians are still fond of calling four hundred years of silence. Our previous scrutiny, dating the last parts of the Tanakh to the second century BCE and their final arrangement to a century later (above, pp. 24–9), has made clear not only that the period was actually a good deal shorter than four centuries, but also that it was not at all silent; it was cacophonous with surviving Jewish sacred literature. Moving forward beyond the last New Testament literature to be written, in the years around 100 CE, historians encounter a different hiatus, but one of equal significance: it is one of the earliest silences in Christian identity-building, indeed one so great as to be deafening. This is the period of the first Christian Great Disappointment, when around sixty or seventy years after the Lord Jesus's Crucifixion and Resurrection, it became obvious that he was not going to return imminently after all. We know very little about this crucial turning point in Christian development, because Christians say a great deal less in their sacred literature about disappointment than the Jews did in the Tanakh.[1]

Yet just as the books of the Tanakh reveal the process of creative responses to disappointment when they refocus prophecy, rethink the afterlife and steadily enrich their meditation on God's purposes, there is much to recover from the history of second-century Christianity.

It is a period in which Christian communities recovered from their trauma and reshaped themselves for new circumstances. We can gather enough fragments of evidence to show how radically different from the first-century Christian groups the later Christian Church came to look: it created a canon of Scripture, credal statements and an institutional clerical ministry for its community life. The closing of the canon involved the exclusion of much of the apocalyptic literature which had formed the matrix of Judaism in the time of Jesus and his first followers; but the process was slow, and Christians never quite forgot this body of texts, or the climate of thought that it had created.

In the middle of the first Great Disappointment around 100 comes the urgent voice of Ignatius, Bishop in Antioch. We met Bishop Ignatius in a moment of continuity with the pre-Christian past, still bathing in a sea of assumptions about the silence at the beginning and end of creation which were the common property of Jewish and Christian apocalyptic texts (above, p. 49). Ignatius was by no means the last Christian to warm to that theme: it is also to be found in the so-called *Protevangelium of James*, a romance around the birth of Jesus, which relates how Joseph looked up 'unto the pole of the heaven and saw it standing still, and the fowls of the heaven without motion', before Christ's birth ended this cosmic freeze-frame.[2] The *Protevangelium* probably slightly post-dates Ignatius, and unlike much of the Christian literature of its age, it avoided total condemnation by the later Church; in this, it was aided by the charms of its engaging supplement to the canonical biblical infancy narratives, and by a useful prompt to later orthodoxy in its precocious insistence that the Mother of the Lord had been ever-virgin. The silence of the cosmos, even when not accompanied by stationary fowls, continued to fascinate those meditating on Christian Scripture and its satellites for centuries to come.

As Ignatius looked forward eagerly to his own martyr's death at the hands of the Roman authorities, he struck more original notes in the precious cache of his letters which have survived. He not only linked the birth of Christ to cosmic silence, but reached below the cosmic and the Christological to the role of leaders like himself in guiding Church communities. In a letter to the Christians at Ephesus, he insisted:

the more anyone observes that the bishop is silent, the more one should fear him . . . It is better to be silent and be real than to talk and not be real. It is good to teach, if one does what one says. Now there is one teacher, who spoke and it happened; indeed, even the things that he has done in silence are worthy of the Father. The one who truly possesses the word of Jesus is also able to hear his silence, so that he may be perfect, so that he may act through what he says and be known through his silence.[3]

Ignatius elsewhere elaborated on this, completing a circle of reference to the bishop, to Jesus and the Church, in association with the first recorded Christian use of a word with a long future: 'Catholic'. 'Wherever the bishop appears, there let the congregation be; just as wherever Jesus Christ is, there is the whole [*katholikē*] Church.'[4]

Ignatius's praise for a leader who is silent may seem puzzling; it is one of the chief sources of scholarly argument about his letters. Henry Chadwick was right to argue that it reflects the bishop's view that God is characterized by silence; Ignatius was clearly sensitive to the Gospel theme of silence in Jesus's ministry and Passion (above, pp. 33–5).[5] Maybe he knew other texts lost to us, which made that motif even clearer. Yet there is more to Ignatius's bundle of thoughts than that. An urgent polemic fuels his arguments: the role of a bishop such as himself was not at all unanimously accepted among Christians of the eastern Mediterranean. Some in the congregations at Antioch, Ephesus and Philadelphia were not impressed with the charismatic authority of the leaders in their congregations called bishops; they looked to others, more like prophets, who were not so 'silent'.[6] We can recall the caution of Paul of Tarsus in writing to the congregation at Corinth: he sought to restrain charismatic enthusiasm, partly because of the offence that he felt that it might cause to outsiders (above, pp. 44–5). Paul's hesitations about charismatic phenomena had clearly broadened in the next generation, as a number of other straws in the wind suggest an increasing worry among local Church leaders about the rival authority claimed by wandering prophets. An extremely early manual of Church life and organization, the *Didachē*, lays down instructions for detecting false prophets who might turn up in a community. It reminds its readers that the local ministry should be given just as much honour as the mobile ministry: 'despise them not: for these are they which are honoured of you with the prophets and teachers.'[7]

A major clash between bishops and prophets broke out in rural Asia Minor a few decades after Ignatius's death. Prophets led by Montanus, many of them (horror of horrors) women, challenged the episcopal hierarchy and made claims to superior prophetic authority. The Montanists were in the course of time isolated, and so the bishops saw off one possible challenge to the growing episcopal structure of the Church.[8] Along with the Montanists there departed for the time being a Christian enthusiasm for prophecy, prophetic performance and the occasional contrasting deliberate enactment of dumbness. Characteristically it has re-emerged in Christian tradition whenever Christians want to challenge existing power structures.

It is interesting that once the Montanists had been excluded from the developing mainstream, no one took up Ignatius's peculiar linkage of silence and episcopal authority. It became dead theology, even though bishops and their adherents eagerly hearkened to his insistence that the bishop was the location of Catholicity in the Church. Perhaps bishops felt that an idea which had meant much to Ignatius had now become distinctly unhelpful to them. One probable reason was that it was too reminiscent of other Christians who were not Montanists, but whose claims to be authentically Christian were likewise soon rejected by Catholic bishops.[9] For now, many forms of Christianity were offering alternative paths away from the original setting of the Jesus cult in first-century Judaism.

GNOSTICS AND SILENCE

Judaism was a moving target in the time of Jesus. It was changing and diversifying, principally because for three centuries Jews had been caught up in a dialogue with Greek culture and thought. It would have been very surprising if the first Christians had not continued and broadened that conversation with the Greeks, as they struggled to interpret what they knew of their Messiah. In their efforts to make sense of the puzzle, they told themselves many more stories than those which crystallized into the Christian canon. At the end of the second century, another bishop who identified himself as 'Catholic', Irenaeus (d. 202), based in Lyon, far to the west in the Mediterranean, scornfully catalogued a miscellaneous heap of these efforts and labelled them as a single *gnōstikē hairesis* ('a choice to claim knowledge'), with adherents whom he called *gnōstikoi*.[10] In reality, as Irenaeus would have well known, there was never a single gnostic movement: just a variety of Christian choices about the adaptation of Greek ways of thought to a Jewish problem, which happened to be different from the choices eventually made by the nascent Catholic Church, whose development in the second century was consciously in reaction to these other possible Christian identities.

In the struggles between Catholic and gnostic Christianity, the opposing themes of silence and noise were the subject of a major tug of war. In favour of silence for Catholics was a twofold consideration: first, silence played a significant part in Jesus's own thinking about himself. Equally important was the fact that it had become a more prominent theme in Graeco-Roman philosophy and culture, without any prompting from Christians. Raoul Mortley, encapsulating the process in the title of his classic study *From Word to Silence*, has observed how in texts from the Hellenistic period (fourth to first centuries BCE), the word *sigē*, silence, is noticeably more frequently used than in the previous age of Classical Greek philosophy, and it is increasingly used systematically in reference to conceptions of God and divinity. Thus that one word exemplified Mortley's theme that '[t]he progress of Greek thought is from logos to *sige*'.[11] Greeks and those who thought like them increasingly found wanting the rationalism of *Logos* which had characterized the systematic thought of the great Classical Greek philosopher Aristotle (384–322 BCE), and explorations beyond *Logos* proliferated.

In early Greek philosophy, a preoccupation with the importance of silence had been a minority pastime, confined to admirers of Pythagoras: it was a corollary of the way that Pythagoreans placed the abstractions of geometry and numbers at the centre of their interpretation of reality. From the third century BCE, Plato's discussion of the 'One' and of 'Being' in his *Parmenides* increasingly seized the imagination of Hellenistic society and took centre stage in both philosophy and discussions of the sacred.[12] God was to be encountered beyond words, indeed by stripping divinity of layers of description or attribution of characteristics. The process has been called 'negative theology', a term which has frequently been treated as a Christian invention. On the contrary: negative theology was well established in the Hellenistic world before Christians gingerly came to consider whether it might help them in their perplexities. Philo of Alexandria, a Hellenized Jew deeply committed to exploring the meanings of *Logos* in relation to the God of Israel, had been wary of negative theology and any attempt to escape from the rationality of language, but many Christians, even those who cherished Philo's notion of *Logos* through its redeployment in John's Gospel, were much less inhibited.[13] None were more enthusiastic in grasping at these possibilities than those with knowledge: the *gnōstikoi*.

One should not look for consistency in the quiverful of gnostic texts which has been so expanded for us by twentieth-century archaeological finds. Rather, within them, we find an interplay between Judaism, the religion of the Hellenistic period and Christianity, which took many turns. Repeatedly, gnostics turned negative theology into stories, seeking to emphasize by their intricate genealogies and spiritual geographies the remoteness of the created world from ultimate being. In these progressions, silence commonly took precedence over noise. Irenaeus said as much in his angry descriptions of gnostic doctrine: he claimed that gnostics had actually made the personified figure of silence into a divine being, and various of the texts found in a library of Coptic gnostic texts at Nag Hammadi in 1945 bear him out.[14]

Works inspired by the gnostic leader Valentinus particularly take this direction: so the Nag Hammadi text now known as the *Tripartite Tractate* is concerned with describing the emanations of being from an unbegotten Father. The Father is characterized in terms of utter transcendence, in a classic form of the *via negativa*: he is without name, even though 'it is possible to utter these names for his glory and honor.'[15] Out of the monad that is the Father comes the Son 'who subsists in him, who is silent concerning him', while alongside him is the Church, which has existed from the beginning. So for this author, already at the first emanation away from the monad, there is division.

In the next emanation, the Totalities (*plērōma*) beyond the Son 'speak about him and see him', but the Father is 'ineffable and unnameable'.[16] It is only now that the *Logos* appears in the narrative, and *Logos* is described as a being with defects: although the good in him returns to the Father for forgiveness, the text mocks him for 'his self-exaltation and his expectation of comprehending the incomprehensible'. This is the same *Logos* whom the Evangelist John had seen in the Beginning, now firmly relegated by a Valentinian to an inferior place in the divine hierarchy below silence.[17] In a further Nag Hammadi text called *Allogenēs*, the first sound to emerge from silence is not the Word, but comic gibberish: 'the power appeared by means of an energy that is at rest and silent, although having uttered a sound thus: Zza Zza Zza.'[18]

As that passage might suggest, a contrary but very significant preoccupation within gnostic literature was with that greatest enemy of silence in human affairs: incongruity and laughter. The Tanakh contains plenty of laughter, which is consistent with its general attitude of reserve towards silence, but alongside the layers of the New Testament which suggest that Jesus deployed silence to deliberate effect there is also plenty to suggest that his ministry was full of irony and jokes. It would take a heart of stone not to laugh at the outcome of the Parable of the Labourers in the Vineyard; equally, one would have to be very dense not to relish the straight-faced advice to those worried about their status that their best strategy at a marriage feast is to make for the bottom end of the table, or to miss the savage irony of God's retorts to the Rich Man in torment begging that Lazarus should bring him a cup of water. There may also be rather more delicate irony at work in that prime focus of contention among biblical scholars, the meaning of Jesus's use of the phrase 'Son of Man'.[19]

To all this, gnostic writers added their own emphasis that one of the characteristics of Jesus Christ was his divine laughter in heaven. This was a major feature of their polemic against Catholic Christians, who, in gnostic eyes, had missed the point of both Christ's life and death. Catholics associated Christ with a false God, and had taken a naively literal view of his life on earth, rather than understanding that it only seemed real: in modern technical jargon, Christ's life was 'docetic', from the Greek *dokeō*, meaning 'I seem'. The point is forcefully made in the Nag Hammadi text entitled *The Second Treatise of the Great Seth*, a tract which assumes the voice of Jesus, whom it identifies with Adam and Eve's third son, Seth. Jesus/Seth ridicules the Cosmocrator God's claim 'I am God and there is no other beside me', saying 'I laughed joyfully when I examined his empty glory . . . And the entire host of his angels who had seen Adam and his dwelling were laughing at his smallness.'[20] The laughter of the Saviour is particularly concentrated on those who read the Passion narratives as Catholic Christians do, for they have missed the great divine joke that it was Simon of Cyrene who actually died: 'It was another upon whom they placed the crown of thorns. But I was rejoicing in the height over all the wealth of the archons and the offspring of their error, of their empty glory. And I was laughing at their ignorance.'[21]

Once more, Irenaeus of Lyon is vindicated, at least in terms of the accuracy of information amid his denunciations of gnosticism: he attributed a similar story of laughter and deception to the gnostic Basilides, and now the Nag Hammadi finds bear him out, both the *Second Treatise* and other texts such as *The Apocalypse of Peter* or the *Hypostasis of the Archons*. The gnostic laughing Christ may not be so far from early Christian mainstream thought as might at first seem, for it could have been part of a train of thought derived from perfectly mainstream Scripture. Rather as the events of the canonical Passion narratives echo passages of the Tanakh, so this cluster of references to the laughing docetic Christ refers back to such texts as Psalm 2.4, 'He who sits in the heavens laughs; the Lord has them in derision.'[22] Moreover, Christians of all beliefs brooding on the Passion of Christ would naturally cast their minds back to the story in Genesis where God orders Abraham to sacrifice his son Isaac. Isaac's very name, according to the commentaries of Philo, Clement of Alexandria and Origen alike, meant 'laughter', in reference to the fact that he had cheated death at the moment that his father prepared to kill him. Isaac had escaped the sacrifice ordered by God: was it so unreasonable to suppose that Jesus had done the same, and then also to celebrate the fact?[23]

That was of course the danger of gnosticism for Catholic Christianity. Far from being remote from each other, the two phenomena were closely intertwined, as both were also with the rival identities of

Judaism and Hellenistic culture. When making choices as to where to draw the boundaries around the Catholic faith, Catholics decided that laughter had been decisively tainted by the fact that it had been so popular among the gnostics. Christians of all varieties would henceforth generally treat laughter with extreme suspicion, particularly anywhere near the liturgy, but with a far wider reference than that. One Syrian word for a monk is *abila*, 'mourner'. One of several Christian spiritual writers who sought to borrow respectability for their works by placing them under the name of the much-honoured fourth-century Syrian ascetic Ephrem insisted that Jesus had cried, but had never laughed; so 'laughter is the beginning of the destruction of the soul'.[24] Umberto Eco's instinct was sound in making a Spanish monk's deliberate destruction of Aristotle's book on comedy the culmination of his great medieval detective mystery *The Name of the Rose*.[25] It has to be said that the one major modern Christian experiment in restoring spontaneous laughter to the centre of communal worship, the so-called 'Toronto Blessing' of the 1980s, has not (at least not yet) produced the dramatic evangelistic results which its early participants confidently expected.[26]

CATHOLIC CHRISTIANITY, SILENCE AND THE PHILOSOPHERS

In contrast to mainstream Christianity's rejection of laughter, by the second century CE the vocabulary and practice of silence were so all-pervasive in the Hellenistic world that it was only natural they should remain strong in Catholic as well as gnostic Christianity. After all, more and more articulate Christians had moved into the social groups which would have received a decent Classical education, and they were living through a major flowering of Greek literature and a new self-confidence in its past achievement, known now as the Second Sophistic. Justin Martyr, writing in the middle of this century, was the first surviving Christian theologian to invest heavily in the proposition that Hellenistic wisdom and Christianity were perfectly capable of being harmonized. Part of this innovative acceptance of Hellenism was Justin's ready deployment of arguments which amounted to a negative theology: God is only to be described in terms of what he is not. When Justin comes to argue with his straw-man Jewish opponent Trypho about how to interpret Moses' conversation with God in the burning bush (Exod. 3.4), his argument hinges on the idea of a hierarchy of beings, in which God the Father is at the summit, the most remote being of all. And to God 'there is no name given'.[27] Any gnostic Christian would find Justin's arguments on this familiar; they amount to the routine language of religious Platonism in that era. Moreover, it may be significant that one of the stages that Justin describes in his spiritual journey towards Christianity is a dalliance with the philosophy of the Pythagoreans, pioneers of such views long before Plato had toyed with them.[28]

An increasingly Hellenistic style of Christianity flourished in step with a growing interest in silence and contemplation which characterized the general religious culture of the Mediterranean. In the generation that succeeded Justin at the end of the second century CE, Clement of Alexandria, who loved in a teasing fashion to call himself a 'true gnostic', was even more regularly insistent on the transcendence of a God whose devotees must worship him in silent wonder. Clement is one of the first Christian theologians to speak habitually of contemplation of the divine beyond language, where, with 'the mind pure', 'we speak in silence'.[29] The problem for Clement, as for all Christians in all ages, was that Jesus himself seemed inconveniently to have privileged spoken prayer, by specifying a form of words which the Evangelists Matthew and Luke had recorded as a model for Christian communities. Clement also made full use of the triumphalist Christian exegesis of the story of John the Baptist's father Zechariah (above, p. 62): Zechariah's return to speech from temporary dumbness, he said, symbolized the way in which the Incarnation of Christ ended the age of ignorance. Clement was not a theologian to worry overmuch about solving apparent contradictions. Convinced that mystery is a necessary veil over the totality of Christian teaching, he said imperturbably: 'the word conceals much.' In suggesting that language is an activity of theology up to the level of the Son but not beyond that, Clement the 'true gnostic' is remarkably close to the propositions behind the mythology presented in the Nag Hammadi *Tripartite Tractate*.[30]

Clement's divided loyalty between words and silence reflects the instability of Christianity's dual parentage in Judaism and Hellenism: Christianity is a religion of historical events, first those of the Tanakh and then of the life of Christ, but it is trying constantly to marry that picture of divinity in historic time with ideas of a transcendent God which trace their ancestry back to Plato. This dilemma was reflected in the everyday life and experience of the second- and third-century Church. Here the evidence suggests that silence played a lesser part than it did in the writings of Hellenized Christian thinkers. First, there was the character of community worship, as it appears in surviving texts going back to Paul's Epistles; it was noisy. Just as in ancient Judaism, and in ancient religion generally (above, p. 14), Christians had to get over a very considerable social prejudice against silent prayer. We can tell this by the often convoluted ways in which a series of Christian theologians try to defend the practice of praying silently: they are arguing against a consensus. After Clement of Alexandria's efforts at justifying it, the North African Tertullian (c. 160–c. 225) took up the challenge, as would his fellow North African, Cyprian, Bishop of Carthage (d. 258), but it is noticeable that Tertullian's first citation justifying silent prayer was drawn not from the Bible, but from wider Classical belief. He quoted an oracle of Apollo as saying that the god understands muteness and hears those who do not speak, before making a slightly desperate further throw: the God of Israel hearkened to the prayer of the prophet Jonah trapped in the belly of the whale.[31]

Bishop Cyprian was more consistent than Tertullian in providing an exclusively scripturally based defence of silent prayer. He hit on the story of Hannah praying wordlessly and tearfully in 1 Samuel 1, which, as we have seen (above, pp. 20–21), had indeed almost certainly been intended by its composers to defend that practice. He went on to annex the Lord's statement in Matthew's Gospel (Matt. 6.6.) that 'your Father knows what you need before you ask him'. This was a slightly more strained effort at justification, since Jesus's observation was the immediate prelude to teaching the disciples the Lord's Prayer. By the fourth century, the weight of opinion on silent prayer was changing, not least because respected Neoplatonist philosophers had become eloquent advocates of the practice, but also because of the phenomenal growth of monasticism. So in the mid-fourth century Cyril, Bishop of Jerusalem, sought to use Hannah's story in an effort to prevent women from praying aloud in church at all: this was now an aggressive rather than a defensive exegesis, a sure sign that many women were not complying with the new expectations. Yet still when the Emperor Justinian tried to codify law for the Church in the sixth century, he forbade liturgical prayers in the administration of the sacraments to be uttered silently. In the Emperor's command we may be hearing an echo of that ancient suspicion that anyone who has to say prayers in silence must have a bad reason for doing so – no doubt he feared the magical abuse of sacramental power, which might have dire consequences even for an emperor.[32]

MARTYRS AND CONFESSORS

Alongside the regular worship of the Catholic Church as it developed through the second and third centuries, another major movement in ecclesiastical life forcefully pulled Catholic Christianity away from silence: the cult of the martyrs. In the quarter-millennium before the Mediterranean Church found itself in alliance with the imperial government, it faced bouts of persecution from the authorities, the most vicious of which occurred in the decade before the Emperor Constantine made his quixotic decision to ally with the Christian bishops in the 310s. As a result, the Church celebrated a considerable series of martyrs, Christians of all ages and status who had stood defiant against the enemies of Christ even as far as death, just as the Maccabean martyrs had laid down their lives for their Jewish faith two hundred years before Jesus's own Passion. Death was usually inflicted to general public approval, and with all the public ferocity that Roman power could manage against dissidents. Martyrs and their admirers came to see themselves as the quintessential Christians, a model for others. After the Constantinian alliance the cult of these martyrs rapidly expanded, with profound effects on the public practice of Catholic Christianity.[33]

Martyrs were laying down their life for their Lord Jesus, but as a rule they did not exactly imitate Jesus in his death; that would have been blasphemy. Rather they were imitating the first Christian martyr, Stephen, even though his public death by stoning had actually been at the hands of the Jewish authorities rather than the Romans; it is described in the Acts of the Apostles (6.8–7.60). What one immediately notices in this exemplary story is that, although it is patently given shape by Jesus's Passion (and indeed may have in return shaped Luke's Passion narrative), Stephen shows no hint of the reticence which Jesus displayed in his trials: the account is primarily of Stephen's setpiece speech expounding a highly uncomplimentary view of Jewish history, plus his description of his vision of Jesus in heaven. That, of course, is the point of the martyr: she or he is a witness, as the Greek word *martyreo*, 'I bear witness', indicates: and what witnesses do is talk.[34] The same was true of those who did not achieve martyrdom during the persecutions, but who had nevertheless not fled arrest and had consequently suffered for their faith. Borrowing the Roman technical legal term for someone who pleads guilty in court, these steadfast Christians were termed 'confessors'. The accounts of the martyrs and confessors are called their 'Acts' (a significant choice of description in itself), and these centre on spirited dialogues with persecutors, who after 70 CE were the Roman authorities.

It is significant that some gnostic Christians strongly disapproved of this reaction to persecution. The gnostics' contempt for the body did not spur them on to sacrifice it in martyrdom; instead they clearly did not think the flesh worth sacrificing. Not only is there a complete absence of surviving stories of gnostic martyrs, but gnostics on occasion opposed martyrdom as a regrettable self-indulgence, and declared themselves furious that some Christian leaders encouraged the naive to embrace it (not altogether fairly: some bishops did try to limit the enthusiasm of the faithful for martyrdom, particularly when would-be martyrs and confessors came to claim their own authority as rivals to episcopal power[35]). Another gnostic text from Nag Hammadi, *The Testimony of Truth*, sneers at '[t]he foolish, thinking in their heart that if they confess, "We are Christians", in word only but not with power, while giving themselves over to ignorance, to a human death', they will achieve salvation as a result. *The Apocalypse of Peter*, also recovered from Nag Hammadi, says that bishops and deacons who send little ones to their death will be punished. And the recently rediscovered *Gospel of Judas,* which probably assumed Judas's name precisely to shock and infuriate followers of the bishops, condemns the apostles because they have led the Christian crowds astray to be sacrifices upon an altar.[36] It is no coincidence that the gnostics were the Christians who most earnestly explored silence in the second century.

We will find other Christians in later centuries taking a similar attitude (below, pp. 179–80), and there were other Christian controversies over the nature of martyrdom. The third century witnessed for the first time empire-wide persecutions of Christians initiated by emperors themselves, first by Decius and two of his successors in the 250s, and then by Diocletian and Galerius from 303, all determined to destroy the religion which was a blasphemy against the old gods. In either case, Christians argued fiercely about the rights and wrongs of fleeing persecution, deceitfully denying their faith or standing firm to face torture and death. Although the extremist advocates of making an uncompromising stand, first Novatianists and later Donatists, ended up excluded from the mainstream Church, the prestige of martyrdom was decisively reaffirmed in a new crop of stories of heroism.[37] During these controversies, scriptural texts were batted back and forth, since the New Testament is unhelpfully contradictory on the subject: in John's Gospel, Jesus recommends his followers to suffer martyrdom bravely, while in Matthew's Gospel, he suggests that they flee from city to city in time of persecution.[38]

An equally poisonous debate on the subject of deceit followed in the late fourth century, although, with the cessation of persecution, the immediate stakes were less urgent. The combatants were two literary giants of Western Latin Christianity, Jerome (*c.* 345–420) and Augustine of Hippo (354–430), and their battleground was the interpretation of a fiery passage in Paul's Epistle to the Galatians (Gal. 2.11–14) in which the Apostle attacks his fellow-Apostle Peter for conforming to Jewish law and seeking to persuade Gentile Christians to conform in the same way. Since Peter himself had previously ceased to observe the Law, Paul accused Peter of cowardice, and piled up on Peter and his companions a series of insults such as 'acted insincerely' (*synypekrithēsan*), 'insincerity' (*hypokrisei*) and 'not straightforwardly' (*ouk orthopodousi*). Jerome, sometime papal secretary and a man not without aspirations to the papacy himself, was clearly appalled at the implications of these aspersions on the man who by the fourth century was being seen as the first pope, and he resolved to defend Peter's reputation in his commentary on the Epistle (c. 387).[39]

This Jerome did by the drastic means of suggesting that the whole passage in Galatians represented a prearranged deal between the two Apostles, designed to preserve peace between warring Jewish and Gentile factions in the Church. Both Peter and Paul were therefore in fact dissimulating in a sham conflict. He reinforced his argument by pointing to another instance of Paul admitting dissimulation on the same topic, and he ranged his way backwards through the Old Testament to find similar examples of heroic dissimulation. Augustine was deeply unimpressed by such arguments, and repeatedly said so, over three decades. In no circumstances, in his view, were Christians justified in lying. These two extreme points of view went on simmering in Christian discussions of dissimulation for centuries to come (below, pp. 172–8).[40]

After the great Constantinian moment of imperial reconciliation and the cessation of Roman persecution, silence remained remote from the burgeoning cult of the martyrs: their shrines were now free to flourish as centres of festival and liturgical celebration. Constantine encouraged this by his extraordinary series of architectural gifts to the Church in Rome: buildings without precedent, principally the large basilicas of the martyrs Peter and Lawrence. These were not conventional basilican designs such as Christians had been building for around a century, nor did they take the shape of a congregational church or cathedral, but rather each was a huge structure intended for burials, funeral feasts and pilgrimages, all under the patronage of the martyr-saint. They were designed to accommodate thousands of people. One vivid reminiscence of how they might be used is a contemporary account from the early 390s of the charity of the ultra-pious multi-millionaire Pammachius, who marked the death of his wife with a vast banquet for a crowd of the poor in St Peter's, with the martyr presiding benevolently over the gargantuan feast from his grave, to the east beyond the festivities. Public self-assertion by one of the city's most prominent families thus combined harmoniously with Christian charity and a suspiciously pre-Christian celebratory occasion.[41]

This was the new face of a religion which had now entered into partnership with the great, on the optimistic premise that the great might also become good as part of the bargain. The martyrs were not at all an embarrassment to the Roman elite, even though in their lives and deaths they had defied Roman power. On the contrary, accounts of the martyrs proliferated, often losing touch with actual historical reality, particularly through the imaginative patronage of Pope Damasus (c. 305–84), who promoted a much-expanded pilgrimage route in Rome in the later fourth century, a matter to which we shall return (below, p. 198).[42] Also during the fourth century, the imperial family sponsored the development of a sacred landscape in a restored city of Jerusalem, centring on the ultimate tomb for Christians, that of the crucified Saviour, in a building large enough to contain both his grave and the site of his Crucifixion.[43] The historian of martyrdom Candida Moss arrestingly comments on Mediterranean Christian worship in this period that '[g]iven the comparative popularity of the cult of the saints, it is plausible that more Christians attended feasts in honour of the saints than Eucharistic rituals in honour of Christ'.[44] Whether travelling just up the road or crossing the seas or seeking far-flung imperial highways, the pilgrim was emerging as a characteristic figure in a Christian landscape.

Ever since this first flourishing of mass pilgrimage, there has been a dichotomy in Christian interest in pilgrimage and holy places. It began in extrovert festival, celebrating the shrines of individuals whose characteristic reason for suffering was that they could not keep quiet. But some Christians actively criticized the cult of pilgrimage and martyrdom, just as gnostics had criticized the martyrs before them, and as some Protestants and radical Christians would do again in the sixteenth-century Reformation. Even among those who have cherished pilgrimage, the practice has within it a potentially contrary element: a search not for a person but for a place, the innate holiness of which promises an intimate approach to the sacred for those who seek it out.[45] That search might not be amid crowds, but, for an individual, in solitariness. The dilemma of how to use a sacred place in crowd or solitude has remained in Christianity – as it has done in the other Abrahamic religions, Judaism and Islam.

THE FIRST ASCETICS AND MONKS

Christians still died for their beliefs after Constantine's alliance with the Church. Sometimes it was at the hands of other Christians vying for control of the Church and turning Roman imperial power on their enemies (below, p. 164); at other times, it resulted from the recurrence of often atrocious violence from the Sassanians, rulers of the great empire across the eastern Roman frontier and dualist Zoroastrian in faith, whose lack of sympathy for their Christian subjects was only increased when the Roman Empire privileged Christianity in the fourth century.[46] Nevertheless, for most Mediterranean Christians, it was increasingly difficult to bear witness to their faith through martyrdom, and alliance with the Roman Empire brought the contrary danger of smug enjoyment of imperial favour. While Christians went on celebrating past martyrdoms, an increasing number turned their attention to practising or celebrating a different sort of specialized religious heroism: a range of ascetic and celibate lifestyles, led singly or in monastic community. The monastic impulse was not new in the fourth century, but solitary ascetic and monastic life now vastly expanded in terms of numbers, energy and self-consciousness. Belatedly, in the next hundred years it developed a literature reflecting on what was involved in this distinctive form of Christian life, reflection which has never subsequently ceased.

It is now apparent that in the fourth and fifth centuries, post-Constantinian monks and hermits rewrote their early history, in order to forget the real origins of asceticism, which seem to have been in second-century Syria. Instead, they highlighted the work of the hermit Antony and the monk Pachomius in fourth-century Egypt.[47] Monks and hermits were quite self-consciously portrayed as successors to the martyrs of the pre-Constantinian period: the lifespans of both Antony and Pachomius conveniently bridged this sea-change in Christian fortunes. Some Syrian ascetics went so far as to throw themselves into fires or into the mouths of wild beasts, in imitation of previous martyrs – though they would also have been galvanized by their knowledge of the continuing bouts of atrocity against Christians over the eastern Roman frontier in the Sassanian Empire.[48] When Bishop Athanasius (c. 296–373) crafted his sensationally successful biography of Antony, he stressed that the hermit was sorry that he had not been martyred in the persecution of Maximin Daia in 311, despite having indulged in some deliberately provocative behaviour in Alexandria, and that Antony's new life was in itself a martyrdom. Once the hermit was out of danger from the authorities, back in his Egyptian desert cell, says Athanasius, he 'each day bore witness [memartyreken] there with his conscience and waged battle in the contests of the faith'.[49] A new species of saint was in the making.

This was just as well for monks, because their fate in Christian history might well have been very different. They could have been permanently excluded from the life of the official Church, like gnostics and Montanists before them. If ascetics lived in supreme solitude, they might rarely or never participate in the eucharist, which had become the centrepiece in the authority of the Church's bishops. Early on, the episcopate had experienced tensions with the most strenuous spiritual athletes in the movement. It isolated them rhetorically as early as the second century by such labels as 'encratite', or, later on, 'Messalian', to promote the notion that their ascetic devotional practices were beyond what was seemly or reasonable, when frequently it may have been their independent spirit which was the chief source of offence.[50] The relationship between bishops and monks has never been entirely easy in Christianity. In one Church of the Christian world, that of Ethiopia, the relationship has been uniquely skewed in favour of the monks and their monasteries until very recent years, since up to the late 1940s the Church's nominal head, the metropolitan bishop or patriarch, was a foreigner from Alexandria, usually of advanced years and frequently with an imperfect command of the languages necessary for daily life in Ethiopia. In such circumstances, the abbots of the major Ethiopian monasteries were generally much more significant in the life and politics of the Church than its bishops.[51]

Undoubtedly some ascetics did represent a Christianity at odds with that of the Catholic Church. Many monks and hermits found themselves on the losing sides in Christian factional strife in Egypt, such as in the early fourth century when they supported the schismatic separation of Bishop Melitius from the more lax members of the Egyptian episcopal hierarchy. Worse still, some might be linked to the new synthesis of older Middle Eastern monotheistic beliefs known as Manichaeism. This was a dualist religion, whose answer to the problem of the existence of evil in God's world has not yet been bettered: evil just is, and that's all there is to it. Traces of a Manichaean monastery excavated in a little town in the Nile Delta called Kellis are contemporary with the first golden age of Egyptian Christian monasticism, and this monastery is unlikely to have been unique. Significantly, these Egyptian Manichees were just as concerned as mainstream Christian monks of Egypt to keep in touch with their fellow-believers in Syria.[52] It was disconcerting for historians of monasticism that the Nag Hammadi cache of gnostic writings on which we have already drawn so much was discovered in close proximity to two chief monasteries of no less a figure than the monastic pioneer Pachomius; the texts are datable to his lifetime, and debate continues as to whether they were part of a library belonging to the Pachomians.[53] There is a still wider perspective to take. It is not fanciful to point out that Syrians were leaders in a flourishing commerce eastwards; they had therefore long been familiar with India and central Asia, and could not have failed to notice the importance of celibate communities in the Buddhist tradition or the solitary holy men of Hinduism, traditions long pre-dating Christianity.

So how 'Christian' was Christian monasticism, given this remarkably eclectic set of connections? It was not straightforward for proponents of the movement to ground monastic activity in biblical precedent, though one of their early great practitioners, John Cassian, did just that around 400 CE, when he crafted a continuous genealogy for monks dating back to the events described in the Acts of the Apostles where the first Christian community pooled their goods to lead a common life.[54] Cassian would not have been sympathetic to the common opinion among modern biblical scholars that this incident never took place, but he could hardly have denied that its denouement in attempted deceit and God striking the deceivers dead was not promising, and in fact there is no further mention of the community of goods in the New Testament.[55] Jesus had indeed told his followers to sell all their belongings, but Paul of Tarsus, as we have seen (above, p. 45), was vocally unsympathetic to those who did not buckle down to earning their living in the community.[56]

Some scholars have tried to push the undoubtedly very early Syrian ascetic movement right back into the age of the Gospel writers, principally to Luke, who among the Evangelists shows the most interest in the renunciation of worldly goods, and who, interestingly, also lays emphasis on Jesus's silences.[57] The chronological connection is not at present quite there, and many strands in the Epistles written in the generation after Paul push in the other direction, with their detailed attention to the organization of family life, and even, in one of the Epistles to Timothy, the observation that the salvation of women will come through their having children.[58] The best that we can say is that Syrian ascetics were much more alert to possible helpful references in the New Testament than other early Christians, and they were also inclined to adjust Gospel texts in their Syriac translations to suit their rigorist agenda.

Why might Syria have been the birthplace of Christian asceticism? One of the most significant early Christian documents from Syria, the *Acts of Thomas*, which is certainly of second-century date, recurrently uses the words 'stranger' and 'foreigner' as a proud self-description for Christians. The reference here is both to the Tanakh, with its recurrent theme of the people of Israel in exile, and also the previous echo of that idea in the New Testament's Epistle to the Hebrews, where the great names of the Israelite past are described as 'having acknowledged that they were strangers and exiles on the earth'.[59] There was an obvious next stage in the implied argument: if not of this earth, then where? That question repeatedly received the same answer, for instance from the fourth-century Syrian writer Aphrahat, in two pithy linked observations: 'We should be aliens from this world, just as Christ did not belong to this world'; and 'Whoever would resemble the angels, must alienate himself from men.'[60]

It is worth observing that Aphrahat wrote this in 337: that same year, the Emperor Constantine died, shortly after becoming the first Roman emperor to receive Christian baptism. The message of the monastic alternative, to become alien in the world, was all the more compelling now that most Christians, including their bishops, had turned to embrace the world and the power it might offer. Aphrahat's second thought, with its identification of alienation from the world with angelic aspirations, had a particular resonance in Syria. Syrian spirituality laid a heavy emphasis on celibacy: too heavy, indeed, for many other Christians, who regarded such enthusiasm as pushing beyond the boundaries of orthodoxy. So angels, sexless beings in heaven, were a useful rhetorical ally for Syrian celibates, and no doubt genuinely provided them with a deeply satisfying inspiration. Luke, favourite Evangelist among the Syrians, was handy, making as he did in his Gospel a stronger statement than Matthew or Mark in his version of Jesus's observation to the Sadducees that those in the next world do not marry, for 'they are equal to angels'.[61]

The Syrians had arrived at an alliance with the heavenly host that was destined to resonate through the history of contemplative Christianity. But some would choose to aim higher than the angels: another Syriac word for an ascetic among the first celibate communities which we can glimpse in second-century Syria, the 'Sons and Daughters of the Covenant' is îhîdāyâ. It has the same root meaning of 'solitary' as the Greek *monachos*, which has descended to us as 'monk'. Given the characteristic Syrian Christian emphasis on celibacy, it would also slide towards its meaning of singleness, but, far more resonantly, Syrians would recall the use of the same word in their New Testament which recurs in the Johannine literature: Îhîdāyâ is the One who is 'Only-begotten'.[62] So the Syrians in their construction of a celibate identity had a peculiarly potent association with the model of Christian life. It would later be expressed forcefully by Athanasius in his prolonged fight with the Arians: the Son of God 'has made us sons of the Father, and deified men by becoming Himself man'.[63] Eastern Christians have always been much more inclined than Westerners to stress the central importance in Christian faith and practice of *theosis*, that is, union with or likeness to God; but ascetics everywhere would eventually be drawn to this idea. An encounter with *theosis* will recur again and again as the story of silence in Christian history unfolds.

We have still not exhausted the range of possible influences on these precocious Christian ascetics. Second-century Syria was a cultural frontier for Hellenism, and its fascination with the celibate and ascetic calling could have had sources other than the Bible. Syriac Christians were close to gnostic Christian discourses with their exploration of silence. The most obvious example of a holy man renouncing the values of the world and making cuttingly wise pronouncements amid total renunciation was Diogenes of Sinope, the first of the Cynics, living three centuries before the time of Christ (*c.* 412–*c.* 321 BCE). The aggressively counter-cultural career of Diogenes inspired significant echoes in a Christian biography of a bizarre Christian ascetic: this was the Cypriot Bishop Leontius's seventh-century life of the sixth-century Syrian saint Simeon called *Salus*, from a Syriac word which might well be translated as 'silly'. St Simeon the Silly was the first in a genre of crazy Christians who, with wary admiration, have been styled holy fools, and who may still be found in Orthodox Christianity today. This notable exception to a general hostility in Christian spirituality towards raucous mirth significantly owes its origin to a pre-Christian and non-biblical source: Diogenes happily residing in a wine-jar on the outskirts of Classical Athens.[64]

DESERT FATHERS?

It should not be forgotten, therefore, that Simeon's spiritual ancestors, and the ancestors of all Christian contemplatives, were Greek philosophers as much as any character in the Christian Bible. Athanasius's *Life of Antony* was closer to historical reality than Cassian was to be a few decades later, for Athanasius made considerable unacknowledged borrowings from a particular genre of non-Christian literature, the biographies of Greek philosophers, whose subjects ranged from Pythagoras to direct competitors with Christianity like Apollonius of Tyana in the first century CE or the even more recent Plotinus, as depicted by his disciple Porphyry. Athanasius did try to distinguish Antony from his philosopher-predecessors by depicting him as illiterate, but, given the recent rediscovery of seven letters from Antony with a distinctly personal theological agenda, it is not clear that this was really the case.[65]

Thanks to the emphasis on 'desert' and 'wilderness' in Athanasius and a host of later writers, it is easy to jump to the label of 'Desert Fathers' to characterize the ascetics and contemplatives of the early Church. The reality was more complex, and more interesting. From the beginning, silence and contemplation were constructed in the midst of ordinary society as much as in solitude. The Syrian 'Sons/ Daughters of the Covenant' remained part of wider Christian communities, and did not embrace the extremes of spiritual athletics that have dominated Christian memory of Syrian asceticism. One of them, the great Ephrem the Syrian (306–73), made his permanent contribution to the Christian musical tradition by composing hymns and training choirs; choirmasters are by nature and calling impresarios and performers.[66]

Even the celebrated Syrian 'Stylites', who took their cue from the first pillar-dweller in the early fifth century, St Simeon the Elder Stylite, were not quite the lovers of solitude that history has made them, for, perched in proto-balloon-baskets atop their pillars, their lives were intimately bound up with the business of preaching to crowds and taking on an active role in the religious and secular politics of their day. Anyone who has visited the wonderful ruined church and monastic precinct surrounding the remains of St Simeon's pillar should note that it is situated strategically above one of the main roads of ancient north Syria: this was no shrinking violet of a saint.[67] In the sixth century St Simeon the Younger Stylite actually found himself the chief exhibit in a grandly architectural pilgrimage site near Antioch when a substantial shrine-church was built around his pillar, while he was still occupying it.[68] The conquering Muslims of the seventh century may well have taken their cue from these Syrian holy men shouting the praises of God from a high pillar when they created the structures which we now know as minarets.

Athanasius, who had a genius for coining a memorable phrase, famously observed in his biography of Antony that 'the desert was made a city by monks', but that same biography makes clear that in reality the early setting of eremetical life was close to the villages of the Nile Delta: it was among the villages that the young Antony wandered, seeking out solitaries and ascetics in the 270s and 280s.[69] There is no question that, later on, he would be the leading figure in the move of solitaries into the desert, but not all followed him there. The earliest known use of the Greek word *monachos* is in a secular petition in an Egyptian papyrus dating from 324, which clearly expected the term to be familiar to any reader. What is interesting about this *monachos* is that he was not living in a wilderness. The reason we know about him is that he was a passer-by in a village street who stepped in and helped to break up a fight.[70] The story is similar for a pair of ladies who might be thought of as 'Desert Mothers', for they were referred to in a papyrus of 400 CE as *monachai apotaktikai*, 'female renouncers'; but the document in question was a rental agreement for an apartment in the Delta city of Oxyrhynchus, which the two proto-nuns were leasing for six months to a Jewish man.[71]

Pachomius likewise set up his exceptionally carefully regulated pioneering monastic community not in the desert, but in the deserted houses of a village which he found conveniently abandoned close to the bank of the Upper Nile. There followed a second takeover of a deserted village, and soon a system of related monasteries grew up which has been described as the most sophisticated and centralized such grouping until the time of Cluny, half a millennium later.[72] One interpretation of what Pachomius was doing is to see it as an effective way of remedying decades of social disruption in Egypt, to which the growing burdens of imperial taxation had significantly contributed; his houses were hives of manufacturing, and the abbot's eye on com-merce was as canny as that of any Victorian Methodist factory-owner.[73] In such communities, but also among solitaries, silence was only one strategy among several in the pursuit and performance of contempla-tion. The community at worship listened to a reader of Scripture, while systematically plaiting mats and ropes from reeds, an activity which one can see as the ancestor of the prayerful repetition of rosary-beads, but which was also one of the staples of community income. One may feel that Pachomius had an unhealthy attention to detail, given that annual financial accounts to the monastic federations required every abbot to provide an exact numerical report on the number of ropes woven at worship.

Outside communal devotion, Pachomian monks apparently carried out a remarkably varied range of useful trades, likewise in silence, and (something which much impressed observers) they also ate their community meals in silence, rapping on the table if they needed some-thing, in an anticipation of the sign practices of the Cluniacs (below, pp. 97–8). The great fourth-century monastic founder Macarius (Makarios) the Egyptian produced a rather startling image for a practice which was to become a much-loved staple of contemplation in Eastern Christianity. He recommended the contemplation and mental repetition of the name of Jesus, remarking that it reminded him of how, when he was young, old women and girls would sweeten their foul breath with chewing-gum. How much more would Jesus's name banish the foulness of demons, he concluded triumphantly.[74]

Silence could be balanced by vocal expression in the pursuit of holiness. The fourth-century Abba John the Little, who lived in the great monastic federation of Scetis on the western edge of the Delta, listed 'weeping and groaning' as an important part of the agenda of the praying monk, for he believed that 'a man should have a little bit of all the virtues'. Many Egyptian and Syrian ascetics later echoed his insistence on the integration of tears and silence.[75] It was an essential part of the life of communities that the younger monks should seek out their elders and demand as of right 'a word', that is, a wise saying. The resulting answers are the basis of much of our literature of the Desert Fathers, particularly the great collection from Scetis, the *Apophthegmata Patrum*. It was quite possible and permissible for such a noted spiritual leader as John the Little to be kept up from dusk to dawn, speaking to a junior monk 'about virtue until they noticed the first light of morning'.[76] Twice a week on the set days of oral teaching (catechesis), Pachomius ordered that his monks enjoy not just instruction from a catechist but also general discussion of what had been taught – maybe to the point of argument, which may have had the incidental advantage of taking the monks' attention away from the fact that they had been fasting all through that day.[77]

Unsurprisingly, hermits were more inclined to privilege silence over the dispensing of verbal wisdom: the hermit Agathon, contemporary of Macarius the Egyptian, was reputed to have spent three years with a stone in his mouth to encourage him in his practice of refraining from speech. Others were inclined to allow the Holy Spirit to decide when they would deliver the word, sometimes remaining deaf to the pleas of their admirers for days. The prerogative to speak or not to speak in such circumstances was, after all, in itself a mark of spiritual authority.[78]

In the later fourth century, monks began to write their thoughts down instead of merely expressing them in conversation in their devotional circles. It is natural that they took up with enthusiasm the existing discussions of silence which were still proliferating and developing around them. One of the most distinctive Syriac voices was a writer known since his modern rediscovery as John the Solitary of Apamea. He appears to have lived in the later fifth century in the part of Syria under Roman rule, and although this dating would place him after the ecclesiastical disruption caused by the Council of Chalcedon (below, p. 54), he remained much esteemed on both sides of the great theological divide in Syrian Christianity about the human and divine natures of Christ which the decisions of Chalcedon failed to solve. John had no hesitation in saying that 'God is silence', but in this affirmation there seems nothing of the gnostic personification of silence as God. John's inspiration arose from his own broodings on the Gospel of his namesake the Evangelist John, where Jesus's conversation with the Samaritan woman culminated in the affirmation that God is spirit, and on 1 Corinthians 14.15, 'I will pray with the spirit and I will pray with the mind also.' The resulting search for the God who was silent impelled him to cry, 'How long shall I be in the world of the voice, and not in the world of the word? ... When shall I become word, in an awareness of hidden things, when shall I be raised up to silence, to something which neither voice nor word can bring?' That was the goal of a life which meanwhile remained part of the worshipping community of the Church: among all the categories of positive silence which John discussed – of whole body, of tongue, of mind, of soul, of spirit – the only exception as a purely negative variety was 'the silence of the tongue' which had no praise for God.[79]

'THAT YONDER'

John the Solitary, appropriately enough, was his own man: not merely without reaching out to a gnostic past, but not even perceptibly a Neoplatonist. Not all discussions of silence went in such a contemplative or mystical direction, and not all of them were Christian, because Neoplatonists were still developing themes which had been the property of Platonists long before Christianity existed. Some of the most radical projections of negative theology came from the fifth-century Neoplatonist Proclus, who passionately hymned the unknowability of God, and his successor the philosopher Damascius (458–538), who fell victim to the Emperor Justinian's Christian vandalism in the final closure of the near-thousand-year-old Athenian Academy in 529. Damascius spent his last days in exile in the Sassanian Empire; it was appropriate, in view of that enforced journey eastwards, that he should sound more like a Buddhist than any previous Greek philosopher in his emphasis on silence and the failure of reason; he could speak of 'hyperignorance' as a desirable goal for the discerning.[80] In a phrase which has great potential in our own time, when Christians argue about whether God should be spoken of in terms of a masculine pronoun, Damascius suggested that ultimate divinity should be referred to as 'that yonder'.[81]

Eastern Mediterranean Christians lived in the same thought-world. In the later fourth century, the 'Cappadocian Fathers' (Basil, Gregory of Nazianzus and Gregory of Nyssa) stabilized imperial Christianity around an extended version of the Nicene Creed and framed much of their debates in terms of negative theology. But so did their opponents in the great arguments about the relationship between Father and Son in the Trinity which have come to be known as the Arian Controversy. The leading historian of Classical negative theology judges that fourth-century 'Anomoean' Arians like Aetius and Eunomius, who stressed the 'unlikeness' of Father and Son, had a rather better grasp of the arguments of Greek philosophy on this matter than did the Cappadocians.[82] That might account for the note of irritation in Gregory of Nazianzus when he remarked on the Anomoeans' unrestrained theologizing on things divine which were best approached by silence, or even by deliberate avoidance of discussion of them: 'Not to every one, my friends, does it belong to philosophize about God; not to every one; the Subject is not so cheap and low; and I will add, not before every audience, nor at all times, nor on all points; but on certain occasions, and before certain persons, and within certain limits.' His Arian opponents could have retorted that they were doing precisely what he sought to do himself, in honouring the silence and unknowability of God.[83]

EVAGRIUS: MEDITATION AND CONTEMPLATION

Even when the Arians had finally been defeated in the imperial Church, much of the discussion of silence in the mystical life remained very tenuously poised on the frontier of what now reframed itself as Orthodox Christianity. One of the Cappadocian Fathers, Basil 'the Great' (329/30–79), was both Bishop of Caesarea in Cappadocia (now Kayseri in Turkey) and creator of one of the first and most widely used Rules for monastic community life. He thus united the charisma of monk and bishop, which as we have seen was one of the potential fault-lines in fourth-century Christianity. Yet his hugely influential younger contemporary from the Black Sea region, Evagrius of Pontus ('Ponticus'; 345/6–99) became officially tainted by his admiration for that riskily adventurous third-century theologian Origen. Evagrius was condemned by a council of the Church in 553, a century and a half after his death, joining Origen in official disfavour. The extent of his suppression within Orthodoxy was far more thoroughgoing than in Origen's case, because his discussion of the impossibility of giving form to a vision of God became entangled in later battles over icons which would have puzzled and saddened him (below, pp. 105–8). The rediscovery and re-evaluation of Evagrius has had to await modern investigators, in many cases retrieving translations of his lost Greek works from Armenian or Syriac manuscripts preserved by non-imperial Churches which continued to cherish his memory.

In a fashion that was to be echoed in the lives of more than one ascetic down to Thomas Merton in the modern age (below, pp. 229–30), Evagrius's rejection of the world sprang out of an unwise early venture into its most heady temptations. From being a rising young clerical star in the imperial capital Constantinople, in 381 or 382 he abruptly fled to Jerusalem, to escape the consequences of an affair with the wife of a senior city official. His flight did not represent a conversion experience: his life continued in chaotic self-indulgence until he suffered a profound breakdown, and only then did he take up the monastic life, in a new withdrawal into the monasticism of Lower Egypt, in the era when Macarius the Egyptian was its most celebrated figure. Thereafter, his fierce resistance to energetic attempts to make him a bishop probably reflected his consciousness that the clerical career ladder had done nothing to curb his headlong rush into disaster in Constantinople and Jerusalem.[84]

Now Evagrius embarked on a path of inner exploration which would lead the ascetic into struggles and torments. The results he expressed in language owing much to the pre-Christian past. The one who struggled would arrive, as might a Stoic, at a state of serenity (*apatheia*) and eventually at a final state for which Evagrius was not afraid to use that word with a 'past', *gnosis* ('knowledge'):

> While the transformations are numerous, we have received knowledge of only four: the first, the second, the last and that which precedes it. The first, it is said, is the passage from malice to virtue; the second is that from *apatheia* to natural contemplation; the third is from the former to the knowledge that concerns the *logikoi* [rational beings]; and the fourth is the passage of all to knowledge of the Blessed Trinity.[85]

Equally resonant for him was another basic word: *nous*, 'mind', which had also been key to many gnostic cosmologies.[86] Mind now became the chief actor in Evagrius's regimen of prayer. He saw it as following that same path towards *gnosis* of the Trinity, in a return to the God who had created it: 'Contemplation is spiritual knowledge of the things which have been and will be: it is this which causes the *nous* to ascend to its former rank.'[87] Quite remarkably, and apparently without precedent, he saw the mind of the individual as the chief arena for prayer. It was a simple and long-established principle for Christian and non-Christian Greeks alike, as far back as Clement of Alexandria, that prayer was a conversation (*homilia*) with God, but Evagrius refined this idea. He said firmly that 'Prayer is a conversation of *nous* with God'; it was the mind's highest activity.[88] Working with this concept of a praying mind, he was ready to develop a system of prayer: it was the beginning of centuries of contemplative practice for communities which at first dared not give him the credit, and in the end forgot him altogether. His descriptions of progress in the spiritual life nevertheless could not and would not be ignored, because they chimed in with the experience of generations of monks to come.

Evagrius was optimistic about the ability of the human mind to receive God's generosity and mercy and grow in grace: 'we come into [this] life possessing all the seeds of the virtues,' he said. 'And just as tears fall with the seeds, so with the sheaves there is joy.'[89] He framed his instruction self-consciously like a physician, prescribing a programme of exercise for *nous*: each day in structured monastic life should have a rhythm, an orderly recital from the Psalms of David followed by a short time of silent prayer (his own practice was repetition of this pattern a hundred times a day). Together with meditation on the Bible, this provided the seedbed in which prayer could grow. But despite his enthusiasm for horticultural and medical figures of speech, Evagrius insisted throughout all his writings, in a fashion unprecedented in previous Christian discussions of the life of prayer, that meditation was only one stage: ultimately, all images must be stripped away from the contemplation of God. What remained in the conversation with the divine was 'pure prayer'.

Such an approach was unmistakably reminiscent of what Neoplatonists were saying in the same era, even though Evagrius's own construction of it was firmly grounded in contemporary Christian battles about understanding the Trinity. His writings infuriated many of his contemporaries in Egyptian asceticism, while it did Evagrius no favours among later lovers of icons, fighting to preserve them in eighth- and ninth-century Byzantium, that he had observed, 'Never give a shape to the divine as such when you pray, nor allow your mind to be imprinted by any form, but go immaterial to the Immaterial and you will understand.'[90]

What Evagrius was describing was a distinction which has become hugely important for later Christianity: the difference was later clarified in the Latin West, with that Latin genius for precise categorization, as between 'meditation' and 'contemplation'.[91] Often these terms are used with much less precision than a Latin taxonomist would like, and often that is because the two states flow into each other, just as Evagrius had described, but it is important to understand that there is a distinction between them. It was well put by a bishop of the late sixteenth-century Counter-Reformation who was condemned to spend most of his career gazing at his own cathedral from afar, because before he was born, it had become embedded in the headquarters of

European Calvinism: he was François de Sales (1567–1622), would-be Prince-Bishop of Geneva.

In his exile from Geneva in nearby Annecy, de Sales was unsurprisingly a fierce (one might say legalistic) defender of Tridentine dogma, but he combined this with a generous spirituality which has rarely been equalled, and which looks back to the distant and very different world of Evagrius – a gulf in other respects as profound as that between Annecy and Geneva in 1600. De Sales emphasized that meditation should be considered to be a form of activity: so he called it 'nothing other than [a process of] attentive thought, either reiterated or voluntarily entertained by the mind, in order to excite the will to holy and salvific affections and resolutions'. By contrast, he spoke of contemplation as beyond activity: 'nothing other than a loving, simple, and permanent attention of the mind to divine things.'[92] Repeatedly, mystics have discovered for themselves that same distinction, which might also be termed a progression. It was a discovery which came in time for it to remain the common heritage of the Christianities which divided in the fifth century – so far, never to reunite.

4

The Monastic Age in
East and West: 451–1100

SILENCE BEYOND CHALCEDON

While Evagrius Ponticus disappeared from the knowledge of imperial Christians, three centuries later his Syrian admirer Isaac, Bishop of Nineveh (d. *c.* 700), addressed the same concerns in a Christian world which had moved virtually beyond the consciousness of the Orthodox and Catholic Churches of the Mediterranean and Europe. Isaac was prelate and monk in the 'Dyophysite' Church of the East, which had rejected a compromise about the human and divine natures of Christ imposed on the imperial Church at the Council of Chalcedon in 451.[1] Christian history cannot properly be understood without appreciating the significance of Chalcedon. In its aftermath, Christianity was split into three because two-thirds of the Christian world refused to sign up to the Council of Chalcedon's compromise decisions, dictated by the then Emperor Marcian and his wife Pulcheria. On one wing of opposite poles rejecting the *via media* reached at Chalcedon were Miaphysites, who emphasized the union of natures, human and divine (they were dismissively referred to by their enemies as 'Monophysites'). On the other were those who emphasized the continuing distinction of these natures, Dyophysites (derogatively called 'Nestorians').

The Dyophysites were subject successively to Sassanian rulers hostile or at best indifferent to Christianity and, in Isaac's own day, to newly established Muslim rulers. They were never to know the experience of establishment and power that had reshaped imperial and Mediterranean Christianity. A bishop of Isaac's Church was not going to show respect for any condemnation by imperial Christians such as had been pronounced on Evagrius at Constantinople in 553, and Isaac enthusiastically explored the implications of Evagrius's teaching, transmitted to him in Syriac versions of the original Greek texts (not all of which translations were accurate). He gnawed away at Evagrius's idea of the progress towards pure prayer:

> Intensity of stirrings in prayer is not an exalted part of pure prayer . . . it belongs only to the second or third rank . . . What is the most precious and the principal characteristic in pure prayer is the brevity and smallness of any stirrings, and the fact that the mind simply gazes as though in wonder during this diminution of active prayer. From this, one of two things occurs to the mind in connection with that brief stirring which wells up in it; either it withdraws into silence, as a result of the overpowering might of the knowledge which the intellect has received in a particular verse; or it is held in delight at that point at which it was aiming during the prayer when it was stirred, and the heart cultivates it with an insatiable yearning of love. These are the principal characteristics of pure prayer.[2]

In her discussion of this fascinating passage, Brouria Bitton-Ashkelony points out how Isaac has moved beyond Evagrius: he marks out pure prayer as subject to levels of individual consciousness. His invocation of the mind's activity is much less metaphysical and much more concerned with awareness. But Isaac also sees even pure prayer as the second in what could be considered as three stages of mystical consciousness in the mind, resulting in the annihilation of all prayer: 'As long as prayer is stirred, it belongs to the sphere of the soul's existence, but when it has entered that other sphere [spiritual existence], then prayer stops.'[3] He describes this final state in terms of an old Syrian theme, 'wonder'. Here Isaac made his own distinctive departure from Evagrius, yet on one occasion he tactfully associates it with the Master by adding the idea to what he claims to be a quotation from Evagrius. In fact it is enriched by his own thought: 'Prayer is the state of the mind which is only cut off from the light of the Holy Trinity by wonder.'[4]

A successor of Isaac in the eighth-century Church of the East, the monk John from the mountains of Dalyatha in what is now a frontier region between Iran, Iraq and Turkey, provides what might be termed one of the termini of monastic triumphalism. John pressed the Syriac emphasis on bodily penance to an extreme: he saw it forming a road back to the original purity of human nature. Through humility and contemplation (especially while physically prostrate), a monk could unite his purged nature not simply with all creation, but with his creator, to achieve a vision of the glory of God himself. '[I]n the same way that fire shows its operation to the eyes,' he wrote, 'so God shows his glory to rational beings who are pure.' John went so far as to deny that a layperson could experience the mystical union with God which resulted from such self-purging: 'Christ cannot live with the world . . . but always, he comes to the soul's home and visits her to live in her, if she is empty of all that is of the world.' It is a repeated pattern in the history of mystic contemplation that, when mystics try to explain their experience of transcendence, the results are not just difficult for others to understand, but seem to overstep the mark between creator and created. In this case, even the Church of the East felt that one of its own had gone too far. Soon after his death, a synod condemned John for his dangerous exaltation of the ascetic life and the view of God which underlay it. Much of what he said has nevertheless found an unconscious echo in later centuries and in other settings, among those who have never heard his name.[5]

DIONYSIUS VERSUS AUGUSTINE

While Isaac and John were shaping Dyophysite views of contemplation and prayer, another writer's influence was working its way through Churches to their west, and taking a very different approach to mystical Christianity, though he was also Syrian. He achieved an extraordinarily long-lived success and influence by the device of hiding his own name and taking the name of another, much more ancient Christian: Dionysius the Areopagite, the chief convert made by Paul of Tarsus in the largely unreceptive city of Athens.[6] The Syrian's real name has never been discovered, and was already being deliberately obscured by writers in his own time in the sixth century.[7] It was politic of the anonymous writer to throw his identity back four centuries, because the most likely setting for him is in the monasteries of Syria which had rejected the outcome of the Council of Chalcedon in 451. He was a Miaphysite, in other words on the polar opposite wing of dissent to Isaac of Nineveh and John of Dalyatha, who belonged to the Dyophysite Church of the East.

There was more to the choice of the Areopagite's identity than mere expediency. This writer really did look back to Athens, in the shape of that long tradition of religious Platonism and Greek musing on silence and absence which we have already surveyed, but he will also have noted that in the rhetorical exercise placed in Paul's mouth by the writer of Acts as his sermon in Athens, the theme was the 'unknown God', whom Paul was now revealing to his largely sceptical audience. Just as much as his contemporary the non-Christian philosopher Damascius (above, p. 79), Pseudo-Dionysius was an exponent of the negative way in approaching the ultimate essence of divinity, although, unlike Damascius, he was also prepared to justify himself by Scripture. He pointed to the fact that Moses had toiled up to the summit of Mount Sinai at a turning point in Israel's history, and still Moses had not met with God himself there.[8] In the fifth chapter of his *Mystical Theology*, there is a hymn which contains one of the most formidable lists to be created in the early centuries of the Church of what God is not – of which this is only a sample:

> Ascending still higher, we say that it is
>   not soul
>   not intellect
>   not imagination, opinion, reason and
>   not intellection . . .
>   not life
>   not being
>   not eternity, not time . . .
>   not divinity
>   not goodness . . .[9]

When one remembers that Pseudo-Dionysius was a Miaphysite, it is clear why he could be so boldly negative. His view of the Second Person of the Trinity swallowed up the humanity of Jesus so profoundly in the divinity of the Christ that no other vision of the divine was necessary in relation to the other Persons, or to the whole of the

Godhead. The negatives of God followed on from his rejection of Chalcedon. And yet those negatives left much to say: strange novelties, which were made palatable by Pseudo-Dionysius's apparent first-century identity, ensuring him a place in the affections of an astonishing variety of later clergy who would have been appalled if they had realized that they were sitting at the feet of an anti-Chalcedonian. Dionysius was as fascinated as any gnostic or Neoplatonist by celestial hierarchies – in fact, he seems to have invented the Greek original of the word 'hierarchy'.[10] The layered procession of beings from high to low which he constructed kept the Deity safely corralled away from created substance. Pseudo-Dionysius did take care to construct his hierarchy in relation to his Miaphysite Trinitarian background, but central to his enterprise was to enrol the angels in a Platonic procession and return, a descent and ascent, which gnostics might have attributed to other powers.

This dragooning of the angels into a celestial hierarchy – Angels, Archangels, Principalities, Powers, Virtues, Dominations and more – was an essential element in Dionysius's theological impact. It appealed to a society which looked like that in everyday life; it appealed to Platonic-minded ascetics; it appealed to clergy generally. The heavenly hierarchy could be matched to the clerical hierarchy on earth. For Dionysius, bishops equated to 'Dominations' among the angels, ranking just below the sacraments of eucharist and baptism, and from there, the clerical orders descended to lay catechumens, whose equivalents among the angels were not dignified with any other particular term of art. This was not merely an ego-boost for clergy. If they were thus to be seen as close to angels, they would have to recognize a frightening responsibility in their conduct, and in their exposition of divine mysteries to the laity.

Dionysius would have a long and very influential afterlife. He gave comfort and sustenance to an extraordinary variety of mystical writers and philosophers, particularly once his thought was transmitted to the medieval Latin West in the ninth century, right down to the Renaissance. The thirteenth-century Italian Franciscan Bonaventure (1221–74) brooded over the Dionysian hierarchies and elaborated them, with the aim of privileging the contemplative over the secular clerical life.

Obsession with Dionysian angels also frequently lined up with the hyper-clericalism of the busiest of medieval secular clergy. A case in point was John Colet, the early sixteenth-century Dean of St Paul's Cathedral in London, who was an austere (though not very success-ful) advocate of Church reform.[11] Rather as Pseudo-Dionysius's contemporaries among Syrian monks had expressed their sense of closeness to God by the most savage mortification of their bodies, so Colet lashed out at the failings of his fellow-clergy with a fierce relish that Protestants later mistook for anticlericalism. It was in fact pre-cisely the reverse, as they would have realized had they perused the manuscript of his commentary on Pseudo-Dionysius's *Celestial Hier-archy*, complete with his secretary's intricate and beautifully written table of the hierarchy which the anonymous one had described.[12] Even those Renaissance humanists of the fifteenth and sixteenth cen-turies who had no vested interest in boosting the role of clergy were seduced by Pseudo-Dionysius: their emphasis was slightly different. Intoxicated with excitement at their rediscoveries in ancient philoso-phy and magic, they saw Dionysius's vision as offering all humans the chance to resemble angels, just as mystics before them had been led to hold out that prospect for fellow-monks.

From the fifth to the ninth century, this contemplative tradition had little purchase among Western Latin-speaking Christians. The contrast between East and West is obvious if one turns to the works of that doyen of theologians in the Latin West, Augustine of Hippo. The theme of silence did not preoccupy Augustine; it played poorly alongside his fascination with language and human psychology as revelations of the nature of God. The one notable exception is Augus-tine's famous description in his *Confessions* of the moment when, in conversation with his mother in a garden in Rome's port of Ostia, only a few days before she died, they had together reached out 'in thought' and 'touched the eternal wisdom'. This was for one moment only, and was the end-result of loving thought and discussion between a mother and her son.[13]

While Augustine retreated from that possibility after his crisis of loss, he was fully alive to the explorations which were opened up by his fascination with written texts. Unlike the Apostle Paul, who had been turned around into a new life by a reproachful question in a blinding light, Augustine associated his Christian conversion experience with the galvanizing effect of the text of a book, Paul's Epistle to the Romans. In the *Confessions*, he described the journey towards that moment of conversion in terms of his previous reading of a sequence of other books.[14] Augustine was also a Platonist, even if he hardly knew the works of the philosopher; it was the Neoplatonists of his own age who shaped his views of self-knowledge. Like them, he deprecated the Aristotelian exaltation of reason or *Logos*, but he was deeply pessimistic about the capacities of humanity after Adam's Fall in the Garden of Eden. His sense of humanity's helplessness, barred by the paralysis of sin from any action deserving God's favour, meant that he was unlikely to be enthused by the possibilities in Neoplatonism which took Easterners down the road to union with God: *theosis* (above, p. 73). Instead he saw a rescue-route for humanity in language: a fragile and imperfect medium, but one that nonetheless offered clues to the divine realities beyond.

Augustine was fascinated by the relation of signs to reality, and words on a page, for all their ultimate inadequacy, are a wonderful system of signs created by humanity's urge to communicate. One supra-literary text, the Bible, is a set of signs imbued with the power of God. It stands in a privileged position to all other literary texts in this search for meaning and reality. How is its message best approached? To answer this question, Augustine reached for aid from the approach to Scripture exemplified in the thought of the great Alexandrian theologians of a previous age, Clement and his successor Origen. Origen was in many respects the opposite of Augustine in theological temperament, but in his pioneering corpus of biblical commentary and in his boldly speculative theological treatises, he had provided a useful strategy for probing below the literal meaning of the biblical text, in order to find more profound layers: allegory, the realities whose shapes could be glimpsed in the literal level of the Bible's words.

In adopting an allegorical method, Clement and Origen were imitating the method long used by learned Greeks to read Homer's *Iliad* and *Odyssey*, or by learned Hellenistic Jews like Philo of Alexandria to read their Tanakh. The innermost meanings, hidden behind the

literal sense of the words on the page, were not only the most important, but were also only available to those with eyes to see: allegory
was to be constructed through the imagination, guided by the Spirit.
Augustine devoted the third of four books in one of his most widely
read texts, *On Christian Doctrine*, to discussing allegory, and the
application of allegory recurs throughout his voluminous discussions
of biblical text elsewhere. 'It is, then, a miserable kind of spiritual
slavery to interpret signs as things, and to be incapable of raising the
mind's eye above the physical creation so as to absorb the eternal
light,' he wrote, and he followed it up with examples.[15] The great
advantage of allegory is that it can draw edifying sense out of passages in the Bible which might give rise to unedifying thoughts – thus,
with careful application of the allegorical method, Augustine was able
to illuminate an incident described in Luke's Gospel which might
alarm or indecorously excite the uninstructed:

> No person in his right mind should ever think that the Lord's feet were
> anointed by a woman with precious ointment in the same way as the
> feet of self-indulgent and evil men are anointed at the sort of banquets
> which we abhor. A good perfume signifies a good reputation: anyone
> who enjoys this through the deeds of an upright life anoints Christ's
> feet in a figurative sense with a most precious perfume by following in
> his footsteps.[16]

Before Augustine, the Western Church had been suspicious of the
allegorical method, but the fact that this giant of Latin theology
encouraged its use (in particular, among monks and nuns) turned it
into a characteristic Western practice: an actively meditative reading
of the Bible, the *lectio divina*. The act of reading the Bible is in Augustinian terms not merely a means of acquiring information on a literal
level; it also involves an engagement with the text on a spiritual level
which brings us closer to God. For a thousand years, this was how the
West read its Bible. Perhaps the method was initially attractive in the
Latin West because readers were ruefully conscious that their Vulgate
Latin text was already at one remove from its original as a translation
from the Hebrew and Greek. This consciousness was to fade as the
centuries wore on.[17]

MONKS IN THE LATIN WEST: THE RULE OF ST BENEDICT

The Western Church in Augustine's time was not yet disastrously isolated from developments in the imperial Church of the eastern Mediterranean, but it built up its own traditions and original approaches to silence and noise in its devotional life, both inside and outside monasteries. The ascetic and monastic founder John Cassian (c. 360–435) brought to south-east Gaul in the fifth century his extensive experience of monasticism in Egypt and Palestine, together with a discreet enthusiasm for the wisdom of his old mentor Evagrius Ponticus, which led to tensions with Augustine and his admirers.[18] In the decades after his death, two successive formulations of a monastic rule appeared in the western Mediterranean, the second of which bears the name of St Benedict, and was with little doubt created by this otherwise rather elusive Italian.[19] The Benedictine Rule described in extensive detail how to construct a single community, living in obedience to its abbot, fully independent of any other. That independence within a wider relationship remains the key characteristic of Benedictine monasteries to this day.

These early monastic Rules in the West tended to discuss silence in moral and pastoral rather than mystical terms. They were not alone in paying attention to such considerations. In the East, the Rule of Basil 'the Great' had already made a distinction between words which built up holiness through instruction and divine praises and words which were useless and potentially harmful, but the Westerners privileged this theme.[20] They saw silence as associated with humility and obedience, virtues always in danger of being threatened by slander and defiance, which not only damaged the individual's spiritual state, but also the life of the community. Valerian (fl. c. 422–39), who joined one of John Cassian's communities in Gaul, was another early example of a monk who became a bishop, in his case of Cemele, now Cimiez in south-east France; he observed that 'To speak and to remain silent, each is a perfection. The case of each consists in holding to the proper measure of words. Silence is great and speech is great, but the wise man sets a measure upon them both.'[21] Benedict laid much more emphasis on silence in his Rule, making it one of his first concerns and devoting his entire sixth chapter to it; he shifted the balance from the attitudes represented by Valerian. His emphasis was not so much on the content of the silence as on its ability to express obedience to the abbot from monks, whose prime purpose was to be disciples. '[P]ermission to speak should rarely be granted even to perfect disciples,' he wrote, 'even for good and holy matters and for edifying thoughts; . . . it is fitting for a disciple to be silent and to listen.'[22] One might observe that, on this basis, Jesus's disciples would not have made very good monks.

Around this silence there was of course the regulated noise which was the framework for monastic life. Monks were now readers of books; indeed they were increasingly expected to read them as part of their monastic life. This was a marked departure from the practice of early Eastern monasticism which can be attributed to the personal preferences and eloquent advocacy of that fourth-century addict of scholarship St Jerome, who had insisted that it was just as arduous and as productive of spiritual growth to read a book as it was to starve in the desert or to sit atop a pillar. There were enough like-minded souls in the monastic world sedulously to promote the view that his argument was good and godly.[23] At least some of that industry of reading was performed aloud, a practice which may have grown more common in monasteries in the medieval period. The historian of philosophy Myles Burnyeat has forcefully argued that reading aloud was not as common in the ancient world as is conventionally believed; nevertheless, the lack of prohibition on reading aloud in monastic regulations indicates that there was a fairly regular danger of hearing the hum of a reader in a monastic library and of not being able to do anything about it.[24]

The sound of bells was also a constant, announcing the further noise of human voices gathered to perform the liturgical round. Ambrose of Milan (c. 339–97), one of the first of the great aristocrat-administrators to turn Christian bishop, contributed one important reflection on the relationship of silence to the Western Church's increasingly elaborate public performance of the liturgy when he observed that 'when a psalm is read, it is itself the instrument of silence for the one who reads. Everyone speaks, and no one interrupts with a clamour.'[25] Ambrose would have envisaged a single cantor reading the Psalms to a silent congregation, but his words would take on a new significance when, in the eighth century, a major liturgical shift took place in Western monasteries. Now the entire monastic community sang the Psalms together. Their combined noise banished other noise from their church and from their minds. The principle was taken even further, with monks now customarily singing the Psalms as they worked in their community or out in the fields. It was an excellent way for an abbot to feel reassured that his brethren were not idly gossiping and that their minds and bodies were concentrated rhythmically on a single task. One is reminded of the same use of communal chanting on military route-marching at the present day.[26]

There are hints by the eighth century that the emphasis on silence set by Benedict was beginning to cause hesitations among some Church leaders, probably because it had been applied over-enthusiastically by some heads of houses. It is at this time that abbots of prominent houses like Monte Cassino and Corbie started issuing regulations providing specified times for conversation in the everyday lives of monks, albeit carefully supervised. The consideration must have been that otherwise silence hindered the need for necessary communication in community life.[27] Moreover the old tension between the life of the Church in its parochial congregations and secular cathedrals, and in monastic communities, also began to find expression in ecclesiastical regulations. Particularly significant in this regard was the work of one great politician-bishop of the mid-eighth-century, Chrodegang (c. 712–66), Bishop of Metz in what is now north-east France. Chrodegang was one of the first bishops in the West to systematize the life of the secular (that is, non-monastic) clergy who served cathedrals. His regulations for them were so effective and widely imitated that cathedral clergy were increasingly referred to as 'canons', from the ordinary Greek word for 'rule'. That did not prevent Chrodegang from being an enthusiast for the monastic life. He promoted a literal observance of Benedict's Rule in a new monastery he established in his diocese at Gorze, so his activity there makes it all the more striking that he did not try to turn his cathedral canons into monks. Silence was useful for canons as one element of their ordered lives, but it was not to dominate their ministry in cathedral churches.[28]

Western monks thus made silence their speciality. When Hildemar, a monk of the abbey of Corbie in what is now north-eastern France, was delivering commentaries on the Rule of St Benedict to the monks of Civate in the mid-ninth century, he took it as axiomatic that laymen and monks would have entirely different attitudes as to how to spend the night: the laity would stay up late chatting and laughing, while monks would be occupied in silent prayer. The two should be kept severely apart.[29] Hildemar's concern had a new urgency, because Western monasteries were now very different from the little communities that John Cassian had created in Gaul or Benedict at Monte Cassino. The Frankish king and self-made emperor Charlemagne (742–814) turned to monasteries as his chief cultural allies in his quest to recreate a Christian version of Roman imperial power in the West, and to rescue what was left of Classical and ancient Christian learning: Jerome's advocacy of monastic scholarship now gained a rich reward. Charlemagne, his successors and their nobility invested massive sums in creating very large monastic communities. These increasingly adopted the Rule of St Benedict, but they did so in the context of a monastic life which was conducted amid a bustle of lay servants, craftsmen, labourers and guests, in grand architectural settings which could outdo most of the palaces of the Western world, and made the Carolingian monastery the equivalent of a small town. The biggest change of all was the wholesale institution of the custom of oblation, that is, the offering of children to embark on a monastic career: and children are, by nature, cheerful foes of silence.

DIONYSIUS AND CLUNY

It is not surprising that old pastoral concerns to establish monastic tranquillity were much renewed in such a world, but further considerations intervened beyond the mere logistics of monastic life. In the ninth century the West recovered much more of the mystical dimension of silence from the East, and to that mysticism it added its own distinctive preoccupation with a theme previously common only in the very early days of Christianity: the end of all things.[30] Two individuals were essential to this change, the first of them long dead. The happily pseudonymous Dionysius the Areopagite jumped the frontiers between Eastern and Western Christianity when John Scotus Eriugena (c. 815–c. 877) came across his text, now three centuries old, fell in love with it and translated it into Latin with an accompanying commentary. Eriugena himself suffered grave ecclesiastical suspicion both during his life and after, because his Platonizing thought was so novel in the West. His work nevertheless represents a remarkable synthesis of Pseudo-Dionysius's negative theology with Augustine of Hippo's reflection on the constitution of humanity as a mirror of the divine.[31]

Several extraneous factors promoted Pseudo-Dionysius's respectability in the Western Latin Church. It was useful that the first manuscript of his work to appear in the West, the actual text used by Eriugena, had been given by ambassadors from Constantinople to Hilduin, a ninth-century abbot of the great Carolingian royal abbey of Saint-Denis near Paris. Hilduin (as the Byzantine Court must have hoped) creatively confused Dionysius with the identically named Gaulish bishop who was patron saint to the abbot's own community. That benevolent elision of identities was as much cause as effect of Dionysius's new popularity in the West. From then on, Dionysius fed a mystical tradition previously little resourced by Western theology.

The second crucial figure was another great abbot in Francia called Odo (c. 878–942), who was born around the time of Eriugena's death. He entered the monastic life at Baume, and later followed its abbot, Berno, to a new foundation of the Benedictine Rule at Cluny, where he became the second abbot in 927. Odo was deeply preoccupied with the idea that monasticism was in steep decline, and he was determined to halt the slide. He was also vividly aware that the first millennium since the birth of Christ was approaching fast. Under Odo's rule Cluny was launched on a path of exemplary monastic life, which attracted extraordinary reverence among contemporaries and made it, by the eleventh century, Western Europe's single most influential monastic community. Its church was the largest on the Continent and its monks were intimately involved in the genesis of Western Christendom's most ambitious and most fatal enterprises, the Crusades to the Holy Land.[32] Abbots Berno and Odo were clearly like-minded souls, and one can detect some of Odo's later preoccupations in the elder abbot's will, which went out of its way to commend the custom of silence among the five virtues.[33] How this worked out for Odo can be reconstructed not only from his own writings and actions, but from the self-conscious apologia created for him by the monk John of Salerno in an admiring biography, which attempted to address a widespread perception among unsympathetic contemporaries that Cluny was going far too far in its innovative view of monastic life.

Silence for Odo was not only a way of calling his monks to be exemplars of holiness, but it also allowed them to play their part in the divine plan for the world, which he expected to end very soon. In a return to a theme which had excited the very first ascetics in second-century Syria, he saw monks as angels, and their life as a discipline of heaven (*coelestis disciplina*).[34] Cluny's round of worship, which became the most elaborate in Latin Christendom, was a deliberate reproduction of the angelic praises in heaven, and the musical solemnity of the liturgy was increasingly surrounded by a profound community silence, especially during the weeks which formed two week-long high points in the year, Christmas and Easter. Odo was a great admirer of the writings of the sixth-century Pope Gregory I, and in his *Moralia* Gregory had given Odo a vital set of links in his programme for Cluny. The pope had observed that it was impossible for humans in this life to apprehend the fullness of divine majesty; it would only be possible for those whom God had chosen at the end of time. Then the spoken word would be replaced with a light to fill every mind.[35] Both Cluny's liturgy and its silence were designed to anticipate this coming state. For a century after the world had failed to end in 1000, the monks of Cluny continued to dwell in a powerhouse of eschatological thought; their sense that the world was entering its last time fuelled the extraordinary burst of reforming energy in the Western Church which culminated in the papacy of Gregory VII (1073–85).

One of the most remarkable fruits of Cluny's regime of silence was its pioneering development of monastic sign language to replace the necessity for speech in everyday transactions. This was widely imitated, not just in the monasteries of Cluny's international federation, but in great Benedictine houses such as Canterbury cathedral priory or the much more austere reforming Order of the twelfth century, the Cistercians. Strictly speaking, it was not a sign language, but a sign system, as it lacked grammar and syntax, but what it did do was to enable work and life to proceed efficiently without speech. Piquantly, its nearest modern equivalent would be sign systems in use in the excessively noisy environments of the Industrial Revolution.[36] Cluny's work took place in three main settings, the kitchen, the library and the liturgy. So the signage had a rich array of words for different types of fish, but no sign for meat, which would not have figured in the monastic diet.

Cluniac sign language regulated thought and action, rather like a benevolent version of George Orwell's Newspeak. One could not gossip nor be malicious in it (at least, that would have required individual ingenuity, and one was not encouraged to supplement signs with gestures involving that dangerous organ, the eye, to supplement meaning). Novices were taught just as much of it as they needed to know and no more: for instance, they did not need to know much of its technical vocabulary about the liturgy, which did not yet involve them. Some of the signs would teach them instructive lessons: for instance, the symbol for angel was the same as for Alleluia, because that was what angels sang in heaven, just like monks in their choir. Contrariwise, the sign for a secular book was derived from the gesture a dog made scratching its ear – those who read secular books were no better than animals. Knowing the signs built up a common monastic identity against outsiders. It also was a comment on the fact that Cluny was the first centralized multinational corporation in European history, so many Cluniac monks would not have understood each other's birth languages anyway.[37] Pedro Ponce, a later monk-practitioner of a system descended from Cluniac signs in sixteenth-century Spain, was a pioneer of a sign system for deaf children: it was a pleasing irony that the system designed to facilitate silence was the agent of their release into communication with the rest of the world.[38]

NEW ORDERS FOR THE WESTERN CHURCH

By the twelfth century the glory days of Cluny were drawing to a close, and most of the considerable number of new Orders created in that era could well be considered an oblique criticism of the sort of monastic spirituality that it represented. Many found the collective opulence of great Benedictine and Cluniac corporations increasingly less palatable. The severity of the Cistercians in architecture, for instance, clearly embodied a comment on the Cluniac decorative style, but silence was not at issue between the two Orders, as was acknowledged by those like the contemporary Benedictine historian Orderic Vitalis, who commented on their other differences.[39] Not so the Carthusians, the one medieval Order to make a permanent success of monastic simplicity. Their foundations were a deliberate repudiation of the Benedictine tradition of communal life. Their key to avoid the temptations to slackness which haunt every religious community was and is their resolve to preserve each monk in solitude in order that he may seek a greater intimacy with the divine. Each member of the community occupies his own walled-in cottage and garden within the monastery, only meeting his fellows for three periods of worship through the day: and, after all, what is a garden but another miniature encounter with paradise?

In the days when Carthusians had servants, even the servants were forbidden from speaking at all, unlike the more moderate silences imposed by Cistercians on their lay brothers (*conversi*). Carthusians thus effortlessly outstripped the Cluniacs in silence, making no great emphasis on liturgical prayer, but they did pursue in full the theme of the eschatological significance of what they were doing: only the direst emergencies interrupted their perpetual meditative silence, and one popular subject of that meditation was how every careless word would be brought to account on the Day of Judgement. The Carthusians even avoided making any imitation of the Cluniac sign system and invented their own, which they called (in a proud reversal of pride) *signa rustica*: no sophisticated sign play on concepts like Alleluia for them.[40]

It is worth comparing Cluniac or Carthusian approaches to silent community life with the classic age of Egyptian monasticism in the fourth and fifth centuries. Cluny, as has already been observed (p. 76), bore a remarkable resemblance to the Nile-valley communities of Upper Egypt so carefully structured by Pachomius. The Grande Chartreuse in the French Alps and its imitators had a different precedent, the scattered colony of hermits in the 22-mile-long valley of

Scetis of Lower Egypt, each in their individual cells but collectively forming a monastic republic looking to the authority of Abbot Macarius the Egyptian and his successors.[41] In both cases, the later Orders showed differences from their predecessors: one can detect that characteristic tidy-mindedness which has been such a feature of the Western Latin Church, in contrast to the Orthodox and the Oriental Churches. Cluny structured its silent life in a more thoroughgoing fashion and gave it a new justification in eschatology, while the Carthusians gathered their hermits in a single precinct, and minimized the opportunity for spiritual conversation almost to vanishing point.

One great continuity with those earlier communities of Egypt was the result of the infiltration of Eastern modes of spirituality through Pseudo-Dionysius in the ninth century. The Western practice of *lectio divina* pioneered by Augustine of Hippo had developed into a contemplative monastic tradition of reading the sacred text which now veered much further into the Eastern concept of union with God than Augustine would ever have envisaged. So the twelfth-century Carthusian Prior Guigo (d. 1193) wrote a brief guide to spirituality, the *Ladder of Monks*, in which he made precisely the distinction between meditation and contemplation which Eastern Christians had inherited from Evagrius.[42]

The four rungs of Guigo's ladder offered an ascent from reading to meditation to prayer to contemplation. He borrowed that scheme from an Augustinian canon of the previous generation, Hugh of St Victor (c. 1096–1141), and behind him there was once more an Eastern source for Guigo's controlling metaphor, that great work of Egyptian contemplation, the *Ladder* of John Climacus (c. 570–c. 659), an abbot who had relished the teaching of Evagrius before it was unsafe to do so.[43] Guigo's language of *theosis* was his own, and a good deal more edgy than anything in Hugh of St Victor. He spoke of God as a loving husband, and he mixed this risky extended metaphor of *theosis* with another very physical image: that of Jacob wrestling in the night with the angel (Gen. 32.22–32). Although a devotee of *lectio divina*, he nerved himself to put reading no higher than the first rung of his ladder: 'reading without meditation is sterile, meditation without reading is liable to error, prayer without meditation is lukewarm, meditation without prayer is unfruitful, prayer when it is fervent wins contemplation, but to obtain it without prayer would be rare, even miraculous.'[44]

Soon other readers of the Bible in their monasteries were taking up Guigo's subversive thoughts in ways which might reinforce the practice of contemplation, but might not. They pressed their engagement with Scripture beyond its text, to the point that they allowed their imaginations to dwell on and wander through the imaginative results of their reading, as the text itself faded away. The process was distinct enough to acquire its own separate name, *lectio spiritualis*, which might simply be translated as 'spiritual perusal', but really it was a form of 'emotional perusal': the exploration of an individual's feelings standing before divinity. This was an unexpected result of the leaching of Eastern Christian thought into the West. The end-product might not so much be contemplation, the vanishing of the soul into the ocean of the sacred, as the free flight and self-assertion of the human imagination.[45] It was, after all, the West that was destined to reinvent the ancient pre-Christian literary genre of the novel.

In generous mood, some Benedictines and Cluniacs could recognize that they had been outgunned in the heroism of ascetic practice by such Carthusians as Guigo. Peter of Celle (*c.* 1115–83), a Benedictine abbot who became Bishop of Chartres, praised the Carthusian Order with what had started life in Psalm 115 as a religious insult: 'mouths have they, and speak not.'[46] This topsy-turvy use of a text that we have already encountered (above, p. 13) is a specimen of the medieval West's genius for twisting any text of the Bible to a new purpose, the product of monks whose practice of *lectio divina* was at the centre of their lives. Yet it was also more than that: a symptom of monastic confidence in this greatest age of the triumph of monastic silence, when Cluniacs and Cistercians could become popes.

Odo of Cluny and his successors assembled a battery of scriptural quotations on silence to justify their way of life. Repeatedly one finds monks whose lives had become structured by silence cheerfully reaching for these biblical texts which had not really been intended for the purpose. A fine example of that comes from one of the letters of Bernard of Clairvaux (1090–1153), whose content incidentally tells us that he was not writing in silence, but dictating to an assistant. We find the great Cistercian in not untypically imperious mood, spending a considerable time and a good many words telling one of his correspondents why it is inappropriate for him to expend such literary labour (and more importantly, mental and spiritual energy) in Lent, when his faculties should be devoted to higher things:

> what a tumult there is in the mind of those who dictate, what a crowd
> of sentiments, variety of expressions, diversity of senses jostle; how fre-
> quently one rejects that word which presents itself and seeks another
> which still escapes; what close attention one gives to the consecutive-
> ness of the line of thought and the elegance of the expression! . . . It is
> for this reason I have fled from the world and abide in solitude, and
> propose to myself with the prophet, 'to take heed to my ways that I
> offend not with my tongue' [Ps. 39.1] since, according to the same
> prophet [the Psalmist], 'A man full of words shall not prosper upon the
> earth' [Ps. 140.11], and to another Scripture, 'Death and life are in the
> power of the tongue' [Prov. 18.21]. But silence, says Isaiah, 'is the work
> of righteousness' [Isa. 32.17], and Jeremiah teaches us 'to wait in silence
> for the salvation of the Lord' [Lam. 3.26].[47]

A particularly engaging example of mystical text-appropriation of Scripture comes from a most individually minded eleventh-century Benedictine, Guibert (1055–1124), who, not entirely happily, became Abbot of Nogent. Guibert seized on that most solemn moment of rest in the Book of Revelation, the famously approximate half an hour which has already exercised our curiosity (above, pp. 47–9), as a good precedent for having a little lunchtime rest from contemplation. He interpreted the text as recommending a variety of divine siesta:

> if there is silence at midday in heaven, our gift of contemplation cannot,
> while we live, remain in a state of unremitting intensity, and so neither, if
> I may say so, can a mind at work remain steadfast in any kind of thinking.
> Thus, we believe that when our hearts are intent upon any object, there
> must be variation in the objects of our intentions, so that while we ponder
> different things in turn, we return refreshed to the one thing to which the
> soul is most attached, as if we had been given some time for recreation.[48]

Evagrius Ponticus or Isaac of Nineveh might well have blanched at this cheerfully pragmatic Western view of how the individual mind sets out on its journey towards divine perfection.

PART THREE

Silence through Three Reformations

5

From Iconoclasm to Erasmus:
700–1500

ICONS: CONTEMPLATION FOR ALL

The first major attempt at Reformation in the Christian world occurred not in the Latin West as is commonly imagined, but in Byzantium, in the eighth and ninth centuries, where it was led by the imperial authorities, in what is known today as the Iconoclastic Movement. The second, also inspired from above but this time by leading churchmen, was the radical reshaping of the Western Church during the eleventh and twelfth centuries undertaken by successive popes. Their work was sent into partial reverse by a third Reformation – by 'Protestants', in the sixteenth century. Each deserves to be given the name 'Reformation' which is generally reserved for the last of them, despite their three very different outcomes.

The Iconoclastic Controversy is generally described as an effort to interrupt the preordained and pre-existing course of Orthodox history: an unsuccessful bid to evict icons from their already central place in Orthodox life. Its defeat, according to this narrative, logically ended in 843 with a 'Triumph of Orthodoxy'.[1] The reality was not quite like that. It was the very struggle over icons that promoted them, after they had eventually been reaffirmed in 843, to the place that they now hold in Orthodox spirituality. It is worth pondering what the underlying issue had been, to produce this success for those who defended icons (the 'Iconophiles'); we shall find it very relevant to the theme of silence.

The ostensible matter of conflict was the role of visual representations of God in churches and society generally. It is important to note precisely that it was representations of God that were in contention.

Byzantine 'Iconoclasts' – those who destroyed these images – were not opposed to art in general. They gladly decorated their churches not only with crosses and vegetable and abstract motifs, but also (if we call into witness an outlying Carolingian survivor beyond the vengeance of later Iconophiles, at Germigny-des-Prés in France) angels and other symbols such as the Ark of the Covenant.[2] Sixteenth-century Reformed Protestants, iconophobes to a man, gratefully seized on the precedent for what they themselves were now doing in the Western Church, even though they went much further in their destruction of sacred imagery than the ancient Iconoclasts. They appropriated and excitedly publicized some of the literature which Western Latins in sympathy with Eastern Iconoclasts had produced during the ninth-century stage of the controversy.[3]

Why were these latter-day Protestant Iconoclasts mistaken in their understanding of Byzantine Iconoclasm? Inevitably they lacked historical perspective: they could not see that the Iconoclastic Controversy had played out against a particular geopolitical background, when a new religion with an absolute prohibition of images of God had been on the verge of conquering the entire Mediterranean. It was understandable that Christians from Spain to Armenia should have decided that there must be some good reason why Muslims were winning God's favour. The Muslim detestation of sacred images must have seemed as good a reason as any. Iconoclasm was thus a rational response to the threat of Islam, and that is why in the course of a century it was repeatedly initiated and supported by emperors who were some of the most competent military leaders in Byzantine history. Yet there was also an internal Christian dynamic to the clash. Peter Brown, with characteristic analytical elegance, has suggested a new perspective on this turbulent and formative period for Orthodoxy: it was an argument about how Christians might reach out to God.[4]

Can that perpetual Christian search be achieved primarily through the Church's liturgy, rather than through the medium of the image? The Iconoclasts said that it could, thus affirming one way in which Byzantine Christianity had developed in the previous three centuries. The empire's liturgical performance looked to a single great church – in fact, THE Great Church, the Emperor Justinian's Hagia Sophia in Constantinople. A steady elaboration of liturgical music had developed both in Hagia Sophia and in major monasteries of the Byzantine world – first those in Palestine and later the immensely influential Stoudite monastery in Constantinople itself. In other words, the Iconoclasts' vision of worship was that it should primarily consist of what clergy did in churches, with the full grandeur of developed choral music. Iconoclasts had little else to offer those for whom the liturgy had become too professionalized and remote to satisfy every spiritual need. Nor would Reformed Protestants, whom we shall find profoundly suspicious of elaborate liturgy and its music (below, p. 131), have found them congenial bedfellows.

The Iconophiles shared the Iconoclasts' love of the liturgy, but they offered alternative routes to the divine. They maintained that believers do not necessarily need the blessing of a clergyman to make something holy: everyone can freely encounter the sacred, because all that God has created is by nature sacred. Icons in particular are available to the entire people of God, and not only those found in church; they have a power in and of themselves. There was already a considerable body of opinion in the Byzantine world before the Controversy which saw icons as containing a perpetual and intimate bond to that which they represented. So a pre-Iconoclastic life of St Simeon the Younger Stylite said about a particular image of the saint that it worked miracles 'because the Holy Ghost which dwelt in him [St Simeon] overshadowed it [the image]'.[5] This was not a power of the Holy Ghost called down by a priest such as took place in the eucharist. Anyone could contemplate an icon and meet the Holy Spirit: layfolk, monks and nuns as well as priests.

The concept of a power-charged contemplation of icons which developed in the midst of the controversy had no precedent in the earlier history of the Church. Iconophiles envisaged a stretching-out of humanity beyond everyday life until it achieved union with divinity, a *theosis* of sacramental significance. The first explicit defence of images in Christianity, which the Cappadocian Fathers (above, p. 79) had pioneered in the fourth century, had relied on the argument that images were useful as a means of instruction for the faithful. From the sixth century, and decisively after the ninth-century Triumph of Orthodoxy, the Eastern Church was moving on to a more far-reaching understanding of the potential function of the icon.[6]

That is why Iconoclasts detested images so much: they felt that they had attracted a new and unwarranted cult, and that this was as blasphemous and un-Christian as the worship of idols. In terms of the first two centuries of Christian history, Iconoclasts might have been right, and powerful voices had gone on making their case in the centuries before the controversy broke out, but now they were being left behind.[7] One of the most persuasive voices supporting their Iconophile opponents was that great Miaphysite champion of silence, Pseudo-Dionysius the Areopagite, who saw visible images as the path leading 'to the contemplation of the divine'. Many Orthodox lovers of visual holiness rapidly took up his arguments, happily oblivious of his unorthodoxy.[8]

One way of reading the Iconoclastic Controversy, therefore, is to see it as a contest between the monopoly claims of holy noise, in the form of the liturgy of the Byzantine Church, and the dissident and democratic voice of contemplative silence. Not all monasteries or nunneries backed the Iconophiles, but monks and nuns who loved icons and used them as objects of their own contemplation could ally with a popular movement rooted among laypeople to save images from the consequences of high clericalism and imperial policy. That became both the strength and the salvation of icons through the years in which the emperors tore them down in churches. They took refuge in peoples' homes, where mothers or grandmothers exercised their customary domestic power to save them. Perhaps such ordinary folk did not have the sophistication of those who had read their Dionysius or Evagrius, but they knew a road to salvation when they saw it, in more senses than one. Equally, icons and their defence became associated with Byzantium's independent holy men – ordinary yet extraordinary, maybe wandering from place to place, yet still claiming the holiness of a monk or hermit. They owed little to the Church hierarchy and its compromises with the emperor's whims.

THE LATIN WEST: A DIFFERENT PATH

These eighth- and ninth-century arguments led to a decisive realignment of what was to become Orthodox Christianity. Of course the liturgy continued in its central place in the Church; why would it not?

But alongside the liturgy was an affirmation of a form of devotion which before the eighth century had been controversial: the use of icons as a democratic complement to clerically dominated worship in church, as a partner in the universal Orthodox search for *theosis*. One might at a superficial level consider that the outcome was the same in the contemporary Latin West. After a brief ninth-century spasm of iconophobia favoured by Charlemagne and his son, wall-paintings and statues in Western churches or at holy sites likewise resumed a career as foci of devotion and prayer, complete with their individual array of votive candles which any layperson or cleric could light either within or outside the liturgy.

Westerners thus stood in prayer before images, but the general dynamic of Western devotion was different from that of the East: the images were generally not icons, but statues or carved panels, and thus graven images, which Orthodoxy, after the turbulence of the Iconoclastic Controversy, took care to avoid. Western graven images became ever more lifelike, bringing the divine down into the middle of life, just as the Western Latin view of the eucharist increasingly emphasized the corporeality and physical presence of the body of Christ, summoned down by divine grace and priestly prayer to the altar.[9] Eastern sacred art, steadily less concerned with exact or realistic representation, took the worshipper in the other direction, towards heaven. Art in Orthodoxy became not a means of individual human creative expression, but an acclamation of the corporate experience of the Church; the artist became a theologian, an interpreter of doctrine through image and story. Every sacred picture was something to be approached in meditation and with an acute sense of tradition.[10]

A famous incident, much cherished by Western Christians, illustrates the difference between East and West, all the more strikingly because it centres on a twelfth-century crucifix of Eastern Christian style which still survives in the church of Santa Chiara in Assisi. This is the crucifix which, in its original position in the church of San Damiano, spoke to the future spiritual leader Francis of Assisi, and told him to rebuild Christ's Church. Francis's reaction to this encounter with his crucified Saviour was the first step in a distinctive Franciscan form of devotion which came to emphasize the human sufferings of Christ, to an extent that even some contemporaries found alarming.[11]

We moderns are likely to look at this crucifix and see something hieratic and unmistakably Orthodox, like much Umbrian art of its period deeply influenced by Byzantium. Yet for Francis, it stirred an intense emotion and a call to action. His reaction to it was that of a Westerner, and Westerners were conditioned by the Romanesque art around them, frequently full of turmoil, vitality and violent distortion.[12] Two centuries later, that unusually noisy mystic Margery Kempe had no doubt as to what she must do when contemplating a *pietà* in a Norwich church: she was moved to 'cryyn ful lowde and wepyn ful sor'.[13]

ORTHODOXY AND HESYCHASM

Once icons had returned to Orthodox churches in triumph in 843, they steadily asserted their place within its physical fabric. During the course of the thirteenth to fifteenth centuries, this resulted in the development of a new piece of church furniture, the iconostasis ('stand for icons'), which has now become the dominant feature of an Orthodox church interior. A complementary set of experiences has developed within communal Orthodox worship. One of these is the liturgy, led by the clergy through a series of preordained stages of formal prayer, sung with whatever degree of solemnity that clergy, choir and people can achieve. In this, the iconostasis serves as a marker of many key stages in the movement of liturgical performance. The other is a myriad of simultaneous small individual acts of contemplation and prayer offered by the faithful, before icons placed on their own stands, or formally ranked amid the assemblage of icons on the iconostasis. Each icon follows a wealth of rules of composition built up since the sixth century to express particular theological or devotional propositions around sacred stories – but crucially, each icon might equally well be found in a humble room in any household, and it could mediate the same individual devotion there: Martha of Bethany busy in her kitchen can be a theologian. This combination has been the one of the great strengths of Orthodoxy, sustaining it through trials which by most reckonings ought to have eliminated it.

It can hardly be coincidence that the first flourishing of the iconostasis in church interiors in the thirteenth century occurred in the period of Orthodoxy which also developed a new approach to silence: 'hesychasm', a word which simply means the practice of silence (*hēsychia* in Greek). During the fourteenth century, amid great argument which assumed political dimensions, hesychasm became the dominant devotional movement in the Orthodox Church, championed by patriarchs, bishops, abbots and the waning imperial establishment, and later treated indulgently by the conquering Ottoman Turks. The practice of contemplation of God in hesychasm was intimately linked to the icon: while disciplining the human faculty of hearing, it emphasized the complementary importance of sight, dwelling on the truths which icons embodied, and the spiritual light which shone through them. Mystics had always been drawn to the metaphor of light, but now, particularly in the cluster of monasteries clinging to Mount Athos on the Macedonian coast, it became much more than a metaphor. For the Hesychasts, it was the vehicle of seeing and knowing God. Gregory Palamas (1296–1359), a monk on Athos from 1318, was chief among the exponents and champions of hesychasm in the fourteenth century. He maintained that, in the practice of hesychastic prayer, it is possible to reach a vision of divine light revealing God's uncreated energy, which is the Holy Spirit:

> when the saints contemplate this divine light within themselves, seeing it by the divinising communion of the Spirit, through the mysterious visitation of perfecting illuminations – then they behold the garment of their deification, their mind being glorified and filled by the grace of the Word, beautiful beyond measure in His splendour; just as divinity of the Word on the mountain glorified with divine light the body conjoined to it.[14]

Gregory was referring to the episode of Transfiguration described in the Synoptic Gospels, in which Jesus was with his disciples on Mount Tabor, and they could see that his face 'shone like the sun'.[15] The Transfiguration, already commemorated with greater elaboration in Orthodoxy than in the Latin West, became a favourite hesychast choice of subject for icons.

Apart from contemplation of the icon, Hesychasts drew on long experience among ascetics of practical, physical ways to structure still or silent prayer. They developed guidelines for appropriate physical posture and correct breathing. One characteristic practice is to exclude noise, either in the outer world or in the mind, by repeating a single devotional phrase, the most common of which has come to be 'Lord Jesus Christ, Son of the living God, have mercy on me'. This phrase or variants on it have become known as the 'Jesus Prayer'. Nothing suggests that the Jesus Prayer had been common in Orthodox Church practice before the thirteenth century outside a few monastic centres like St Catherine in Sinai. And yet it was a direct descendant of that devotional repetition of Jesus's name which, nearly a millennium before, St Macarius the Egyptian had affectionately compared to the women of his childhood enjoying their chewing-gum (above, pp. 76–7).[16]

There is no doubt that the hesychast approach draws on a venerable and vigorous tradition within the Christian eastern Mediterranean, but to grant that does not explain why the hesychast bundle of ideas and practices emerged and then triumphed in Orthodoxy just when it did. Hesychasts did, after all, face formidable opposition within Byzantium from distinguished and sophisticated theologians such as Barlaam the Calabrian (c. 1290–1348), who felt that the movement was dangerously innovative and destructive of the monastic tradition which he loved. Those opposing hesychasm were just as loyal children of the Church, but nevertheless they found themselves thrust aside and discredited by powerful political and clerical interests, who allied with popular devotion to establish hesychasm as a normative expression of Orthodoxy.[17]

It is possible to explain this triumph in terms of the dire contemporary political situation in the fourteenth century: hesychasm has been called 'part of a chain reaction among reflective souls across the Orthodox world to the shortcomings of earthly institutions'.[18] The Byzantine Empire had never recovered from the criminal Western vandalism of the Fourth Crusade of 1204. Even when the Latins were expelled from Constantinople, Byzantium was irretrievably divided and continually diminished by military pressure from the Ottoman Turks, until the final conquests of Constantinople and Trebizond in the fifteenth century. Moreover, at the height of Gregory's and Barlaam's struggle over hesychasm in the 1340s, Asia and Europe faced the baffling terror of the Black Death. What more natural amid such miseries than to turn inwards to seek the light and comfort of God? It probably helped that the Ottomans, busily digesting the former Byzantine Empire piece by piece, were well disposed to a movement that encouraged their new Christian subjects to introspection and political passivity. Gregory Palamas himself was notably well treated when he was an involuntary guest at the Ottoman Sultan's Court in 1354; equally significantly, the Ottomans left in place and even allowed expansion in the monastic republic which is still in existence on Mount Athos, the original chief stronghold and continuing power-house of hesychasm, when so many other great monastic centres were dispersed or declined into oblivion.[19]

One should not neglect a more positive possible influence from Islam: the mystical movement known as Sufism, with its quest for a special friendship with God, and its conviction that ecstasy provides a path to knowledge of divine truth. Sufism predates the late thirteenth-century rise of hesychasm: its final acceptance into the Islamic mainstream had taken place two hundred years before, through the writings of the great mystical philosopher al-Ghazali. There is a not-able similarity in the suspicion of the intellect expressed by Gregory Palamas and such earlier masters as al-Ghazali, and in the fact that both movements emphasize the recitation of the divine name.

We have seen how, back in the eighth century, Muslim iconophobia had touched off ancient iconophobic themes from Judaism which the Tanakh had bequeathed to Christian sacred Scripture; in the same way, the impressive example of the Sufi mystics in the steadily encroach-ing Muslim dominions may have stimulated a Christian rediscovery of ancient Christian resources to produce the hesychast movement. If there is a direct relationship between the hesychast approach and Suf-ism, there remains acute controversy, with an obvious contemporary political charge, as to which way the influence travelled: Muslim to Christian, or vice versa? The chronology suggests the priority of Islam – and not merely Islam, but what lies beyond it. Once more, it is worth emphasizing that, when considering Christian mysticism, it is never wise to confine one's gaze to the Mediterranean: it should travel eastwards, as far as the Buddhism and Hinduism of India and China, because that is what ancient Christians themselves did.[20]

There is one significant difference between Sufis and Hesychasts. During the fourteenth century, the Hesychasts reined in their early emphasis on the physical aspects of silent meditation: by contrast, the Sufis had greatly developed it, particularly in the thirteenth-century Sufi Mevlevi Order, still famous for the dancing of its 'whirling dervishes'.[21] Maybe, if there had been a more exuberant survival of imperial Byzantium, Hesychast Orthodoxy would also have developed its dervishes. In the short term, such practices as contemplative navel-gazing would have been unhelpful in the desperate Byzantine military and theological negotiations with the West which preceded the fall of Constantinople in 1453; they would not have endeared Byzantium to the Western Church. In the long term, equally, the Ottomans were unlikely to have tolerated such public and extrovert expressions of Christianity. In any case, the religion which had turned its face against the theological use of laughter back in the second century (above, pp. 59–61) was not likely to look kindly on liturgical dance. As in so many things, the Ethiopian Church has over the centuries been the exception to prove this general rule, though its practice probably owes more to its reverence for the Old Testament's commendation of dancing before the Lord than to any influence from Sufism.[22]

GREGORIAN REFORM IN THE WEST

The era which produced the triumph of hesychasm, the thirteenth and fourteenth centuries, took a very different turn in the Latin Church of the West, where a first effort at Reformation had taken place during the eleventh and twelfth centuries. Like the earlier attempted Reformation in the Church of Constantinople, it was a movement of reform primarily led from above, by a series of popes of whom one, Gregory VII, has lent his personality to the enterprise. Gregorian reform defined more rigidly the boundary between clergy and laity, and drew jurisdictional power to Rome. In the context of monastic life, it encouraged new foundations and reformed Orders. The Western Church thus became both increasingly centralized and compartmentalized; silence and contemplation were increasingly regarded as the business not of layfolk, but of Orders founded to make such practices central to their lives. Not all monks were clergy, and the great success of the new Cistercian Order in the twelfth century was partly thanks to the opportunity it offered illiterate or semi-literate laypeople to be integrated into monastic life. Yet the frontier between a life 'in religion' and a life in ordinary lay society became increasingly clear: so much so that even clergy who were serving in the parish or cathedral system were referred to as 'seculars'. Western Christianity had already taken a different line from the East as early as the time of St Benedict, by setting its face against wandering ascetics, who have continued to be so prominent in Orthodoxy. Western asceticism has classically been practised in community or by carefully regulated hermits, given a fixed home, often in virtually permanent enclosure.[23]

This was all of a piece with the Western Church's imposition of universal and mandatory celibacy on its clergy, an imposition unique in the Christian world: no other Church has ever extended this monastic discipline in compulsory fashion across the whole clerical body. The Orthodox, by contrast, institutionalized the difference between monks and parish clergy, making the monastic life the exclusive road to episcopal office while strongly encouraging parish clergy to marry. In the West, the prestige of monasticism impelled the Church to banish wives and children from parsonages, as well as more logically from monastic precincts. This separation of clerical from lay status, together with an assumption of clerical superiority and the superiority of celibacy over marriage, are distinctive features of the medieval Western Church, and these characteristics have lingered on into modern times (below, pp. 206-7).[24]

Having set up its own structures, Western monasticism continued to flourish and proliferate different forms. Alone among monastic Orders, the Carthusians never warranted reform, thanks to their proudly maintained austerity.[25] While never numerous anywhere in Europe, they spread widely across the Continent: the increasing architectural magnificence of their 'Charterhouse' monasteries, a mark of the esteem which the European secular elites felt for their holiness, was a paradoxical setting for their heroic solitary asceticism. Kings and noblemen paid for these stately buildings because they valued the counsel of the solitaries; admiration from great men whose lives were mired in the everyday sordidness of politics was probably tinged with wistful envy of hermit simplicity. By the fifteenth century, Carthusians across Europe were producing manuals of conscience for the powerful, some of which survive in copies evidently painfully written out by noblemen or noblewomen themselves.[26]

Beyond the ability of the Carthusians to maintain their austerity, much criticism of the Church was absorbed through a process of regular innovation: official papal sanction for new institutions. Up to the fourteenth century, the Western Church was remarkably creative in inventing new forms of asceticism to complement the old. So those impresarios of Western silence, the Cluniacs, had produced a reaction of austerity in the Cistercian Reform (above, p. 99), and when the mass of twelfth-century monastic reforms in turn failed to satisfy popular hunger for holiness, a new version of the regular life emerged in the form of the various Orders of friars which gained papal recognition in the thirteenth century. The daily lives of the friars was in itself something of a criticism of the enclosed regular life, since their ministry focused on constant contact and communication with the laity. Since they tried with relative success to avoid accumulating the great estates which monasteries had gathered for their endowments, friars made their living by gathering funds from the laity in return for the spiritual services they provided: hence their proudly borne label as 'Mendicants', beggars.

One of the most influential of these organizations was that created by St Dominic. For an exemplar of silence in the medieval Western Church we might not look to the Dominicans, who were indeed officially called the Order of Preachers, yet it is worth remembering that friars offered a variety of services to layfolk, both in their innovatively designed and welcoming churches and out in the parishes. They did not simply provide preaching, but also votive Masses, and individual confession. Parish clergy were able to perform all these functions, but the friars were widely seen as the specialists. The practice of individual auricular confession had been a growing practice in the Western Church since the ninth century.[27] Innocent III, the same pope who so encouraged the formalization and recognition of the main Orders of friars, was instrumental in making regular individual confession to a priest mandatory for all faithful Catholics.

The point and the power of this encounter between priest and

layperson was that it was a conversation which then completely vanished from the record. This silence of the confessional, a principle
peculiar to the Western Church, was an essential element and indeed
a validation of the experience, however much it might be breached in
practice. It was also one more building-block in the growing accumu-
lation of sacred power by the Western clergy, regular and secular, both
now officially marked off from the laity by their celibacy. Their power
also centred on a penitential system which was increasingly associated with that peculiarly Western doctrine, purgatory, and these two
distinctive features of the Western Latin Church, celibacy and the
industry that purgatory became, were eventually to prove flashpoints
to tear it apart.

The Orders of friars included one of the strangest of religious
Orders in any part of Christendom: the groups who came together as
the Order of the Brothers of Our Lady of Mount Carmel (Carmelites).
They began as an informal group of hermits in the Latin Kingdom of
Jerusalem living on Mount Carmel, where they probably went as refugees when Jerusalem was first recaptured by the Muslims in 1187.
Conditions grew impossible for them when the whole kingdom col-
lapsed, so during the mid-thirteenth century they migrated westward
across the Mediterranean. Now they would have to find a role for
themselves in a Church which looked with deep suspicion on new
religious movements, but which also offered them a route out of possible condemnation, in the shape of the recently contrived identity of
Mendicancy. When the Palestinian ascetics reached Europe, they not
only succeeded in forming themselves into an accredited Order of
friars, but crucially accounted for their odd history to a wary Church
hierarchy by the ingenious if drastic means of inventing an origin even
more exotic than the already unusual reality: they backdated themselves to the time of the prophet Elijah, a much earlier enthusiast for
Mount Carmel. Thus they became the only Christian religious Order
ever to claim a pre-Christian past, as well as the only Order of contemplative religious to have taken its origins among the Latin Christian
settlements of the East. Carmelite pseudo-history was ridiculed even
at the time, particularly by their fellow-friars the Dominicans, but
enough influential people chose to believe Carmelite fictions to ensure
their survival as a respected section of the Mendicant world.[28]

There was indeed a distinctive value in the Carmelites' stubborn adherence to their story of Elijah, who had heard the whisper of God on a mountain. Since they kept their collective memory of contemplation on Mount Carmel, they brought with them to the West a love of rural solitude and its beauty. The Cistercians in their early years had independently discovered the value of contemplating the European countryside, but the Carmelites came to outstrip the rather instrumental attitude which even the earliest Cistercians took to their wildernesses, which supported their foundations with large-scale farming. The Carthusians had chosen to make a myriad of little paradises out of the enclosed individual gardens cultivated by their hermit-monks. The Carmelites, by contrast, remembering their mountain-wilderness, saw paradise in nature unspoilt by fallen humans.

We have already compared Cluniac and Carthusian silences with those of early Egyptian asceticism (above, p. 99); there are different comparisons to draw between the Cistercian and Carmelite enthusiasm for desert places and the mindset of the Desert Fathers. From Antony onwards, Egyptian monks and hermits had rarely seen deserts as anything more than places of struggle against demons and physical discomforts, or escapes from the sins of the world. They were not places in which to admire the beauty of creation and see paradise beyond it. Carmelites added to an existing Cistercian literature on natural beauty, and eventually surpassed it. True to the Mendicant ideal, they were not interested in accumulating landed estates such as sustained Cistercian life, but like all the Orders of friars, they soon disagreed among themselves bitterly about their strategy for the future. Many of the first refugees in Europe headed for solitudes such as Carmel had been, but within a few decades the Carmelites were building their houses in busy towns just like the Dominicans and Franciscans.

One of the Carmelite old guard, Nicholas Gallicus, Prior-General between 1266 and 1271, wrote a bitter diatribe against the general tendency of the Order to ape their fellow-friars; he called his bilious work the 'Fiery Arrow', *Ignea Sagitta*. Gallicus's sheer love of nature provides some of the few moments where the *Ignea Sagitta* forgets its anger. He urged his brethren to return to the wilderness, not least because its natural beauty is a poem in worship of God: 'The roots germinate, the grass grows strong, leaves and branches rejoice and praise in their own way for us.'[29] He spoke lyrically of the stars and the singing of birds, passionately contrasting all this with the vicious and violent life which surrounded Carmelites in their urban friaries.

It is likely that Nicholas's work was little known among the Carmelites until the fifteenth century, but from then on it had a dramatic effect on the Order: the Carmelites rediscovered their roots in the wilderness, particularly under the stimulus of the remodelling of the Order in Counter-Reformation Spain. Two tremendously influential Spanish Carmelites, John of the Cross and Teresa of Avila, would introduce a new conception of contemplation in the sixteenth century: their version of the Order was called 'Discalced' because its members either went barefoot or only wore sandals. In order to enjoy the divine pleasures of creation, Discalced Carmelites began encouraging their donors to create rural wildernesses for them, not to farm for profit as Cistercians had done, but simply for contemplation. These were the first wild gardens or sacred theme parks to appear in the history of ascetic silence.[30]

MONKS AND MYSTICS

The rapid institutionalization and enclosure of the Carmelites in the thirteenth century reinforces the great contrast between East and West. While individual asceticism and lay itinerant mysticism outside monastic communities continued to flourish in Orthodoxy, similar ascetics faced ambiguous and sometimes fatally punitive reactions from a Western Church which from the mid-twelfth century had become much more intolerant of deviant behaviour, in what R. I. Moore has famously called 'the formation of a persecuting society'.[31] Notable in the precarious profession of medieval Western mystic was the fact that many were women. One reason for this was a structural change in education and scholarship in the twelfth-century West: the growth of universities. Imitations of Islamic centres of higher education, universities in Latin Christianity were a necessary means of processing the flood of Classical learning arriving in the West via

Spain and the Crusades. Crucially, like their Islamic predecessors, these were all-male institutions. They arrogated to themselves most of the intellectual activity of Western Latin culture, including the practice of a new intellectual discipline which during the twelfth century gained a name previously unknown: theology.[32]

This put women at a grave educational disadvantage. Since the great days of Carolingian monastic foundations, nunneries had possessed as good a chance of being home to scholarship as male Benedictine communities. The most notable example, right at the end of that era, was the polymath and visionary Hildegard of Bingen, Abbess of Rupertsberg (1098–1179). But once men dominated higher learning and embarked on the adventures of formal theology with the aid of a rediscovered corpus of the works of Aristotle, it was decided that learning was not for ladies. Perhaps that is why women were now so attracted to mysticism: it is a mode of spirituality independent of formal intellectual training, that enables both mind and imagination to seek out the hiddenness of God, beyond doctrinal propositions or the argumentative clashes of scholasticism. Many of the writings which conveyed mystical experience in this period were in various European vernaculars, consciously directed towards people whose command of Latin, the international language of Western culture, was shaky or non-existent (as was likely to be the case with most women). Particularly in late medieval England, the anchoritic life became unmistakably a female-dominated profession.[33]

Perhaps this distance from male-dominated scholasticism explains why mystics, through their independent personal experiences, hit on themes which were familiar in Orthodox spirituality, but which had not been given nearly as much official encouragement by the Western Church. The mystic could meet God without needing the mediation of the male Church hierarchy, and in ways which involved remarkable metaphorical or imaginative appropriations of physical contact with the divine.[34] Characteristic in mystical writings of the period are expressions which emphasize the human vulnerability, frailty and virginity of the subject, but which also celebrate the capacity of human frailty to unite with divinity. It is not surprising that such mysticism, springing from free choices by individuals, attracted hostile attention from the inquisitions which became a feature of Western Christianity from the thirteenth century onwards. One of the most well-known mystics, Marguerite Porete, wrote of her experiences in a work in French entitled *Le Mirouer des simples âmes* (*The Mirror of Simple Souls*). Its first modern edition, in 1927, received a papal imprimatur, a gracious partial amends for the fact that Marguerite had been burned at the stake in France as a heretic in 1310.

There was a fine line between such a fate and eventual honour in the Church. One who managed to step just the right side of the line, more by luck than judgement, was the German Dominican Meister Eckhart (*c.* 1260–*c.* 1328). He was an associate of Marguerite Porete during his years in France and was similarly accused of heresy, but he died while inquisition proceedings against him were under way. Simply because his works eventually escaped full condemnation, they could survive and have wide influence, but one can see why an inquisitor would have been suspicious, particularly in view of Eckhart's robust criticism of monastic life and of clerical pretensions to spiritual superiority generally.[35] Writing once more in the vernacular, a vigorous German, Eckhart insisted that after abstracting the particular 'this' or 'that' and achieving 'detachment' – *Gelassenheit* – the soul can meet God in the 'ground' (*Grunt*) of all reality. There she (as he put it) can achieve an inseparable union with the divine, 'the unplumbed depth of God [which] has no name'. 'Life can never be perfected till it returns to its productive source where life is one being that the soul receives when she dies right down to the "ground", that we may live in that life where there is one being.' It is startling, against the background of Western and Augustinian theology, to read in Eckhart that 'God begets His only-begotten Son in the highest part of the soul'.[36]

Gelassenheit sounds remarkably like the *apatheia* of Evagrius Ponticus, but the centuries roll back much further than Evagrius in Eckhart's discussion of the depth of God which has no name, or in the procession and return of the soul, and moreover a soul who is female. Philo, gnostic Christians and Neoplatonists would all have given such themes a welcome. Eckhart offers a mingling of conversations, probably beyond any recognizable ordinary intellectual contact, which is the recurrent ecumenism of the mystic. Such mystics, often inspired by the elusive Pseudo-Dionysius the Areopagite, reversed the normal priorities of Western spirituality, which privileges the positive knowledge of God and affirms what Christian doctrine says about him. They joined Easterners in emphasizing silence and otherness. One of the best-known works to emerge from this tradition is an anonymous meditation probably by a priest, *The Cloud of Unknowing*, which is remarkable for its saturation in the Dionysian text and in its silence on the common apparatus of Western Latin dogma and devotion. It goes directly and consciously to Dionysius when it says that 'the most godlike knowledge of God is that which is known by unknowing'.[37]

At the other extreme of fortune from Marguerite Porete's death at the stake was the fourteenth-century Swedish noblewoman Birgitta or Bridget of Sweden (*c.* 1303–73), who in her widowhood founded a papally approved monastic Order for women and attendant priests. She drew the considerable detail of her foundation out of a single vision of Christ, who considerately spoke to her in Swedish. The Bridgettine Order, like the Carthusian Order with which it was closely associated, became much favoured by Bridget's fellow-nobility and monarchs all over northern Europe. It represented late medieval piety at its most lavishly funded, intense and sophisticated, particularly in England in its single royally sponsored house at Syon in Middlesex, packed with aristocratic ladies and (suitably segregated) retired Oxbridge dons.[38] Bridget and her visions survived by finding a place within the established structures of the Church; her socially elevated status was a helpful factor in her survival.

The role of the Carthusians and the high esteem for the community of Syon among the late medieval English elite illustrate the continuing ability of the Western Church, particularly in that unusually well-ordered part of it, the kingdom of England, to draw on the resources of monastic life for the benefit of a wider lay audience. There was clearly a hunger among the laity for a meditative spirituality which had become primarily confined to the cloister. One theme which served the purpose was for a layperson to imagine him- or herself as an embodied monastery: it is well exemplified in two popular vernacular English devotional texts of the fourteenth century, *The Abbey of the Holy Ghost* and *The Charter of the Holy Ghost*.[39] The *Abbey* re-imagines the building of the soul as the construction of a monastic architectural complex, lovingly itemized; when the abbey is finished, it is still vulnerable to attacks from sin, a theme which is taken up with relish in the *Charter*. The two works are clearly by different authors, the first much more of a mystic than the second in setting out a meditation to shape a life of spiritual exercises, but they are very frequently found paired in manuscripts. Together, they made a precocious joint appearance in print in the 1490s; nearly two centuries after their composition, the new entrepreneurs of the print trade clearly regarded them as still very saleable.

Although some copies of these paired tracts in manuscript or print are associated with monastic libraries, the *Abbey* is aimed at laypeople, whom it comfortingly assumes 'wolde ben in religioun but they mowe nowt [may not] for poverte or for awe or for drede of her [their] kyn or for bond of maryage'.[40] That is an interesting reflection of the way in which Western spirituality had come to see marriage as a second-best, indeed a competitor with or hindrance to a proper spiritual life. It also fits the concerns of women rather than men; women were much more likely to be at the mercy of their kindred in their aspirations. When *The Abbey of the Holy Ghost* started its career in the French vernacular, it was specifically addressed to a woman: the abbey it describes is a nunnery. Perhaps the first work was conceived as an effort to pull would-be mystics more securely back into the mainstream of the Church, given the fate of Marguerite Porete; what better mental image could there be for that purpose than building a monastery? It is noticeable how many of even the surviving English copies are part of manuscript anthologies which appear to have been the prized possessions of women, judging by the accompanying lives of female saints or Marian devotional tracts bound up alongside.

One wonders how far down the social scale such literary imaginings could travel in a world of limited literacy: certainly not so far as the icons of Orthodox hesychasm. And it is worth observing that despite the rich flowering of female spirituality in the two centuries after 1300, the Western Church canonized (that is, officially declared to be saints) remarkably few women in the same period. One of them was Bridget of Sweden, and the other was her Italian contemporary and fellow-visionary Catherine of Siena (?1347–80), another wife and mother, who, in much the same spirit as *The Abbey of the Holy Ghost*, envisaged the building of a monastery of the mind: 'To attain charity, you must dwell constantly in the cell of self-knowledge.'[41] Both canonizations were deeply controversial – indeed, in the case of Bridget, the process had to be repeated three times. It was utterly alien to the normal medieval Western expectations of mystical piety that such people should be seen as qualified for sainthood, but there was one good reason for Catherine and Bridget breaking through the canonization barrier. Prominent among the prophecies of both women was their insistence that the papacy, which had relocated from Rome to Avignon in the early fourteenth century, was destined to return to the city of St Peter: predictions whose fulfilment did not harm their chances of long-term favour from popes, once they had achieved this goal.[42]

THE *DEVOTIO MODERNA* AND ERASMUS

One movement of the late fourteenth century developed beyond this assumption that the spirituality of laypeople in their families was a second-best to the monastic life: the style of personal piety known as the 'present-day/modern devotion', *Devotio Moderna*, so important in north-west Europe up to the sixteenth-century Reformation. The *Devotio* was never a purely clerical movement, despite attracting such distinguished clergy as the great mystical writer Thomas à Kempis (*c.* 1380–1471), the philosopher-theologian Gabriel Biel (*c.* 1420–95) and even one estimable though briefly reigning sixteenth-century pope, the Dutchman Adrian VI (1459–1523). The Brethren of the Common Life, the nearest thing to a formally organized religious Order to emerge from the movement, discouraged members from becoming ordained clergy. The Brethren took care to put their houses of Sisters and some of their own communities under the control of local urban corporations rather than the Church authorities.[43] Notably, married couples (and of course their children) might be involved on an equal basis in a lifestyle inspired by the *Devotio*. Its promise was that serious-minded laity could aspire to the programme of practical action and organization of one's thoughts and life which was summed up in the title of Kempis's famous devotional treatise *The Imitation of Christ.*

The idea of imitating Christ related uneasily to Augustinian beliefs about fallen humanity; it could be regarded as standing in a different line of theological descent, linking with the Christ-centred piety of the Franciscans and, before them, Pseudo-Dionysius. It was also a solvent of that Western assumption that clergy and religious had a better chance of getting to heaven than laypeople. A combination of these thoughts might have represented an alternative future for the Western Church to the destructive reality of the sixteenth-century Reformation, but one young Dutchman brought up at the heart of the *Devotio Moderna*, Desiderius Erasmus (1466/9–1536), standard-bearer for late medieval Christian humanism, helped to ensure that this was not so. He developed the ethos of the movement into an attitude of mind deeply subversive of the whole monastic enterprise.

Erasmus was a failed monk who only belatedly, in the years of his international celebrity, obtained a papal dispensation for his absence from Augustinian enclosure. He had good personal reasons for loathing and denigrating monastic life, some of which were probably twinges of guilt.[44] His attack on monasticism, deeply meditated over the years after he quitted his monastery at Steyn in 1495 and not published until 1518, took the ingeniously oblique form of praising marriage. His *Encomium matrimonii* was a sustained sneer at celibacy, whose flavour can be gained from its observation that the single state is 'a barren way of life hardly becoming to a man . . . let us leave celibacy for bishops . . . the holiest kind of life is wedlock, purely and chastely observed'.[45] The *Encomium* was only the centrepiece of a flotilla of writings from Erasmus which brutally asserted that laypeople in everyday society could be as holy as monks. 'What is the state [*civitas*] but a great monastery?' was his rhetorical question, whose answer logically removed the need for monasteries.[46] This was a profound reversal of nearly a millennium of Western assumptions about the relationship between ascetics and laypeople. Erasmus's enormous prestige in the early sixteenth century gave a new impetus to three centuries of existing anti-monastic polemic, most of which had previously been inspired by secular clergy in tension with the regulars, and it was to prove a potent weapon.[47]

The alternative direction of piety which Erasmus sought to encourage throughout the Western Church was a cut-down, sanitized, Spirit-filled version of the exuberant devotion of his own time. Fatefully, it was to prove more palatable among the pope's foes than in the Vatican. His emphasis on that classic text of the Spirit in John 6.63 ('The Spirit gives life, but the flesh is of no use') proved to be a theological time bomb in the Western Church. Likewise his discreet but unmistakable preference for Origen over Augustine of Hippo was to be an inspiration for Western Christians who sought to take their faith in new directions, away from the *éminence grise* of Latin theology. But the faith which he advocated was cerebral, not mystical: Erasmus never joined those humanists who delighted in cabbalism or any of the ancient magical variants on the thought of Plato. As a scholar should, he took an intellectual interest in the antiquity of Pseudo-Dionysius's writings, but he also followed the best scholars of the previous generation in seeing that the mystic was not who he said he was.[48] After that, it is almost comic to watch Erasmus busily applying Dionysian hierarchies to the utilitarian purpose of justifying the power of temporal rulers in society; he was never slow to write what monarchs wanted to hear.[49] Some of Erasmus's later admirers, as independent and original as him in their spiritual explorations, nevertheless parted company from his reductionist view of mystical silence. Yet there were many who listened to his sneers about monks and their contemplation, and built them into the movement of reform which burst apart the Western Church in the sixteenth-century Reformation.

6

The Protestant Reformation:
1500–1700

JUSTIFYING PROTESTANT NOISE

Both the papacy and the Western Latin Church were to meet their nemesis in the sixteenth century, not in the first instance at the hands of the failed monk Erasmus, but from a monastic success story. Martin Luther (1483–1546) was a deeply conscientious churchman who had defied his father to enter the cloister, but came to reverse everything symbolized by that decision. Ironically, he joined a rigorously reformed section of a religious community which is the only religious Order ever to have been founded by a pope: the Observant Augustinian Eremites. That fact, so much part of the young Luther's consciousness of his community's identity, is too often forgotten when assessing his momentous career in launching the third in our sequence of Christian Reformations.[1]

Historians are interestingly vague about whether to call Luther a monk or a friar: the answer seems simple, and especially to anglophones, since the sister-Order of Luther's Observant Augustinians in England was commonly known as the Austin Friars. Yet as their name of 'hermit' implies, the Augustinian Eremites were friars who behaved like monks, exhibiting the same ambiguity as the Carmelites as to whether they should be withdrawn from the world or Mendicants within it. The Austin Friars placed a high value on mystical contemplation: one of their number, the English semi-hermit William Flete, was a major influence on Catherine of Siena after he relocated to Italy, and Flete had previous associations with the Bridgettine community of Syon.[2] Luther himself, while still in the cloister, was excited by his discovery of the anonymous fourteenth-century vernacular German mystical text known as the *Theologia Germanica* (*A German Theology*). He published editions of it the year before and the year after his public demonstration in 1517 against Johann Tetzel's notorious campaign selling indulgences.[3]

Yet Luther's theology was destined to pull in a different direction. In 1521, at the height of his first defiance of the papacy, he published his own discussion of monastic vows, *De votis monasticis Martini Lutheri iudicium*. This was not a total condemnation of monasticism nor a recommendation for its abolition. Like Erasmus, Luther emphasized that the monastic life unjustly relegated married life to a second-class status in the Church. For Luther, drawing on a much more visceral experience of failed expectations than Erasmus, there was something much worse to say: monastic vows fostered an unhealthy obsession with performing pious works which were irrelevant to salvation.[4] Luther's tract was extremely influential: these were to become the twin themes which dominated the sixteenth-century Protestant Reformation. Modern Protestants easily remember justification by faith, but are inclined to forget that the first of Luther's preoccupations, cutting clerical celibacy down to size to exalt marriage, particularly clerical marriage, was equally significant at the time. Luther's own later happy marriage and family life, though not quite the first in the Reformation, became a model for that characteristic Protestant social formation, the clerical dynasty.[5]

Monastic life was not entirely extinguished in Lutheranism, but its survival was minimal and largely thanks to accidents of aristocratic preference in certain territories of the Holy Roman Empire.[6] Other non-Lutheran Protestant Churches simply annulled the regular religious life with thoroughness and satisfaction. Luther's own ambiguous feelings about the vocation which had sustained him for more than a decade were swept aside during the 1520s in a huge outpouring of popular fury at the cloisters, which was to alienate Protestantism from monasticism for more than three centuries. To ancient clerical rivalries and Erasmian sarcasm was now added the angry zeal of converts to the cause of total reformation for a corrupt Church. Much of the most eloquent fury came from former friars, who were by vocation the star communicators of the Western Church, and who in rejecting their Mendicant life, felt most keenly and personally the sense that they themselves had cheated and betrayed the faithful in their fraternal careers. Luther was not slow to encourage their repentance.[7]

The loss of the regular life concentrated the practice of worship and devotion in established Protestant Churches more or less exclusively on the parish, which can only be regarded as a diminution of the rich variety of religious experience within Western Christianity. It is possible to argue that, in the long term, German Pietism and British Methodism were both attempts to make good the deficit.[8] One of the immediate consequences was the inauguration of one of the noisiest periods in Christian history since its first two centuries; noise was the characteristic of the mainstream Protestant Reformation. That was the result of the twin messages of Luther's *Iudicium*.

The emerging Protestant Churches now had a clergy among whom celibacy was the exception, and who had before them the example of cheerful and convivial family life reflected in Martin Luther's *Table Talk*. When these new pastors led worship, it was above all to preach, repeatedly hammering home the message Luther had rediscovered in his reading of Augustine of Hippo, and, through Augustine, Paul of Tarsus: justification by faith. This was a theme common to all the mainstream or 'magisterial' Protestant Reformers – 'magisterial' because, unlike more radical spirits in sixteenth-century Europe, they sought to replace the medieval Western Church, which embraced all society, with another equally universal Church. They did not succeed in this, because these 'masters' of the Reformation themselves rapidly divided. Besides Lutherans, there were those who gradually gained a distinct description as 'Reformed' Protestants, a group which needed a label of differentiation because in so many ways, apart from their shared belief in justification by faith, they deeply disagreed with what became developed Lutheranism.[9] Particularly among the Reformed, the Reformation embodied not just a return to Pauline themes, but a rediscovery of strands in the Tanakh which the Church in both East and West had found uncongenial and had quietly forgotten. One of those rediscoveries was inevitably an encounter with the various degrees of reserve in the Tanakh towards silence. This was to be an era of words, relentlessly clarifying the Word of God.

Lutheran or Reformed, worship became sermon-centred. The pulpit became as visually and symbolically dominant a feature of reordered church interiors as was the iconostasis in Orthodoxy. In Reformed church buildings, this was the absolute norm, but the earliest purpose-built Lutheran church, the Castle Chapel of 1544 at Torgau, was also completely focused on its pulpit.[10] It is even more remarkable that in the Church of England, the Protestant Church most wedded to set liturgical forms, where the altar or communion table still had the possibility of remaining a visual focus, there were a good many instances where the pulpit stood directly on an axis in front of the altar, obscuring it from general congregational view. The liturgical and theological changes of the last two hundred years in these churches have swept away most examples in fastidious distaste, but a few remain.[11]

A feature of all Protestant churches was the destruction of medieval devotional furniture, triggered by a rapid embracing of iconophobia and Iconoclasm. This mood was soon curbed among Lutherans, since early in his career as a Reformer Luther found theological reasons for destroying as little as possible of medieval ecclesiastical art, but it was a constant preoccupation in varying degrees throughout the Reformed world, most pronounced on the geographical fringes, in the Reformed Churches of Scotland and Ireland.[12] The pioneer was the first notable exponent of the Reformed tradition, Huldrych Zwingli (1484–1531) and his fellow-Reformers in Zürich, and soon Reformed Protestants established a vocabulary and theological rationale for their destructive activities.

As we have noted (above, pp. 105–6), Reformed Protestants took a great interest in the Iconoclastic Movement of the eighth and ninth centuries, but chiefly they relied on the Old Testament. It is hardly surprising therefore that the gleeful abuse of dumb idols by the Psalmist figured highly in condemnations of images from the pulpit, or in the roar of psalm-singing as French and Dutch Reformed Protestant crowds smashed up images in the Protestant uprisings of the 1560s. Even King Henry VIII of England, proud at his destruction of a great many images in his monasteries, cathedrals and parish churches, complacently endorsed the iconophobic opinions of his fellow-monarch and *Doppelgänger* King David, in scrawled annotations to his beautifully illuminated personal psalter.[13]

MUSIC AND CHURCH BUILDINGS

Protestants valued a second type of noise in their congregational worship besides preaching: new forms of music. Most musical noise was the property of the whole congregation. The one significant exception was the surviving professionally performed choral tradition in the cathedrals of the Church of England (echoed in generally attenuated form in the Church of Ireland), but English cathedral worship gave no more room for communal silence than did the contrasting parish developments in Lutheranism and Reformed Protestantism.[14] With Luther as impresario, Lutheranism joyfully developed vernacular hymnody, while from the 1550s the metrical psalms of the Reformed proved a major weapon in spreading their brand of Protestantism across the Continent. Some Lutheran hymns crossed the boundary into Reformed Churches as well. Only one major Reformer kept music at bay from the communal worship of his community and it was that pioneer of Reformed Protestantism himself, Huldrych Zwingli.

It is interesting that all three leading Protestants, Luther, Zwingli and John Calvin, were exceptionally musical. Zwingli was perhaps the most talented of all of them. Precisely for that reason, he felt acutely suspicious of the seductive power of music, because he felt it himself: music was as liable to lead to idolatry as devotional images. In his *Conclusions* (*Schlussreden*) of 1523, two years before Zürich officially banned the Mass, he set out his justifications for this extreme position: 'when one prays, mouth and mind are not long on the same track, much less so mind and song.'[15] So music had to be ejected from the services of the Church, just like images and vestments. Zwingli took very seriously the Lord's admonition in Matthew 6.6, 'When you pray, go into your room and shut the door and pray to your Father who is in secret; and your Father who sees in secret will reward you.' When he read another command about worship, Ephesians 5.19, 'sing and make music in your hearts to the Lord', it was the phrase 'in your hearts' that he emphasized.[16] Not surprisingly, he also returned repeatedly and approvingly to the story of Hannah and her silent praying, regarding her witness as far more obviously pleasing to God than the cacophony of sacred music one encounters elsewhere in the Old Testament. The truest prayer was silent prayer; the problem was how to apply this to public worship.[17]

Not even Zwingli could follow through his own logic to envisage completely silent services in his city. He did stipulate that people should normally recite their psalms or prayers, not with music or vocalization at all, but silently, while the pastor explained to them what the texts of Scripture meant. The strategy recalls Bishop Ambrose of Milan's observation more than a thousand years previously that the public reading of a psalm was 'the instrument of silence' in a congregation (above, p. 93); one wonders whether Zwingli himself remembered that precedent. Zürich's newly purged communion services did exhibit real silences, with the bread and wine being taken silently, and with pauses for silent prayer around the scriptural readings, pastor's prayers and sermon. Services in the city became virtually a ministerial monologue.

The most musical vocalization Zwingli would allow in church was simple recitation by the pastor on a single note, presumably to aid audibility in large buildings. The three songs he is known to have written himself were strictly for use at home, just as pictures became permissible in Zürich only in domestic or civic settings.[18] Zürich's excellent schools resounded to hymns and psalms, including in the newly founded music school presided over by the noted Swiss organist Johannes Vogler – but not its churches. What one heard in church was the voice of the minister, some passages of silence, and occasional set responses from the congregation. In 1527, the organs of Zwingli's own collegiate church, the Grossmünster, were finally dismantled after three years of disuse.[19]

At first, Zwingli seems by the power of his personality to have gained general civic consent for his remarkable revolution, though the banning of music impressed none of his fellow-magisterial Reformers elsewhere. His loyal and long-lived successor as presiding minister in the city, Heinrich Bullinger (1504–75) – yet another musician – made no change in direction for city worship. In his major systematic collection of sermons, the *Decades*, as influential in England through its translation as in the clergy-houses of central Europe, Bullinger devoted a substantial passage to defending a complete ban on music in the liturgy, which he regarded as reflecting not just apostolic practice, but his conviction that Jesus was never recorded in the New Testament as singing anywhere, in or out of church. In order to sustain this tendentious view, he indulged in some unhappy casuistry around the incident recorded by Matthew and Mark, 'when they had sung an hymn, or psalm, they went out into the Mount of Olives.' 'For if godly men persevere in the study of godliness, and in daily prayers; though they sing not, yet remain they nevertheless the sons of God,' he said, clearly conscious that respected fellow-churchmen did not agree with him.[20]

As a result, right to the end of the sixteenth century Zürich's services were entirely without the metrical psalms which were already being developed the other side of Switzerland, in Protestant Basel during Zwingli's lifetime, and which printers in Zürich were only too happy to publish for other Reformed Churches. It was not until 1598 that the ministers of Zürich finally gave way to pressure from bored congregations and allowed the metrical psalm to triumph in the city, as it had done throughout the rest of the Reformed world from Ireland to Transylvania. In what may have been intended as a theological gesture of graceful capitulation, they allowed the first psalm-singing in the Grossmünster on the Christian feast of many tongues, Pentecost. Zürich did keep the pipe organ at bay until 1848, and local opposition prevented that lonely pioneer from being played for another five years.[21]

The general Protestant attitude to the use of church buildings was deeply symbolic of a new rupture between individual and communal prayer in the Reformation. Particularly among Reformed Protestants, churches were now seen solely as shelters for congregational worship, with its diet of sermons and hymns: individual private prayer outside the communal context provided by services was regarded with grave suspicion as potential popery. This meant that normally most church buildings were kept locked when there was no service in progress. Regulations enacted by the city authorities in Geneva in 1547 specifically ordered that apart from the appointed times of worship, '[church] buildings are to remain shut . . . in order that no one outside the hours may enter for superstitious reasons. If anyone be found making any particular devotion inside or nearby, he is to be admonished; if it appear to be a superstition which he will not amend, he is to be chastised.'[22] Those familiar with the frustrations of church-crawling amid the Reformed Churches of the Netherlands, Scotland or Transylvania will know that, in such settings, the locked church is still generally the norm.

There were, it is true, notable exceptions. Some major churches remained unlocked, but for purposes which negated devotional silence even more effectively than any official prohibition. The general public, where they were allowed to, used such spacious church interiors for recreational walking and conversation, a particularly useful social function in the uncertain climate of northern Europe, when in the Catholic south or even in sunny Geneva they might have enjoyed the market square. The most famous English example, familiar in the literature of the period, is the long Romanesque nave of Old St Paul's Cathedral in London, which, despite the great changes of the Reformation, seamlessly retained its role as 'Paul's Walk' for every variety of social transaction, both licit and illicit.[23] Similar practices in the United Provinces of the Netherlands are much more familiar to us in art than literature: that distinctive Dutch genre of paintings and drawings of church interiors which became popular in the early seventeenth century, among which the works of Pieter Saenredam are probably the best known.

What is clear in these Dutch pictures is that the greater urban medieval churches of the United Provinces were too large and complex to be used as a single unit for Reformed congregational worship, now that their side chapels or choir enclosures had been emptied. Where there was an enclosed congregational and preaching area in the building, it might be surrounded by people strolling and chatting even in service time. There was not much that the ministers of the Dutch Reformed Church could do about this, as many such churches belonged to the local town council, which was not inclined to concede power unnecessarily to the Reformed clergy. Frequently town corporations maintained pipe organs, both old and brand new, to drive home the same point to the ministers, for these large and expensive fixtures of church interiors played no part in Reformed worship. Instead they were used for secular concerts. Indeed, the Dutch seem to have invented the secular organ recital at this period, as a by-product of the tensions between Church and State in their argumentatively pluralist commonwealth.[24]

The Protestant scheme of salvation pioneered by Luther was, naturally, not hospitable to the theological themes that had sustained Christian mysticism in East and West. It emphasized the 'imputation' of righteousness by a gracious God to humans who, as far as their salvation was concerned, would never be righteous in themselves. The idea of human righteousness as effectively a fiction was not promising ground for exploring that traditional mystical preoccupation with union with the Godhead, *theosis*.[25] Luther knew his *Theologia Germanica* and the works of Meister Eckhart, but he radically reapplied the principle of *Gelassenheit* or *apatheia* to the logic of justification by faith: justification led to a letting-go of guilt, a surrender to the power of God which was in turn manifested in an active life in the world, not by any unhealthy descent into the nothingness beyond prayer. Luther's own break with the mystical tradition, despite his early enthusiasm for the *Theologia Germanica*, was summed up in his hostility to the works of Pseudo-Dionysius, on whom he commented as the culmination of a brisk rhetorical cudgelling in 1520, 'he is downright dangerous, for he is more of a Platonist than a Christian.'[26] In this, Luther was destined to share an uncommon moment of unanimity with that central textbook of Reformed Protestantism, Calvin's *Institutes*, in which Calvin craggily dismissed Pseudo-Dionysius as 'nothing but talk. The theologian's task is not to divert the ears with chatter, but to strengthen consciences by teaching things true, sure and profitable.'[27]

The Lutheran theologian who came closest to asserting the possibility of divine 'impartation', an actual gift of righteousness by God rather than an 'imputation', was Andreas Osiander of Nuremberg (1496/8–1552), and for his pains he found himself ostracized through most of the Lutheran world. Archbishop Thomas Cranmer (1489–1556) had reason to be grateful to Osiander, as his wife was the pastor's niece; they married in Nuremberg in 1532 while Cranmer was on a diplomatic mission abroad. Twenty years later that did not stop Cranmer cold-shouldering his benefactor and relative when Osiander needed a refuge; Osiander's theological solecism was just too serious to overlook.[28] The case of the Lutheran shoemaker and glove merchant Jakob Böhme (1575–1624) is also significant. At the end of the sixteenth century, Böhme rediscovered for himself the visionary dimension of Christian faith. When he applied it to his own devout Lutheranism, he aroused intense hostility among Lutheran clergy, and, while there was Continent-wide interest in his writings, it did not find a home within mainstream Protestantism. One of Böhme's enthusiastic followers, the visionary millenarian poet Quirinus Kuhlmann (1651–89), met his death burned at the stake in Moscow, alongside one of his German admirers. Kuhlmann was a sadly paradoxical victim of Russian Orthodox lack of sympathy with one outcome of Western mystical thought, but his execution for heresy was also the result of his being denounced by local Lutheran pastors.[29]

PROTESTANTS, INNER SILENCE AND TOLERANCE

What did this turning-away from the mystical tradition mean for the inner devotional life of Protestants in the new Churches of the Reformation? With the passing of the monasteries, there disappeared any structured forum for either meditation or contemplation. The whole tradition of *lectio divina* (above, p. 91) no longer had a home, and Protestants were indeed generally extremely suspicious of allegorical readings of Scripture unless it suited their purposes to draw on them.[30] Not only had Protestants lost any institution in which meditative or contemplative silence could be treasured, but to begin with they found it difficult even to create literature which might be a vehicle for meditation. Hence the surprising popularity in the Church of England under Elizabeth I and the early Stuarts of a devotional work minimally adapted in 1583 by the Puritan clergyman Edmund Bunny from a treatise on self-examination by Robert Parsons or Persons, the Jesuit probably most hated and feared by Elizabethan Protestants. Through the medium of Bunny's adaptation, Parsons was able to turn briskly in his second chapter to emphasize to a large Protestant readership 'How necessarie it is to enter into earnest consideration and meditation of our estate'.[31]

Bunny, a Yorkshireman by descent, emphasized in his dedication to no less a figure than his metropolitan, the veteran Protestant Edwin Sandys, Archbishop of York, that the tactfully unnamed original author had produced a text which was 'willingly read by diverse, for the persuasion that it hath to godlinesse of life, which notwithstanding in many pointes was corruptly set downe'. He spent the rest of his preface justifying what he had done to Archbishop Sandys, pointing to the work of one fellow-Puritan in producing a purged version of that *Devotio Moderna* classic, Thomas à Kempis's *Imitation of Christ*, 'taking onely that which was sound'. In a further preface to the general reader, full of further justification of his bold step, he struck a wistful note, rare in the Reformation, and remarkable in a man who had been forced into exile under Mary Tudor:

> whereas inordinate contention is not onely unseemely for the Church of God, but also hurtfull to the cause of religion, a special point of wisedom it is when God hath bestowed any good gift of any of us all, that other should esteeme thereof, as that they make the same a mean to moderate the bitternes of their affections towards all those that gladly would live peaceably withall.[32]

Bunny's would-be ecumenism to moderate Roman Catholics was not especially productive of results amid the polarization of the English Reformation, but his Protestant version of Parsons's treatise was a commercial success; it supplied a real lacuna for Protestant devotion, and greatly outsold the Catholic original which it had plagiarized.[33]

All this gives the lie to the old cliché about the individualism of Reformation Protestant faith. Rather its problem was the opposite, that it was too communal: it gave little place for the individual to be alone with God. One exception to this Protestant rule was the work of Isaac Ambrose (1604–64), a minister of the Church of England who was sufficiently in the Reformed mainstream to become a prominent Presbyterian after the collapse of English episcopal structures in the 1640s. Despite this theological identity, he seems to have sought to understand the self-confident Roman Catholicism of his native Lancashire, and used what was good in it for Reformed purposes. His writing testifies to his systematic practice of meditation, and lovingly explores the theme of the believer's mystical marriage with Christ.

Although there is some effort in Ambrose's writings to distinguish meditation from contemplation, he shows little awareness of much spirituality that is any more radical than might be found in Jesuits of his generation; he stands in a recognizably Western and Latin meditative tradition. Perhaps for that very reason, and because there was so little on the market to rival his work, it was much reprinted, and for longer than Bunny's bowdlerized Parsons, right up to the time of John Wesley's extensive reprints of devotional works in the mid-eighteenth century. He answered a continuing need which few others seemed capable of filling.[34]

Protestants were naturally encouraged to cultivate inner resources of devotion, but the thrust of their thoughts at home was expected to be a personal appropriation of the truths of Holy Scripture: the making of biblical words into a Gospel of salvation for themselves, in preparation for their communal worship in church. Private devotion should centre on Bible-reading, generally annotated with previously prepared commentary such as that of the English Geneva Bible. Protestants were universally encouraged to be literate – or, more accurately, they were universally encouraged to learn to read, so that they could read the Bible. Writing was of secondary importance in terms of understanding Scripture, but Reformed Protestants laid more stress on it than Lutherans, as it formed a useful adjunct to the particular Reformed preoccupation with election to salvation. In England they put it to a particular purpose in personal devotion which had important and lasting literary results in the confessional private diary, still so familiar a part of our everyday cultural experience.[35]

William Perkins, Cambridge don and doyen of English Puritanism (1558–1602), took up John Calvin's passing thought that the Lord in his mercy had given some of those destined for damnation (the 'reprobate') a merely temporary faith, which should sharply be distinguished from the saving faith given to the elect by divine grace. Perkins concluded that it was important to test out one's life for genuine proofs of election. To achieve this, writing an analysis of daily thoughts and actions could serve as a useful vehicle for private examination of one's conscience. So, particularly in Reformed Protestant England at the end of the sixteenth century, clergy and literate laity pioneered the use of the private diary to enumerate proofs that they truly were among the elect (or, unhappily, that they were not). Diaries were part of a vast industry of literary self-examination which has not ceased since, even if it has often left its spiritual origins behind. This in turn produced an infuriated backlash among some English Puritans, who regarded it as precisely the pathology from which Martin Luther had been concerned to free himself: those whom Christ has saved should not be fretting about laws and regulations. The mainstream opponents of these independent-minded folk christened them 'antinomians' (opposers of law), and regarded them as dangerous radicals, which indeed some became, in the great English national upheaval that struck England from 1640 to 1660 (below, pp. 144–50).[36]

The noise of theological controversy bore all before it in the official religion of sixteenth-century Europe, despite the occasional sound of alternative voices such as that of Edmund Bunny. A number of rulers at first tried to step aside from commitment to one side or the other; even Henry VIII of England in his brutal and clumsy way tried to find a middle path. Yet the failure of various negotiations between Rome and the Protestants, and then the increasingly bitter cleavage between the Lutherans and the Reformed, forced commitment to confessional identities. Landgraf Philipp of Hessen, sometime protector of Luther and long a mainstay of Protestants in the Holy Roman Empire, always refused to sign up to any Protestant confessional statement, and kept Hessen out of the poisonous theological debates in the Empire until his death in 1567.[37] Landgraf Philipp was not alone in seeking to keep his options open even after the Peace of Augsburg in 1555 had tried to force choices on imperial princes and territories: another notable example was set in Wesel, chief city in the duchy of Cleves, Protestant but not confessional.[38] Wesel allowed most of its Catholic convents to stay open, only stipulating that they should not ring their bells or keep their doors open when celebrating Mass. The chief pastor in the town from 1559, the duke's court chaplain, Nicholas Rollius, expressed his repugnance at Protestant internal bickering: 'by nature I shy away from accusations and, since I was not baptized in the name of Calvin, Beza, Bullinger, Luther, etc., but in the name of the Son of God, why is it necessary to rage against this or that person?'[39] Thanks to Rollius, it was possible for a parishioner to witness (in his case, with fury) monks singing Catholic hymns in Latin before the altar during the

Protestant liturgy in the principal church of the town. It was the end of the century before Wesel's compromise between Catholics, Lutherans and Reformed faded. By the outbreak of the Thirty Years War in 1618, it had gone for ever.

Some communities in the Empire and the Low Countries still found themselves with an unavoidable balance of opposing confessional sides, in terms of either populations or legal jurisdictions over church buildings. In such places some remarkable solutions for public worship were created on the ground, an arrangement which was known as the *Simultaneum*. Church buildings could be shared in use between Catholics and Protestants, generally by splitting the complicated medieval structures up with a wall, but sometimes by careful expedients in sharing the same space. Dutch Protestants in the territories of Overmaas increasingly brought in large curtains for their churches, so that during their preaching services in the nave they could blot out the annoying sight of a Catholic high altar to the east. The good folk of Biberach in Swabia thought long and hard about their shared parish church, the only major space for worship in their town. They eschewed complete physical divisions, instead creating a scheme of decorative imagery which had a Lutheran theme in the nave and a Catholic theme in the choir, plus a large clock above the nave crucifix, to remind the Lutherans several times a Sunday to get a move on in their singing before the bell started to ring for the Catholic Mass. St Martin Biberach is an enjoyable setting in which to contemplate how even the greatest efforts of the Reformation at tolerance still came to embody division in an alternation of confessional noises.[40]

RADICAL PROTESTANTS: WORD AND SPIRIT

If one seeks silence among those who separated from Rome in the European Reformation, it is not 'magisterial' Protestants who have the most to offer, but more radical spirits, who rejected the assumption of Luther, Zwingli and Calvin that Christianity should be a public affair, supported by the magistrate, and embracing everyone in society. This may seem surprising, because among the many varieties of radical Reformation which evolved in the sixteenth century there was much to lead them away from silence and contemplation. Many radicals were just as inclined as magisterials to banish silence from their worship with their preaching and their own variety of hymnody. Common among radicals, though as we shall see not universal, was a revival of the universal adult baptismal practice of the first Christians. So a public testimony of informed faith, to be repeated regularly in public, and an acute sense of identification with a gathered community of 'saints', was for many the essence of the true Church.

Some radicals went further and turned their activism to militancy: from the wild pronouncements of the 'Zwickau Prophets', who so alarmed but also fascinated Luther's colleague Philipp Melanchthon in 1521, through to those like Thomas Müntzer who contributed to the 'Farmers' War' (*Bauernkrieg*) of 1525, on to the various groups whose excitement about the imminence of the Last Days led to the tragedy of siege and massacre at Münster in 1534–5, and, in the decade after that, to the guerrilla violence in the Netherlands movement known as the Batenburgers.[41] Defenders of infant baptism invented a hostile Graeco-Latin label to describe radicals, whether militant or not, calling them *anabaptistae*, 'rebaptizers' – a term which of course no proponent of adult baptism could accept. 'Anabaptist' became a scattergun term of abuse during the Reformation.

Yet powerful forces moved some radicals in another direction: towards Christian quietness. It is significant that the *Theologia Germanica*, the medieval mystical work which had once so engaged Luther, became a taboo work for mainstream Protestants, because a whole raft of radical leaders whom we are about to meet became fascinated by what it contained.[42] One apparently noisy aspect of Swiss radicalism in the 1520s terrified even some radical leaders: women began reconstructing Christianity for themselves. Opinions previously confined to mystics and nuns were now heard in the streets. Medieval women had often turned in their imaginations to intimate encounters with God which were not fettered by the Church structures created by males: as a result some had been made to suffer like Marguerite Porete, but others had been satisfied in more conventional ways through the reading of approved popular works like *The Abbey of the Holy Ghost*, or the measured contemplation encouraged by the

Devotio Moderna. With no rules holding them back, some of these explorations now turned in strange directions.

In 1524 demonstrations of ecstatic religion broke out in north-east Switzerland. Women were prominent in these, sometimes going so far as to offer themselves in sexual freedom within their elect circle, as a sign of the new age which was dawning. Such feminine assertions were nearly as disturbing and confusing for male Reformers as the violence of the 'Farmers' War', the cluster of popular uprisings which traumatized much of central Europe a few months later. They can be seen as having a formative role in the creation of that famous early statement of Anabaptist belief, the Schleitheim Articles of 1527, which seem like an attempt to restrain the radicalism of radicalism. Thus, as so often in Christian history, a revolutionary movement started by suggesting new possibilities to women and then soon slid back into conventional male-dominated paths.[43]

Radicals, even those who were not pushing the boundaries of medieval female piety like the women of Appenzell and Sankt Gallen, did have the advantage (if that is the *mot juste*) of generally not following Luther in stressing justification by faith. Many of them took up spiritual themes stressed by Erasmus, emphasizing the Spirit over the Word. That emphasis was liable to turn them in on themselves, to hear the call of the Spirit within. One of the first of such 'Spirituals' was in Luther's eyes a renegade supporter whose defection was all the more infuriating because of his elevated social status. Caspar Schwenckfeld (1489–1561) was an independent-minded Silesian knight of the crusading Teutonic Order who, unlike most of those under vows of celibacy who joined the Protestant cause, maintained his celibacy throughout his life, despite rejecting the old Western Church. It may be relevant to the subsequent turn of his theology that from 1523 he became severely deaf; certainly he later mocked the noise of evangelical preaching with the tart observation that the problem with the occupants of Lutheran pulpits was that they 'wish to bring more people to heaven than God wants there'.[44]

That scepticism was by no means the most dramatic element in Schwenckfeld's break with Luther, for he embraced a thoroughgoing silence on the sacraments. He was hardly the only person to take exception to Luther's idiosyncratic opinions on the Lord's Supper, but his disgust at the Continent-wide disagreements on a sacrament which was at the centre of his devotional life took him in a remarkable direction. In 1526 he decided that this unseemly bickering justified a complete suspension of the eucharistic liturgy, a halt or 'standing still' (*Stillstand*) which replaced the physical reception of bread and wine. Since there was no agreement on the eucharist, he proposed that believers should feed on Christ's heavenly flesh in their hearts. At first Schwenckfeld saw this suspension as only necessary on a temporary basis, while some general renewal of the Church took shape across the already divided Reformation, but then, in his dismay at the continuing bitterness about the nature and significance of the eucharist, particularly between Luther's party and the Swiss theologians led by Zwingli, he came to see the *Stillstand* as a long-term necessity, which must endure until the Spirit of God might choose to reveal the true nature of the sacrament. For the rest of his life, he never once received the eucharistic elements of bread and wine.[45]

Spiritual reformation as envisaged by Schwenckfeld revealed a startlingly new approach to Christian silence. Those who followed him, the 'Silesian Brethren' or 'Schwenckfelders', were now to form a Christian group without any outward practice of the eucharist or indeed, at first, baptism. It was not until the late nineteenth century that they ended their self-imposed ban.[46] Many other 'Spirituals' among the radicals throughout Western Europe hearkened to Schwenckfeld's call for *Stillstand*; but now he found a different opponent from Martin Luther. His theology and that of Spirituals like him clashed profoundly with other radicals to whom the term 'Anabaptist' had direct relevance, because they insisted on adult baptism. Mainstream Protestants had no hesitation in calling Schwenckfelders Anabaptists, but Schwenckfeld's followers deeply resented this, and fiercely criticized Anabaptists for usurping God's prerogative of restoring the sacraments before he had sufficiently prepared his Church. Schwenckfeld was perfectly ready to take up the abusive term to describe radicals who rejected his 'standing still', as he made clear when in 1530 he produced a tract bluntly entitled *Judgement on the Anabaptists* (*Judicium de anabaptistis*).[47]

Modern observers confused amid these disputes may be forgiven for being intimidated by the variety of early Reformation radicalism.

Once the boundaries provided by the medieval Western Church had been breached, every traditional doctrine was worthy of re-examination and reformulation, especially doctrines which had been decided after what all radicals saw as an un-Christian alliance at the time of Constantine between the once-persecuted Church and the power of the Roman Empire. As a result, radicalism contained not so much a series of neat parties as a spectrum of radicalisms, stretching between the two extreme poles of conviction as to how authority should be viewed. Were Christians to be guided primarily by the promptings of the Spirit or by Scripture? The Spiritualist intellectual, historian and former priest Sebastian Franck (1499–c. 1543) provided a memorable put-down to Scripture when he characterized its common use without the benefit of the Spirit by both magisterial Protestant and Anabaptist contemporaries as creating a 'paper Pope'.[48]

For Franck, the inward word inevitably trumped the outer word. By contrast, scriptural Anabaptists, for all their disagreements with Luther, prioritized the authority of the Bible over the Spirit. There were infinite gradations between extreme positions in this debate, and Caspar Schwenckfeld came to find himself out-radicalized by Sebastian Franck. Franck simply rejected all external forms of religion; his mystical version of Spiritualism went beyond Schwenckfeld's hopes for a purer Church in which the sacraments would be restored once more. The theological chasm between the two men led in the 1540s to an irretrievable breach; yet both were seeking to create a form of Christianity which gave priority to inwardness in the individual's encounter with God.[49]

STUART ENGLAND AND THE QUAKERS

A century later, a new flowering of radical Spiritualism carried this quest for spiritual inwardness further. It emerged in a different part of Europe: the Atlantic kingdoms of the Stuart dynasty, Scotland, Ireland and England. Radicalism gained its chance through the political upheaval caused by the collapse of Charles I's royal authority in 1640–41, which was rapidly followed by the collapse of coercive authority in the Church of England. Charles's defeat in 1646 by the armies of the Parliament in Westminster and of the Presbyterian Scots left more than a decade of freedom for new configurations of radicalism to take shape. But this new wave of radicalism did not emerge fully formed from nowhere in 1640: Cambridge University in particular had exhibited a number of interesting undercurrents in the previous twenty years, some of which have been largely forgotten. David Como, an intrepid intellectual archaeologist, has recently rescued from oblivion the writings of John Everard (?1584–1640/41), a wildly independent-minded Cambridge-educated cleric and alchemist who was preaching as parish lecturer in London at St Martin-in-the-Fields and Kensington in the 1620s and 1630s. Everard went far beyond Isaac Ambrose's one-man revival of Western Latin meditative practice for Reformed Protestants. It was not until twelve years after his death that an admirer published a rich selection of Everard's sermons; they had been forced to await the disappearance of the ecclesiastical and royal courts which had frequently harassed him into prison on charges of heresy and sedition.[50]

Around 1622, Everard had been transformed from a conventionally aggressive Puritan preacher by a mystical conversion experience which sprang out of his considerable and unconventional reading. It led him towards the antinomianism which was emerging from Puritanism at that time (above, p. 139). He published English versions of the *Theologia Germanica* and Pseudo-Dionysius. His printed sermons are a cornucopia of allusions, direct or oblique, both to these and to other names already familiar in this book, such as Sebastian Franck – but also, beyond them, to the great Jewish medieval philosopher Moses Maimonides and to works of alchemy hovering on the edge of gnosticism, stretching back to the hermetic literature of the first Christian centuries. Everard's confident message in one sermon reached an extraordinary climax of *theosis* in metaphors of roaring fire and great oceans. Faithful Christians must travel past the superficial meaning of Scripture, and if they allowed Christ the persistent fire 'to burn up your dross', he told his listeners, '. . . at length you may be Swallowed up and Emptied into him: Even into that *Ocean* whence ye came, as all the small *rivulets* which come from the *Sea*, never rest till they return into the Sea'.[51] The old Platonic themes of procession and return, distilled by Pseudo-Dionysius, were sounding again in an

English pulpit. By the time his sermons reached print, they found eager readers, and if Everard did not go on to found a branch of Christianity to promote his thoughts, one equally radical thinker did.

In the immediate aftermath of the English Civil Wars, a new radical grouping emerged which, after a century of divergence in mainland Europe, represented a reconciliation between Spiritualist silence and the Anabaptist insistence on costly public witness. Those associated with it came to call themselves 'Friends of the Truth', while others sneeringly nicknamed them Quakers, after an incident in which their most prominent figure, George Fox (1624–91), told a judge trying him in a law court to tremble at the name of the Lord. Quakers, like the Spirituals of the previous century, formed only part of the spectrum of radicalism in the English Interregnum. It took time for them to separate out from antinomian activists whose public celebration of their exemption from law, in the form of prophetic nudity, fornication, swearing and tobacco-smoking, spawned yet another abusive name from a horrified public, the Ranters. Recent debate about the reality of Ranterism, much of it remarkably bad-tempered and extending to the charge that Ranters were invented by contemporary journalists, has led to a balanced conclusion: there was a reality amid the exaggeration, as much as there had been in the ecstasy of radical women in the cantons of north-east Switzerland in the 1520s.[52]

George Fox was not above exploiting the name of Ranter as a negative description of those Friends who did not agree with him, and in fact the early history of Ranterism and Quakerism is more linked than traditional Quaker historiography has been prepared to admit. Quakers too were known to go naked in a symbolic return to Eden, and noisily to disrupt public worship in English parish churches. In one notorious incident in 1656, the Quaker James Naylor made a symbolic triumphal entry into Bristol in imitation of Christ's entry into Jerusalem on a horse (in default of a donkey), with devotees casting garments before him: the height of blasphemy. No wonder so many in England applauded when their neighbours beat up Quakers, or the authorities rounded them up and imprisoned them. Even one Irish Quaker's attempt to confront the pope in person and convert him to Quakerism might have been seen by English Protestants as meriting the three years in an Italian lunatic asylum which was John Perrot's reward.[53]

Yet part of Fox's determination to draw boundaries around the Friends' movement was precisely because of the value he placed on the contemplative exploration of 'inner light'. This concept meant as much to him as it did to Hesychasts in Orthodoxy, but for Fox and the Friends it had a very different outcome. He was only one in a chain of Protestant radicals who since the 1520s had cherished the idea of inner light. Among those who had affirmed the central importance of believers' baptism, there were Dutch Mennonites and the first English Baptists, emerging in England from Puritan roots, largely independently of Anabaptists across the North Sea; the earliest group to gather round Fox at Mansfield (Nottinghamshire) in 1648 had previously been Baptists.[54] These Baptist groups complemented the theological contribution of pre-Civil War English antinomians like John Everard.

Fox's contribution was to apply the principle of inner light to congregational worship. He created a society which considered that it had no need for outward sacraments, for there were sacraments to be experienced within oneself. He was not completely original in his rejection of outward sacramental forms; part of the prehistory of his movement as he puzzled how to move forward was his contact with those who called themselves Seekers, an unusually diffident self-designation amid the competing self-confident dogmatisms of the Reformation.[55] During the war years, the Seekers, even more elusive and suspicious of organization than the Ranters, had followed Caspar Schwenckfeld in seeing all existing forms of Church, together with the performance of the sacraments, as invalid. They waited on the Spirit to inaugurate a better age when formal worship might begin again. When the Seekers gathered as a congregation, it was for long periods of fasting and silence.[56]

All this Fox carried into his own new congregations, together with a will to organize which was very far from the ethos of the Seekers, and which did not exhibit their tentative approach to the divine. He spoke a great deal of the Spirit, as one would expect from an 'Inner Light' Christian, but he and a subsequent generation of tidy-minded leaders were anxious to manage enthusiasm into safe channels. So they also characterized independent-minded Friends or obstreperous meetings disrespectful of their authority as bearing 'an unruly, disorderly, lyeing spirit ... a darke willfull spirit' – even 'a durty spirit'.[57] In an urgent pamphlet of 1657, addressed equally to his own Friends and to sceptics, Fox promised to set out 'the difference betwixt silence and speaking'. Very soon he fastened onto the ancient association between light and silence in passive contemplation, and to that he yoked a familiar symbol from the Book of Revelation as a practical expression of his Friends' superiority over the magisterial Reformation:

> there is none upon the earth that come to have their spirits quieted, but who come to the light that Christ Jesus hath enlightned them withal, and so comes here every spirit to have a particular satisfaction and quietness in his own mind ... their spirits and minds are quieted in silent waiting upon God, in one half hour, more peace and satisfaction, then they have had from all other Teachers of the world all their life time.[58]

Fox, endowed with the prophet's enviable gift of supreme lack of doubt, contrasted the apocalyptic Quaker silence with a century of magisterial Protestant preaching: 'give over your railing and bauling, and backbiting in the Pulpits all people, for that is not to preach the Word of God.'[59] He directed a formidable battery of scriptural citations to those who 'stumble at the silent waiting upon the Lord', all of which will be familiar from our survey of references to silence in the Tanakh and New Testament. In the midst of it all, he moved to the complementary aspect of Quaker worship, contrasting 'the time of waiting' with 'the time of receiving ... a time of speaking' in the gift of tongues at Pentecost as described in Acts 2. In an ecstatic leap to the Book of Ezra which also alluded to the popular nickname of the Society, Fox linked Pentecost, and Christ's commendation of two or three gathered together, with those who 'trembled at the word of the God of Israel; because of the transgression of those that had been carried away, and sate astonished till the evening sacrifice'.[60] These are classic justifications for the shape of Quaker meetings which Fox created in the face of internal and external opposition, and which have endured to the present day.

One can glimpse the pride that Quakers felt in their sense of rediscovery of a truly biblical way of worship in the title of a frequently reprinted early Quaker tract of William Britten, repenting of his ministry first in the national Church, then among the Baptists: *Silent meeting, a wonder to the world*.[61] The results can also be seen in the surviving architecture of Quaker meeting houses, though the earliest are slightly later than these founding years: they date from the period after the English Act of Toleration of 1689, when for the first time Quakers could legally build their own places of worship. The striking difference from the architecture of Reformed Protestantism is the absence of any pulpit. No preacher should dominate Quaker meetings. There was no minister; all had the same prerogative of speech, praise, or simply of silence. This was a very powerful weapon against hostile outsiders in bad times. The American Church historian Horton Davies put it strikingly: 'Drums might be beaten to stop the meetings of other Dissenters at worship, but could do nothing against the silence of the Friends.'[62]

Quakerism could be seen as a rediscovery of the monasteries destroyed by the Protestant Reformers, but in fact it represented a relocation of them, away from the ruins which after a century still perforated the skyline all over England, into the hearts of convinced Friends. So William Penn (1644–1718), who was to become one of the Friends most active in the world, to the extent of founding an American colony bearing his own name as a haven for his fellow-Quakers, wrote in 1669 in condemnation of the 'recluse Life', 'The *Christian* Convent and Monastery are within, where the Soul is encloistered from Sin ... True godliness does not turn Men out of the World, but enables them to live better in it, and excites their Endeavours to mend it.'[63] The interior monastery was hardly a new theme; we have encountered it, without Penn's polemical edge, in *The Abbey of the Holy Ghost* back in the fourteenth century (above, p. 122), and any medieval friar sneering at his monastic rivals would have recognized Penn's argument. Yet it was a remarkable rediscovery for a radical Protestant.

Why has the Society of Friends managed more than any other Reformation radicalism to maintain its balance between contemplation and social activism to the present day? One good reason may be that Quakerism was yet another case in the history of Western Christianity where mystical themes made a particular appeal to women, but, uniquely among European radicalisms, Quakers did not wholly reject female activism in the long term. They were not like the Anabaptist men at Schleitheim in the 1520s, emphatically distancing themselves from the female testimony they met in Sankt Gallen and Appenzell. The most prominent surviving Anabaptist groups, the family of Mennonite Churches which include the Amish of North America, have (with honourable exceptions) commonly decided to withdraw from mainstream society to varying degrees to preserve their version of their radical past. Vital in that withdrawal has been their strenuous effort to preserve antique patterns of family life and gender relations.

The Quakers, by contrast, have never quite lost the memory of their rather unconventional beginnings. George Fox formed a spiritual partnership with Margaret, the wife of a long-suffering Cumbrian judge, Thomas Fell, a partnership which after the elderly judge's death was converted into marriage. The formidable Mrs Fell had in a manner reminiscent of Caspar Schwenckfeld the consciousness of a higher social status than most of her fellow-Quakers. She was one of the leaders within the movement until her death in 1702, though in later historiography she has been rather relegated to the role of helpmate and hostess for George Fox.[64] In the early years of the movement, there were a very considerable number of female Quaker prophets, and they suffered as grievously as the men. Although the Society made a remarkable turn towards social respectability from the 1670s, and did to some extent rein in the leadership of women, the fact that it stubbornly resisted the introduction of a male clerical ministry meant that its tradition of female assertion never experienced the rejection that befell women leaders in other successor-Churches to the sectarianism of the English Civil Wars.[65]

TRIDENTINE CATHOLICISM: DEFENDING TRADITIONS

The radicals of the European Reformation thus cherished a rejection of the noisiness of magisterial Protestantism. Opposing them both was the surviving part of the Western Church still loyal to the pope. For decades after Luther's rebellion, there was a struggle about the way forward among papal loyalists: should there be some attempt to listen to what the rebels had to say, and press for reunion with them, or should the reaction be a firm assertion of traditional certainties? Those positions represent two ends of a spectrum rather than two easily definable parties, but it is possible to use names which were used at the time for those who gathered at either end of the spectrum: *Spirituali* and *Zelanti*. The eventual outcome was a defeat for the *Spirituale* strategy of accommodation with Protestants, though, as we shall see (below, p. 168), the *Spirituali* left some unexpected legacies to Western Christianity. From 1545, the Council of Trent did its best to build a new 'Tridentine' Church on the old foundations; a 'Counter-Reformation', based on further centralization of the Western Church in Rome, was launched.[66]

Since the future of the Roman Catholic Church was set against the backdrop of a structurally unaltered celibate clericalism, it was not surprising that auricular confession and its secrecy was part of the Counter-Reformation's intensification of past ecclesiastical and clerical patterns. To emphasize the importance of this sacrament in the Roman Church's arsenal of saving grace, a new item of furniture appeared, first in Milan under its hyperactive Archbishop Carlo Borromeo, and then universally throughout the Tridentine world: the confessional, inside which the sins of an anonymous penitent could disappear, after they had been whispered to a priest.[67] The Catholic Reformation saw a newly systematic imposition of another sort of silence: that of universal censorship. Various Church institutions, first the Sorbonne in Paris, then the Spanish Inquisition, then the Roman Inquisition, compiled lists of books which the faithful were forbidden to read. These lists were known as the Indexes, the last of which was abolished by Pope Paul VI as late as 1966.[68] Book-destruction could be justified by a good New Testament precedent. In a somewhat implausible story in Acts 19.19–20, during what the narrator presents as a spectacularly successful missionary visit to Ephesus, the Apostle Paul presided over a holocaust of books of magic arts, worth in total fifty thousand pieces of silver. 'So the word of the Lord grew and prevailed mightily', the writer concludes triumphantly. More than one painter of the Counter-Reformation, or his inquisitorial patron, came to find this book-burning an edifying subject for art.[69]

Equally important was a reaffirmation of monasticism. Eager to refute Erasmus's oblique attack on the regular life through a praise of marriage, the Counter-Reformation insisted anew that celibacy was better than marriage. One corollary was that contemplation was an activity best left to the celibate and clerical professionals; not only the subversive shade of (the celibate) Erasmus but also those of the rene-gades Sebastian Franck and (the celibate) Schwenckfeld hovered behind that thought. In the very last stages of the Council of Trent in 1563, despite the vexation of the Habsburg emperor, who hoped to concili-ate married Lutheran clergy within his dominions, the bishops declared the inviolability of vows for nuns and male clergy and pro-nounced anathema (the most solemn curse possible) on anyone claiming that 'the married state excels the state of virginity or celibacy, and that it is better and happier to be united in matrimony than to remain in virginity or celibacy'.[70]

This theology was starkly reformulated in 1597 by Cardinal Rob-erto Bellarmino ('Bellarmine'), who, after being made Cardinal Inquisitor only a year or two later, came to embody the new direction in the Roman Church. Bellarmine's widely used 'larger' catechism, intended for public lay education, naturally discussed the Church's seven sacraments. The only sacrament to receive anything but unquali-fied praise and commendation was the sacrament of marriage, over which there hovered something of a health warning: 'Mariage is a thing humane, virginitie is Angelical. Mariage is according to nature, Virginitie is above nature. And not only virginitie but widowhood also is better than mariage ... the holie Doctors have declared, that the thirtie fold fruite is of Matrimonie, the three-score fold of widow-hood, the hundereth fold of virginitie.'[71] With this distinction between the natural and the angelical, we are back in the world of the fourth-century Syrian ascetic Aphrahat (above, p. 72). He had written within a Christian culture which at the time had often been regarded with suspicion by other Christians, not least in the western Mediter-ranean, for its excessive enthusiasm for celibacy, but now Rome would have welcomed his extreme position. The consequences of this new imposition of a real universal celibacy on the Roman Catholic clergy, instead of its often nominal medieval observance, will become apparent in Chapter 8.

It is hardly surprising that the sixteenth and seventeenth centuries therefore saw not merely the defence of existing religious Orders in Roman Catholicism, but also their continuing renewal in medieval fashion. Particularly significant were the successful moves in France to restore a purified observance in the Cistercian Order, thus renewing the silence on which the Order had prided itself.[72] One Cistercian house in Normandy went much further; it was rescued from two centuries of decay in the 1660s by Armand de Rancé, a commendator-abbot with an unusual sense of his spiritual duties. As a godson of Cardinal Richelieu, he was also a suitable symbol of the return to self-confidence in French Catholicism. Under de Rancé, La Trappe seized its independence from the parent Order, so that it could return to the strictest possible observance of monastic silence outside the Carthusian fold. For the time being, de Rancé refused to allow his house to become a centre of a congregation of monasteries as the abbey of Cîteaux had been in the twelfth century; that only changed at the end of the nineteenth century, when Trappists became an Order with monasteries distributed throughout the world.

The Trappist observance was actually so austere in its return to early Cistercian values that it revived a conflict within the Benedictine tradition which monasticism might have considered settled back in the fifth century through the advocacy of St Jerome: the relationship between contemplation and the life of the intellect (above, p. 93). De Rancé banned the pursuit of scholarship within his community. Perhaps this might be regarded as the exercise of a gift of discernment appropriate to a monastic superior, seeing through Jerome's venerable but self-serving arguments in favour of scholastic pursuits, but it brought him into acute conflict with Benedictine monks of the Congregation of St Maur, who were at the forefront of contemporary Catholic historical research. The great Benedictine scholar-historian Jean Mabillon found the Trappist Abbot's anti-intellectualism shocking, and a heated literary debate followed between the two men. Apart from the fact that de Rancé perforce demonstrated his own intellectual ability in his debates with Mabillon, he was exhibiting a strange myopia towards the scholarly achievements of his Order back to the time of Bernard of Clairvaux, and the Trappists have since quietly set aside his prejudices.[73]

Nevertheless, much of the most effective promotion of the Counter-Reformation on a worldwide scale was not so much the work of medieval monastic Orders as of two brand-new organizations, which became closely associated in their work and aims: the Society of Jesus and the Ursuline Sisters. Both just pre-dated the Counter-Reformation, but they were swept up into it and one cannot now imagine Tridentine Catholicism without them. Neither were conventional religious Orders: in the case of the Jesuits, the name 'Society' suggested their rather amorphous origins as something like a religious gild, albeit with an unusually gifted and talented first membership, while the Ursulines spent more than two centuries deftly defeating the plans of anxious bishops to turn them into a well-regulated enclosed Order of nuns, such as the fathers of Trent had felt was appropriate for women. What the Jesuits found useful in Ursuline groups was their ability to undertake pastoral work among women and poor children, the first of whom invited scandal for male priests, while the second did not fit with emerging Jesuit priorities.[74]

Neither Jesuit nor Ursuline spirituality could be called contemplative: they were both activist groups with a ministry in the world. The Jesuits emphasized their difference from the enclosed religious Orders and even from the Orders of friars by eliminating two normal features of religious community life: regular decision-making gatherings in chapter, and a daily structure of worship 'in choir' in the community church. They also refused to develop a distinct uniform dress. Ignatius Loyola was one of the greatest spiritual directors of any Christian age, but his most important writing, the *Exercises*, is not a work of contemplative spirituality: it is a systematic effort to train the mind for the purposes of the soul, deploying an extraordinary variety of literary genres in the process – 'directives, meditations, prayers, declarations, procedures, sage observations, and rules', in the affectionate listing by one of its informed admirers.[75] One of its recommended methods of meditating on the Gospels, visualizing the incidents in them, might well stimulate contemplation, but that would only be one of many possible outcomes in exploring the *Exercises*. Silence is a word conspicuous by its absence from the writings and letters of Loyola. This may well be precisely because he was determined to keep a distance between his new organization and monasteries, and silence was too closely associated for him with the monastic tradition.[76] His successors in leading the Society were determined to uphold this tradition: when some of their fellows tried to move towards a contemplative life, it caused fierce debate. In the 1580s and 1590s, the leadership took firm steps to prevent this and to maintain the active missionary strategy of the Society.[77]

That is not to say that the Jesuits neglected private prayer. Far from it: they used their pastoral ministry to recommend to the humblest folk the traditional techniques and forms of prayer known in the West. They encouraged the practice both of recitation of familiar prayers and what they were slightly awkwardly wont to call 'mental prayer' to complement attendance at the liturgy.[78] This emphasis was an essential part of their highly successful public ministry; but it represented a democratization of prayer, rather than of silence. Once more we are seeing the distinction between meditation and contemplation which we first encountered in the fourth-century writings of Evagrius Ponticus (above, pp. 80–83). If mystics from Evagrius to the Tridentine age and beyond regarded meditation as only a preparation for contemplation, a step on the journey, the Society of Jesus decided not to encourage either its members or its pastoral charges to take that further step.

TRIDENTINE MYSTICS AND THEIR TRIALS

Not so the monastic Orders, which, once they had recovered from the shock of Protestant disruption, renewed their exploration of the contemplative ethos. In Spain this was best seen in the renewal of the Carmelite Order which was the life's work of John of the Cross (Juan de Yepes, 1542–91) and Teresa of Avila (1515–82). John of the Cross, in quiet contrast to the Jesuits, referred to the 'dryness' which might result from a failure to move from meditation to contemplation.[79] Teresa, one of the most down-to-earth explorers during centuries of search for silence, revelled in her rediscovery of Carmelite impulses to delight in divine and human creativity. She made contemplation seem disarmingly possible even for those with little confidence in themselves:

For those who walk the path of silent prayer, a book can be a useful device to prompt recollection. I have also found it helpful to gaze at meadows, flowers and water. Creation reflects the Creator. These things have awakened me and brought me back to recollection, as a book would. They also remind me to be grateful and good. My mind was so dense that I could never imagine sublime things until the Beloved showed them to me in a way I could understand ... Other people are able to use their imaginations to recollect themselves in prayer, but mine is no use to me. I could *think* of Christ as a man, but I couldn't really *see* him.[80]

Might one see in such apparently artless words a subtle critique of the tidy and systematic approach to meditation through use of the imagination set out in Ignatius of Loyola's *Spiritual Exercises*?

The glory of the Counter-Reformation is often seen in these Spanish Carmelite mystics who embarked on the journey from meditation to contemplation. John and Teresa represent some of the heights of Christian engagement with the silence of the divine. They pulled the Carmelites back to their desert roots; behind their thought lurks once more not only Evagrius, long forgotten in Catholic Spain, but also Pseudo-Dionysius, who was not. John of the Cross explored the negative way to God in language which owes much to the Areopagite. Dionysius had spoken of ridding the mind of its contents, so that it could pass out into the night, an image which meant much to the Spanish friar a thousand years later.[81] Teresa too can reach out to the thought of Evagrius in his discovery of the mind at the centre of his search for silence, when she speaks in her no-nonsense way of getting beyond joy and thankfulness in the higher levels of contemplation:

All the soul needs to do during these times of quietude is be still and make no noise. What I mean by noise is rushing around with the intellect trying to rustle up reflections of gratitude and words of praise for the gift you are being given. It's that impulse of mind to catalogue your transgressions to convince yourself that you do not deserve to receive such grace. It's that commotion the faculties create, the intellect trying to conjure up images and the memory rushing to store them. These faculties wear me out. I may have a poor memory, but sometimes I seem to be incapable of subduing it.[82]

Yet the relationship of mystic contemplation with Counter-Reformation Catholicism is as problematic and complicated as that between mystics and the medieval Western Church. Teresa faced much infuriated opposition to her efforts to remodel Carmelite life: John of the Cross suffered nine months of exceptionally unpleasant imprisonment at the hands of other Carmelites who saw no need for reform of their Order. Yet the complication is not simply thanks to the habitually uncomfortable fit between mystical piety and episcopal Christianity. One cannot understand the troubled careers of John and Teresa without the background of late medieval Spain and Portugal, violently transforming themselves from a peninsula of three world faiths into a Christian monoculture, its new character enforced by the Spanish and Portuguese Inquisitions, operating respectively from 1478 and 1537.[83] The expulsion of the Jews in 1492 and the steady marginalization of Muslims up to their final expulsion in 1609 left a great many people of the Iberian peninsula in the category contemptuously known by more long-established Iberian Christians as *conversos*. For many, that represented a spiritual limbo, gradually losing contact with their ancestral religions of Judaism and Islam, and trying to find some compensatory place in the only religion legally left to them. One element they might bring with them was the tradition of mystical silence deeply rooted in these other faiths. It is therefore no surprise to find that both Teresa and John of the Cross were from Jewish *converso* backgrounds, and one should see their mystical experiences in the light of a mystical heritage beyond purely Christian resources. Like Bridget of Sweden, they both had bumpy rides towards canonization: Teresa got there only thirty years after her death, but accompanied by much political infighting, while John of the Cross had to wait as late as 1726.[84]

At least they achieved their sainthood. Less fortunate were the leading figures in the mystical grouping known as Quietism, which took its inspiration from Teresa of Avila and John of the Cross, but suffered much more lasting hostility than they did. Quietism's chief protagonist in the eye of the storm was yet again a woman, indeed a married woman, usually known to history as Mme Guyon (Jeanne Bouvier de la Motte; 1648–1717).[85] The principal battleground was Catholic France. It has been described as having been subjected to a 'mystical

invasion' in the half-century before Mme Guyon's birth, as knowledge of the Spanish mystics spread and fuelled a remarkable
indigenous movement of devotion, joining with the native reform of
the Cistercians. We have already compared the thought of Evagrius
with that of one of the earliest heralds of this French mysticism,
Bishop François de Sales (above, pp. 82–3). The mystical invasion
claimed patrons at the highest levels of French society, thanks to
Henri IV's chaplain Cardinal de Bérulle, who might be seen as the last
Dionysian thinker, at the end of a millennium's exploration of the
anonymous Miaphysite.[86]

Quietism was much more controversial, and its eventual fate represented a defeat for the mystical invaders in this French spiritual golden
age. It was not exactly a movement, more a national stirring of interest and bitter controversy around a single short book. Immediately
before the troubles which were to befall Mme Guyon, there had been
warning signs of what might happen to a Quietist. One of the
great influences on her was yet another Spaniard, Miguel de Molinos
(c. 1628–97), who was imprisoned and whose writings were condemned in both Italy and France; he died in the Inquisition's prison in
Rome. Significantly the Jesuits were his chief accusers, and his fate
was to be echoed in that of Mme Guyon. Only five years after de
Molinos was first denounced in 1681, she published a book – short,
but not as short as its title implied, *A Brief and Very Easy Method of
Mental Prayer*.[87] It soon became notorious.

Mme Guyon had the misfortune to win the admiration of some
extremely powerful people at the French Court, who had in turn some
extremely powerful enemies, freshly triumphant from de Molinos's
disgrace. There were religious as well as political considerations. Now
that France had officially returned to a monopoly Catholicism with
Louis XIV's revocation of the Edict of Nantes in 1685 and his expulsion of defiant Huguenots, a newly assertive episcopate was alert for
attempts to foster devotions beyond clerical control, and it hearkened
to Jesuit denunciations. Not only was there the shadow of the campaign against de Molinos: Guyon also fell victim to that prejudice
against women writing theology or biblical commentary which is as
old as the founding of universities in the West (above, pp. 119–21).
The very title of her little treatise was an explicit invitation to the

lowliest French peasant, even those who could not read, to explore the mystical way, which she had proclaimed to be 'very easy'. While the Jesuits had sought to bring 'mental prayer' to the poor, even the illiterate, Mme Guyon meant something rather different when she used that Jesuit phrase, for she spoke of contemplation rather than meditation. In a classic fashion which Evagrius Ponticus would have understood, she described a path to union with God though surrender and passivity. 'Abandonment is a letting go of every concern for ourselves, so as to let ourselves be led entirely by God . . . Being indifferent to everything, as much for the body as for the soul, concerning the good of this world and that of the world to come.'[88]

Mme Guyon's treatise alighted perhaps predictably on the story in Luke's Gospel of Mary and Martha entertaining Jesus in their home in Bethany. This incident, which witnesses to Luke's particular interest in the silences around Jesus, had long been a favourite theme of contemplatives, particularly in the Counter-Reformation, when the contrast between the two sisters gave them a rhetorical weapon against Jesuit activism. Christ had praised Mary sitting passively at his feet, not busy Martha in the kitchen. As Guyon saw it,

> Martha was doing good things; but because she did them in her own spirit, Christ rebuked her. The spirit of man is turbulent and uneasy; that is why it achieves little, even though it might seem to achieve much . . . what then did Mary choose? Peace, tranquillity and rest. Outwardly, she stopped working, in order to let herself be stirred by the spirit of Jesus Christ; she ceased to live, in order that Christ might live in her.[89]

Another of Guyon's long-unpublished works, *Les torrents*, took as its eponymous controlling metaphor the theme which had so fascinated the antinomian Englishman John Everard half a century before: in it, Mme Guyon describes the journey to union with God in terms of the journeys of various rivers which flow into the sea.[90] The consequence of all this was her frequent imprisonment over the course of two decades, and her works eventually ended up more esteemed by Protestants than French Catholics. The discrediting of mysticism in the French Catholic Church which resulted from the condemnation of Quietism left the Church with one less spiritual resource against the outburst of destructive fury which it was to face in the French Revolution.

The first two Reformations surveyed here, the Iconoclastic Controversy in the Eastern Church and the Gregorian reforms in the West,
had succeeded in uniting their respective Churches in one path to the
future. The third, the sixteenth-century Reformation, confounded the
confident hopes of the Protestant Reformers through disagreements
and failure to destroy the Roman Church completely. It created a division in Western Christianity which still shows no sign of ending.
Traditionally, and particularly in the last century of ecumenical
endeavours, this fragmentation has been seen as tragic, but it is possible to view matters differently. Western Europeans who know
anything about their history tend to take the united medieval phase of
the Western Latin Church for granted, just as, when we are growing
up, we take for granted the environment around us as the norm by
which everything else is judged. But this obscures the fact that it is
unique in human history for a region to have been so dominated by a
single form of monotheistic religion and its accompanying culture for
a thousand-year period. Islam has the concept of the overarching
ummah, the community of all Muslims, but this has none of the unity
possessed by medieval Western Christendom.

In other words, the dominance of a single Western Church which
looked to the Bishop of Rome was a freakish occurrence in human
experience, albeit a freak with profound consequences for the present
day. Its break-up in the sixteenth century was a return to normality in
human and religious history, rather than some unexpected or even
undesirable accident. The division was agonizing, and it aroused the
most destructive emotions. In the midst of the struggles, devotional
silence proved one of the greatest casualties. But there were other varieties of silence that flourished in that most turbulent of Christian
eras. They must now take their place in a different narrative that cuts
through the layers of Christian history, and takes us right back to its
beginnings. In its course, it will lead us to some dark places.

PART FOUR

Reaching behind Noise in Christian History

7

Silences for Survival

NICODEMISM: NAME AND THING

So far we have traced what might be termed the official history of silence, which has tended to focus on the positive utterances and actions of public Christianity. There are further, more oblique, varieties of silence to consider in this and the next chapter, few of which reflect very well on the bodies which call themselves Churches. The Catholic Christianity which we observed emerging in the second century was marked by an exclusivity and intolerance of rivals, which may have been one reason for its great success in the later Roman Empire, but which would have dramatic effects once bishops had made their alliance with the secular power. Now Christians really could aspire to exclude the 'Other'. In such circumstances, groups which represented the 'Other', some Christian, some not, have repeatedly made themselves invisible simply in order to survive: they have become what John Calvin in the sixteenth century contemptuously called 'Nicodemites', in allusion to Jesus's timorous disciple Nicodemus, who, according to John's Gospel (John 3.1–2), would only visit his Lord by night.

Christianity is not alone in creating Nicodemism by its actions and assumptions. It is a melancholy truth about the human race that groups who have suffered oppression are inclined to forget the experience, once given the chance of power. Islam has its Nicodemites too: they are as old as the division between Sunni and Shia, when the persecuted Shi'ite followers of the murdered Caliph Ali created their own Nicodemism *avant la lettre*, with its doctrine of legitimate dissimulation, *taqiyyah*.[1] Many subsequent Muslim minorities have borrowed that concept in hard times. One significant example is the Alawi offshoot of Shi'ism in Syria: it has been suggested that in a perverse reversal of the secrecy of the oppressed, the concept of *taqiyyah* has provided a sense of legitimacy to the secret police, the *mukhabarat*, who have brutally sustained the Alawite Syrian Presidents Hafez and Bashar al-Assad in power.[2]

Mediterranean Christians of the first five centuries were no exception to the rule; they seem to have learned very little tolerance in the long term from their experiences of being persecuted by the Roman Empire. Medieval inquisitors did not invent the concept of heresy: it is embedded in New Testament literature in a series of bilious references to 'sects',[3] and the exclusionary attitude went on to flourish richly as Catholic Christianity created boundaries around its beliefs from the second century CE. So Christians enthusiastically oppressed and imprisoned one another wherever the imperial authorities gave them the chance, first during the Arian controversy in the fourth century, and right up to the present day: witness some of the troubles of various Protestant groupings and of Jehovah's Witnesses in post-Soviet Russia and other former Soviet republics, inspired principally by officials intent on promoting the interests of state-sponsored Orthodoxy.[4]

It was not long after Constantine's conversion before a Christian Roman emperor persecuted Christians to the point of execution on charges which included heresy. The chief victim was the unfortunate monastic leader and bishop Priscillian, who was beheaded with several of his followers in 385 on charges which were ostensibly about the practice of magic, but which were in fact more to do with what many Church leaders regarded as his excessive committment to asceticism. At the time several of Priscillian's fellow-bishops, including the formidable Martin of Tours, had the grace to feel that his execution was a bad idea.[5] That did not stop Christianity refining the precedent when, in the eleventh century, it belatedly borrowed the method of execution by burning at the stake from the Emperor Diocletian; that great third-century enemy of Christianity had decreed burning for his equal pet hate, the Manichees (above, p. 71).[6] Christian leaders were just as offended as Diocletian by Manichaeism and later dualist religious systems, and carried out their first burning for heresy in Orléans (France) in 1022. The great advantage of burning a human being to death is that it does not infringe ancient prohibitions on churchmen shedding blood.[7]

Soon the Western Church, in the wake of the Gregorian reforms of the eleventh century, faced various new movements of dissent through-out western and southern Europe, including the Free Spirit, the Waldensians and Albigensians. The response, particularly fostered by the Dominicans and Pope Innocent III (1160/1–1216), was the inven-tion of inquisitions to inquire into the beliefs of those whom the Church chose to label as heretics, preferably to bring them back to the Church, but, if not, to arrange for their punishment. Inquisitors would insist that they did their work on good biblical principles; after all, was not the first act of inquisition the expulsion of Adam and Eve from paradise – and was not Christ, the giver of the new Law, thereby the greatest of inquisitors?[8] An inquisitor's first effort was always to persuade and reconcile the erring. It was not his fault if the erring obstinately continued to err (that is the strict definition of a heretic, after all); but it was then his duty to rid society of such pollutants.

This attitude of constant vigilance might be considered justified by the length of time it took to eliminate the Albigensians – over two centuries – let alone the amorphous groups of the Free Spirit. The Waldensians managed to maintain a precarious but coherent existence till rescued from possible oblivion by the sixteenth-century Reformation, and they were the most successful clandestine group of the medieval West. More-over, by their survival, they have been able to refute a consistent charge of medieval inquisitors which has stuck remarkably tenaciously to other medieval dissident groups: that all this dissidence originated in a dualis-tic Eastern religion imported to the West via Byzantium. The Albigensians had disappeared, and could not defend themselves from a canard which many modern historians now see as an invention of inquisitors intended to discredit them: that dissident Christians had embraced an alien, intru-sive belief-system, fundamentally at odds with the Christian principle of the incarnation of Christ. It is possible to argue that there was in fact little or no dualism in the medieval West, but that it was attributed by the authorities to Western Christians whose real error was to seek to extend the logic of the Gregorian reforms further than Gregorian reformers in the Church hierarchy thought appropriate. As in so many other situations, this was a dispute about authority rather than about faith itself. Hidden groups in every age are very vulnerable to the public calumnies of their enemies who wield authority.[9]

IBERIAN JEWS: *CONVERSOS*

Medieval Christian clandestinity was dwarfed by the strategies employed by Jews in the medieval Iberian peninsula, which gave many clues to Christians in later centuries about preserving an identity. Judaism faced determined ecclesiastical efforts to eliminate it through a royal inquisition newly created in the late 1470s by Queen Isabel of Castile and (less enthusiastically) her husband King Fernando of Aragon. From the first large-scale forced conversions to Christianity in the wake of widespread Spanish Christian pogroms in 1391, *converso* Christians frequently really remained secret Jews. Christians often gave them another, far more offensive name than *conversos*: 'pigs' (*marranos*). It would not be the last time that this epithet would be bestowed on a minority in order to represent it as sub-human.[10] It is hardly surprising that the Spanish Inquisition was so paranoid about the hidden menace of Judaism when one realizes that the first two Inquisitors-General of the institution, the Dominican Tómas de Torquemada and his successor, Bishop Diego Deza, were both from families which had very recently been Jewish: such officials had a great deal of personal baggage to dispose of through their busy activity.[11]

It is nevertheless remarkable, and a heartening tribute to the obstinacy of the human spirit, to see how long clandestine Judaism survived in Iberian culture. In Brazil, it managed to outlive three centuries of the Portuguese Inquisition, and to re-emerge in the nineteenth century. That success came largely by adopting a thoroughgoing version of the strategy which had served Byzantine Iconophiles well in the Iconoclastic Controversy of the eighth and ninth centuries (above, pp. 105–8): crypto-Judaism retreated into the female sphere, the household, where external male society was less sure in its ability to coerce, and less interested in looking, long after the menfolk had lost their normal Jewish prerogative of dominating their communities.[12] That survival is an ironical reflection of an old African-American Christian community saying: 'If it wasn't for the women, you wouldn't have a church.'[13]

By its nature, Iberian crypto-Judaism's influence on Christianity is difficult to trace, but its very dispersal through the rest of Europe gave cues to many Christians facing similar trials. In the eastern Mediterranean and beyond, Christians hardly needed such lessons. As Spanish and Portuguese Jews travelled eastwards to the hospitality of the Ottoman Empire in the 1490s, they encountered Christians who had already developed their own clandestinities over centuries, as they sought to survive in an increasingly Islamic landscape. Although Islam had not been a proselytizing faith in the first two centuries of its conquests in the Middle East, it did move towards seeking mass conversions, and encouraged them by reserving economic and social privileges for Muslims not available to the other religious communities in Muslim lands. It was very tempting for both Christians and Jews to convert outwardly to gain such advantages, and persist more or less in practising their old faith in private. A considerable literature, including hagiographies of those who thought better of their conversion and suffered accordingly, developed from the eighth century onwards, particularly among Syrian and Arab Christians.[14]

Jews, remembering their experience in their old homeland, must have relished the irony when they encountered such Christian subjects of the Sublime Porte, who were in effect *conversos* within Islam. Cases lasted until the disintegration of the Ottoman Empire in the nineteenth and twentieth centuries. Generations of Orthodox Christians were able to sustain a covert life of faith for extraordinary lengths of time. On the island of Cyprus, finally captured from the Venetians by the Turks in 1570, a large proportion of those who converted to Islam were said to be like a cloth in which cotton was covered with linen, so it looked different on either side; they were evocatively known as 'the linen-cotton folk' (*Linovamvakoi*). Such double allegiance survived right up to 1878, when the British ended Ottoman power in Cyprus. There are similar stories of generations of crypto-Christians from Asia Minor, numbering tens of thousands: even some Christian priests functioned outwardly as mullahs.[15]

NICODEMITES IN REFORMATION AND COUNTER-REFORMATION

One of the most exciting reappraisals of Christian history in recent years has been the recognition of what a large part clandestine Iberian

Judaism and Islam played in that cataclysm of Western Christianity, the sixteenth-century Reformation and Counter-Reformation. As we have seen, the Reformation has few rivals in any era of Christian history in its extremes of noise and silence, of proclamation and concealment. It represents an end to nearly a millennium of ecclesiastical unity. The resulting traumas produced more violence of Christian against Christian than in any other period, but many of the responses to that violence were conditioned and shaped by the earlier story already in train: the violence of Iberian Christians against Jews and Muslims.

One of the phenomena of dissent in early sixteenth-century Spain which infuriated the Inquisition was that of the *alumbrados* or 'enlightened ones'. Like the Ranters of Interregnum England a century later (above, p. 146), *alumbrados* were half a reality, half a construct of inquisitorial paranoia. Certainly they numbered among their most prominent spiritual guides a more than coincidental number of *conversos*. Like crypto-Jews, *alumbrados* examined by the inquisitors exhibited an indifference to how they practised outward religion, privileging an inward spirituality. Latterly the first voices of northern Protestantism ('Lutheranism', Iberians consistently called it) became one of their inspirations, and in due course they repaid the debt.[16]

The streams of hidden Iberian religion flowed towards Rome itself. One of the chief impulses came via the *converso* and *alumbrado* theologian Juan de Valdés, who fled from the Spanish Inquisition to the Spanish Italian territories around Naples, where the Inquisition had no jurisdiction. Despite his distinct heterodoxy (notably his remarkable lack of comment on the doctrines of the Trinity and of the role of an institutional Church) and his covert sympathies with Protestant theology, Valdés was one of the chief inspirations of the amorphous groups of Italian Christians interested in inner devotion and outward reformation of Church structures, who during the 1530s became known as *Spirituali*. When the clash between *Spirituali* and Italian hard-line clerics like Giampietro Carafa (later Pope Paul IV) turned to a rout of the leading figures in the *Spirituale* movement in the early 1540s, a stream of refugees began to leave Italy for the safety of Protestant Europe to the north, or for the more religiously varied eastern lands of Hungary and Poland. This had extraordinary long-term results: not merely modern Unitarianism, but much of the early Enlightenment, can be traced to the influence of these Mediterranean refugees.[17]

Valdés was not the only potential victim of the Spanish Inquisition to make his escape eastward: none other than Ignatius Loyola had at one point been its prisoner, and his creation, the Society of Jesus, was also at first embedded like the Valdesian circle in the *Spirituali* grouping which was so prominent in the first moves at renewal in the Roman Church. The defeat of the *Spirituali* may belatedly have prompted a silence in the Jesuit archives. One curious feature of Ignatius's voluminous surviving correspondence is that it is almost exclusively preoccupied with matters of business; one would find it difficult to gauge from it what spiritual qualities singled out the writer to be a saint, this man who wrote that key text of Tridentine spirituality, the *Exercises*. This silence suggests a huge missing body of letters systematically fed into a Jesuit stove. Evidently an efficiently comprehensive hand, probably in the 1560s, refashioned the earlier years of the Society. The aim was to delete large portions of the story that would have been embarrassing in a Church which was by then dominated by the bitter foes of the shattered and dispersed *Spirituali*.[18]

The most famous dissident escapee from the Iberian hothouse was the physician and theologian Michael Servetus, who spent his truncated career doing his best to create a single religion of one God out of the three monotheisms of the Iberian peninsula. He made the mistake of angering John Calvin, particularly by his provocative imitation of the title of Calvin's *Institutes* (*Institutio Christianae Religionis*) in his own reconstruction of Christian faith, *Christianismi Restitutio* (1553), which proved the tragic culmination of three decades of independent thought. After slipping from one refuge to another, hubris overtook him and he abandoned any discretion on his visit to Geneva in 1553: his fiery death there soon afterwards was the result of a barely concealed collaboration between the Roman Catholic Inquisition of Vienne and Calvin himself.[19] Servetus's fate demonstrates what happened when Iberian clandestinity refused to remain silent. He was the extreme and most candid example of a consistent tendency away from orthodoxy among those who fled Iberia and, later, Counter-Reformation Italy.

Many of those who took shelter in institutionalized northern European Protestant Churches showed this same capacity for independent thought, which often alarmed their hosts. It rarely pushed the authorities to the brutality which Servetus had faced in Geneva: since these refugees from southern Europe personified the effects of popish cruelty, there was generally a certain constraint in lighting the inquisitorial fires too readily. A remarkable example who infiltrated the Church of England was Antonio del Corro (1527–91), who became minister of the Spanish exile congregation in London in the late 1560s, and one of the least silent of these southern European radicals. Here was a man who moved from opposing the prevailing assertion of predestination in the Reformed Protestant Church of England to cautious but unmistakable statements of Unitarianism. He was prepared to officiate at the burial of someone he knew to be a crypto-Jew, and was reported as having once said that 'If you are a Jew, you are blessed; if you are a Turk, you are blessed; if you are a Christian, you are blessed and will be saved.' It is astonishing that he got away with it all, let alone end his days in comfort as a prebendary of St Paul's Cathedral in London. It all suggests that del Corro had some very powerful friends, whose protection must have nerved him to unusual public candour, but all this was nevertheless only a fraction of what he might have said.[20]

By its very nature, clandestine religion might seem unlikely to produce justifications, but an interesting feature of this period which launched so many clandestinities was that politics as much as religion spawned an unprecedented torrent of talk about dissimulation and the reasons why it might be desirable or despicable. The political discussion in fact pre-dated the Reformation by half a century. Much of it involved an increasingly sophisticated discussion of secrecy and dissimulation, making explicit themes which had no doubt been obvious to cynical monarchs for centuries, but which now took both wider currency and a new practical urgency, thanks to the increasing bureaucratic sophistication of late medieval secular government. The simultaneous flowering of humanism provided politicians with a bonanza of newly available ancient literature which had little to do with Christian theology. What the humanists rediscovered ranged from analytical discussions of politics by Cicero to the hermetic literature which, like gnosticism, had hovered on the frontiers of Judaism and of early Catholic Christianity.[21]

Humanists could point out to the reading public of Europe that Classical Egypt, Greece and Rome had elevated silence to the status of a god. This provided a fruitful series of images for those wishing to commend or discommend silence, or simply to discomfit other politicians. For instance, in *Pasquil the Playne*, a satirical English conversation-piece for three voices that gained nationwide popularity, the learned English humanist Sir Thomas Elyot (*c.* 1490–1546) mocked his former fellow-diplomat and sometime friend Thomas Cranmer in a thinly disguised portrait as Harpocrates, the Egyptian god of silence. Cranmer had something important to hide at the time: Elyot published his *jeu d'esprit* in 1533, not long after that notoriously tight-lipped cleric, newly chosen as Archbishop of Canterbury, had broken his vows of celibacy by his clandestine marriage to Andreas Osiander's niece in Nuremberg (above, p. 135).[22]

Elyot's text was little more than playfulness, although with a very serious and malicious political purpose. Occult literature promised much more to its readers. The very essence of the wisdom ascribed to the Egyptian priest Hermes Trismegistus, in a whole series of ancient texts eagerly explored by the cognoscenti from the fifteenth century, was that it was hidden, esoteric: that was its attraction, its promise of power to its adepts. Hermeticism comfortably straddled the frontiers of theology, astrology, medicine and magic. One of its chief practitioners, Cornelius Agrippa (1486–?1535), magician, astrologer and historiographer to the Emperor Charles V, and a man who attracted denunciation by John Calvin and Catholic inquisitors alike, commented (oddly enough, in the same publication year of 1533 as *Pasquil the Playne*) on the value of silence in communicating with God: 'Now that is the best prayer, which is not uttered in words, but that which with a Religious silence and sincere cogitation is offered up to God, and that which with the voice of the mind and words of the intellectuall world, is offered to him.'[23] Agrippa was echoing Plato in this thought, but in the sixteenth century there was no question but that silent prayer was certainly the safest. Small wonder that Agrippa should be translated into English at the beginning of the 1650s, that strenuous decade of competing raucousness and quietness in the troubled Atlantic archipelago.

In the new secular literature of what came to be known as statecraft, the writings of Niccolò Machiavelli (1469–1527) were the most notorious. It was soon generally considered good form to express public disapproval of Machiavelli for his cynicism, particularly after his work became one of the first books to be placed on the Roman Inquisition's Index of Prohibited Books, in 1559, but that did not stop courtiers and would-be courtiers finding a pressing need for the sort of political analysis which Machiavelli provided. A useful evasive ploy for such men was to dwell on the political cynicism of the first-century Roman historian Tacitus, rather than show a too obvious direct interest in Machiavelli – the same reliance on safely remote Classical authors can be found in those who wanted to discuss those highly dangerous topics, atheism and sodomy, without showing too obvious an interest in them.[24]

Tacitus came to enjoy a Continent-wide vogue among those interested in history and politics, which included just about any leading figure in the Reformation and Counter-Reformation. He was popularized through a great edition of 1574 by Justus Lipsius (1547–1606), a more-or-less Catholic scholar from the Low Countries whose career exhibited an exemplary discretion, though that did not stop Lipsius's works eventually joining those of Machiavelli on the Roman Index. Not only did Tacitus's name, in a happy coincidence, suggest the theme of silence, but he provided a convenient talking point in his careful (though not approving) picture of the tyrannical Emperor Tiberius, a constant if not always effective practitioner of dissimulation. Even Cardinal Borromeo's secretary, Giovanni Botero (1544–1617), a priest at the heart of the Counter-Reformation, can be seen to exploit the strategy of talking about Tacitus when he wanted to discuss Machiavelli. Botero's work became a standard political treatise; published in Venice in 1589, it popularized that new phrase 'reason of state' thanks to its title, *Della ragion di stato*.[25]

Melding with this secular discourse of the chattering classes of Renaissance Europe was an equally noisy debate among theologians. It took its cue from that fourth-century conflict between Jerome and Augustine of Hippo on the question of lying (above, p. 66), and, predictably, the fiercest defender of absolute truthfulness and un-compromising religious witness was the arch-Augustinian of the Reformation, John Calvin.[26] In 1537, two years after he had fled from France into what proved to be permanent exile, Calvin began address-ing a series of fierce rebukes to those who were not prepared to follow his own drastic action. In his sights to begin with were two personal friends who sympathized with reform, but had not broken with the papal Church. Calvin made the resonant coinage 'Nicodemites' in the title of a pamphlet of 1544, *Excuse à messieurs les Nicodémites sur la complaincte qu'ilz font de sa trop grand rigueur*, which stigmatized those of his contemporaries whom he sarcastically saw as following the timorous example of Nicodemus.[27] Calvin's consequent demoniz-ing of Nicodemites managed to ignore the significant fact that ultimately John's Gospel narrative (John 19.38–42) awards Nicode-mus what appears to be an honourable mention. He is one of two leading Jews who arrange dignified though clandestine burial for Jesus, and thus provide the setting for his Resurrection (the other, Joseph of Arimathea, has generally received a much better press in Christian history than Nicodemus).

Calvin had a talent for inventing such loaded neologisms for those of whom he disapproved (such as 'libertine' for all the many and var-ied inhabitants of Geneva who resisted the exact imposition of his will on that much-tried city). His message had its supporters, not least the compilers of Reformation Europe's many martyrologies. Many read with horrified fascination the numerous versions of the cele-brated cautionary tale of Francesco Spiera, a Nicodemite who got caught, and then recanted his evangelical faith when arrested by the Venetian Inquisition. The detailed account of Spiera's tormented death in 1548, convinced that he was damned for his treachery to godliness, was still frightening Protestants in the nineteenth century.[28] Nonetheless, not everyone approved of such intransigence even among the mainstream Reformers, and some were not slow to point out that it was all very well for Calvin to take such a line from his comfortable study behind the high walls of Geneva. Among the doubt-ers was Martin Bucer, long the chief minister of Strassburg until forced to flee to England in 1549, where he became much involved in the developing Reformation of Edward VI.

Bucer was a man whom Calvin regarded in many other respects as a mentor, but Bucer's opinion of his protégé's attitude to discretion in religion can be gauged by a long private treatise which he wrote on the subject probably around 1541, at a time when there was a real prospect of reuniting the Roman and Protestant Churches. It cautiously sanctioned attendance at popish services where there was no other option, justifying it by the scandal and misunderstanding which would be caused among ordinary people in the community by withdrawing from public worship: 'since they will not know the reason for your separation, you are stirring them up against yourself and your cause, and thus leaving them further from the Gospel; and moreover you will take on yourself as a private individual that which is a public matter, and only pertains to the public ministers of the Gospel.'[29] Bucer went so far as to say, in direct contradiction to Calvin's barbs against Gérard Roussel, that 'pastoral office may properly be exercised in papist churches at the moment'.[30]

ENGLAND: A VARIETY OF NICODEMITES

Bucer's opinions were not altered by the failure of the Church reunion negotiations in which he enthusiastically participated at Regensburg that same year, for there are copies of his treatise made after 1541; some carry dates up to 1544. Though he never put it into print, it is extremely interesting that two manuscript copies are to be found in England, one of them in the library of a future Protestant Archbishop of Canterbury, Matthew Parker, a friend and admirer of the Strassburg reformer.[31] Bucer did not live to see the restoration of Protestantism by Queen Elizabeth I in 1558, which reversed the restoration of papal authority in England by her half-sister Mary, but with his sensitivity to the English political scene, he would have instantly recognized in Elizabeth's religious Settlement of 1559 something unprecedented among the official Reformations of sixteenth-century Europe. It was planned and executed entirely by former Nicodemites, Protestants who had nevertheless conformed outwardly to the Roman Church from the moment Mary had secured her throne.

Foremost in this group was the Queen herself, ably assisted by two secular politicians, the brothers-in-law William Cecil and Nicholas Bacon (whose emphatically Protestant wife had been among Queen Mary's ladies-in-waiting). Their counterparts among the leading clergy were Matthew Parker, Elizabeth's first Archbishop of Canterbury; William May, her first nominee for Archbishop of York; the new Dean of Westminster Abbey, Gabriel Goodman; and the new Dean of the Chapel Royal, her former chaplain George Carew: all those clergy had served actively in the Church of Mary Tudor, though they now did their best to cover their tracks for the benefit of later historians. To a man, they were undoubtedly convinced Protestants, but they had also all been, in practical terms, Nicodemites. If William May had not died prematurely in 1560, that Nicodemite team would have entirely kept at bay from the very top of the Elizabethan political and religious scene all those Edwardian Protestants who had gone into exile under Mary for their faith.

Elizabeth's notorious detestation of all things Genevan is often attributed to the political ineptitude of John Calvin's Scottish admirer John Knox, but the fact that her Primate of All England was the custodian of one copy of Bucer's aggressive tract against Calvin's arguments raises the possibility that she may have been angrily conscious that Calvin would see her as the object of his principled contempt.[32] Her affirmation of her English *Messieurs les Nicodémites* in her plans for her Church also tells us much about her conduct as Supreme Governor of the Church of England, whose original parliamentary Settlement she preserved with fierce determination against all attempts to change it over the next forty-four years.

Continuously from the 1570s, Elizabethan England was clandestinely or openly at war with Catholic Europe. As a result, it judicially murdered more Roman Catholics than any other country in the continent – over forty-five years, nearly two hundred, all on charges of treason – producing tales of religious heroism and fortitude to equal any of the Protestant stories emerging from Mary Tudor's Catholic persecution: a new phalanx in the array of Christian martyrs. Yet Elizabeth's government behaved very differently towards those Catholics who did not seek to defy her as 'recusants' (those who refused to attend Protestant services). Catholic Nicodemites went to their parish churches and kept their counsel, particularly the male heads of gentry households, while their wives might stay at home and, in the fashion of crypto-Jewish mothers in Iberia, quietly nurture Catholicism in their families. Even most declared Catholic recusants, as far up the social scale as Philip Howard, Earl of Arundel (now canonized by the Roman Catholic Church), for some of their career occupied this ill-defined middle ground between resistance and the established Protestant Church, and many more found this a congenial solution to their religious dilemmas.

From at least 1582, these deliberately evanescent folk were abusively known as 'church papists', although, among various other dismissive labels, the Jesuit Father Henry Garnet's adroitly and bitterly paradoxical 'Protesting Protestants' deserves a revival. All in all, it was a highly successful stance from the Protestant English government's point of view, and, as a result, full-blown Catholic recusancy and Roman Catholicism in Reformation England did not become coterminous till as late as the 'Glorious Revolution' in 1688.[33] What is fascinating about Catholic Nicodemism is that both sides of the new religious divide had an interest in loudly condemning it in public. The middle way, church papistry, threatened all those who were seeking to build and define religious identities in a time of struggle. Mainstream Western European religious commentators, saddled with the assumption of a religious monopoly in society, portrayed religious division in terms of binary opposition, and they were happiest when this opposition was most effectively demonstrated; hence the frequent sneering characterizations by Catholics of the eucharists of the Church of England as 'Calvinist' – that is, not properly English: alien, other. There was an amusing concurrence between Puritans and Jesuits that recusancy was the right thing to do for Catholics; at least, thought Puritans, a firm upholding of the Mass showed principle, even if it was a principle 'verye badlye applied', as the Puritan Perceval Wiburn sourly remarked.[34]

Church papists broke the rules which religious polemicists were trying to create. Such equivocation was bad enough for hardline Catholic missionary clergy, who were risking their lives in order to stiffen the flabby resolve of the faithful, but there was an additional agony for Puritans. They suspected, quite rightly, that many leaders of the established Church, not least its Nicodemite Queen, were happy to tolerate merely formal adherence from equivocators; Puritans were thus forcibly reminded of their own worries about the inadequacies of the Elizabethan Settlement. By the 1590s, many Puritans were becoming aware that there were new polemical defences of the Church of England from the likes of the sacramentalist cleric Lancelot Andrewes (1555–1626); such treatises took a kindlier view of the Church's Roman past than the writers who had first championed the Church by stressing its Reformed Protestant character. In the seventeenth century, the debate over church papistry merged with anger at 'Arminianism' and its dire implications for Reformation purity, and this combination eventually cost King Charles I his throne.

The parallel and awkward reality was that even those who advocated steadfastness, critics at opposing poles like Jesuit Father Garnet and Puritan Mr Wiburn, were just as much caught up in the sixteenth-century industry of dissimulation as any church papist. In general, both sides preferred living to fight another day to making an exemplary death on the scaffold, and, in the face of determined interrogation by a ruthless authority like the Elizabethan Church of England, that required careful thought. In the case of the Society of Jesus, the English mission was the first great proving-ground for that essential element in Jesuit pastoral training, the resolving of particular cases of conscience – casuistry. For example, since Jesuits could not recognize Elizabethan authority as legitimate, because of the papal excommunication of the Queen by Pope Pius V in 1570, English official interrogations were not legitimate and pretence was thus lawful: after all, had Christ not pretended to his disciples at Emmaus (Luke 24.28) that he was going to travel further with them? So 'pious equivocation' was not the same as lying. Silence or returning a question were certainly not lying.[35] In the mouth of a Jesuit such as John Gerard, who could also describe in horrible detail the tortures he had suffered during interrogation, such arguments for 'mental reservation' had considerable authority, even though they gave polemical weapons not merely to Protestants but to that considerable number of fellow-Catholics right across Europe who hated Jesuits.[36] The disapproving adjective 'Jesuitical' is not an exclusively Protestant usage.

The strategy's plausibility was increased by a similar though slightly belated move among English Protestants to develop casuistry. They had their own troubles with authority, as they sought to push the logic of the Elizabethan Settlement to match the development of the other Reformed Churches of Europe. Particularly uncomfortable for Puritans if they were summoned to ecclesiastical courts was to be faced with the demand that they should observe normal (but pre-Reformation) legal Church procedure, by swearing an oath to reply truthfully to all questions (technically, an ex officio oath). Puritans could, like Jesuits under Protestant interrogation, deny the lawfulness of this popish demand, as 'contrarie boeth to the lawes of god, and of the land, to require such an oath, especiallie of a minister' – that last thought was an interesting reflection of the new clericalism of the Reformed pastor.[37]

Those Puritans who did take the ex officio oath frequently turned to strategies which would have been instantly recognizable to those teaching casuistry in the English College in Rome. They were also prepared to extend the practice beyond the courtroom. Perhaps the most striking example of constructive casuistic silence in Reformation England, and the most long-lasting in its effect on historians, came from the colourful and humorous Puritan gentleman Job Throckmorton, almost certainly the principal author of the outrageously successful series of attacks on the English Church establishment, the 'Martin Marprelate' tracts of 1588–9. Generations of gullible modern scholars have taken Throckmorton at his word in denying his authorship of these sprightly libels, but both his latest biographer, Leland Carlson, and Perez Zagorin, chief recent analyst of Reformation lies, have shown just how easily those denials can be knocked down by applying the rules of casuistry. 'I am not Martin,' said Job – true, because he was Job Throckmorton. 'I knewe not Martin,' he added – true as well, because Martin was a literary invention, not a real person.[38]

REFORMATION RADICALS:
WORD AND SILENCE

As one might predict, the greatest glorying in casuistry and concealment among Western Christians of the Reformation came from radicals beyond the pale of the magisterial Protestantism within which festive Puritans like Job Throckmorton, for all their bad manners to bishops, still sheltered. By no means all this Nicodemite impulse can be attributed to the line of descent from Iberian Judaism via Juan de Valdés and the Catholic *Spirituali* of the 1530s. Some was native to north-west Europe, with its distinctive radicalism fostered in northern Switzerland, Strassburg and the Low Countries.[39] We return to the early radical Spirituals, and recall the angry disagreement which separated their chief spokesmen, especially Caspar Schwenckfeld and Sebastian Franck, from Anabaptists who maintained the Protestant insistence on the authority of Scripture (above, pp. 143–4). It is that chasm on authority which illuminates the different attitudes of Spirituals and Anabaptists to concealment and the visible Church.

Western European Anabaptists looked keenly at the New Testament. There they saw a Church that passionately anticipated the imminent return of Christ in the Last Days and urgently needed to proclaim Christ's message to the world before his arrival. They were concerned to play their part in restoring the primitive purity of the early Church, which included biblical descriptions of the sufferings of the proto-martyr Stephen and his fellows (above, p. 65). Schwenckfeld considered his Anabaptist opponents profoundly mistaken in this train of thought. For him, the Church in the present generation was too imperfect to indulge in activism, which could only be justified in God's good time. Anabaptist critics of Schwenckfeld's insistence on his *Stillstand* saw it as a coward's way out in the face of the persecution which had quickly faced radicals during the 1520s. It became a prime tenet for Anabaptists that the true Church was authenticated by persecution from the ungodly: after all, that had been the experience of the early Church, and, in the same way, present-day Christians should demonstrate their faith by public endurance of suffering.

For Anabaptists, martyrdom became as central, and as dependent on the history of pre-Constantinian Christianity, as it was for contemporary mainstream Protestants or for Roman Catholics, who from the 1550s were greatly to expand their veneration of relics and shrines of the Christian victims of ancient persecution. More so, indeed: Anabaptists might be said to be the ultimate anti-Nicodemites, since they made public suffering the chief mark of the true Church.[40] Spirituals were by contrast inclined to consider such public witness to be as misguided in radical Christians as it was in Protestants or Catholics: it was a distraction from the true tranquillity with which Christians ought to live out their sufferings in the world. Running through many of the writings of the Spiritualist radical Sebastian Franck is that resonant word 'resignation', *Gelassenheit*, which had meant so much to Meister Eckhart two centuries before, and which united medieval mystics to early ascetics like Evagrius Ponticus who had spoken of *apatheia*.[41] There is another interesting echo in these arguments between Spirituals and Anabaptists about persecution: they recall the stand-off between certain gnostics and the episcopally organized Catholic Church in the second century (above, pp. 65–6). Those who believed in activism and public witness were once more pitted against those who placed a particular value on silence and on avoidance of inappropriate and unnecessary conflict.[42]

The most extreme Nicodemites of the sixteenth century, and arguably the most successful despite their apparent disappearance in the seventeenth century, were the adherents of a small mystical sect known as the Family of Love. They were a product of the same wide skies and open landscapes of the Low Countries which had bred the enigma that was Desiderius Erasmus; their founder Hendrik Niclaes habitually signed himself in his writings by his initials H. N., which by a happy or divinely inspired coincidence also stood for *homo novus*, 'New Man'. His version of *theosis* was radical indeed: he told his followers that they were so full of God's spirit that they were actually part of the Godhead. Thanks to his own missionary journeys to England in the time of Edward VI and perhaps even during the unpromising reign of Mary, his movement became unobtrusively established on both sides of the North Sea from the 1550s.[43]

The Family of Love upset the magisterial Protestant stereotype of radicals as crazed illiterate wretches. Niclaes himself had made a comfortable living as a merchant, and his Familist followers were often precisely those who might feel within themselves the creative call of the Spirit – artists, musicians or scholars – among their number, for instance, was the great Flemish painter Pieter Brueghel the Younger. Familists also had a distinct liking for the powerful, which was helpful for their survival. In Antwerp, chief commercial city of the Spanish Netherlands, King Philip II of Spain's printer Christophe Plantin was a Familist: by day he printed the King's Catholic breviaries for the Counter-Reformation Netherlands, and by night Familist literature (he also printed the local edition of the Roman Index of 1570 which banned some of Mr H. N.'s books). One of King Philip's Spanish councillors, Benito Arias Montano, a close collaborator with Plantin in the production of the prodigious officially sponsored Antwerp Polyglot version of the Bible, also became a Familist sympathizer: thanks to his Jewish *converso* descent, he knew all about concealment.[44] Both Plantin and Montano died in their beds, much honoured; and in Plantin's stately house in Antwerp one can still see the carefully preserved favourite room of his great friend, that carefully ambiguous Tacitean and serial Catholic, Justus Lipsius (above, p. 172).

Later, the first Quakers combined silent worship with noisy public proclamation and self-advertisement, and it has been suggested that the Familists, with their extreme commitment to a doctrine of 'inner light', faded into the Quaker movement in the seventeenth century. That is possible, but the two movements were in fact very different. The Familists' urgent desire to spread their good news was confined to quiet conversations and unobtrusive pamphlets; otherwise they were happy to meld with whatever established Church they found, confident in the divine status which put them above normal ethical considerations. One extraordinary example of their success was their parasitism of the established Church of England in the little Cambridgeshire village of Balsham. The Rector there was Dr Andrew Perne, a very senior academic, Master of Peterhouse, Cambridge. He has remained famous as one of the most shameless floor-crossers in the English Reformation, but he might well have had special sympathies with those who had things to hide, if we are to believe Martin Marprelate's (or Job Throckmorton's) not altogether implausible insinuations that Perne's lifelong friendship with John Whitgift, the Archbishop of Canterbury, was more than just friendship.[45] Certainly Perne did nothing to impede the Familists' near-takeover of his parish, even after he had himself investigated their activities. He would not have been the only Familist clergyman to serve the Church of England.[46]

There were other places in Cambridgeshire and the Isle of Ely where Familists were so embedded in the parish that they regularly served as parish officers, but Balsham was home to the most blatant Familist colony in all Europe. In 1609, to the fury of Balsham villagers not in the clique, the Familists gave one of their leaders, Thomas Lawrence, an especially sumptuous burial-site, reusing the stone tomb of a medieval priest in the churchyard, a very special honour which implied that he was the local Mr H. N. One may still climb Balsham church tower to view the three bells given that same year, probably as a memorial to Lawrence: one of them bears the unusual inscription in Latin *non sono animabus mortuorum sed auribus viventium* – 'I do not sound for the souls of the dead but for the ears of the living.' Or to be precise, that is not the inscription: the three words for 'souls of the dead' and 'ears' are written the wrong way round, in a piece of private impudence towards those deadened souls in Balsham who did not hear aright. How the Familists must have smiled (inwardly) as they heard Balsham's church bells ringing.[47]

Concerning the Familists, there is a still greater cause for wonder, which turns back full circle to the arch-Nicodemite of magisterial Protestantism, Elizabeth I. Great was the public consternation in the 1580s when some of the Yeomen of the Guard, the Queen's personal security force, turned out to be Familists. Puritans raged: Elizabeth, most enigmatic of monarchs, did nothing, and Familists continued to flourish at her Court. What does that say about the Queen's own involvement with these ultra-loyal Nicodemites?[48] There were still Familists among her successor James I's Court officials, including his keeper of the lions in the Tower of London.[49] Somewhere in this may be one of the greatest silences of Christian history, which conceals the possibility that the woman most responsible for Anglicanism's existence may have lent a sympathetic ear to pantheist heretics who were among her most faithful servants. Certainly it is not part of the founding story of the Anglican Communion to which Anglicans have decided to listen, up until now.

What this story of Reformation concealment reveals is that there was a pleasing complexity and hesitancy among the reactions to the deep fissures which opened up in the Western Latin Church after Luther's defiant protest in 1517. There were of course those who wished to turn the lives of all Europeans into an unending fight between truth and error, good and evil, with as destructive effect as

Mao's unleashing of the Cultural Revolution on Chinese society. Towards the end of the English Interregnum, the Presbyterian minister Daniel Cawdrey denounced a proposal for general national toleration by one of his Independent rivals as 'the last and most desperate *Designe* of Antichrist, and his *Agitators* the Jesuits, to destroy this Church and State, and to subdue it to *Antichrist*'.[50] But enough people were prepared in practice to make the situation much more complex and untidy, to create out of a myriad of small silences a practical neighbourliness and toleration.

The vital factor was that neither side, Catholic or Protestant, decisively won the war against Antichrist in Europe. In fact there was no one Protestantism, so that Reformed Protestants and Lutheran Protestants often hated each other just as much as both of them hated Catholics, and they could be wonderfully petty to each other as a result. The vital principle was formalized when, in 1555, the Peace of Augsburg ended one round of destructive European religious warfare: each ruler subject to the Holy Roman Empire could decide his people's official religious practice (*cuius regio, eius religio*). Because so many political units in central Europe were very small, the local authority might turn a blind eye to its religious dissenters slipping over the border for worship. This practice became formalized in various places: the Catholic Habsburgs became very fed up when thousands of Viennese Protestants ostentatiously trooped out of the city Sunday by Sunday to worship in a privileged Protestant castle nearby, but it was a long time before they managed to summon up the legal and military resources to stop it happening.[51]

In England and Wales, geography and the Church of England's official monopoly status combined to make it impossible for similar things to occur so openly, but people may love the sinner while hating the sin. Late medieval English bishops sought to swell crowds at the burnings of Lollard heretics by granting forty days' indulgence to all who attended, which may suggest that ordinary people often needed some incentive to see their neighbours die horribly in public. Even conscientious dissent had its limits. As late as the last years of the seventeenth century, recusant Catholic wives in Shropshire habitually attended their Protestant parish churches for a 'churching' ceremony, to give thanks for childbirth. This was not a sacrament, so it could hardly be considered as sinful as taking Protestant communion; it might be regarded as a permissible use of an amenity offered by and for the whole community. Equally, Sussex Baptists, among the most intransigent of English Dissenters, although predictably enough choosing overwhelmingly to marry within their own confessional group, mostly stooped to wed their Baptist brides in their parish churches, and they certainly did not shun their neighbours in everyday life.[52]

GAY ANGLO-CATHOLICS: LET HE WHO HAS EARS TO HEAR

We have drawn many lessons from Reformation and Counter-Reformation Nicodemisms. They can all be applied afresh to another remarkable phenomenon of Christian history which has persisted from the mid-nineteenth-century up to the present day: the existence of a Nicodemite homosexual sub-culture within High Church Anglicanism or Anglo-Catholicism. It has been a voice within the Anglo-Catholic movement which, like Familism in the bell-tower at Balsham, is simultaneously audible to those with ears to hear, and not heard by others. Its history was first properly described by the Australian church historian David Hilliard in pioneering research published in 1982: I remember Dr Hilliard reminiscing to me that his initial presentations of his findings were repeatedly greeted with incredulity in history departmental seminars, and acknowledged with cautious familiarity in more ecclesiastical academic gatherings.[53] Gay male Anglo-Catholicism (traditionally lesbians have seldom been shown hospitality) is a perfect example of Christian Nicodemism: John Calvin would undoubtedly have recognized the character of the Nicodemite in the closet gay man of the twentieth century.

Why did gay male Anglo-Catholicism feature in the Oxford Movement from its earliest days in the 1830s? Homosexuality is a word with a short history.[54] In the minds of some modern historians who should have more common sense than to buy into reductive nominalism, that has obscured the obvious likelihood that varied patterns of behaviour and various homosexual identities are as old as the human race. Among these varieties, one which we might term the modern Western Enlightenment form, centring on same-sex relationships between equals, is first detectable from the 1690s, with the Netherlands and England pioneering what became a more general phenomenon. It became visible quite suddenly, as part of a rapid and extraordinary shift in attitudes towards sexual behaviour generally, which in the succeeding three centuries has come to privilege privacy, mutual emotional fulfilment and equality over punitive religious discipline.[55] Nevertheless, a homosexual subculture could not immediately find a home in the eighteenth century within the Protestant Church of England. Gay activity associated with English churchmen was of the variety which still sells the Sunday tabloids: the story of Oxford's Robert Thistlethwayte, the vanishing Warden of Wadham (1690–1744), who might be considered fortunate in having pre-dated the invention of the limerick; or the abrupt downfall in 1822 of the portly and hypocritical Percy Jocelyn, Bishop of Clogher (1764–1843), previously active in various societies for moral improvement.[56]

The change came with the Oxford Movement. It was inspired by a group in Oxford University, mostly consisting of academics (in Regency and Victorian Oxford, necessarily nearly all single men by legal requirement). Promoting their views in a series of 'Tracts for the Times' (hence another name for them, 'Tractarians'), they sought a new identity for the Church of England, although of course, in their eyes, their campaign was the rediscovery of an old identity. They aimed to make the Church 'Catholic' in far closer approximation to the Church of Rome than would have been tolerated by earlier High Churchpeople in England, Ireland and Scotland, who generally still gloried in the name of Protestant.[57] The group stirred a wider national movement initially largely consisting of clergy; its ripples spread outwards from Oxford 'Tractarianism' to another newly named identity, Anglo-Catholicism, and into a wider renewed High Churchmanship. As Protestant episcopal Churches spread from Britain and the United States to become a worldwide faith with yet another new name, Anglicanism, so Anglo-Catholicism became a worldwide movement too, and from its earliest years it took with it a strong homoerotic element.[58]

There has been nothing quite comparable in Roman Catholicism, at least until the transfer of Anglo-Catholic clergy to Rome in recent years.

The homosexual identity of the first chief spokesman of the Movement, John Henry Newman (1801–90), has been the subject of intense controversy. It has been made much more tangled by enthusiasm for his canonization among some of the most ethically conservative in the present-day Roman Catholic Church, since Newman and many of his early admirers ended up transferring their ecclesiastical loyalties thither. After a survey of Newman's emotional life – his passionate friendships with other single men (of whom his companion in the grave Ambrose St John was just the most longlasting), his tortured opinions about his own sinfulness, his obvious revelling in the homosocial world of early Victorian Oxford, it is difficult to avoid applying to him that useful variant of Ockham's Razor: 'Looks like a duck, waddles like a duck, quacks like a duck – can it be a duck?' Other members of Newman's circle, such as the extrovert F. W. Faber (1814–63), can much less controversially be identified as homosexual. We should remember that in such cases, the question is one of identity – not necessarily of sexual activity – among deeply pious clergy, many of whom were committed to physical if not emotional celibacy. That consideration does not lessen the intensity, the reality or the importance of the emotions involved.[59]

It is indeed that very emphasis on clerical celibacy which is key to understanding why homosexual men gravitated to Anglo-Catholicism as promptly as they did. Celibacy was one of the innovative borrowings which Anglo-Catholicism made from Rome; it had never been a significant feature of traditional High Churchmanship. Newman had at least initially regarded celibacy as only optional for Anglican clergy, indeed best avoided by country parsons, but 'a high state of life, to which the multitude of men cannot aspire . . . the noblest *ēthos* is situated in that state'.[60] That was in 1832, before the Tractarian Movement had gathered momentum, but over the next two decades there was an increasing insistence on the superiority of celibate vocation to the priesthood. It entered partnership with High Churchmen's creation of privately run theological colleges, to promote both a properly trained clerical ministry and a Catholic party among Anglican clergy. The surviving 'Catholic' training colleges such as Mirfield and St Stephen's House Oxford continue to fulfil this function for the Anglican Churches of the Atlantic Isles. Victorian Anglican Evangelicals, not to be outdone, created their own theological colleges (St John's Nottingham and the London Bible College are descendants of such efforts), while some other colleges have actually tried to avoid the party spirit.[61]

The result was a professionally trained clergy: Victorian England's only profession in which, thanks to the Anglo-Catholics, lifelong abstention from marriage did not cause too much raising of eyebrows. Anglican priesthood was a safe haven for those who found that abstention personally congenial. Soon they were spreading out into the parishes, and many of these churches became permanent strongholds of the movement, known throughout the land to friend and foe alike as providing 'Catholic privileges'. By the 1870s the Anglo-Catholic campaigning organization the English Church Union was publishing a gazetteer of 'sound' churches right across the kingdom, whose dedications and locations aficionados would habitually be able to recite with as much spiritual comfort as devotion to the Rosary.[62]

The early clergy of the Oxford Movement were commonly rebels by temperament, conscious that they were overturning the complacent certainties of their day. They were as a consequence likely to be powerful, charismatic personalities, who attracted admirers to their churches and the doctrine which they preached. Another borrowing from Rome which they introduced to the Church of England was individual auricular confession. That caused terrible fears for the moral welfare of young ladies in many a Victorian paterfamilias, but it is likely that the silence of the confessional was much more significant in building up some sort of self-awareness in confused homosexual males, as they talked through their personal confusions to those whom they trusted, in the secure knowledge that what they said would not be repeated, and felt their isolation evaporate in the presence of the like-minded.

There were plenty of insinuations from the unsympathetic about the result. Tractarians adapted more and more extravagant outward liturgy from Rome, and gained public notoriety in the process. In 1868 an Evangelical visitor to the demonstratively Anglo-Catholic church of St Matthias, Stoke Newington, no doubt conventionally bewhiskered as Victorian gentlemen were, commented with daring innuendo about the vestments and appearance of the clergy there that the 'style of dress and the close-shaven face, favoured so greatly by English imitators of Rome, do give to most men a rather juvenile, if not womanly appearance'.[63] A more sympathetic early twentieth-century description of the atmosphere at a thinly disguised St Stephen's Bournemouth is to be found in the once-popular novel *Sinister Street* by Sir Compton Mackenzie (1883–1972), a writer who had reason to be familiar with that sub-culture. Mackenzie portrays what amounts to a pick-up of the teenage hero Michael at Solemn Evensong by a slightly older bank-clerk called Prout, closely followed by Michael's initiation as a processional torch-bearer into the exotic world of the Anglo-Catholic sacristy: 'The sacristy was crowded with boys in scarlet cassocks and slippers and zuchettos, quarrelling about their cottas and arguing about their heights. Everybody had a favourite banner which he wanted to escort and, to complicate matters still farther, everybody had a favourite companion by whose side he wished to walk.'[64]

There were plenty of women in Anglo-Catholic parish congregations, but female relationships with 'Father' were given careful boundaries by priestly celibacy: it made the clergy safe and sexless. Moreover, Father's ambiguous sexuality combined frequently with an Oxbridge articulacy and extravagantly camp wit: a welcome contrast to prosaic domesticity. All were assets in providing a non-threatening and pastorally objective ministry to female parishioners; there was no need to name the Love that Dare not Speak its Name. Particularly in urban parishes, gay male Anglo-Catholics were part of a society which effortlessly crossed social boundaries – that was how Mr Prout the young bank-clerk could befriend the upper-middle-class public schoolboy Michael, and socialize with him at such events as the London reception for the legitimist Emperor of Byzantium at Clifford's Inn Hall, at a shilling a head.[65]

Anglo-Catholic clergy in such parishes, often sharing a clergy-house between parish priest and curates like Roman Catholic presbyteries, lived in an overwhelmingly homosocial male world. The Anglo-Catholic gay network provided many working-class boys with small glimpses of glamour and status as altar-boys and servers, and it might prove a means of social advancement, as they met patrons who took them to social circles to which they would not otherwise have had the entrée.[66] They could even embark on ordination training; that took them to theological colleges which provided them with further inculturation into an erotically charged same-sex society. Anglo-Catholicism was fun, hospitable to extrovert mischief in its ritual, and generally full of delight at the annoyance that it caused bishops by its extravagant borrowings from Roman Catholic ritual. Clerical studies and drawing rooms frequently resounded with howls of laughter at the latest expression of episcopal or archidiaconal outrage.[67]

Not all was laughter. The need for conscientious avoidance of physical expression of one's sexuality was a very real problem for many. Geoffrey Clayton (1884–1957), Anglican Archbishop of Cape Town, was really speaking to himself when, in a confirmation sermon, he urged, 'There may come a time when you are very greatly tempted, when this will be the one thing you want to do more than anything else, when your whole being will cry out, "I want to do this". But you must *never, never, never* give in.'[68] Perhaps Clayton would have been able to fight harder in his opposition to the onward march of apartheid in South Africa if historical circumstances had not forced so much of his energy to be diverted into that other, more personal struggle. Instead, he raged at braver souls like Bishops Trevor Huddleston and Ambrose Reeves, who are the men now remembered as actors in the long-drawn-out destruction of apartheid, rather than Clayton.[69]

Gay Anglo-Catholic clergy, pledged by their vocation to preach truth and integrity, constantly faced the debilitating necessity of compromising their integrity by concealing a major part of the truth about themselves. It was the same cruelty of concealment that crypto-Jews had faced in medieval Spain. It is a structural affliction for all Nicodemites, apart from that minority of Spirituals like the Family of Love who glory in their secrecy. For some such clergy, sometimes at very senior levels in the Church, there was the extra burden of blackmail. Yet when all the negatives have been placed on the scales, the gay male Anglo-Catholic ghetto in Britain long provided a reasonably safe and sympathetic area of male homosociability and emotional release in a nation which up to the 1960s had one of the most repressive attitudes towards homosexuality in all Western Europe.[70]

Despite many gains in respectability and influence during the twentieth century, Anglo-Catholicism as a whole continued to enjoy outsider status inside the Church of England – the best modern sociological analysis of the movement is subtitled 'a study in religious ambiguity'.[71] Gay male Anglo-Catholics were one step further out than the rest, a sub-culture within a sub-culture: rather like the status of gay men in the wider world, but boasting better organization. Nemesis came in the 1960s. Rome changed drastically with the Second Vatican Council, particularly in its liturgy, leaving the extrovert liturgical precision of the Anglo-Catholics in uncomfortable isolation. Gay society changed also, steadily emerging into the open in the Western world over the next three decades. Bewilderingly for traditionalist Anglo-Catholic gay men, it included lesbians in its message of liberation.

At that point, the comfortable gay male Anglo-Catholic network across the globe ran into problems of identity and credibility. I can well remember from the 1970s and 1980s the often unhappy clash of cultures and personalities which resulted, as gay liberation (especially in the form of the Gay Christian Movement, later the Lesbian and Gay Christian Movement) collided with what the prominent Anglo-Catholic Socialist Fr Kenneth Leech acerbically termed the world of 'gin, lace and backbiting'.[72] The problem was only exacerbated in the 1990s, as Anglo-Catholics had to face up to a different gender crisis in deciding how to react to the Anglican campaign for the ordination of women. Many conversions to Rome resulted, many gay clergy among them. One aspect of such conversions might be seen as a strategic personal retreat from the new open sexual freedoms offered by the wider world.[73] After a century and a half, as the various parties within Anglicanism realigned and struggled over how to relate to a reconfigured sexual landscape, a Nicodemite Christian sub-culture had outlived its usefulness within the Church of England. Its obsolescence has left a great deal of confused noise in its wake.

8

Things Not Remembered

BUILDING IDENTITY THROUGH FORGETFULNESS

Nicodemism or the science of dissimulation is not the only Christian silence to consider behind Christian noise. The remaining great silences to examine can be grouped in a general category of silences of forgetfulness or oblivion: things not remembered, for both worthy and unworthy motives. The history of Christianity is full of things casually or deliberately forgotten, or left unsaid, in order to shape the future of a Church or Churches. Institutions religious or secular create their own silences, by exclusions and by shared assumptions, which change over time. Such silences are often at the expense of many of the people who could be thought of as actually constituting the Church; institutional needs outweigh individual needs.[1] Some are conscious silences of shame and fear at the institution of the Church not living up to its own standards of truth and compassion; and there has often been a particular pain meted out to those who make the silences end. Life is rarely comfortable for the little boy who says that the emperor has no clothes.

We all have a tendency to hear what interests us and pass over what does not, so we should not be too ready to attribute sinister motives to past omissions. In the Church, no less than in other, more avowedly human institutions, history has been written by the winners – fortunately, not usually with so much skill that alternative stories cannot be recovered. Those recovered memories may represent a battleground in the self-image of Christianity as a whole which raises very basic questions. One austere point of view on the murky origins of episcopacy, which for so many Churches is nevertheless seen an essential badge of authenticity linking them to an apostolic tradition instituted by Christ himself, is that 'The establishment of orthodoxy has less to do with history than with memory . . . In the end, the idiosyncratic and anachronistic episcopal claims of Ignatius [of Antioch] coupled with the use of legal language by men like Cyprian [of Carthage] to assert authority altered the course of history and memory.'[2]

Repeatedly, Churches have built up their identity by forgetting things which it was no use remembering. To begin with an example from the very frontiers of Western Christianity, it is instructive to see the gradual and purposeful forgetting of an important element in the eleventh-century establishment of Christianity in Iceland. The surprise which emerges from the earliest sources on this process is the part played by Armenians: there were three Armenian bishops active in Iceland at the time of the first Catholic bishop, Ísleifr. By the time that a later chronicler was writing around 1200, the Armenians had become a group of anonymous foreign bishops supported by local evil men, and in a chronicle of half a century later they had simply disappeared from sight. The reason is evident: the presence of the Armenians in the conversion years could only have been thanks to Christian contacts with the Orthodox East, via Kievan Rus' and Novgorod. By the thirteenth century, Icelandic Christianity had become absorbed into the episcopal system of the Western Latin Church, and Catholics and Orthodox Christians were increasingly hostile to each other, to the point of warfare which the Western Church dressed up as crusading. For safely Catholic Iceland, the Armenians were not worth remembering.[3]

Such history as that is inevitably present-centred: it repackages the past in order to make it useful to contemporaries. One recent re-examination by Robin Vose of the Dominican role in the extension of Christianity through medieval Spain provides an interesting parallel case of this phenomenon. The Dominicans have had a reputation in Spanish historiography as standing in the forefront of the conversion of Jews and Muslims in territories newly reconquered by Christians. That seems logical, since proselytization was the original main aim of the Order of Preachers, and later, the Dominicans would be the backbone of the Spanish Inquisition. The reality turns out to be rather different, once one does not assume (in Vose's perceptive phrase) 'that the friars always did what they were legally permitted to do'.[4] In fact there is little evidence of medieval Spanish Dominicans preaching to Jews, and none at all of their preaching to Muslims. Their interest in learning Hebrew and Arabic was sporadic and apparently mostly directed towards their own scholarly pursuits. In the sixteenth and seventeenth centuries, these earlier realities became a non-story for Dominicans, who were now in the vanguard of aggressive Christian missionary efforts, and who needed to hear that that had always been the case. To make a historical correction to that myth-making is not to let medieval Dominicans off some modern liberal hook, it is simply to get a story right.

It is easy to point out the ways in which many of those particularly esteemed in the history of Christianity have after their death been annexed for causes which in life they would most probably have repudiated. Nowhere is this more true than in the Orthodox world, always prone to see itself as representing uncomplicated authenticity in Christian tradition, and therefore smoothing over difficulties in its story of the past. In 451, as we have seen (above, p. 84), Christianity was split into three on the question of the relationship between the divine and human natures of Christ: there were those who accepted the Council of Chalcedon's compromise dictated by the imperial advisers, and the two groupings on either pole of it who did not: the 'Miaphysites' and the 'Dyophysites'. It is probably the hostility of these anti-Chalcedonians towards imperial Chalcedonian Christianity that is the major factor in the rapid military success of Islam in its early years; anti-Chalcedonians of either stripe had no reason to defend what they regarded as a corrupt and imperially dominated version of their faith. Chalcedon should be seen as one of the great disasters in Christian history, not one of its triumphs.[5]

These uncomfortable facts about Chalcedon have been forgotten by most Chalcedonian Christians, even those who know enough about their history to remember Chalcedon at all, because the decisions of the Council eventually won through in that third of the Church which was based around the Mediterranean. Anti-Chalcedonian Christians were henceforth regarded as heretics by the self-styled

'Orthodox' or Western Latin Christians of the Mediterranean basin, later Protestants included. But many of the anti-Chalcedonian refuseniks were just too good and saintly to ignore: once they were safely dead, the imperial Church reconstituted them within the Chalcedonian fold. The first great Syrian 'pillar-dweller', St Simeon the Elder Stylite, maintained a prudent silence through the Chalcedonian crisis, but, very soon after his death, his vast popularity in the Middle East made a Chalcedonian-sympathizing emperor finance the largest church building in the East around his pillar, in a desperate bid to shore up the Chalcedonian cause (the Syrian faithful were very pleased with the church, but generally continued to dislike Chalcedon).[6] The fifth-century Georgian founder-saint Peter the Iberian was a great deal more aggressive than Simeon in his hatred of Chalcedon, as one of the chief and most effective campaigners against its decisions during his time as a bishop in Palestine. Although the Georgian Church has in later centuries become Chalcedonian, Peter is so important as a pioneering evangelist, not least because of his Georgian royal blood, that his furious rejection of Chalcedon is treated with indulgence or obfuscation.[7]

The Byzantine empress Theodora, wife of the great Emperor Justinian I, was likewise a promoter of dissent against Chalcedon, but she has been given consistent honour by the Orthodox, because of her status. The emergence of Procopius's *Secret History* of the reign of Justinian from the Vatican Library in the seventeenth century, providing a vivid picture of the Empress's colourful sexual past among much else to her discredit, was too late a discovery, and from too suspect a source in Orthodox eyes, to alter their favourable perceptions of Theodora.[8] Most influential non-Chalcedonian of all is of course a name thoroughly familiar to us by now: Pseudo-Dionysius the Areopagite, a Syrian Miaphysite monk whose real name we shall probably never know. His vast influence on Christian mysticism has been possible because of the cloak of anonymity over his origins amid the rebellion against the Council of Chalcedon.

All these examples of historical amnesia are the result of two centuries or more of gradual reframing of the past, but it is worth noting just how suddenly, on occasion, Christians have been affected by attacks of purposeful forgetfulness. Once more, the great watershed is in the decades around 1700, when we have already seen Western Europeans change their outlook on sexual freedoms. Much else changed then, as well. Some in that eventful period felt the need to self-censor, because they sensed the intellectual shift in Christianity away from the authority of scriptural and private revelation, towards a stress on the benevolent and transparent rationality of the divine creator's purposes.

No less a figure in the scientific pantheon than Robert Boyle (1627–91) was concerned to edit out of his public activities his considerable interest in what he called the 'supernatural' or 'cosmical' – God's purposes as demonstrated by magic, astrology and the occult. The same concern was even more marked among subsequent admirers who wrote his biography and curated his private papers, in order that they might provide a less complicated portrait of one of empirical science's early patron saints. On the eve of the early Enlightenment, Boyle had not forgotten or repudiated his interest in the supernatural: he lived in what his contemporary and acquaintance Sir Thomas Browne (1605–82) cheerfully called 'divided and distinguished worlds'. Boyle's occultist Nicodemism in the late seventeenth century concealed an intellectual preoccupation which would have been considered perfectly intellectually respectable only half a century earlier, but which now seemed to him to be a potential source of social embarrassment.[9]

There were those in that same age who rewrote other people rather than themselves, for present-centred purposes. A prime exhibit is the drastic reshaping of the memoirs of the Interregnum radical republican and regicide Edmund Ludlow (c. 1617–92) by the Irish radical of the next generation John Toland (1670–1722). Toland much admired Ludlow for his political radicalism and stern adherence to republican principles, and he wanted to present him in the best light for his own contemporaries, but there was a big problem with the manuscript he proposed to publish: he was a rational Protestant deist, whereas Ludlow had been a providentialist and millenarian Reformed Protestant. The very title of Ludlow's original memoirs, 'A voyce from the watch tower', set the wrong tone, let alone its belief in the imminent destructive appearance of Antichrist in the world. This was not the Ludlow whom Toland wished to present, so he set about eliminating as many of Ludlow's references to religion as he could. The end-result, published in 1698–9, still runs to three volumes, rather less excitably entitled *The Memoirs of Edmund Ludlow*, and virtually every sentence in it has been altered from the original.[10]

SILENCE, SEX AND GENDER

One of the most striking and recent examples of an extremely sudden turn is the very recent disappearance from Western Christianity of one of the most consistent of prohibitions in Christian history, the banning of menstruating women from participation in the sacraments, or even from approaching the altar. The ban is first to be encountered in the writings of Dionysius, Bishop of Alexandria at the beginning of the third century, and although the problem faded from the minds of the less sacramentally centred Protestant Churches in the Reformation, it survived semi-articulated in sacramentalist Lutheranism and Anglo-Catholicism till the 1950s, and could still be encountered in 1970 in the Roman Catholic Church's regulation excluding women lectors from the sanctuary during their menstrual periods.[11] The time lag in this belated recognition of the revolution of the 1700s might be attributable to the conservatism of Christian sacramental liturgy.

An honourable exception – one of very few – to the unexamined consensus on this was Pope Gregory the Great, writing soon after launching his mission to England under the monk Augustine in 597. He justified his generous view on scriptural grounds: 'We know that the woman who suffered an issue of blood, humbly approaching behind our Lord, touched the hem of his robe and was at once healed of her sickness. If, therefore, this woman was right to touch our Lord's robe, why may not one who suffers nature's courses be permitted to enter the church of God?' Alas, the Pope's open-mindedness on this matter was probably conditioned by his evident irritation with Christians encountered by the Anglo-Saxon mission who not only pre-dated but resisted Augustine's authority: it was the rigorism of these native Christians on the matter of menstruating women which provoked his liberal ruling.[12] Now Western Christendom has forgotten an issue upon which Church leaders were near-unanimously agreed, almost without discussion, for seventeen hundred years.

As this last example indicates, the great distorting factor in Christian history, which transcends denominational and many other ecclesiastical divisions, is that most of it has been written by men. The role of women in the earliest stages of building Christianity has faded, as the Church assimilated itself to the customarily male-dominated societies of the last two thousand years. Clues to an alternative story are present in the earliest Christian records we have: the letters of the Apostle Paul. Despite Paul's confused statements about women and worship in his seven indisputably authentic letters (above, p. 43), he is a major witness to female office-holding in Pauline Churches before it was gradually banished to the margins and then to oblivion. Amid the large number of people whom Paul lists as sending greetings to the Romans are Phoebe the deacon (administrative officer or assistant) in the Church of Cenchreae (a port near Corinth), Prisca, a 'fellow-worker', and Tryphaena and Tryphosa, 'workers in the Lord' – descriptions which Paul also applies to men in the same passage.[13] That is hardly surprising, since there are several similar testimonies from Hellenistic synagogues of the Jewish Diaspora to active female leadership in synagogue councils, and synagogues were after all still close to the first Christian communities. Jewish women were acting alongside men as 'elders', in appropriately gendered variants on that Greek word *presbyteros*, which Christians would soon borrow and apply to a newly created priesthood.[14]

Most strikingly, Paul's greeting list for the Romans includes Junia, a female 'apostle', so described alongside another 'apostle' with a male name. The obviously feminine ending '-a' was considered such an appalling anomaly by many later readers of Romans that in the recopying of manuscripts, Junia's name was frequently changed to a masculine form, or was simply regarded without any justification as a man's name. Early biblical commentators, given a strong rhetorical lead by the great fourth-century preaching Bishop of Constantinople John Chrysostom, were honourably prepared to acknowledge the surprising femininity of Junia, but there was a sudden contrary turn in the thirteenth-century Western Church which had been shaped by the Gregorian reforms, prompted by the theologian Giles of Rome, and it took until the twentieth century to rectify this among biblical commentators. Likewise, biblical translators and therefore historians have

SILENCE

tended to view Phoebe's status as that of a 'deaconess'; but this is probably reading back from the third and fourth centuries, when female deacons were restricted to roles necessarily reserved for women, like looking after scantily clad females during baptisms. First- and second-century Christians may not have made such a distinction between male and female deacons or the part that either played in the life of the Church.[15]

Paul's remarks, innocent of the later turn in Christian Church formation, are witness to a consistent pattern in Christian history. In times of trial and conflict, or of rapid innovation in theology, men fall away from their accustomed leadership roles, partly because they are more likely than women to be victims of male punitive violence. Female leadership thus re-emerges as a survival strategy for the Church: during the Reformation years and their aftermath, Protestant gentlewomen sustained exiles in the reign of the Catholic Mary Tudor, Catholic recusant gentlewomen in the reign of Elizabeth I performed much the same service for persecuted Catholicism and, later, women were prominent among radical dissenters during the English Civil Wars and Interregnum.[16] Men took over again when life returned to more tranquil patterns, and the Church conformed once more to the expectations of society around it. The historical record was then adjusted to match those expectations.

The stories of the early Christian martyrs and their later modifications provide evidence of this process. The Canadian scholar Nicola Denzey has pieced together a fascinating story from the well-known activities of Pope Damasus in reorganizing the Christian shrines of Rome for Christian pilgrimage in the later fourth century. Damasus was taking on a well-populated sacred landscape in Rome; some specimens of his programme of inscriptions at various shrines describing their sacred associations survive. They have long been recognized as characterized more by elegance than by historical accuracy, but Denzey's analysis shows how he accentuated Christian Rome's masculine history, and made sure that male martyrs predominated. Most of the men thus honoured were those martyrs who had refused military service under non-Christian emperors, while the few sites that remained in commemoration of martyred women after Damasus's rebrandings placed a particular emphasis on a different sort of denial: virginity was the quality pilgrims were bidden to associate with the women who had suffered.[17]

And so the pattern continued over the centuries. Protestants were no better than Catholics. The treatment of Lutheranism's pioneer female hymn-writer is symbolic: Elisabeth, wife of Martin Luther's colleague Caspar Cruciger, was author of one of the best-loved Lutheran hymns, 'Herr Christ der einig Gottes Sohn' (Lord Christ, the only Son of God), which Miles Coverdale translated into English as early as 1535. Yet within a generation, the hymn was usually attributed to a male pastor of faraway Riga, Andreas Knoepken.[18] The tendency to erase women from the record was as true of English Catholic recusants in the reigns of Elizabeth and the early Stuarts as of radical Christians in the English Civil Wars. Even the Quakers, the most successful practitioners of quiet counter-culturalism in their survival after 1660, downplayed their early female activism in later accounts of their history. One very recent reversal of this characteristic pattern can be credited to the Vatican. On 7 September 2011, L'Osservatore Romano featured a short article by the Italian historian Lucetta Scaraffia pointing out that the inspiration behind the Roman Catholic Church's first eucharistic conference in 1881 had been not a priest but a French laywoman, Emilie-Marie Tamisier (1834–1910). Mlle Tamisier had spent more than a decade energetically lobbying clergy, but her work had never previously received any public recognition from the Church which had so often repeated that pioneering event. It was interesting to watch this report going viral on the Internet in the wake of its publication.[19]

Protestantism's greatest subtraction of the feminine from Christianity was perpetrated on the person of Mary, whose cult had been such a major part of pre-Reformation devotion that it was immediately the subject of a great deal of destructive Protestant hatred in the sixteenth-century Reformation. Even those Reformers like Martin Luther who tried to establish Mary in a new devotional role failed to take their Churches with them, and the studied hostility of Reformed Protestants went much further, much encouraged by John Calvin. The fact that Mary could be regarded as the guarantee of the Incarnation, and was therefore a bulwark against the rethought Christologies of Melchiorite or Unitarian Radicals, only increased Protestant perplexity as to what to with her. As a result, a sullen Protestant silence fell on the subject.[20] It is sobering, for instance, to listen afresh to that magnificent Protestant musical meditation on the birth, death and resurrection of Jesus Christ, Handel's *Messiah*, after one has realized that its libretto by the Englishman Charles Jennens (1700–73) is so constructed as virtually to ignore the Blessed Virgin, who might be considered to have had some importance in the Nativity story. She is met obliquely through a prophecy of Isaiah, and that is it.

In the wake of such deliberate neglect, Mary had a hard time stealing back into the centre-ground of nineteenth- and twentieth-century Anglicanism. She did so in the end through one of its great worldwide success stories, the Mothers' Union. This still-flourishing organization, one of the very few in modern Anglicanism not to be seriously affected by theological party strife, was founded in 1876 by Mary Sumner, an Evangelical parson's wife who had little time for Our Lady's simultaneous recovery of esteem among Anglo-Catholics. Mrs Sumner did institute an annual day of prayer on the Feast of the Annunciation, which as the traditional Prayer Book and legal feast-day of Lady Day, held few terrors for Protestant Englishwomen, but in the earlier years of her movement, St Monica, the formidable mother of Augustine of Hippo, was generally thought of as a more suitable maternal role-model for members than the Mother of God. Queen Victoria, who was patron of the MU from 1897, was safer still, and there was of course always Mrs Sumner herself. After 1912, the society's icon became Raphael's Sistine Madonna, which, despite its alarmingly popish title, was by then housed in safely Protestant Dresden. Raphael's image nevertheless still needed careful trimming before it was usable: the accompanying papal tiara at bottom left had to go, as well as the flanking saints, which might suggest the idea of Mary as mediatrix (necessarily, alas, the two famous bored cherubs in the same area of the picture went too: Anglican mothers would have given them a brisk talking-to). This was a splendidly selective piece of recovered memory.[21]

There were other good reasons for a rewriting of history in relation to women. Too close an association with females sometimes caused problems for men of the cloth. That is the case with John Wesley (1703–91), a man with an unusually well-developed urge for self-publicity, who surprisingly early on in his public ministry began publishing his private diaries, suitably edited. Comparison with the manuscript originals is illuminating on many matters. The American Methodist historian Richard Heitzenrater has produced some striking statistics: in the unpublished entries for his time as a missionary in the new British colony of Georgia in 1736–7, Wesley mentions women four times more often than he does men, while in the published version, that statistic is spectacularly reversed. Men are mentioned ten times more often than women, and some of these allusions actually involve gender reassignments of names and pronouns.[22] Why might this be? Wesley was only too conscious that his time in Georgia had been marred and indeed brought to a premature end by some injudicious emotional involvement with women (a pattern that recurred more than once in his long itinerant ministry). Some massaging of the narrative for public consumption would thus be helpful.

Wesley's self-editing is a comparatively mild instance of the recurrent and melancholy fact that purposeful forgetting in Christian history has involved the excision of sexual scandal or perceived scandal from the record. Another example is instructive: the career and afterlife of the Victorian Anglican clergyman F. W. Robertson (1816–53), who enjoyed a series of spectacularly successful preaching ministries in various Evangelical strongholds such as Cheltenham, St Ebbe's Oxford and Trinity Chapel Brighton, winning golden opinions before his early death for his liberal version of Evangelical certainties and for his eloquence – enough to inspire a memorial stained-glass window in his old Oxford college. Various edifying biographies of him appeared, and Gordon Fallows (1913–79), Bishop of Sheffield and an open-minded Broad Churchman in Anglican terms, was proposing to add to them, when to his alarm he was made privy to a volume of Robertson's diaries, for 1849. When decoded, this revealed in explicit detail the preacher's passionate and very physical affair with a married woman, eight years into his marriage, along with his wife's furious reaction. Other papers revealing Robertson's quest for marital separation at the time of his death only made matters worse.

Bishop Fallows continued to work on his biography, but, even before his own death brought the project to an end, he had decided to suppress the contents of the diary in his account. Robertson's latest biographer, Christina Beardsley, has been more committed to a rounded narrative than Fallows. She discovered that the Bishop had deliberately concealed the existence of the diary and other compromising material from her, while affording her access to other, innocuous documents. Some may find Robertson's adultery rather less reprehensible than the Bishop's attempt to hide historical evidence.[23]

SHAME: A DARK THEME

Fallows's conduct might seem a trivial instance of *trahison des clercs*; after all, which of us under examination should 'scape whipping? Yet much more profound ethical issues lurk behind this Evangelical storm in a Victorian teacup. They are pitilessly pursued in one of Donald MacKinnon's bleakest and most profound miniature theological essays.[24]

MacKinnon briefly scans the career of three bright stars of modern philosophy, biblical scholarship and theology: Gottlob Frege (1848–1925), Gerhard Kittel (1888–1948) and Paul Tillich (1886–1965). He convicts the first two of systematic racism – which, in Kittel's case, extended to active membership of the Nazi Party – and the third of shameless and heartless sexual promiscuity (alas, Tillich was a Gifford Lecturer, albeit at Aberdeen). MacKinnon devotes particular attention to Tillich, whose career he places in the context of the experimental ethos of the Weimar Republic, seeing in it a 'calculated, elaborately defended, yet always elaborately hidden perpetuation of a lifestyle involving an unacknowledged contempt . . . for the elementary, demanding sanctities of human existence'. In the conduct of his life, with his neglect and humiliation of his wife and children, Tillich was as antinomian as any seventeenth-century Ranter. Given MacKinnon's indictment, and given this lack of integrity, one wonders how far any of Tillich's theological work can be taken seriously. One can without too many ethical problems rely on the professional expertise of a hypocritical car mechanic, but the stock in trade of theologians is honesty, and the same rules do not apply.[25]

MacKinnon, himself an engagingly adventurous theologian, suggests that one lesson to be learned from the career of Paul Tillich is that 'we have to reckon with the built-in risk of a deep corruption in a theology that would cultivate a temper of exploration'. He goes on to articulate a still deeper problem, which all charismatic preachers (and, sadly, many have followed down the primrose path of Robertson or Tillich) would do well to ponder: 'how far the heroic is a Christian category'.[26] Once more, we hear the gnostic question, or the question posed by the Nicodemite Spirituals of the Reformation, to Christian martyrs and their admirers. MacKinnon's essay is a tribute to the value of the historical discipline in pulling mislabelled saints from their pedestals. No man is a hero to his valet, and it is always worth remembering when visiting shrines that one definition of a saint is someone who has not been researched well enough.[27]

What is true of individuals is equally true of Churches. They are perfectly capable of collectively knowing that they have done wrong, even by the standards of their own time, in circumstances which no amount of historical relativism can condone. Their acts of forgetting, their silences, can be the result of quite justified shame, either because they have realized even at the time that shame is appropriate, or because they have come to realize it later. Of many possible examples, I offer three in ascending order of generality: the concealment of clerical child abuse in the Roman Catholic Church, the relationship of all Western Churches to the Nazi Holocaust of the Jews, and worldwide Christian attitudes towards slavery, particularly as they have affected African-Americans. Although all these instances involve conscious shame, it is exhibited in a tangle of contemporary and retrospective silences.

CONCEALING CLERICAL CHILD ABUSE

It would be unjust to suppose that historically the main perpetrators of child abuse are clergy, let alone Roman Catholic clergy, so what aspect of the revelations of the last two decades has made them so painful, apart from the very considerable numbers of victims and perpetrators involved? What shocked and repelled very many faithful Roman Catholics, driving countless numbers away from active participation in the Church of their birth, was the repeated attempts by the clerical hierarchy until very recent years at cover-up. The clergy seemed to regard the good name of the Church as more important than the damage done to the young victims.

One of the justifications belatedly offered by a humiliated Church leadership from the late 1990s was that all this was the result of the corrupting influence of the permissive society of the 1960s, coupled with a lack of understanding of the issues involved in child abuse in earlier decades. This line of argument seemed a good deal less convincing with the publication in 2004 of Karen Liebreich's meticulous study of an extraordinary neglected monastic archive from the seventeenth century, which she found in Florence: it concerned the first Order to be founded in the Christian world to provide free education for the poor, the Order of the Clerics Regular of the Pious Schools, or Piarists. The Piarists were also the only Order of the Counter-Reformation to be closed down by papal command, for reasons that will become apparent.[28] The Piarists' early papers were much weeded in the seventeenth century, soon after the events which they catalogued, but such had been the size of the original archive that Dr Liebreich soon realized that the weeding had not been very efficient.

The story begins with a Spanish priest, Joseph Calasanz (1557–1648), who spent a quarter-century developing a network of free schools for the poor before, in his old age, in 1621, he gained papal approval for the foundation of the new Piarist Order. Calasanz was a deeply austere man, and he was never himself accused of any sexual misbehaviour. His Order, which spread as far as Poland, showed a pleasing interest in new mathematical advances and in the research of Galileo, and it was also characterized in its early years by the extreme self-denial of its lifestyle. Unfortunately the twin weaknesses of the Founder-General were to indulge particular favourites among his brethren, and to be a poor judge of character.[29]

Sexual scandal began to gain publicity only six years after the Order's formal papal approval, but the real trouble awaited the rise within its ranks of a rich Roman lawyer's son, Stefano Cherubini, a pleasure-loving young man whom Calasanz quickly over-promoted. Cherubini soon set out drastically to modify the Order's strict mode of life in terms of personal possessions, diet and leisure, but in 1629 Fr Calasanz was urgently informed of far more serious sexual offences involving pupils of Cherubini's school in Naples. The old man, brow-beaten by Cherubini and fearful for the future of his Order, took no action, despite a raft of evidence in explicit detail from Piarist col-leagues. He wrote to Cherubini: 'There is no one in the world today that wishes more than I that this rumour would disappear . . . because I have at heart the honour of the Order and of the individual people in it more than anyone else . . . The Lord make everything disappear as I wish and pray to his divine Majesty.' Repeatedly in Calasanz's letters comes another theme: 'it seems best to me, that if we are allowed to be the judges of this case, we will not permit it to come into the hands of outsiders.' In later years, Calasanz added another reason for what he freely admitted had been a cover-up: it was out of respect for Cherubini's distinguished family. At the time, in a pattern all too familiar in later centuries, Fr Cherubini was promoted to visitor-general to get him away from the scene of his misdeeds. Joseph Calasanz was the man whom in 1948 Pope Pius XII named as patron saint of Christian schools.[30]

Despite the cover-up, the scandals continued to proliferate. Cheru-bini, far from being grateful to his former patron, became a central figure in a mostly youthful circle of Piarists who in 1642 deprived the aged founder of his office, and contrived his humiliating and terrify-ing arrest by the Inquisition. Soon the clique was running the Order, and Cherubini was back as headmaster of the Order's most illustrious school in Rome itself. The results there were predictable, and others in his circle with equally dark reputations were put in charge of visit-ing other Piarist schools. In the end in 1643, with support from the Inquisition and the Society of Jesus, Cherubini was promoted to be Universal Superior of the Order. Now the chorus of outrage from the great majority of conscientious Piarists across Europe was too great to ignore, but Pope Innocent X's solution in 1646 was simply to decree the Order's dissolution. Several decades passed, and all the principal actors were dead before it was refounded; the Piarists went on to educate a swathe of European great names from Mozart to Goya to Pius IX to Egon Ronay. Apart from the first honest and angry historical notes on the Order by a contemporary Piarist, Vincenzo Berro (1603–65), which were not published at the time, historical notices of the Order buried the scandal in oblivion until now.[31]

There was no question but that throughout this sorry saga contemporary Italian society was perfectly aware of what child abuse, as we would understand it, actually was. That had been a concern in monastic Orders since the days of the Desert Fathers, and the Order's own rules had plenty of provisions to prevent it.[32] There was certainly a purposeful circle of perpetrators in this particular case, but there is no evidence that the recurrence of child abuse in the Roman Catholic Church has a continuous Nicodemite semi-institutional character, in contrast to gay male Anglo-Catholicism since the 1840s. The institutional circumstances are different – what we are looking at is a repeated but discrete series of individual reactions to a structural problem: the emotional constraints of universal compulsory clerical celibacy on the Roman Catholic Church. It is very different from the effects of the 'opt-in' celibacy of modern clerical Anglicanism.

The timing of the emergence of Catholic clerical child abuse in the early seventeenth century is significant, and can be attributed to the malign effect of combining two very different outgrowths of reforming zeal in the Counter-Reformation. First, clerical celibacy became a generally enforced Tridentine reality, as it had not been in previous centuries, despite its theoretical universalization in the twelfth century. The Church now waged a determined campaign against clerical heterosexual partnerships, goaded precisely by the emphasis which Protestants placed on clerical marriages, not to mention the obvious general success of such marriages. Crucially, the Tridentine authorities persuaded the Catholic laity to be their eyes and ears in enforcing the new dispensation against a frequently reluctant clergy.[33] Second, the Counter-Reformation brought an impressive wave of social activism throughout European society on behalf of the poor and the vulnerable, not the least of which was the commitment to educate the young on a far greater scale than Christian Europe had ever before attempted.

That conjunction arguably lies behind the repeated clandestine pattern of child abuse in the Roman Church since the Counter-Reformation. One of the lessons learned about such abuse in recent years is that it is as much, if not more, about the exercise of power as about sex, and the exercise of power can (in the short term) be very emotionally consoling. Suddenly, around 1600, the three major clerical Orders of the Church, even bishops and cardinals, found themselves faced with the reality of celibacy. That left them struggling to cope with emotional consequences which had not been so inevitable in the more relaxed disciplinary atmosphere of previous centuries. It is probably no co-incidence that, among the kaleidoscope of rulers in the Holy Roman Empire at the time, it was some of the German Catholic prince-bishops who presided over the most extreme manifestations of the witch-craze: their personal anxieties about their own newly regulated sexuality might be relieved by punitive action against women who were symbols of disordered sexuality.[34]

Lower down the clerical scale, clergy were forced into a celibacy which by no means all found natural or acceptable, and which many could observe played no part in the clerical ministry of Protestants. Some of these unfortunates took out their frustrations by exercising power over vulnerable young people, given the opportunity in pastoral educational situations in which the Church authorities had little recognition of the problem, and no developed procedure to deal with it. The Counter-Reformation emphasis on the special ontological status of priesthood did not always encourage clergy to attempt proper moral reflection on their actions. It is easy for those with privileged status to come to justify what they do with reference to that privilege, especially if they think that their status has been conferred by the Holy Spirit.[35]

WESTERN CHRISTIANITY
AND THE HOLOCAUST

When it comes to the record of both Catholic and Protestant in relation to the Holocaust, it is difficult to know where to begin. Perhaps the best place is the Gospel of John. Here 'the Jews' are presented as a party entirely separate from Jesus and his disciples, and in the course of one of his most bitter discussions with them Jesus tells them that 'you are of your father the Devil, and your will is to do your father's desires'.[36] The Evangelist Matthew is equally unhelpful in quite unhistorically shifting blame for Jesus's death from the Roman authorities to the Jewish crowds, who in his narrative roar out to a disgusted Pontius Pilate, 'His blood be on us, and on our children!'[37]

This is a real problem for all Christians, because it acutely raises the question of scriptural authority. Rabbi Michael Lerner, brooding on the effect of Mel Gibson's notorious film *The Passion of the Christ* (2004), pointed out that 'if Christians have not confronted anti-Judaism as effectively as they have tackled other "isms", then that is because doing so requires them to question the historical truth of their own scriptures.'[38] Professor James Dunn has observed to me in the same vein that it takes a liberal biblical critic to put those anti-Jewish statements in the New Testament in a proper historical and textual context. By contrast, a fundamentalist is stuck with their literal meaning, and that reflects the interpretation of very many Christians for nearly two millennia.[39]

On a literal reading, Jews are not just the enemies of God and Christ, but Christ-killers, and it is not surprising that one vicious outcrop of this notion was the 'blood-libel' developed in England during the twelfth century and extending to modern times, in which Christians fantasized about Jews repeating Christ's Crucifixion on helpless Christian boys.[40] It is painful but necessary to remind Christians of the centuries-old heritage of anti-Semitism festering in the memories of countless ordinary twentieth-century Christians on the eve of the Nazi takeover. In the 1940s, this poison led not just Christian Germans but Christian Lithuanians, Poles and many others gleefully to perpetrate bestial cruelties on helpless Jews who had done them no harm. Without the long Christian centuries of characterizing the Jews as Christ-killers, the Nazis would not have been so easily able to manipulate otherwise decent ordinary folk.[41]

It would have been difficult for even the most articulate and determined Christian opponents of Nazism within Germany to make the leap of imagination required to incorporate a proper defence of the Jews into their defiance. Notoriously, the ecumenical Lutheran and Reformed alliance of pastors who created the Confessing Church made no reference to the plight of the Jews in their Barmen Declaration in 1934: something for which, three decades later, one of the leading actors, Karth Barth, expressed personal regret.[42] The Confessing Church took an official stand only on the question of racial discrimination via its statements on ecclesiology (its theology of the Church): it refused to accept that the State could determine Church membership by excluding through racist legislation ethnic Jews who had become Christians. Many Confessing Church members went so far as to feel that such Christians ought to have their own separate parishes.

The Confessing Church experienced the difficulty of all well-intentioned Christians in a nation-state dominated by an evil whose dimensions were difficult to comprehend, and certainly to anticipate. But its members were also still exhibiting that greater and more profound shackling of the Christian mind which in 1878 had led the Court Chaplain of the Kaiser in Berlin, Adolf Stoecker, to create the Christian Social Workers' Party, the first political party in modern German history to stand on an anti-Semitic platform. This was not simply a German sin, as some particularly clear-sighted and independent-minded modern Christians were beginning to point out in the 1930s. In the Church of England, one of the earliest honourable voices was Herbert Hensley Henson (1863–1947), latterly Bishop of Durham, and never one to spare the feelings of the myopic. As early as 1935, Henson not only squarely confronted the Church of England's Church Assembly with the dangers of Nazi anti-Semitism, but also suggested that Christianity had to bear some responsibility for the development of that anti-Semitism.[43]

Besides Henson, there was James Parkes (1896–1981), an Anglican clergyman who can be regarded as the chief systematic pioneer of the late twentieth-century revolution in Christian attitudes towards Jews. Significantly, Parkes spent most of his ministry in positions which were slightly outside the mainstream of the Church of England.[44] He faced a great deal of hostility even from those who might have been expected to know better, such as the leading English Presbyterian missionary, ecumenist and sometime pacifist William Paton, who called Parkes 'barely Christian'. Paton's Anglican counterpart in missionary organization John McLeod Campbell accused Parkes of an irrational and over-emotional reaction to the situation of the Jews in Nazi Germany. Even the normally far-sighted Archbishop William Temple, who much esteemed Parkes and actually recommended him (unsuccessfully) for a peerage, could not accept his analysis of the biblical roots of anti-Semitism, saying in private correspondence that he did 'not think that the reading of the passages in the New Testament describing the crucifixion can themselves without comment create ill feeling against the Jews'.[45]

The recurrent failure of imagination among conscientious and well-informed British opponents of Nazism like Temple was to misread the problem. They regarded Nazism even in its anti-Semitic atrocities as an assault on Christian rather than on Jewish civilization. Bishop George Bell (1883–1958), whose generous spirit made him rather too inclined to assist after 1945 in rehabilitating German churchmen who had been close to the Nazi regime, passionately believed that Germany was a Christian country occupied by Nazis; that conviction lay behind his celebrated denunciations of RAF bombings of German cities.[46] It was indeed a Christian country, but one in which the majority of Christians, Protestant as well as Catholic, in the Lutheran State Churches in particular, had come to acquiesce in a regime which systematically dehumanized and murdered German Jews, and millions of other Jews throughout Europe.

In the wake of the collapse of Nazi Germany in 1945, it was easier to begin a retrospective assessment of Christian complicity in or silence about its crimes against the Jews, but in practice it was still very difficult. The Council of the Evangelical Church in Germany issued what has become celebrated as the Stuttgart Declaration of Guilt in October of that year, one of the first such acknowledgements by any German community. Apart from the fact that only a small minority of German provincial Churches adopted the Declaration at the time, two features of it are noticeable: first, it does not explicitly mention Jews at all, and, second, the sins that it confesses are primarily sins of omission, not of commission: of not doing enough to help, rather than of doing the wrong thing in the first place. So it speaks of 'not having confessed more courageously, prayed more conscientiously, believed more joyously, and loved more ardently'.[47]

That calls to mind the famous quasi-prose-poem first formulated soon afterwards by the Confessing Church pastor Martin Niemöller (1892–1984), who was much less evasive than most German clergy about his own emotional and personal entanglement with the Nazi regime. It begins, 'First they came for the Communists, and I did not speak out because I was not a Communist . . .' The Jews figure prominently in his compact exemplary list of his own sins of omission.

Niemöller was vague about the exact origins and form of his text, but he used it frequently through the rest of his long life, and it remains the classic confession of silent inaction, so adaptable that many have reformulated it in ways of which Niemöller would instinctively have disapproved. In the United States, the opening reference to the Communists frequently disappears.[48]

Unhappily at the centre of attention both before, during and after the Second World War was Eugenio Pacelli (1876–1958), who became Pope Pius XII, by nature a taciturn and solitary man. His part in the war generated debate which is still not ended, but the Pope's own silence is easily heard above that considerable and frequently angry noise.[49] It has several aspects, for the Pope was silent to the German government when he learned of an army plot to assassinate Hitler in late 1939, and he was discreetly communicative to the Allies about what he knew of the plans. That is one testimony that the description of Pius as 'Hitler's Pope' is grossly off the mark.[50] Yet already, on becoming pope in 1939, he had also been responsible for suppressing a draft encyclical of his predecessor Pope Pius XI, 'On the unity of the human race' (*Humani generis unitas*). Pius XI would have condemned all racism, with direct reference to Germany and Mussolini's Fascist Italy, and had envisaged ordering Church action against it.[51] As the Holocaust unfolded, and circumstantial and horrific reports reached the Vatican, Pius XII remained silent in public about the Jews. While a variety of Vatican agencies helped thousands of Jews to escape round-ups in Italy, the Pope only once nerved himself to make a public statement about their plight. Even then, in his Christmas radio broadcast in 1942, his mention of those 'put to death or doomed to slow extinction, sometimes merely because of their race or their descent' failed to put a name to the chief sufferers.[52]

Pius's last near-silence was that of any significant public reflection on his actions after 1945. It lasted through the thirteen years of his pontificate after the war, and it included some deliberate if understandable obfuscation. The first pope to make much use of radio and even television in his last years, Pius XII spent his time energetically pronouncing on a vast variety of subjects, some of which might be considered not best calculated to showcase expertise on the part of the Supreme Pontiff, but he showed no inclination to seek any public reconciliation or make any public apology to Jews. His refusal to speak out on this shocked that devout Catholic convert Jacques Maritain (1882–1973), appointed French Ambassador to the Holy See after the Liberation of France; Maritain frankly regarded Pius's response to his pleas as evasive, and resigned his diplomatic posting in protest. The Pope's most explicit step, which can hardly be described as radical, was to order that any translation of the Latin word in the Church's prayer for the Jews which characterized them as *perfideles* should be 'unbelieving' rather than 'perfidious'. That stands in counterpoint to a memorandum of 1946 passing on to the French bishops the instruction that Jewish children baptized during the war should be brought up as Catholics, even if it might keep them from their birth-families.[53]

It is ironic that Pacelli's ecclesiastical career was shaped by service to his great patrons Cardinal Pietro Gasparri (1852–1934) and Pope Benedict XV (1854–1922). Benedict was bitterly criticized during the First World War by both combatant blocs for his failure to speak out in their favour, and governments treated with contempt his dogged efforts at diplomacy in the interests of a balanced peace. A sympathetic view of Pacelli's strategy in the Second World War might be that he was only seeking to apply lessons of neutrality and the preservation of lines of communication that he had learned from Benedict's pontificate. Benedict's stock has risen since: there is no sign of that happening to Pius XII, beyond his confessional admirers within a particularly 'Ultramontane' section of Roman Catholicism.

CHRISTIANS, THE BIBLE AND SLAVERY

Our last example of historical amnesia once more raises questions about traditional Christian ways of looking at the Bible: it is the issue of the morality of slavery. Modern Evangelical Christians are particularly pleased with themselves in having been associated with the movement to abolish slavery. There is a mantra of late eighteenth-century English names to recite; John Newton, Thomas Clarkson and William Wilberforce head the pantheon, given their successful campaign first to abolish Britain's participation in the slave trade, then to end Britain's acceptance of slavery, then to end the acceptance of slavery generally throughout Christendom. It was a narrative much encouraged and commemorated by British liberal imperialists during the nineteenth century, providing a fine moral justification for the 'altruistic presence' of empire.[54] There is more than one problem with this narrative. In terms of origins, it ignores the fact that, beginning with a Dutch Quaker petition against slavery in Pennsylvania in 1688, the earliest credit should actually be given to late seventeenth-century and early eighteenth-century Quakers, who would not have inspired Evangelical approbation at the time.[55]

There was a good reason why Quakers should have arrived there before other Christians, and that reason should also give Evangelicals pause. As we have seen, Quakers were Spirituals, who believed in the prime authority of the 'inner light'. Many of their earliest activists, particularly the cosmopolitan Quaker missionary Samuel Fisher, had through their sharp critique of the problems of the scriptural text, pioneered the modern Enlightenment discipline of biblical criticism.[56] That was the corollary of a movement which depended on a rejection of the overriding authority of the scriptural text as understood in the seventeenth century. The Quakers' disrespect for the established conventions of biblical authority was the reason that they could take a fresh perspective on biblical authority and reject it. It took original minds to kick against the authority of sacred Scripture. What was needed was a prior conviction in one's conscience of the wrongness of slavery, which one might then decide to justify by a purposeful re-examination of the Bible.

The distressing fact for modern Christians, particularly Evangelical Christians, is that slavery is taken for granted in the Bible, even if it is not always considered to be a good thing, at least for oneself. One would have had to have been exceptionally independent-minded and intellectually awkward to face up to the consensus of every philosopher in the ancient world, and the first Christians did not rise to the challenge. Paul's Epistle to Philemon, in which the Apostle asks his correspondent to allow him the continued services of Philemon's slave Onesimus, is a Christian foundation document in the justification of slavery. There are very many modern Christians who would vehemently disagree with that assessment, and they should be given credit for their generous wish to absolve the text and affirm its value for the modern age, but their case is not strong.[57] In fact it can be argued that early Christians were rather better at inventing theological reasons for accepting slavery than the non-Christians around them.[58] Slave-owners in the Deep South in nineteenth-century America were perfectly entitled to look to the Bible to justify their slave-owning, and they were right to be surprised that other Christians disagreed with them. It is only in less than three out of twenty Christian centuries that Churches have come round to saying that slavery is bad in all circumstances, full stop. Nowadays, Christians take this for granted. They have forgotten the huge moral revolution that has taken place to get to where they are now on this subject, and how much effort it took some maverick souls, over more than a century, to persuade fellow-Christians that this was the only way to think about slavery.

That process was by no means complete by the end of the nineteenth century, and that is a very important part of the 'abolition' narrative often forgotten. We need to remember the extraordinary story of Nachash theology, or, perhaps more accurately, encounter it rather than remember it, because this set of beliefs is still current in the United States.[59] It is a racist theology, which sought to justify the subjection and inferior status of African-Americans, ironically with reference to the early stirrings of modern biblical criticism. Nachash theology made sense to a significant section of mainstream American society well into the twentieth century, and still has its fringe advocates. It took its origin from an innocent suggestion by the English Methodist biblical commentator Adam Clarke which he made in the heyday of abolition in the early nineteenth century, in 1810 (Clarke himself was a fervent abolitionist). He speculated that the very articulate 'serpent' (nachash) who tempted Eve in the Garden of Eden (Gen. 3.1) was in fact 'a creature of the ape or ouran-outan kind'. This attracted general scorn among British biblical scholars, but within a few decades it was taken up with enthusiasm by some in the United States with a very particular reference to the urgent question of what to do with the African-American population, most of which was still enslaved.[60]

The schismatic Mormon Charles B. Thompson (ironically, a former Quaker) made an identification which Clarke had not: he said that the seductive *nachash*/ape was a Negro, hence the primordial sin of the *nachash* could justify Negro enslavement. In the age of Charles Darwin, some American defenders of Negro slavery saw it as potentially offering a more scientifically respectable and cogent explanation of Negro origins than the long-standing attribution of Negro descent to Ham, which had the disadvantage from the racist point of view of relating Negroes to Adam. From the fringe Mormon Thompson, the idea spread to mainstream Christians in the South, because, for the likes of President Jefferson Davis of the Confederacy, it was a welcome theological accompaniment to secession and the defence of slavery. In effect, since the Negro was not fully human, there was no slavery of human beings in the South, and abolitionists were wasting their energy.

After the Confederacy's defeat, the Southern merchant and writer Buckner H. Payne (1799–1883) and his assiduous publicist Charles Carroll (b. 1849) both used this distorted biblical exegesis to say openly on occasions that it would be good to annihilate African-Americans, who were, after all, only apes, and particularly degraded and threatening ones. So *Nachash* theology lived on in respectable Southern circles into the twentieth century: decades, indeed, after the achievement of Civil Rights. It still fuels the thinking of American white supremacist groups, and sometimes there are traces of it in more central parts of American society. Thus have the well-meaning critical speculations of a Methodist abolitionist been perverted to a new use which would have appalled him.

The importance of reciting this dismal genealogy is that it reminds us that the task of remembering the Christian record on slavery is still incomplete. There have been honourable amends made, such as the belated recognition by the oldest Anglican missionary society, the United Society for the Propagation of the Gospel, that its predecessor, the Society for the Propagation of the Gospel, was involved up to its neck in slavery, to the extent of having its own West Indian plantation and its own branding iron for those enslaved Africans working for it. Nevertheless, the United Society's website now appears evasive on the subject of its involvement in slavery, despite the incentive to continued acknowledgement provided by an excellent and pitiless recent academic study of its past published in 2011, which overturns previous, more optimistic estimates of its humanitarian record in the age of slavery.[61]

Selective memory will always invite further probing, to find the silences which still demand an ending. The issue of British involvement in the slave trade brought a dramatic example of that in the most solemn of English liturgical contexts, a national service in Westminster Abbey, in March 2007. This commemorated the bicentenary of the abolition of slavery; it was envisaged as an event which would combine thanksgiving, remembrance, penitence and perhaps, out of that, healing. Present were the Queen, the Prime Minister, the Archbishop of Canterbury, plus the political and religious elite of the nation, including representatives of black communities. As the service proceeded, the Dean of Westminster's conduct of an Act of Penitence was suddenly both shatteringly interrupted and given a more vivid colouring: Toyin Agbetu of the African rights organization Ligali walked into the centre of the Abbey from the south transept to add noisy protest to the liturgical mixture. There was pushing, struggling, a blow or two, as Mr Agbetu pointed at the monarch, shouting, 'You, the Queen, should be ashamed!', and to Tony Blair 'You should say sorry!'[62]

Agbetu was then forcibly escorted out of the Abbey to the accompaniment of a mixture of deep embarrassment, heart-searching and barely suppressed excited fascination among the congregation. This being Britain in all its flawed attempts to do the right thing, he was able to preface his arrest outside the Abbey by an improvised press conference, setting out why such an event should apologize for two and a half centuries of English involvement in the slave trade. Not all will agree that Agbetu was justified in that particular extension of the day's ceremonial, but one interpretation of his actions is that they were a necessary completion of what was missing in the bicentenary service: an ending of silence which had not otherwise been planned for. Silences such as Christian involvement in child abuse, anti-Semitism, slave-owning, demand constant rupture. On such noise does the health of Christian society depend.

9

Silence in Present and Future Christianities

RETROSPECT: WILD-TRACKS

Those who have been involved in set-piece interviews on radio and television will be familiar with the concept of the 'wild-track'. Belying its restless name, the wild-track is in fact the recording of silence, and it forms a welcome and relaxing finale to what is normally a much longer, more tedious and exhausting ordeal than neophyte interviewees will have imagined beforehand. It is an essential part of the production process, since it provides an aural patching for any untoward noises that need to be cut out, or it becomes the accompaniment to the panning shots which television adores. My most entertaining experience of the wild-track was after a sequence of interviews and location-shots with Fr Christophe Lazowski, one of the brethren of the Benedictine monastery of Saint-Wandrille-de-Fontenelle in Normandy. At the end of our interview, the sound-man as usual asked for us to stand in complete silence for three minutes while he captured his wild-track. I much relished observing our monastic interviewee's fascination with Roger Lucas's statuesque custodianship of the microphone amid the medieval cloister, as twenty-first-century technology demanded its own version of what Odo of Cluny had decreed long before.[1]

Fr Christophe, a man of wisdom and experience of the world, would have enjoyed the ironies involved, but would also have appreciated the deeper lessons to be drawn. The point of the wild-track is that every silence is different and distinctive. Each is charged with the murmurs of the landscape around it, with the personalities of those who have entered it and remain present within it, together with the memories of conversations which have come and gone. It has been well said that silence 'has no opposite and is the ground of both sound and the absence of sound'.[2] It is an ambassador between the mundane and the sublime, solving tensions and miseries which words cannot touch. That role was exemplified in the visit of the Blessed Virgin Mary to the remote village of Knock in the rural west of Ireland, in August 1879. Fourteen people in the village witnessed a vision of Our Lady on the gable of the local Roman Catholic church; she was accompanied by St Joseph and a third figure, whom a consensus identified as St John the Beloved Disciple; the Lamb of God himself looked on. The Knock appearance is one of the few from the period which has gained official recognition from the Vatican, confirmed by a visit by that great Marian devotee Pope John Paul II very early in his pontificate, on the centenary of the vision in 1979.[3]

Our Lady's hundreds of appearances in nineteenth-century Europe were unprecedented in their frequency, testimony that the era was as much a time of re-enchantment as disenchantment, and part of the renewal of Western Christianity after the traumas of the French Revolution. She was a woman of her time, zestfully embracing the new democratic spirit in the egalitarianism of her appearances to the humblest and most marginal in European society, and evincing the readiness of the period's 'first-wave feminism' to make her views known on the political and theological issues of the day. That is what makes one special feature of Our Lady's visit to Knock so interesting: she said nothing. At Lourdes (France) in 1858, she had brusquely exercised the prerogative of the Queen of Heaven to transcend Western logical categories, announcing 'I am the Immaculate Conception.' At Marpingen (Germany) in 1876, she had stooped to accommodate herself to the rules of European syntax in the statement 'I am the Immaculately Conceived.'[4] Three years later at Knock, she showed that she knew her Wittgenstein, for whereof she could not speak, she remained silent.

Why might that have been? The latest and most subtle of scholarly considerations of Our Lady of Knock provides some very convincing reasons through a detailed examination of the circumstances of County Mayo and the Catholic Archdiocese of Tuam in the previous decades. It was a poverty-stricken and deeply divided region, still traumatized by the memory of the great Potato Famine of the 1840s. The dominant Catholic Church was riven with disputes between clergy and faithful laity over its demands for financial support. There was widespread lay anger that the clergy were officially hostile to militant Irish nationalism, symbolized by the Catholic hierarchy's much-resented order that dying members of the republican Fenian Brotherhood should not be given the last rites unless they repudiated their membership. Through her silent vigil, Our Lady of Knock demanded reconciliation and regrouping amid the bitter noise of provincial Catholic politics.

Moreover, Our Lady's silence neatly sidestepped an acute question in the west of Victorian Ireland: what language should she speak? At Lourdes and Marpingen, she had experienced no problem over this: she used the appropriate local patois to convey her emphatic theological message. That was much less possible in Knock in 1879, because the village was one among many linguistic battlegrounds between a dying Irish Gaelic and an English which was rapidly being adopted across rural Ireland. Though virtually everyone still understood Gaelic, many clearly felt that it had become a language for losers. Under the circumstances, silence was the best policy. The taciturn appearance of the Blessed Virgin on a church wall was not simply the naive construction of simple rural folk who had just discovered the excitements of the Magic Lantern, or even an actual use of the Magic Lantern, as some cynics have suggested in the past.[5]

Silence is always contextual. We have seen it steal gradually into the consciousness of the people of Israel through the silences of the Temple liturgy, a growing appreciation of the silence of the cosmos, and the peculiar concerns of the second prophet known as Isaiah in a time of rebuilding and restoration. Judaism was formed in dialogue with the cultures around it: Jews who talked to Greeks picked up Plato's fascination with the silence of the divine. They meditated afresh on their own creation stories with that thought in mind: they linked first things to last things, and they found silence in both.[6]

Then came Jesus, whose distinctive, original voice I have argued can still be heard through the conversations of his followers which have shaped the Gospel text. Jesus's actions, such as his retreat into the Wilderness and his lack of words at crucial moments in his ministry, are purposeful silences which united him with the 'minority report' of the Tanakh. The silences of Jesus do not seem greatly to have resonated with the sort of Christian communities in which Paul of Tarsus played so prominent a part, but they bore great fruit in later Christian centuries. For more than a century, Pauline or Catholic Christianity contended with many other Christian identities, some of them labelled 'gnostic' by Catholic Christians. Both sides fished in the pool of Hellenism which lent the new faith so many different probings of silence, but some gnostics further stressed themes which Pauline Christianity rejected: the cosmic importance of laughter, the irrelevance of martyrdom.

What Catholic Christianity did not escape was a thought sprouting from the meditation on divinity of both Pythagoras and Plato: God was not the passionate God of the Jews and their Tanakh, merciful and loving one moment, angry and righteous judge the next. He was so perfect that he was beyond description, beyond words, beyond even a human concept of silence, since he was beyond being.[7] The Christian problem was how to relate this idea to the stories in their sacred literature about Jesus, because it did not feature strongly within that sacred literature. The resulting four centuries of increasingly bitter debate never managed to generate answers that would satisfy all who call themselves Christian.

Christianity as it emerged in the later second century, its gnostic forms firmly excluded, was a religion of congregational worship and occasional public witness that took the form of martyrdom at the hands of the Roman state; those martyrdoms were proudly remembered. Only gradually did an ascetic or solitary tradition find a place in this Church; asceticism came from the eastern frontiers of the Roman Empire and found its first home in Syria, just as the Catholic structures of the Church were taking shape. Just like negative theology, its sources were more likely to come from outside the biblical deposit of faith than from within. It would not have been obvious until the end of the fourth century that this movement was to find a respectable place in the Catholic Church beyond Syria. It is only during the fourth century that we can hear the practitioners of silence reflecting on what they were doing, and conveying what was involved to others in devotional texts. With Evagrius of Pontus, we find the first comprehensive picture of the progression from public prayer to meditation to contemplation.[8]

All the while, the steady conversation with the world around continued. Christianity plagiarized other experiences of divinity beyond itself, drawing from dialogues with Greeks, particularly Neoplatonists, whose discussion of the absent, silent God grew ever more radical, and with the Asian religions to the east. Both these two diverse sources had long known the truths of the ascetic, world-denying life which now also found a home in Christianity. As we have heard in so many different mystical voices over the course of this survey, the same metaphors and themes sound again and again in mystic discourse, like a muffled peal of bells in English change-ringing. Many mystics through the centuries have spoken and written about the impulse to move towards a goal, to travel onwards, even though frequently to the worldly eye they are people steeped in stillness and immobility. Stillness may be the goal; on the way, there is much toil. Beyond the labour are to be found light; water; silence – metaphors which Platonism and Eastern religions discovered long before Christianity, out of the constant human striving to describe the indescribable.

Christians reshaped or rediscovered these truths for themselves, always conscious of their God whom they experienced in threeness as well as oneness. Repeatedly they returned to the idea of union with that God, *theosis*. The progress of embedding *theosis* in world Christianity was not straightforward. The theological and political upheavals of the fifth century brought multiple disruptions to the Christian world. Of the two greatest exponents of silence and *theosis* in the Church, Evagrius was eclipsed, and the anonymous Miaphysite felt the need to hide his identity behind the name of Dionysius the Areopagite. Only in the ninth century did Pseudo-Dionysius come to play an increasingly significant part in the thinking of the West. Even then, he contended with Augustine of Hippo's lifelong fascination with words, and ultimately also with the West's inveterate fascination with the individual imagination. It was not just the Council of Chalcedon that tore Christianity apart: Eastern and Western Chalcedonians drifted apart in their monastic practice.[9]

One of the most under-recognized and significant differences between East and West resulted from the monastic founder St Benedict's dislike of wandering monks, which meant that this variety of ascetic was virtually excluded from the Western Church, while remaining honoured in the East (admittedly, always with the exercise of some worried episcopal vigilance). When the Byzantine Church was riven by the Iconoclastic Controversy, wandering monks were a significant factor in the victory of the icon, and so were ordinary laypeople, for whom the icon could represent a personal road to divinity. The dividing line between the professionally 'religious' and the laity was much more blurred in Orthodoxy than it was in the West. These two elements in Orthodoxy meant that contemplation and the search for union with the divine were never confined to the formal institutions of the Eastern Churches. The search was open to anyone who made the effort to take it up. All that was needed was a picture, the icon, which was so much more than a picture: a little gate to heaven. In the West, meditation and contemplation became far more associated with a specialist technology, the act of reading: *lectio divina*.[10]

Given that combination of circumstances, Eastern spirituality has always been more democratic, less clerically dominated, than that of the Latin West. The sixteenth-century Reformations in the Western Church were an attempt to redress the balance for Westerners, but the success was only partial. Protestant congregations threw off the old clericalism of Rome, only to embrace a new clericalism, together with one of the noisiest forms of Christianity – the least attentive to the silence of God – in Christian history. Word overwhelmed silence. Attempts to the contrary in magisterial Protestantism, like the shape of public worship created by Zwingli, achieved very little lasting success.

VARIETIES OF MODERN CHRISTIAN SILENCE

The problem was that, in the course of their efforts to rid the Church of what they saw as the great clerical cheat perpetrated by late medieval Catholicism, Protestants had destroyed the institutions which had cherished contemplation, and they had no idea how to replace them. The problem remains today, both in the inveterate Word-centred noisiness of Evangelical Protestantism, and equally in the constant striving after joyful Spirit-filled celebration which has so far characterized the worship life of worldwide Pentecostalism. It is not a characteristic that will change soon; one of the great attractions of Pentecostalism for so many in the world is that worship is often almost the only possible arena for celebration and emotional release amid lives of poverty and deprivation.[11]

We should also remember that in twenty-first-century Asia, millions on millions of Christians in the Indian sub-continent and in China are still effectively Nicodemites, crypto-Christians, prevented by government power or by the hostility of non-Christian neighbours from practising their faith openly. One well-informed commentator has suggested that their combined number might be around 120 million, around 6 per cent of the world's total population, capable of being recognized as the world's fifth largest religion in their own right.[12] Their experience remains to be reintegrated into the life of the world's public Christianities. It is likely to contain the joyous expression of a great deal of previously suppressed noise, but as yet, we cannot know. As Christianity welcomes crypto-Christianity back into the open, if that is what historical circumstances allow, it would be worth remembering that just like negative theology and the monastic life, the history of Nicodemism takes little more than a name from the Bible: it is from gnosticism, hermeticism and the *converso* Jews of Iberia that Nicodemism can trace its outlook and modes of behaviour.

Some of the radicals of the sixteenth- and seventeenth-century Reformation, privileging the Spirit over a 'paper Pope', saw a way through the Protestant hullabaloo of the period, notably the Schwenckfelders and the Quakers. Maybe they have lessons to teach the heirs of magisterial Protestantism.[13] The mid-twentieth century saw a notable turn in the Christian West to a discussion of the silence of God which had previously been more familiar in mystical than in pastoral theology. The great Anglican New Testament scholar Canon John Fenton (1921–2008) was remembered as remarking to Oxford ordinands in one lecture, 'The most obvious characteristic of God is his silence.

He does not cough or mutter or shuffle his feet to reassure us that he is there.'[14] And a fruitful piece of Anglican-Methodist co-operation from the same generation produced a celebrated remark often diversely credited, but taking its genesis from that distinguished English Methodist historian Professor Gordon Rupp (1910–86). It was subsequently given a more pithy and general form by the wise and crustily conservative Anglican spiritual guide Canon W. H. Vanstone (1923–99): the Church is like 'a swimming pool in which all the noise comes from the shallow end'.[15]

The birth and death dates of these theologians are significant. They were becoming adults when the full horror of the Holocaust became apparent. What could one say about God in the face of what had happened in Christian Europe? Their Scottish Episcopalian contemporary Donald MacKinnon (1913–94) was said by his friend George Steiner to see 'no justifiable future for Christianity so long as Christian theology and practice had not faced up to, had not internalized lucidly, its seminal role in the millennial torments of Judaism and in the Holocaust. Primarily, this signified coming to terms with the horror of Golgotha, a horror unredeemed – this was Donald's compulsive instinct – by the putative wonder of resurrection or by any promise of celestial reparation.'[16]

Themes of divine silence which had meant so much to mystics, ascetics and reclusives over centuries suddenly assumed an immediate, practical significance for Christians in the world, as they came to a horrified realization of what a supposedly Christian European civilization had done between 1933 and 1945. They were hardly alone in this: Jewish writers such as Eliezer Berkovits likewise struggled to answer the bitter questions of so many Jews who had experienced the grotesque violence perpetrated in the Nazi empire. Berkovits was not inclined to listen to anything that Christians might have to say on the matter, but such understandable anger does not stop Christians from still turning to Jewish experience in this most perplexing of moral questions. Christianity has spoken much of Christ's suffering for his people on the Cross. Now it can appreciate more clearly two millennia of Jewish meditations on the sufferings of God, which reach back into the Tanakh's psalms and lamentations. Now it might understand more fully the wintry scepticism of Qoheleth.[17]

WHISTLE-BLOWING

Contrariwise, one particular modern variety of breaking Christian silence is much to be cherished. It is a heartening feature of Christianity in the last 150 years that it has produced so many whistle-blowers who have drawn attention to the discreditable or misconceived features of the Christian past and present. A good deal of credit for that should go to historians, who have provided the tools for them to tell their stories and be heard. The Enlightenment practice of history, part science, part story-telling and pragmatic observation of human nature, is a great gift to Christian truth, and it has found a fruitful ally in a new frankness in the public discussion of sex, which the West owes to that otherwise frequently misguided pioneer of psychiatry and psychoanalysis, Sigmund Freud (1856–1939). As we have already seen, very many of the silences in Christian history have been about sex, but by no means all; there has also been a 'great transformation' in Christian understanding of slavery, and the beginnings of an equal transformation in Christian acceptance of guilt in anti-Semitism.

Those involved in whistle-blowing seldom get thanked at the time. James Parkes, whose achievement in seeing through Christian anti-Semitism we have already celebrated (pp. 209–10), got off comparatively lightly, hovering in jobs in the Church of England which in his time would have been construed as marginal. The life of Parkes demonstrated that whistle-blowers are not infrequently awkward by nature, sometimes even anti-social characters, but their very awkwardness and refusal to accept convention and lazy commonplaces has become a providential virtue in a good cause.[18] Often they are additionally cursed with an endearing naivety about the commitment of other Christians to absolute truth, and have been bewildered by the harsh reaction to their revelations. Such has been the fate of Fr Richard Wagner, an American priest within the Order of Missionary Oblates of Mary. In the late 1970s, he decided to undertake an academic study of how fellow-Roman Catholic priests who were gay reconciled their sexuality with their pastoral vocation in a Church committed to universal celibacy; in 1981 he submitted the results as a doctoral thesis. His findings had come as a shock to him: of his sample of fifty self-identifying gay priests from across the USA, forty-eight spoke in some detail, and with a rich variety of reflection, about the fact that they were sexually active.[19]

If Dr Wagner was surprised by the data underpinning his doctorate, his superiors as far up as the Vatican were appalled at the public revelation of this unpalatable reality, particularly when Wagner was unwise enough to present his findings in a television interview. There were suggestions that, like his interviewees, Wagner had broken his vow of chastity, something he always strenuously denied, but, since he would not keep quiet, the suggestions were turned into complete exclusion from his Order. He found himself in a situation very like that which had faced Martin Luther in the two or three years after 1517: 'the more I insisted that the past be remembered, the more the leadership would press the insinuation that I had difficulties with my vow of obedience.'[20] It is a classic confrontation in the history of Christianity, but it has countless echoes in other recent stories which arise out of the relatively sudden confrontation of ecclesiastical institutions with openly gay people. Wagner's sad tale has for instance close contemporary parallels with the treatment which the Church of England has meted out to those among its gay clergy who over the last few decades have refused to keep silence about themselves within the confused official Anglican guidelines on sexuality.[21] Many modern Western-based Churches would dearly love not to speak about homosexuality at all, but they end up talking about little else.

Christianity's travails about sex are always really about another issue: authority. Historically, Church leaders have loved to claim a particular authority to make pronouncements on society, doctrine and the Church, and they have done so by reference to another sort of authority, that of the biblical text. This means that historical investigations of ecclesiastical authority are just as potentially explosive as any historical study of sexuality: there can be few aspects of research in ancient history which are more likely to stir emotions than investigation by historians of Christianity's earliest years. The same is true for historical research on Christian Churches with shorter pedigrees than others: they were founded in periods when the abundance of documentary sources of all varieties makes for a great deal more triangulation than will ever be possible for the first two Christian centuries.

Two Churches which emerged in the USA in the nineteenth century, the Mormons and the Seventh-Day Adventists, have experienced particular problems over historical analysis of their origins, not least because they have developed authority-structures with claims to obedience and conformity as high as any that the Vatican might make. Any challenge is therefore explosive and liable to result in casualties. The problem is ever more acute in these Churches, because of changes in their culture brought them by their very success. In the early days of the Adventists and Mormons, few of their members had any experience of higher education, with its tendency to nurture Enlightenment conceptions of how history works in relation to theology, whereas, over the last century, more and more of the faithful worldwide have achieved Western-style prosperity and sent their children off to be educated at university level. It is not surprising that some have turned an interested but historically analytical eye on the founders and foundation literature of their Churches. The Seventh-Day Adventists experienced a growing crisis from the 1960s through to the 1980s, particularly concentrated in Australia and New Zealand, which resulted in the expulsions of several professional historians and scores of Adventist clergy. The tide towards acceptance of at least some historical realities over fierce denominational piety only began to turn after the first textbook on Adventist history written by a trained historian was published in 1979.[22]

The Church of Jesus Christ of Latter-Day Saints has faced the same problem. So far, the leadership has repeatedly found a solution by excommunicating such Mormon members as Fawn M. Brodie, whose biography of the Prophet Joseph Smith remains after more than six decades one of the best overviews of his career: she was expelled in 1946.[23] The most dramatic case of recent years occurred in September 1993, when six Mormon intellectuals and academics were simultaneously and very publicly excommunicated or disfellowshipped. Their crime had been publicly to advocate various revisionist views on present-day Mormon doctrines and past history, all of which relied on an Enlightenment view of how history works. All those thus excluded regarded what they were doing as for the benefit of the Church that they loved, but they had all come up against a different view of authority and truth, summed up seven years before their final expulsion by the Mormon Apostle Russell M. Nelson: 'In some instances, the merciful companion to truth is silence. Some truths are best left unsaid.'[24]

Such instances are powerful arguments as to why the discipline of history should feature in the Gifford Lectures series, with their brief 'to promote and diffuse the study of Natural Theology'. Repeatedly, religious leaders, whether in the Vatican or Salt Lake City, find that their efforts to silence dissidents armed with historical evidence have the temporary success and long-term failure of the child on the seashore defending a sandcastle against the tide. It is interesting to watch ecclesiastical leaderships struggling to find ways of dealing with this new reality, which is not going to go away. Maybe I am affected by professional hubris, but I still speculate as to whether we are witnessing worldwide the opening stages of a new 'Axial Age' in the understanding of religion and religious authority. The phrase is famously that of the German psychiatrist and philosopher Karl Jaspers. More than half a century ago, he sketched a picture of a first Axial Age of six centuries beginning at the end of the ninth century BCE, in which four civilizations of Israel/Judah, Greece, India and China, for the first time in human development, all discovered common religious themes: self-reflection, scepticism about defining truths about the absolute, willingness to embrace suffering and compassion. I would suggest that a present-day Axial Age, reassessing some of the dogmatic religions whose emergence Jaspers described, is rather more coherently grounded in historical reality than was his original hypothesis.[25]

ECUMENISM IN SILENCE

If that is felt to be too ambitious a claim, we should at least celebrate a new Christian ecumenism which is not making the mistakes of the twentieth-century Ecumenical Movement in diverting its energy into committees and agreed doctrinal statements. This is an ecumenism of Christian experience which peers across ancient divides, not ignoring such barriers but excitedly exploring the wealth that has been hidden by them. Thanks to the researches of historians, the full breadth of the Christian past is starting to flow into a common stream. So Evagrius

Ponticus has been rescued from his long exile amid anti-Chalcedonian Christianity, and he is celebrated once more by the spiritual descendants of the Chalcedonians who condemned him, because of the riches of what he said about the practice of silence. Accompanying him back into honour and appreciation are such anti-Chalcedonian giants of the spiritual life as Isaac the Syrian of Nineveh, and the ever-evasive Pseudo-Dionysius. Even some Reformed Protestants have braved the hostility of their twentieth-century theological giant Karl Barth to explore devotional outlooks which might part from the priority of the inspired Word: they have turned to their admittedly somewhat exiguous heritage of mystical piety, represented for instance by the English Presbyterian Isaac Ambrose (above, pp. 137–8).[26]

Another significant feature of the last century has been the democratization of spiritual exploration, centred for so long in the West on the clerical Orders and the regular life. Now the quest for silence and mystical union with God has moved beyond the formal bounds of Christian Churches and, for the first time since the spiritual explorations of the gnostics, even unites adherents of different world faiths. It is always dangerous to take one individual as symbolic of any major shift in historical development, but the life of the monk Thomas Merton (1915–68) offers a very tempting example. His first four decades read like a classic devotional biography of the Counter-Reformation: spiritual struggle through libertine years ending in the embrace of Trappist vocation. Then there is a departure from the script: a sea-change wrought by Merton's struggles with his own temperament and with community discipline, a transformation which predated the great if still incomplete changes in Roman Catholicism triggered by the Second Vatican Council. In the end, Merton repudiated what he more than once called the 'Carolingian' view of the world. By this he meant that particular Western monastic ethos formed from the ninth to eleventh centuries, which we have seen associated with the great Benedictine expansion in the age of Charlemagne, leading to the apocalyptic denial of the world personified in Odo of Cluny (above, pp. 95–8). Merton embraced the anguish of the modern world while in no way repudiating his solitariness. He extended that status outwards and took it way further than his Western spiritual formation, into East Asian religion. He would say to the many who had read him outside the monastic enclosure of Gethsemani in Kentucky, and who might be bewildered at the change from the rather priggish Tridentine anti-Modernist of the early 1950s, 'I *am* the world just as you are! Where am I going to look for the world first of all if not in myself?'[27]

Hospitality has always been a basic principle of Benedictine monasticism: now that monastic precept has blossomed into a veritable industry of retreats and guides to spiritual direction. Monasteries appeal because of their patent counter-culturalism: they are devoted to 'that yonder' in a self-centred world. They are not alone as Christian assets stretching out to a wider society. Christian Churches have been very good at creating holy places, and often they have simply become the latest custodian of sacred sites which have had meaning over many preceding centuries. Holy wells, like the monastic life, would struggle to find much justification in Scripture, but that has not hindered their ubiquity in the landscape of the former Christendom. In some much-visited shrines across the Christian world, it is not easy to find silence, but there are plenty of others. The latest and most comprehensive gazetteer of such sites throughout England, Scotland and Wales chronicles hundreds of them, and it is clear that they are now more visited and cherished for spiritual purposes than at any time since the sixteenth-century Reformations did their best to eliminate them from the religious scene.[28] Once more, these may be the salvation of a Christianity not dependent on words.

It is easy for Christians to sneer at the bulging shelves on 'Spirituality' of 'Mind, Body and Spirit' in the bookshops of the Western world, but they should be grateful for the countless searches for seriousness which these represent. In particular, many seekers are united in a shared search for silence, and, through it, sanctuary. Structured religion, and not just Christianity, has a formidable armoury of approaches to silence to aid societies which have been growing intolerably noisy since the first spread of steam power in the Industrial Revolution. A secular campaign for silence has been growing since the first complaints of the Scottish historian Thomas Carlyle (1795–1881), although its targets change with every shift of technology: a major concern of the first public campaigner for noise abatement, the German Jewish philosopher Theodor Lessing (1872–1933), was the omnipresent beating of domestic rugs in public, no longer a major environmental hazard in the developed world.[29]

Silence has now become the highest symbol of community action in secular liturgy. It unites those of diverse faiths and those of none, and it is chiefly manifested in the growth of the public remembrance of the dead in silence. This is something without much precedent in previous periods of recorded world history, but it is the mark of an irretrievably pluralist society, in which any specific religious statement is bound to exclude someone. Readers will have experienced the small silences of meetings in which deceased friends or colleagues are recalled. They are miniature versions of the public communal silences which began in Canada with the commemoration of those dead on the *Titanic* in 1912, and then coalesced after 1919 in the remembrance of the unprecedented numbers who had died in the course of a war whose moral justification seemed in retrospect dubious to many.[30]

MUSIC AND SILENCE

Silence is allied to wordlessness, and wordlessness is allied to music, which has made sporadic guest appearances throughout this study. Music plays the role of mediator between silence and words, because it stretches between and melts into either polarity. Michael Pisaro (b. 1961) is par excellence the composer who has creatively experimented with silence in music in the wake of the better-known experiments in musical silence by John Cage (1912–92). Pisaro expresses that function with admirable precision: 'Music traces the border between sound and silence. It erases and redraws the boundary with a fine line, or, erects a wall which is soon knocked down – thus determining the breadth of the expanse by building obstructions. We measure distance by limiting it; we grow by pushing this limit as far as we can imagine.'[31] Christians considering that tense border-zone between word and spirit should recognize this secular meditation as describing the same frontier.

Music has emerged in modern Western society as one of the great sustainers of spiritual exploration, as well as one of the great ambassadors of Christianity to the wider world. There is a completeness or givenness about a musical composition, well captured in a passing remark of the formidable Anglican theologian Bishop Charles Gore (1853–1932). After emerging from a concert performance of one of Bach's Brandenburg Concertos, Gore was heard gruffly to observe, 'If that is true, everything must be all right' – which seems to me rather an improvement on Mother Julian's 'All shall be well, and all manner of thing shall be well'.[32] Anglicans have good reason to point complacently to their development and protection of Choral Evensong in cathedrals after the Reformation. Thomas Cranmer's Prayer Book service, put to musical uses of which he would undoubtedly have disapproved, has become one of the principal present-day vehicles of devotion for many who cannot accept forms of words which contain the orthodox propositions of Christianity; such attenders may still discover and explore their Christian identity through music, and in fact they have been attending the Anglican cathedrals and greater churches of England in ever larger numbers through the first decade of this century.

Music has been the colour and often the backbone of the liturgy through most of Christian history: policing that frontier-zone between eternity and the fragility of human words. Many of its practitioners, following Ambrose of Milan (above, pp. 93–4), have seen it as effectively a form of regulated celestial silence, banishing any rival noise. Liturgical music has reached its greatest intricacy in the Western liturgical tradition, which took its own direction out of the inheritance of chant; up to the fourteenth century, this was largely common to both the West and Byzantium.[33] From that great parting of the ways onwards, the centre of the Western musical tradition in liturgy has been the setting of the Mass. Precisely because the words of the Proper, the unchangeable parts of the service, are so familiar to Catholic priest and people, the composer, performer and listener enjoy the maximum freedom to soar away from words in the music. That is precisely why those sensitive musicians Huldrych Zwingli and John Calvin brusquely banned such distractions from the hearing of words, but the mood of disapproval can be traced back to Erasmus, and it was as characteristic of reforming papal Catholicism as of Archbishop Cranmer, until routed by the Counter-Reformation.[34] One can have some sympathy with the austerity of the Reformers when dealing with some eighteenth-century European Mass settings, which exhibit infuriatingly operatic and deeply inappropriate settings of that congregational plea for peace in the Agnus Dei, 'Dona nobis pacem'. Wolfgang Amadeus Mozart (1756–91) is a prime offender in this respect. There is a decorum to be observed in sacred music which such solecisms violate; I will not point to more modern instances in which that decorum has been forgotten.[35]

Music is so personal an enthusiasm that one can only be arbitrary in pointing out some of the ways in which the supposedly godless twentieth and twenty-first centuries have used it to reach beyond the borders between belief and unbelief. I offer merely one extraordinary work by Sir Michael Tippett (1905–98), an agnostic English composer who was drawn by his fascination with transcendence to set to music that extraordinary fragment of Western spirituality which we have already encountered, Augustine's conversation with his mother Monica in the garden at Ostia (Confessions 9.10), a passage which had fascinated the composer since his schooldays.[36] Tippett said that he conceived of The Vision of Saint Augustine as describing the door of heaven opening and closing. One of the most intricately layered works of a composer who delighted in intricacy, and often unwisely wrote his own libretti, it preserves its coherence by setting long sequences of Augustine's Latin text unaltered.

Underneath the soloist's narrative, the chorus repeatedly chant a hymn of Augustine's mentor Ambrose of Milan, 'Deus creator omnium', declaimed in Tippett's own recomposition of the chant of the Western Church. Ambrose's hymn suggests the certainties of Christian doctrine, but its foursquare appearance here always stirs a storm in the music, contending with Augustine's text. Tippett has grasped the importance of the fact that the culminating passage seeking an understanding of eternal joy is presented by Augustine as make-believe: 'suppose, we said', is the hinge of the vital sentence.[37] So in the alternating tranquillity and violence of the Vision, eternity contends with provisionality. Out of Augustine's Latin emerge extended choral passages of glossolalia, the most extended examples of which come from the word 'Alleluia'; as we have already observed, that is the highest music of the angels (above, p. 98). Timelessness is suggested by overlapping ostinato passages in percussion, piano and trumpets.

Then there are the all-important silences in the work. Silence is a vital shaping quality for all music, all speech, all sound. In Tippett's setting, it is first conjured around the subjunctive verb *sileant*, 'were they to be silent'. This rings repeatedly through Augustine's text, and Tippett's repetition of it causes the syllables '-*leant*' to rush in a choral crescendo out of complete silence – a reverse echo. Tippett may have noticed that the syllable thus left silent from *sileant* is '*si*': an 'if', the provisionality of the vision. The work reaches a thunderous climax in the moment when mother and son might have comprehended the eternal joy. Tippett creates a brief storm of anger in Augustine, conscious after his fleeting contact with paradise that the moment has passed. What follows is all supposition, a provisional idea wistfully imagined by mother and son. The vision ends after this rueful tranquillity with the first and only English text of the work, the chorus whispering the King James version of words in Philippians 3.13, 'I count not myself to have apprehended'. Then complete silence falls.

PATTERNS IN SCRIPTURE,
SILENCE AND SIN

My message in this book might charitably be seen as standing alongside the classic negative theologies of silence devised in the early Church: that apophatic approach to divinity which portrays what God is not, rather than what he is. Another way of viewing my report on silence within Christian history is as a necessary penitential work of stripping the altars, or, more cheerfully, the anticipatory clearance of the house before the party begins. I have certainly made many negative observations, not just through stories of institutional evasion, shame and forgetfulness, but by trying to show that silence itself has been constructed and reconstructed in the life and thought of the Church in ways which most of the writers in the library of Christian Scripture would not have expected or wanted. I have questioned many of the ways in which authority has evolved in the Church, and I have drawn attention to stories which suggest that the fixity of doctrine is not all it seems.

None of the more negative silences I have surveyed are unique to

Christianity: they are products of how human beings construct the world around them and negotiate their way through the embarrassments and opportunities created by our search for power and control, over others and over ourselves. Yet still the tidy-minded, particularly those who style themselves Christian traditionalists, often react to questioning both of dogma and of ecclesiastical structures like G. K. Chesterton's dog on the beach: they howl in perplexity and anger because they feel the patterns of their world to be unravelling. They would be better to follow the example of Holmes's dog, and recognize that there is nothing unfamiliar. These have been questions for Churches through two thousand years.

Apophatic Christianity or negative theology is a religion of spirit, of looking inwards. The Spirit may well find itself privileged over Scripture, which is a collection of words, even if they may be seen as inspired words. Reading Scripture emphasizes one human sense: sight; paying attention to silence involves a different sense, hearing. Wittgenstein's dictum was effortlessly anticipated by Isaac of Nineveh, the seventh-century theologian of awareness and wonder: 'Love silence above all things, because it brings you nearer to the fruit that the tongue cannot express . . . and then, from out of this silence something is born that leads to silence itself.'[38] This fruit might be discovered in the manner of the first Quakers, out of the silence of their meetings. It freed them to consider questions of authorship and formation in the biblical text, and numbered them among the first people to see through the biblical writers' unthinking acceptance that slavery as an institution was a permanent feature of the sublunary world.

At the very least, there is a tension in these two ways of approaching the sacred, through Spirit and Text. That is not to say that an apophatic Christianity could ever be detached from the Christian Bible. How could it be? It would be like denying one's parents. The relationship between parent and child is one that cannot be abrogated, though natural disasters or the man-made catastrophes of war and slavery have often done their best to do so. It is like no other relationship; it is not dependent on shared interests or opinions or even liking; it is just there – just so – a given. It is in the nature of such a profound, ineradicable relationship that it does not always betoken agreement. That is also the true meaning of 'canon'. There can be no

Christianity without the canon of Scripture, and the Christian life has characteristically demanded a searching and researching of it. The great gift of the Enlightenment to Christianity, contextual criticism of the text, has not sought to deny that demand, only to enrich it.

There are three very important themes on which my own experience has led me to see the majority of mood-music in the New Testament as just plain wrong: on homosexuality, anti-Semitism and slavery. In stating matters that bluntly, I am heartened by the example of the early Quakers, who feistily challenged what they saw as wrongly conceived views of the authority of Scripture, but did so in pamphlets and treatises oozing with scriptural texts. Looking further into the past, I observe how Martin Luther, the great prophet of *sola scriptura*, felt free, because of his fierce engagement with Scripture, to play fast and loose with its plain meaning and its canonical boundaries. He created loaded readings of key phrases in the Psalms when translating the text into German, sneered on occasion at the writing of James as 'an epistle of straw', scorned the Book of Esther and felt free to relegate a whole category of biblical books into a reserved category which he had no hesitation in terming Apocrypha.[39]

We can push back beyond Luther to find help from the man who formed his mature theology, Augustine of Hippo. Augustine, with his consuming interest in his Latin literary inheritance, his shaky Greek and his very selective knowledge of Greek philosophy, represents that age in the fourth and fifth centuries when eastern and western Mediterranean Christianity were already drifting apart. He hardly influenced future Greek theology at all, in contrast to his profound influence on the Latins.[40] Nevertheless, on one occasion Augustine did comment positively on a very important Eastern use of Scripture, which moves beyond the Augustinian West's active meditation in the *lectio divina* towards the practice of contemplation in the East. This was in the course of a famous letter on the Lord's Prayer which he addressed to Anicia Faltonia Proba, one of those serious-minded and fabulously wealthy ladies who were so important to Latin Christianity in the last years of the Western Empire.

Augustine reminded the Lady Proba of the practice of contemporary Egyptian ascetics who concentrated their contemplation through the use of rapid prayers 'thrown like javelins, so that the alert attention, which is necessary in prayer, does not fade and grow heavy during long-drawn-out periods of time'. These sudden, savage launches of short prayers against Satan the Great Distractor have come to be known as 'arrow prayers', as that passage of Augustine is often taken as referring to arrows. It does not: Augustine speaks of the throwing of javelins.[41] Nowadays the javelin evokes hearty school sports days or the Olympics on television rather than the horrors of war: bar-lovers will be equally familiar with the javelin's cheerful miniature cousin, the dart. For Augustine, the javelin or dart was a weapon of death, far more basic than the bow and arrow. We lose the brute phys-icality of his metaphor if we shift from the original meaning.

Augustine the inveterate Westerner is describing here a form of prayer which much later blossomed within hesychasm in the Greek East, particularly in the form of the Jesus Prayer (above, p. 112). He does not actually mention the use of Scripture in his invocation of 'javelin prayer'. That connection is made by that great and now once more happily familiar Greek contemplative Evagrius Ponticus, one of Augustine's contemporaries. Evagrius recalls that greatest moment of Jesus's silences which was also the greatest contest in his ministry before his final contest on the Cross: his Temptations in the Wilder-ness. Evagrius uses the same metaphor of the javelin or dart as Augustine before him, reminding his readers that Jesus 'passed on to us what he did when tempted by Satan. In the moment of struggle, when the demons attack us with pricks and darts, we must answer them with a verse from Holy Scripture.'[42] Jesus ended Satan's chatter with deadly thrusts from the text of the Tanakh; the contemplative should follow his example.

The arrow prayer or javelin prayer should not be equated with that nervous tic of Evangelical Protestant Christianity, the proof text from Scripture, which seeks to deal with everyday situations as if the Bible were a collection of instructions in a computer manual fixed for all time. Thomas Fudge's dismissal of such misuse of Scripture is worth savouring: 'A text without a context is a pretext for a proof text.'[43] That is not the point of the javelin prayer. As meditation gives way to contemplation, and perhaps also before that, the ground bass in a Christian context will still be the Christian's consciousness of Scrip-ture, shooting out bursts of words like lava from a queasily dormant volcano. In other approaches to the silence of the divine, in different great religious traditions of the world, other sacred texts will bear the same function: to be parents of those countless millions who have been formed in their images. All of them fire into the silent ecumenism which approaches the divine.[44]

Any negative theology has to take into account the positive reality of sin, which ordinary observation seems to suggest is one of the distinctive characteristics of the human race, along with humanity's sense of wonder and its capacity for laughter. It is worth recalling Donald MacKinnon's reflections on the profound sin which came from deliberate deception, built into the career of a theologian as celebrated as Paul Tillich once was (above, p. 202). Tillich's mendacious silence demanded exposure, in words; and words are commonly the way to reveal sin for what it is. Can a negative theology or a theology of silence carry a comparable burden in fighting evil in human society? The example of the Quakers, activists and contemplatives alike, might suggest that it can. Behind them are the ghosts of the Desert Fathers, helping to rebuild the torn fabric of Egyptian society, and behind them are spirits which fade smilingly behind the text of the Bible, as far back as Diogenes of Sinope, squatting in his wine-jar, and telling Alexander, the latest aspirant master of the world, to step out of his sunlight. The task of combating the sin of the world is for humanity, not humanity's creator. If silence has no contending opposite, then neither has divinity. Least of all is the polar opposite of divinity the power of evil. That proposition is the most respectable reason why Catholic Christianity set its face against Manichaean dualism; but negative theology points to the same message.

In the end, I hope to have offered my readers natural theology as required by Adam, Lord Gifford for his lecture series. Among the many silences both creditable and discreditable which we have explored is the assertion, heard in Sebastian Franck, John Everard or Samuel Fisher, that the inner light is the prime path to the divine, as much as any revelation offered by the 'paper Pope'. That should not stop Christians finding what they seek in the texts that prompt their glimpses of Jesus Christ. Let us stay with Donald MacKinnon, wrestling with the ultimate failure of Paul Tillich as a moral human being, and broodingly conscious of the vile parody of Golgotha which the

Nazi regime had created in the mid-twentieth century. After that dismal contemplation, MacKinnon turns his eye on Jesus's vital decision, made in solitude in the Wilderness, to reject the temptation to cast himself from the pinnacle of the Temple, the culmination of all his tempations in Luke's Gospel – that same story which we have seen so galvanizing contemplatives from Evagrius to the present day.[45]

The point of Luke's tale is that Jesus rejects the quick fix of glory or death, the noisy proclamation of Good News in a jump from the pinnacle. In this, MacKinnon sees the Christ as accepting 'unbearable ambiguity', a 'refusal to accept the "either/or" of total emancipation from ambiguity'. He sees all human faith as depending on a 'hardly decipherable *mimēsis*' of Christ's faith in God, 'that is itself human expression of God's total fidelity to himself and his creation':

> And this faith of Christ we have most painfully to see as something that if we rest our hope upon it, and find in it the source of our flickering charity, we must affirm for what it was, and through the Resurrection, eternally is: response after the manner of God's being and of human need, no wilful wresting of an unambiguous triumph over circumstance that will, by its seeming transparency, satisfy our own conceit.[46]

MacKinnon's faith of flickering charity, unbearable ambiguity, beckons the seeker of faith towards a Resurrection silence. The silence in the aftermath of Golgotha has transcended the din of the triumphant. It may still be enough to nerve those immersed in it to return to the fight against all that is Satanic in creation. We began this long exploration with Margaret Atwood's observation that '[t]he living bird is not its labelled bones'. That is her amplification of what has gone before: 'What isn't there has a presence, like the absence of light'.[47] Over the course of this book, I hope that the reader may have been persuaded to appreciate the central importance for religious faith of this presence in absence: the divine wild-track.

Further Reading

This is designed to provide general introductory reading or classic works in English in the various sections of the book. Detailed reading on particular topics is cited in the notes relating to each chapter, including works in languages other than English, and is not necessarily repeated here; the same applies to books listed in the abbreviations at the head of the notes.

INTRODUCTORY

Always useful for reference on particular matters historical is F. L. Cross and E. A. Livingstone (eds), *The Oxford Dictionary of the Christian Church* (4th edn, Oxford, 2005). One attempt to cover the whole subject is D. MacCulloch, *A History of Christianity: The First Three Thousand Years* (London, 2009).

An extraordinary book through which to wander amid silences is M. Picard, *Die Welt des Schweigens* (Erlenbach/Zürich, 1948), translated by S. Godman as *The World of Silence* (London, 1952); it is the discursive voyage of a Platonically inclined Swiss Roman Catholic in the aftermath of Satanic Nazi noise. Sara Maitland, *A Book of Silence* (London, 2008) is a memorable book, combining autobiography with reflections on silences both sacred and secular. A different combination of the two, of considerable merit, is G. Prochnik, *In Pursuit of Silence: Listening for Meaning in a World of Noise* (New York, 2010). Equally fertile, including interesting discussions of religious silence (chs 8–9) and of constrained silence (ch. 6) is C. Kenny, *The Power of Silence: Silent Communication in Daily Life* (London, 2011).

For an excellent exploration from an anthropological perspective of various ways of communicating beyond conventional language, see E. T. Hall, *The Silent Language* (New York, 1973). A. Jaworski, *The Power of Silence: Social and Pragmatic Perspectives* (London and New Delhi, 1993) is informative, if rather more in the style of a sociological textbook. Case studies are assembled in Jaworski's edited collection of essays, *Multilingua*, 24, pts 1–2 (2005), and in D. Tannen and M. Saville-Troike, *Perspectives on Silence* (Norwood, NJ, 1985).

For general background on religion, W. James, *Varieties of Religious Experience: A Study in Human Nature*, Centenary Edition (London and New York, 2002) is still tremendously useful; the material on mysticism is entertaining as a tremendous effort of fair-mindedness from an author who made no bones about his own temperamental distance from it. L. Bouyer, *A History of Christian Spirituality* (3 vols, London, 1968–9) is a monumental survey. The Paulist Press 'Classics of Western Spirituality' series, with volumes now running into triple figures, is a user-friendly series of translations presenting a rich variety of Western spiritual writers.

Of an infinite number of books with a devotional purpose, a very good starting point would be K. Leech, *True Prayer: An Invitation to Christian Spirituality* (San Francisco, 1980). M. Laird, *A Sunlit Absence: Silence, Awareness and Contemplation* (Oxford, 2011) is also full of practical good sense, as is a book which was echoed in a widely popular BBC television documentary, C. Jamison, *Finding Sanctuary* (London, 2006); a concise Dominican perspective on contemplative prayer comes from lectures published as P. Murray OP, *In the Grip of Light: The Dark and Bright Journey of Christian Contemplation* (London, 2012). A contemporary solitary writing under a pseudonym provides a set of essays vigorously championing the centrality of silence to Christian practice: M. Ross, *Writing the Icon of the Heart: In Silence Beholding* (Oxford, 2011). A significant book by a Quaker theologian with a feminist perspective, reflecting in particular on the significance of divine silence, is R. Muers, *Keeping God's Silence: Towards a Theological Ethics of Communication* (London, 2004).

PART ONE: THE BIBLE

One could not do better for introductory commentary on the biblical text than J. Barton and J. Muddiman (eds), *The Oxford Bible Commentary* (Oxford, 2001). One classic introduction to the period of the Tanakh is H. Jagersma, *A History of Israel in the Old Testament Period* (London, 1982), translated from Jagersma's *Geschiedenis van Israël in het Oudtestamentische Tijdvak* (Kampen, 1979), and J. Barton, *Reading the Old Testament: Method in Biblical Study* (London, 1984) helps to clarify how the Bible relates to this history. S. E. Balentine, *The Hidden God: The Hiding of the Face of God in the Old Testament* (Oxford, 1983) is a very technical but very thorough treatment of that theme. C. Rowland, *The Open Heaven: A Study of Apocalyptic in Judaism and Early Christianity* (London, 1985), and C. Rowland, *Christian Origins: An Account of the Setting and Character of the Most Important Messianic Sect of Judaism* (London, 1982) lead the reader into what Christians have called the 'Inter-Testamental period'. M. Hengel, *Judaism and Hellenism: Studies in their Encounter in Palestine during the Early Hellenistic Period* (2 vols, London, 1974) is a masterly if austere survey of its subject, translated from M. Hengel, *Judentum und Hellenismus: Studien zu ihrer Begegnung unter besonderer Berücksichtigung Palästinas bis zur Mitte des 2 Jh.s v. Chr.* (2nd edn, Tübingen, 1973). C. M. Tuckett, *Reading the New Testament: Methods of Interpretation* (London, 1987) will orient the reader trying to understand that collection of literary genres, and no one seriously interested in the Gospel accounts of Jesus should fail to have to hand K. Aland (ed.), *Synopsis of the Four Gospels; Greek–English Edition of the Synopsis Quattuor Evangeliorum* (9th edn, Stuttgart, 1989), derived from the German original of 1964, K. Aland (ed.), *Synopsis quattuor Evangeliorum, locis parallelis Evangeliorum apocryphorum et patrum adhibitis*. G. Vermes, *Jesus the Jew* (London, 1973) and E. P. Sanders, *Jesus and Judaism* (London, 1985) will help make sense of the texts set out there.

PART TWO: THE TRIUMPH OF MONASTIC SILENCE

H. Chadwick, *The Early Church* (London, 1967) is still an excellent start on study of the first five centuries of Christianity, and could be followed at much greater length by W. H. C. Frend, *The Rise of Christianity* (London, 1984). To understand Christianity's Greek background, one should turn to O. Murray, *Early Greece* (rev. edn, London, 1992), or, for the wider picture, M. I. Finley, *The Ancient Greeks* (London, 1963). R. Mortley, *From Word to Silence* (2 vols, Bonn, 1986) is austere, but indispensable. A fine introduction to the Nag Hammadi material is J. D. Turner and A. McGuire (eds), *The Nag Hammadi Library after Fifty Years: Proceedings of the 1995 Society of Biblical Literature Commemoration* (Leiden, 1997), while the original texts are easy to encounter in J. M. Robinson and R. Smith (eds), *The Nag Hammadi Library in English* (3rd edn, Leiden, 1988). W. H. C. Frend, *Martyrdom and Persecution in the Early Church: A Study of a Conflict from the Maccabees to Donatus* (Oxford, 1965) introduces a theme competing with silence in the early Church.

There is much to be gained from the essays in W. Skudlarek (ed.), *The Continuing Quest for God: Monastic Spirituality in Tradition and Transition* (Collegeville, Minn., 1982). W. Harmless, *Desert Christians: An Introduction to the Literature of Early Monasticism* (Oxford, 2004) does precisely what it says on the tin, and does it superbly. T. Vivian and A. N. Athanassakis with R. A. Greer (eds), *The Life of Antony by Athanasius of Alexandria* (Kalamazoo, Mich., 2003) is an excellent edition of one of the most influential texts of late antiquity. Of the many fine editions of spiritual writers by Sister Benedicta Ward SLG, these are samples: B. Ward (ed.), *The Wisdom of the Desert Fathers: Systematic Sayings from the Anonymous Series of the* Apophthegmata Patrum (Oxford, 1975 and 1986); *The Sayings of the Desert Fathers: The Alphabetical Collection* (London, 1975). S. A. Ivanov, *Holy Fools in Byzantium and Beyond* (Oxford, 2006) will provide entertainment as well as instruction.

K. Parry (ed.), *The Blackwell Companion to Eastern Christianity* (Oxford, 2007) is a fine set of essays on Churches which have much to teach Western Christianity. A. M. Casiday (ed.), *Evagrius Ponticus* (London, 2006) is a flagship among efforts to rehabilitate this much-maligned spiritual writer, and equally valuable is L. Dysinger, *Psalmody and Prayer in the Writings of Evagrius Ponticus* (Oxford, 2005). We are rediscovering the riches of anti-Chalcedonian Christianity just as those ancient Churches are facing their worst ever crisis of survival in their homelands. S. Coakley and C. M. Stang (eds), *Re-thinking Diony-sius the Areopagite* (Chichester, 2009) is a useful place to start in understanding a much more elusive figure of both Eastern and Western spirituality. P. Hagman, *The Asceticism of Isaac of Nineveh* (Oxford, 2010) is one of the first large-scale scholarly treatments of Isaac in English.

D. Turner, *The Darkness of God: Negativity in Christian Mysticism* (Cambridge, 1995) is an exhilarating tour of how the Western mystical tradition took its cue from Dionysius, but still managed to found itself in Augustine; it takes the spiritual tourist down to the time of St John of the Cross. B. Stock, *After Augustine: The Meditative Reader and the Text* (Philadelphia, 2001), treating the medieval Western tradition of *lectio divina*, is one of those rare books that would have benefited from expansion, but the work of M. Carruthers also brilliantly brings back to life the context and practice of *lectio divina*; to choose from many riches, a start might be made with her *The Craft of Thought: Meditation, Rhetoric, and the Making of Images, 400–1200* (Cambridge, 1998). S. G. Bruce, *Silence and Sign Language in Medieval Monasticism: The Cluniac Tradition c. 900–1200* (Cambridge, 2007) is the model of everything that a monograph should be. A deeply engaged and engaging account of the last days of traditional Carthusian life in Parkminster, a twentieth-century English Charterhouse, is N. Klein Maguire, *An Infinity of Little Hours: Five Young Men and their Trial of Faith in the Western World's Most Austere Monastic Order* (New York, 2006).

PART THREE: SILENCE THROUGH THREE REFORMATIONS

P. Brown, *The Rise of Western Christendom: Triumph and Diversity AD 200–1000* (Oxford, 1997) will provide much wisdom on the period which encompassed the Iconoclastic Controversy, and K. Ware, *The Orthodox Church* (London, 1994) provides a reliable guide from a bishop of that tradition firmly grounded in Enlightenment scholarship. C. Barber, *Figure and Likeness: On the Limits of Representation in Byzantine Iconoclasm* (Princeton, 2002) is a perceptive study. Some may find N. J. Chumley, *Mysteries of the Jesus Prayer:*

Experiencing the Presence of God and a Pilgrimage to the Heart of an Ancient Spirituality (New York, 2010) overly chatty and personal, reflecting its companion television series, but it is a well-informed guide to the past and present of the subject.

R. W. Southern, *Western Society and the Church in the Middle Ages* (London, 1970) could be read as a starter on the Western Church and the Gregorian reforms, while the Gregorian Church's development of definitions of heresy is fascinatingly re-examined in R. I. Moore, *The War on Heresy: Faith and Power in Medieval Europe* (London, 2012). Desiderius Erasmus can be met through the classic J. Huizinga, *Erasmus of Rotterdam* (London, 1952), a translation of the Dutch original of 1924, and L.-E. Halkin, *Erasmus: A Critical Biography* (Oxford, 1993).

D. MacCulloch, *Reformation: Europe's House Divided 1490–1700* (London, 2003) seeks to introduce the third Reformation and Counter-Reformation across the whole continent and beyond. C. Garside Jr, *Zwingli and the Arts* (New Haven and London, 1966) helpfully clarifies Zwingli's distinctive attitude to liturgical silence. G. H. Williams, *The Radical Reformation* (original edn 1962; 3rd edn, Sixteenth Century Essays and Studies, 15, 2000) is an indispensable mine of information and comment, and in later editions has ridden back considerably from Williams's original analytical categories, which were not altogether helpful. A. Bradstock, *Radical Religion in Cromwell's England* (London, 2011) provides a way into subsequent crucial developments. A fine recent treatment of Quakerism in extracts from the writings of Quakers over four centuries, with commentary, is G. Durham (ed.), *The Spirit of the Quakers* (New Haven and London, 2010). A. Weber, *Teresa of Avila and the Rhetoric of Femininity* (Princeton and London, 1990) presents a fresh view of one of the great mystics of the Christian tradition, while a different perspective on her is given by one of the modern masters of spiritual exploration, R. Williams, *Teresa of Avila* (London, 2003). M. Furlong, *Merton: A Biography* (London, 1980), chs. 8–13, gives a good picture of Tridentine Trappist life, while R. Parish, *Catholic Particularity in Seventeenth-century French Writing: 'Christianity is Strange'* (Oxford, 2011) sensitively provides the wider background.

PART FOUR: REACHING BEHIND NOISE IN
CHRISTIAN HISTORY

A very useful collection of essays is S. Radstone and B. Schwarz (eds), *Memory: Histories, Theories, Debates* (New York, 2010): the introduction by the editors (pp. 1–9) is a good orientation for what follows, including case studies, and not too heavy a dose of post-modern theory, mercifully not presented as an overarching system. D. Cupitt, *The Sea of Faith: Christianity in Change* (London, 1984) cuts a different swathe through Enlightenment Christianity in narrative form.

On particular themes, P. Zagorin, *Ways of Lying: Dissimulation, Persecution, and Conformity in Early Modern Europe* (Cambridge, Mass., and London, 1990) introduces debate on Nicodemism, while A. Hamilton, *The Family of Love* (Cambridge, 1981) is the starting point for this theme, and can profitably be read in conjunction with B. J. Kaplan, *Divided by Faith: Religious Conflict and the Practice of Toleration in Early Modern Europe* (Cambridge, Mass., and London, 2007). I have avoided including articles in this bibliography, but the discussion in D. Hilliard, 'UnEnglish and Unmanly: Anglo-Catholicism and Homosexuality', *Victorian Studies*, 25 (1982), 181–210, has not so far been bettered at book length. J. A. Harrill, *Slaves in the New Testament: Literary, Social and Moral Dimensions* (Minneapolis, 2006) is gritty and sensible, and has a wider reference than its title suggests.

J. Micklethwait and A. Wooldridge, *God is Back: How the Global Rise of Faith is Changing the World* (London, 2009) looks at the new and sometimes alarming shapes which are emerging in Christianity across continents. A rich collection of reflections on silence in modern Christianity with a particular eye on modern experience is in O. Davies and D. Turner (eds), *Silence and the Word: Negative Theology and Incarnation* (Cambridge, 2002). M. Furlong, *Merton: A Biography* (London, 1980) is one of the best of countless studies of one of the most significant and dynamically progressive contemplative lives of the twentieth century. One of the most important modern Christian whistle-blowers can be encountered in H. Chertok, *He Also Spoke as a Jew: The Life of the Reverend James Parkes* (London and

Portland, Ore., 2006). R. Harries, *After the Evil: Christianity and Judaism in the Shadow of the Holocaust* (Oxford, 2003) effectively positions the role of silence in post-Holocaust Christianity in his discussion of a wider realignment of Christianity and Judaism. M. D. Jordan, *The Silence of Sodom: Homosexuality in Modern Catholicism* (Chicago and London, 2000) usefully enters the tangle of contradictions in the relationship of the modern Roman Catholic hierarchy and homosexuality.

Notes

ABBREVIATIONS

Bruce, *Silence and Sign Language in Medieval Monasticism*

S. G. Bruce, *Silence and Sign Language in Medieval Monasticism: The Cluniac Tradition c. 900–1200* (Cambridge, 2007)

Harmless, *Desert Christians*

W. Harmless, *Desert Christians: An Introduction to the Literature of Early Monasticism* (Oxford, 2004)

HTR — *Harvard Theological Review*

JEH — *Journal of Ecclesiastical History*

JRH — *Journal of Religious History*

JTS — *Journal of Theological Studies*

Luther's Works

J. Pelikan and H. T. Lehmann (eds), *Luther's Works* (55 vols and companion vol., Philadelphia and St Louis, 1958–86)

MacCulloch, *A History of Christianity*

D. MacCulloch, *A History of Christianity: The First Three Thousand Years* (London, 2009)

MacCulloch, *Reformation: Europe's House Divided*

D. MacCulloch, *Reformation: Europe's House Divided 1490–1700* (London, 2003)

Mortley, *From Word to Silence*

R. Mortley, *From Word to Silence* (2 vols., Bonn, 1986)

NPNF — *Nicene and Post-Nicene Fathers*

PG	*Patrologia Graeca*
PL	*Patrologia Latina*
Robinson and Smith (eds), *The Nag Hammadi Library in English*	J. M. Robinson and R. Smith (eds), *The Nag Hammadi Library in English* (3rd edn, Leiden, 1988)
RSTC	A. W. Pollard and G. R. Redgrave, rev. W. A. Jackson and F. S. Ferguson and completed by K. F. Pantzer, *A Short-Title Catalogue of Books Printed in England, Scotland, and Ireland and of English Books Printed Abroad before the Year 1640* (3 vols, London, 1976–91)
SCH	*Studies in Church History*
SCJ	*Sixteenth Century Journal*
Stevenson (ed.), rev. Frend, *Creeds, Councils and Controversies*	J. Stevenson (ed.), rev. W. H. C. Frend, *Creeds, Councils and Controversies: Documents Illustrating the History of the Church* AD 337–461 (London, 1989)
Stevenson (ed.), rev. Frend, *New Eusebius*	J. Stevenson (ed.), rev. W. H. C. Frend, *A New Eusebius: Documents Illustrating the History of the Church to* AD 337 (London, 1987)
TRHS	*Transactions of the Royal Historical Society*
WA	D. *Martin Luthers Werke* (Weimar, 1883–) [*Weimarer Ausgabe*]
Wing	D. G. Wing (ed.), *Short-Title Catalogue of Books Printed in England, Scotland, Ireland, Wales, and British America, and of English Books Printed in Other Countries, 1641–1700* (4 vols, New York, 2nd edn, 1972–98)

THE BIBLE
Books of the Tanakh

1 Chron.	1 Chronicles
Deut.	Deuteronomy
Eccles.	Ecclesiastes
Exod.	Exodus
Ezek.	Ezekiel
Gen.	Genesis
Hab.	Habakkuk
Hag.	Haggai
Isa.	Isaiah
Jer.	Jeremiah
Judg.	Judges
Lam.	Lamentations
Lev.	Leviticus
Mic.	Micah
Num.	Numbers
Prov.	Proverbs
Ps. (pl. Pss)	Psalms
1 Sam.	1 Samuel
2 Sam.	2 Samuel
Zech.	Zechariah
Zeph.	Zephaniah

Books of the Apocrypha

2 Bar.	2 Baruch
2 Esd.	2 Esdras
Wisd. of Sol.	Wisdom of Solomon (= Wisdom)

The New Testament

Acts	Acts of the Apostles
Col.	Colossians
1 Cor.	1 Corinthians
2 Cor.	2 Corinthians

Eph.	Ephesians
Gal.	Galatians
Heb.	Hebrews
John	John (Gospel)
1 John	1 John (Epistle)
Matt.	Matthew
1 Pet.	1 Peter
2 Pet.	2 Peter
Phil.	Philippians
Rev.	Revelation (= Apocalypse)
Rom.	Romans
1 Thess.	1 Thessalonians
2 Thess.	2 Thessalonians
1 Tim.	1 Timothy

INTRODUCTION:
THE WITNESS OF HOLMES'S DOG

1. 'Silver Blaze', in A. Conan Doyle, *Sherlock Holmes … the Complete Short Stories* (London, 1928), 331.
2. 'The Oracle of the Dog', in G. K. Chesterton, *The Father Brown Stories* (London, 1929), 643.
3. M. Atwood, *The Blind Assassin* (London, 2000), 395.
4. Chesterton, 'The Oracle of the Dog', 648. For an acerbic comment on the myth of this supposed quotation, see D. Johnson, 'Overrated: Umberto Eco', *Standpoint* (March 2012).
5. W. James, *Varieties of Religious Experience: A Study in Human Nature*, Centenary Edition (London and New York, 2002). For James's discussion on the characteristics of mysticism, see ibid., lectures 16 and 17 (pp. 294–332).
6. The paradox is perceptively discussed in J. G. Finlayson, 'On Not Being Silent in the Darkness: Adorno's Singular Apophaticism', *HTR* 105 (2012), 1–32, especially at pp. 9–10, with reference to Adorno's critique of Wittgenstein, *Tractatus Logico-Philosophicus*, proposition 7: 'What we cannot speak about, we must pass over in silence.'
7. A. Momigliano, *The Classical Foundations of Modern Historiography* (Berkeley and Los Angeles, 1990), 136–7 (I am indebted to Sam Baddeley for pointing me towards that observation). The characterization of Momigliano is to be found in his obituary by O. Murray, in *Journal of Roman Studies*, 77 (1987), p. xi.

8. In his pioneering essay on noise pollution, Theodor Lessing pointed to the Christian proselytizing programme announced by the omnipresence of church bells: T. Lessing, 'Ueber den Lärm', *Nord und Süd*, 97 (April 1901), 71–84, at pp. 79–80, quoted in L. Baron, 'Noise and Degeneration: Theodor Lessing's Crusade for Quiet', *Journal of Contemporary History*, 17 (1982), 165–78, at p. 166.

9. 1 Cor. 13.1–3.

I. SILENCE IN CHRISTIAN PREHISTORY: THE TANAKH

1. A wise and helpful commentary on method in biblical encounters is J. Barton, *Reading the Old Testament: Method in Biblical Study* (London, 1984), particularly pp. 4–6.

2. MacCulloch, *A History of Christianity*.

3. Reliable and sensible commentary on biblical dating will be found throughout the articles in J. Barton and J. Muddiman (eds), *The Oxford Bible Commentary* (Oxford, 2001), starting with p. 6.

4. A. Cruden, *A Complete Concordance to the Holy Scriptures of the Old and New Testament: in two parts. Containing, I. The Appellative or Common Words in so full and large a manner, that any Verse may be readily found by looking for any material Word in it ... To which is added a concordance to the Books, called Apocrypha ...* (London, 1738), pt i, s.v. 'Silence'.

5. W. McKane, *A Critical and Exegetical Commentary on Jeremiah* (2 vols, Edinburgh, 1986), vol. 1, p. 190.

6. Amos 8.2–3. H. W. Wolff, *Joel and Amos* (Philadelphia, 1977), 317, 320, translates v. 3 with an exclamatory imperative demanding strictest silence, otherwise death itself may hear the sounds of mourning and renew his work: 'On that day (utterance of the Lord Yahweh) there will be many corpses. They will be cast everywhere. Hush!'

7. Isa. 47.5. 'Deutero' is simply the Greek preface-word meaning 'second', a usage to be found also in discussion of the Bible in the conventional Greek name 'Deuteronomy' used for the book of the 'second Law' in the first five books of the Tanakh (the Pentateuch). Sometimes the term is also used for certain major epistles in the New Testament attributed to Paul of Tarsus but probably not actually written by him: Colossians, Ephesians and 2 Thessalonians: the 'Deuteropauline' epistles. 'Deuterocanonical books' are those books not present in the Tanakh but included in the

Roman Catholic version of the Old Testament, otherwise known by Protestants as the Apocrypha.

8. Ps. 31.17–18. RSV's 'the wicked go dumbfounded to Sheol' is better read with the KJB: 'and let them be silent in the grave'. Cf. e.g. P. C. Craigie with M. E. Tate (eds), *Word Biblical Commentary 19: Psalms 1–50* (2nd edn, Dallas, 2004), 257, 262.

9. Ps. 115.4–5, 8. A. Weiser, *The Psalms: A Commentary* (London, 1962), 714–16, is a good discussion of this cultic psalm, and rounds up the Tanakh's generous cluster of similar references to the powerlessness of other gods, probably drawing on liturgical tradition, Deut. 4.18, 1 Sam. 12.21; Hab. 2.18 f; Jer. 10.3 f; Jer. 16.19 f; Isa. 40.19 f; 44.9 f; Pss 96.5, 135.15 f. Interestingly, the Apocryphal Wisd. of Sol. 15.15, a text probably from Alexandria and of the later first century CE, repeats the topos on idols in very traditional terms, but omits any reference to the mouths of idols or their dumbness. That might relate to the growing devotional discussion in Judaism and embryonic Christianity of the silence of God; on that, see above, pp. 25–9.

10. Ps. 115.17–18.

11. Isa. 35.5–7. Richard Coggins comments that these reversals are 'the restoration of the community to full humanity': Barton and Muddiman (eds), *Oxford Bible Commentary*, 462.

12. See P. W. van der Horst, 'Silent Prayer in Antiquity', *Numen*, 4 (1994), 1–25, esp. pp. 1, 6–9.

13. Ps. 30.8–9.

14. P. Joyce, *Ezekiel: A Commentary*, Library of Hebrew Bible/Old Testament Studies, 482 (New York and London, 2007), 82–3, following up the line first suggested in R. R. Wilson, 'An Interpretation of Ezekiel's Dumbness', *Vetus Testamentum*, 22 (1972), 91–104, esp. at pp. 96–8, and elaborated in G. Y. Glazov, *The Bridling of the Tongue and the Opening of the Mouth in Biblical Prophecy* (Sheffield, 2001), 24–74, 335. I find this much more plausible than the explanation of the puzzle advanced by J. Galambush in Barton and Muddiman (eds), *Oxford Bible Commentary*, 539, who suggests that it was a way of justifying the innovation of producing prophecies in writing, to win over those who regarded prophecy primarily as an oral genre.

15. Judg. 18.7; 1 Chron. 4.39–40: the words for peaceful and quiet are respectively šōqêṭ and ûšelêwâ.

16. Deut. 12.9. See also the association of the idea of peace with the birth of Solomon the builder of the Temple, 1 Chron. 22.9: 'Behold, a son shall

be born to you [David]; he shall be a man of peace. I will give him peace from all his enemies round about; for his name shall be Solomon, and I will give peace and quiet [KJB quietness] to Israel in his days.'

17. Isa. 14.7: 'at rest [*nāḥâ*] and quiet [*šāqeṭâ*]'.

18. Gen. 2.16–19.

19. C. Westermann, *Genesis 1–11: A Commentary* (London, 1984), 111. G. F. Hasel, 'The Significance of the Cosmology in Genesis I in Relation to Ancient Near Eastern Parallels', *Andrews University Seminary Studies*, 10 (1972), 1–20, esp. pp. 9–12, while usefully describing the relationship of the Priestly Creation account to Egyptian sources, seems to display rather too much conservative Evangelical anxiety to distance it from their magical verbal systems.

20. Gen. 1.20–22: cf. Westermann, *Genesis 1–11*, 134.

21. Gen. 2.2–3.

22. 1 Kings 22.19–23.

23. See Ps. 82, well discussed in S. L. Terrien, *The Psalms: Strophic Structure and Theological Commentary* (Grand Rapids, Mich., 2003), 586–91; and cf. Job 1–2; Isa. 6.1.

24. e.g. 2 Sam. 22.8–9: 'Then the earth reeled and rocked; the foundations of the heavens trembled and quaked, because he was angry. Smoke went up from his nostrils, and devouring fire from his mouth . . .' Cf. the similar scene in Hab. 3.3–6, which carries the interesting comment, 'His ways were as of old.'

25. Num. 22.24–40. M. Noth, *Numbers: A Commentary* (London, 1968), 171–2, particularly points to the parallel in Gen. 16.7–13.

26. 1 Kings 19:12; C. F. Burney, *Notes on the Hebrew Text of the Book of Kings* (Oxford, 1903), 231. A useful summary discussion of the episode is C. Kenny, *The Power of Silence: Silent Communication in Daily Life* (London, 2011), 237–44.

27. J. Lust, 'A Gentle Breeze or a Roaring Thunderous Sound? Elijah at Horeb; I Kings XIX.12', *Vetus Testamentum*, 25 (1975), 110–15. See the discussion in D. J. A. Clines, *Job 1–20* (Dallas, 1989), 112, of the parallel quasi-theophany to Eliphaz at Job 4.15–16.

28. S. E. Balentine, *The Hidden God: The Hiding of the Face of God in the Old Testament* (Oxford, 1983), ch. 2, esp. pp. 36, 124, 158–60.

29. Ibid., 45.

30. Mic. 3:4. Cf. also Pss. 28.1, 35.22, 83.1; Balentine, *The Hidden God*, 134–9, 145, 150–57.

31. Job 29.7–10, 21–2.

32. Exod. 15.16; for Mesopotamian precedents as well as echoes in the Tanakh, see N. M. Waldman, 'A Comparative Note on Exodus 15.14–16', *Jewish Quarterly Review*, 66 (1976), 189–92.

33. Ps. 37.7. On 'Wisdom' literature, see the thorough and informative treatment in R. B. Y. Scott, *The Way of Wisdom in the Old Testament* (New York, 1971). Eric Heaton, former Dean of Christ Church Oxford, was fond of saying that this strand of the Tanakh was about 'the ability to cope'.

34. Hab. 2.18–20. Cf. the echo of this passage's universal theme in Zech. 2.13, a text of a century later, in the Persian period after the fall of Jerusalem, and in another text almost certainly later than Habakkuk, Zeph. 1.7. F. I. Andersen, *Habakkuk: A New Translation with Introduction and Commentary* (New York, 2001), 256, notes that there is little in Habakkuk's writings to indicate any close link to the formal cult in Jerusalem: hence perhaps the originality of his concept of the universality of Yahweh.

35. 1 Sam. 1.9–17.

36. There is good discussion of the effect of the story on Judaism and Christianity in van der Horst, 'Silent Prayer in Antiquity', 12–14.

37. As is observed by J. Goldingay and D. Payne, *A Critical and Exegetical Commentary on Isaiah 40–55* (London, 2006), 'Isaiah 52.13–53.12 has had a more colourful afterlife than most of the OT.'

38. Isa. 53.7.

39. Jer. 11.19.

40. K. Baltzer, *Deutero-Isaiah: A Commentary on Isaiah 40–55* (Minneapolis, 2001), 414.

41. Ps. 39.1–3, 9. Weiser, *The Psalms*, 328, emphasizes the strangeness and remoteness from tradition of this psalm and comments that that singer 'provides us with a deep insight into the struggles of his soul in a way almost unique in the Psalter'.

42. Eccles. 12.3–13; for useful comment, Balentine, *The Hidden God*, 162, 167–70.

43. Goldingay and Payne, *A Critical and Exegetical Commentary on Isaiah 40–55*, 284–6, is a useful summary discussion of the relationship of Messianic ideas to this passage.

44. D. S. Russell, *The Method and Message of Jewish Apocalyptic* (London, 1960) is still an excellent introduction to this literature.

45. Mortley, *From Word to Silence*, vol. 1, p. 39.

46. Plato, *Republic* 509b, trans. and ed. P. Shorey, *Plato: The Republic* (2 vols, Cambridge, Mass., 1969), vol. 2, pp. 107–8; Plato, *Timaeus* 28c,

trans. and ed. R. G. Bury, *Plato VII: Timaeus, Critias, Cleitophon, Men-exenus, Epistles* (Cambridge, Mass., 1929), 50–51.

47. G. Stroumsa, 'A Nameless God: Judaeo-Christian and Gnostic "Theologies of the Name"', in P. J. Tomson and D. Lambers-Petry (eds), *The Image of the Judaeo-Christians in Ancient Jewish and Christian Literature* (Tübingen, 2003), 230–43, esp. pp. 231–4.

48. C. Rowland, *The Open Heaven: A Study of Apocalyptic in Judaism and Early Christianity* (London, 1982), 78–87, 94, 182, 274–5.

49. Philo, *On the Cherubim*, 27–28 (sect. IX), trans. and ed. F. H. Colson and G. H. Whitaker, *Philo II: On the Cherubim; The Sacrifices of Abel and Cain; The Worse attacks the Better; On the Posterity and Exile of Cain: On the Giants* (London and New York, 1929), 24–5.

50. Plato, *Timaeus* 34b, trans. and ed. Bury, *Plato VII*, 64–5.

51. Helpful discussion of Philo's relationship to Plato can be found in Mortley, *From Word to Silence*, vol. 1, pp. 39, 103–5, 120, 124; vol. 2, p. 243. M. Hengel, *Judaism and Hellenism: Studies in their Encounter in Palestine during the Early Hellenistic Period* (2 vols, London, 1974), vol. 1, pp. 210–18, illuminatingly places developments in Jewish religion from the third century BCE to the earliest formation of Christianity in the context of changes in Hellenistic religion more generally.

52. Jubilees 2.16–17, 31 (H. F. D. Sparks (ed.), *The Apocryphal Old Testament* (Oxford, 1984), 16), and cf. Jubilees 50 (Sparks (ed.), *Apocryphal Old Testament*, 138). See Rowland, *The Open Heaven*, 121.

53. 2 Esd. 7.29–33 (this is part of the apocalyptic section of 2 Esdras and is also known as 4 Ezra). Certain textual elements in this passage are contested and altered in detail in the present Christian sources because of their bearing on the significance of Jesus Christ.

54. Cf. 2 Bar. (the Syriac Apocalypse of Baruch) 3.7–8 (Sparks (ed.), *Apocryphal Old Testament*, 842) and the *Biblical Antiquities* of pseudo-Philo of Alexandria 60.2, ed. M. R. James (London, 1917), 232, works roughly contemporary with 2 Esdras. Sparks (ed.), *Apocryphal Old Testament*, 838, argues plausibly against these works being dependent on 2 Esdras, seeing them rather as representative of widespread religious opinion in the late first century CE.

2. THE EARLIEST CHRISTIAN SILENCES: THE NEW TESTAMENT

1. J. Hollander , 'Psalms', in D. Rosenberg (ed.), *Congregation: Contemporary Writers Read the Jewish Bible* (New York, 1987), repr. in D. Jasper,

S. Prickett and A. Haas (eds), *The Bible and Literature: A Reader* (Oxford, 1999), 176–9, at p. 176.

2. Frank Kermode, *The Genesis of Secrecy: On the Interpretation of Narrative* (Cambridge, Mass., 1979), 18. A very useful discussion of the consequences and problems for modern homiletics is M. J. Salmon, *Preaching without Contempt: Overcoming Unintended Anti-Judaism* (Minneapolis, 2006): I am grateful to Derek Jay for drawing my attention to this work.

3. Rom. 16.25–6. For complications in the interpretation of this passage, obvious in Origen and in other theologians wanting to emphasize the ongoing mystery of God against Paul's theme of the end of mystery, see Mortley, *From Word to Silence*, vol. 2, pp. 64–5.

4. G. Vermes, *Christian Beginnings: From Nazareth to Nicaea, AD 30–325* (London, 2012), 163–4, notes that the earliest known such usages are in the second Epistle of Clement of Rome, of *c.* 140 CE.

5. It must be noted that 'its present form' includes an interpolated phrase, 'and the Father', *filioque*, of later date than the fourth century and of Western origin, which has never been accepted by the Churches of the East.

6. I say more about this in MacCulloch, *A History of Christianity*, 77–8. A useful introductory compilation of viewpoints is W. Telford (ed.), *The Interpretation of Mark* (London, 1985); note particularly Siegfried Schulz's remark at p. 158: '[Mark's] central significance [among the Evangelists] lies in the fact that he was the first and the only one to write a Gospel.'

7. Luke 1.5–80.

8. Origen, *Homilies on Luke* 5.1, quoted in Mortley, *From Word to Silence*, vol. 2, p. 63. For a discussion of Clement of Alexandria's enlargement of this standard early Christian interpretation of the story of Zechariah, to incorporate the increasing Christian interest in negative theology at the end of the second century CE, see ibid., 37.

9. Jesus does not reply when mocked and beaten at Matt. 26.67–8, Mark 14.65 and Luke 22.63–5. He does not answer the Chief Priests when he is accused of saying that he will destroy the Temple, Matt. 26.63 and Mark 14.61. Matt. 27.12–14 is an expansion of Mark 15.3–5: Jesus before Pilate. Luke 23.6–12 is an independent passage about Jesus and Herod.

10. Mark 15.34; Matt. 27.46–7; Luke 23.46.

11. Ps. 69.21; cf. Matt. 27.48; Mark 15.36; Luke 23.36; John 19.29.

12. S. Gillingham, *Psalms through the Centuries I* (Oxford, 2008), 14. Gillingham also notes that Pss 22 and 69 as Psalms of lament and questioning

of God are rarely employed in the literature of another first-century Jewish sect, the Qumran community, even though they do commonly use other Psalms of lament; that suggests that in this respect, Jesus was branching out in a new direction. The Synoptic Gospels are so called because all three present the basic story of Jesus in a similar way, quite differently from John's narrative – so they 'see together', the root meaning of the Greek *synopsis*.

13. John 19.8–12: 'When Pilate heard these words, he was the more afraid; he entered the praetorium again and said to Jesus, "Where are you from?" But Jesus gave no answer. Pilate therefore said to him, "You will not speak to me? Do you not know that I have power to release you, and power to crucify you?" Jesus answered him, "You would have no power over me unless it had been given you from above; therefore he who delivered me to you has the greater sin." Upon this Pilate sought to release him . . .'

14. An apparent exception, John 8.1–2, Jesus's solitary night-long prayer on the Mount of Olives, is part of an anomalous semi-detached section of text, John 7.53–8.11. In its general resemblance to the Synoptic Gospel texts, it is in more than one respect the exception to prove the rule in John's Gospel. As René Kieffer comments of this fragment of text in J. Barton and J. Muddiman (eds), *The Oxford Bible Commentary* (Oxford, 2001), 999, '[T]he style reminds us of Luke', and Luke's Gospel text shares this interest in Jesus's solitude. A contrary strand on silence in John's narrative is his ultimately sympathetic treatment of the secret disciple Nicodemus, a Christian character who, as we shall discover in Ch. 7, has played a highly important role in Christian history.

15. Luke 22.61.

16. For early Syrian interest in Luke's Gospel for its prompts to asceticism, see above, p. 73.

17. Isa. 53.7.

18. F. F. Bruce, *The Acts of the Apostles: The Greek Text with Introduction and Commentary* (Grand Rapids, Mich., 1951), 193; on Isaiah in lectionaries, see J. Sawyer, *The Fifth Gospel: Isaiah in the History of Christianity* (Cambridge, 1996), 25.

19. Matt. 26.36–46; Mark 14.32–42; Luke 22.39–46; John 18.1. In the following discussion I am indebted to the sensitive and wide-ranging commentary in S. Covington, 'The Garden of Anguish: Gethsemane in Early Modern England', *JEH* (forthcoming).

20. For the afterlife of 'Man of Sorrows' in medieval Western Christendom, see Sawyer, *The Fifth Gospel*, ch. 5.

21. John 12.27.

22. e.g. Mark. 3.13–19a, 6.45–6; Matt. 5.1 and 14.22–3; Luke 6.12; John 8.1–2.

23. Matt. 5.1 f.; Luke 6.12 f.

24. Matt. 4.1–11; Luke 4.1–13; both are expansions of Mark 1.12–13.

25. Matt. 4.3–4: the quotation is from Deut. 8.3.

26. M. Laird, *A Sunlit Absence: Silence, Awareness and Contemplation* (Oxford, 2011), 12.

27. F. W. Faber, *Growth in Holiness, or the Progress of the Spiritual Life* (2nd edn, London, 1855), 147. Faber would probably not have known and certainly not have approved of the direction in which Goethe took the same sentiment: 'Jesus felt purely and thought / only of the One God in silence; / Whoever makes him into God / does outrage to his holy will' (J. W. von Goethe, *West-östlicher Divan*, 1819, quoted in Vermes, *Christian Beginnings*, 243–44).

28. Good summary discussion in J. Fenton, *The Gospel of St Matthew* (London, 1963), esp. p. 48, and see also ibid., pp. 51, 66, 194–6, 242–3, 255, 262, 408.

29. W. Wrede, *Das Messiasgeheimnis in den Evangelien: Zugleich ein Beitrag zum Verständnis des Markusevangeliums* (Göttingen, 1901), translated as *The Messianic Secret in the Gospels* (London and Cambridge, 1971). C. Tuckett (ed.), *The Messianic Secret* (Philadelphia and London, 1983) provides an excellent introduction to the subsequent debate.

30. Mark 13.14. Here I use the KJB text, to retain the familiar phrase 'abomination of desolation'.

31. For summary discussion, see MacCulloch, *A History of Christianity*, 105–6, 113.

32. Quotation from J. B. Tyson, 'The Blindness of the Disciples in Mark', in Tuckett (ed.), *Messianic Secret*, 35–43 (repr. from *Journal of Biblical Literature*, 80 (1961), 261–8), at p. 36: Tyson makes a crisp statement of the case. Tuckett includes emphatically contrary views: J. D. G. Dunn, 'The Messianic Secret in Mark', in Tuckett (ed.), *Messianic Secret*, 116–31, at p. 119, and E. Schweizer, 'The Question of the Messianic Secret in Mark', in Tuckett (ed.), *Messianic Secret* (tr. and repr. from 'Zur Messiasgeheimnis bei Markus', *Zeitschrift für die neutestamentliche Wissenschaft*, 56 (1965), 1–8), 71 n. 17. I do not find these perspectives persuasive.

33. Mark 3.33, 35.

34. I say more on this in MacCulloch, *A History of Christianity*, 93–6.

35. Mark 16.8.

36. See P. W. van der Horst, 'Can a Book End with a ΓΑΡ? A Note on Mark XVI. 8', *JTS* 23 (1972), 121–4; his example is Plotinus, *Ennead* 5.5,

from the third century CE, by a writer who would almost certainly have known about Mark 16.8.

37. Kermode, *The Genesis of Secrecy*, 66–9. Tyson, 'The Blindness of the Disciples in Mark', 42, comes to the same conclusion. For a contrary view, see L. Hurtado, 'The Women, the Tomb, and the Climax of Mark', in Z. Rodgers, with M. Daly-Denton and A. Fitzpatrick-McKinley (eds), *A Wandering Galilean: Essays in Honour of Seán Freyne* (Leiden, 2009), 427–51, and for discussion of the problem taking a usefully varied set of positions, see D. A. Black (ed.), *Perspectives on the Ending of Mark: Four Views* (Nashville, 2008).

38. C. Markschies, *Kaiserzeitliche christliche Theologie und ihre Institutionen: Prolegomena zu einer Geschichte der antiken christlichen Theologie* (Tübingen, 2007), 32. For Islam, see T. Holland, *In the Shadow of the Sword: The Battle for Global Empire and the End of the Ancient World* (London, 2012), ch. 1. A judicious survey in a superb miniature study, A. J. Silverstein, *Islamic History: A Very Short Introduction* (Oxford, 2010), ch. 4, puts a similar case in rather more emollient language.

39. J. B. Phillips, *Letters to Young Churches: A Translation of the New Testament Epistles* (London, 1947). The question of authorship and authenticity among Paul's Epistles, which is vital to sorting out which messages are likely actually to be his own, from those foisted on him by his admirers, is crisply dealt with by Terence Donaldson, in Barton and Muddiman (eds), *Oxford Bible Commentary*, 1078–83, and in comment on subsequent individual Epistles. Those generally agreed to be written by Paul himself are Romans, 1 and 2 Corinthians, Galatians, Philippians, 1 Thessalonians and Philemon (the longer Epistles, Romans and Corinthians, may be composites of a number of letters addressed to these communities, a possiblity which does not greatly affect the following discussion). Colossians is the subject of much more disagreement, and that leaves a still more dubious status for Ephesians, 2 Thessalonians, 1 and 2 Timothy and Titus.

40. For the category of non-Jewish *theosebeis*, see MacCulloch, *A History of Christianity*, 98–9.

41. Eph. 5.19; Col. 3.16.

42. 1 Cor. 12.2–3.

43. 1 Thess. 5.20–21; my italics.

44. 1 Cor. 14.27–33.

45. See C. S. C. Williams, in M. Black and H. H. Rowley (eds), *Peake's Commentary on the Bible* (London, 1962), 963. For further discussion of the 'women question', see Ch. 8.

46. I Cor. 14.21: 'By men of strange tongues and by the lips of foreigners will I speak to this people, and even then they will not listen to me, says the Lord.' Compare the version of the same quotation in Isaiah 28.11–12, which has passed into the canonical textual tradition of the Old Testament.

47. I Cor. 14.23. P. Cox Miller, 'In Praise of Nonsense', in A. H. Armstrong (ed.), *Classical Mediterranean Spirituality: Egyptian, Greek, Roman* (London and New York, 1986), 481–504, at p. 485, points out that the verb for being mad that Paul uses here, *mainomai*, is the same as is commonly used for the oracular utterances of Delphi and of the Sibyls and followers of Dionysos (Bacchus). Perhaps there is also an element of reproach to those who use glossolalia that their behaviour may be grouped by outsiders with these alien phenomena; but still that does not deny the sacred character of glossolalia in Paul's eyes.

48. I say more about this in MacCulloch, *A History of Christianity*, 104, 931–41.

49. I Tim. 2.1–2.

50. I Pet. 2.13–15; 3.3–4. The latter thought is picking up prophetic and Wisdom themes from the Tanakh: cf. Isa. 3.18–24 and Prov. 11.22, 31.10–30.

51. I Thess. 4.10–11. For further comment on Paul's attitude to work contrasted with a common message in the Gospels, see MacCulloch, *A History of Christianity*, 113–14.

52. 2 Thess. 3.11–13. Neither *ataktōs*, 'in a disorderly manner', nor *periergazomenous*, 'being busybodies', are words found elsewhere in the New Testament.

53. I Thess. 5.13.

54. James 3.18–4.1.

55. Gal. 5.19–23.

56. Phil. 4.4–7. *Epieikēs*, 'forbearance' in the RSV, was better translated by KJB as 'moderation'; its meanings range from that through to 'kindness'.

57. In Black and Rowley (eds), *Peake's Commentary*, 988.

58. 2 Esd. 8.21.

59. 2 Cor. 12.2–4; on Origen's reaction to this passage, see Mortley, *From Word to Silence*, vol. 2, pp. 64–8.

60. Rev. 8.1; *hōs* ['as long as', or 'about'] *hēmiōrion*: the latter word does not occur elsewhere in the New Testament.

61. N. Turner, in Black and Rowley (eds), *Peake's Commentary*, 1050.

62. C. Rowland, *The Open Heaven: A Study of Apocalyptic in Judaism and Early Christianity* (London, 1982), 416–17, gives cogent arguments for

seeing the sequence of three groups of seven events as sequential rather than happening in parallel: he points to Rev. 15.1, which explicitly states that the plagues of the seven bowls are the last of the plagues to come.

63. Rev. 8.3. See J. Sweet, *Revelation* (London, 1979), 158–9, and discussion of Talmudic tradition in the Tractate *Hagigah* 12b by R. H. Charles, *Revelation* (2 vols, Edinburgh, 1920), vol. 1, p. 224, that 'in the ma'ôn (or fifth heaven) are companies of angels of service who sing praises by night, but are silent by day because of the glory of Israel'. Richard Bauckham, in Barton and Muddiman (eds), *Oxford Bible Commentary*, 1294, chooses to make the reference to Temple ritual the principal explanation.

64. Wisd. of Sol. 18.14–15.

65. See above, p. 28, and especially n. 54 to Ch 1.

66. John 1.1; see comment in Mortley, *From Word to Silence*, vol. 1, p. 50.

67. Ignatius, *Magnesians* 8.2, tr. M. W. Holmes, *The Apostolic Fathers in English* (3rd edn, Grand Rapids, Mich., 2006), 104.

68. Ignatius, *Ephesians* 19.1–2, tr. Holmes, *The Apostolic Fathers in English*, 101–2.

3. FORMING AND BREAKING A CHURCH: 100–451 CE

1. A perceptive discussion of the latter theme is R. P. Carroll, *When Prophecy Failed: Reactions and Responses to Failure in the Old Testament Prophetic Traditions* (London, 1979).

2. *The Book of James, or Protevangelium* 18.1–2, 19.1–2, tr. M. R. James, *The Apocryphal New Testament* (Oxford, 1924), 46.

3. Ignatius, *Ephesians* 6.1, 15.1, tr. M.W. Holmes, *The Apostolic Fathers in English* (3rd edn, Grand Rapids, Mich., 2006), 98, 100. Cf. also comments in Ignatius, *Philadelphians* 1.1, ibid., 117: '[the bishop] accomplishes more through silence than others do by talking.'

4. Ignatius, *Smyrnaeans* 8.2, ibid., 123 (slightly altered).

5. H. Chadwick, 'The Silence of Bishops in Ignatius', *HTR* 43 (1950), 169–72.

6. An excellent summary overview of the case is provided by L. Pietersen, *The Polemic of the Pastorals: A Sociological Examination of the Development of Pauline Christianity* (London, 2004), 98–100; further useful discussion in C. Trevett, *A Study of Ignatius of Antioch in Asia and Syria* (London and New York, 1992), 128–9.

7. *Didachē*, 15.2, quoted in Stevenson (ed.), rev. Frend, *New Eusebius*, 12.

8. For summary discussion of the Montanists, see MacCulloch, *A History of Christianity*, 138–41.

9. For another important theme in Ignatius's letters which went nowhere in subsequent rhetoric, that of 'image-bearer', see A. Brent, 'The Enigma of Ignatius of Antioch', *JEH* 57 (2006), 429–56.

10. D. Brakke, 'Self-differentiation among Christian Groups: The Gnostics and their Opponents', in M. M. Mitchell and F. M. Young (eds), *The Cambridge History of Christianity I: Origins to Constantine* (Cambridge, 2006), 245–60, at pp. 247–9.

11. Mortley, *From Word to Silence*, vol. 1, p. 162 (his italics), and cf. ibid., 110.

12. Ibid., 112, 126–30, containing a useful survey of modern views of the *Parmenides*, some of which frankly regard it as satirical; Mortley nevertheless emphasizes the seriousness with which it was treated in the Hellenistic world.

13. Ibid., 39–43, 156.

14. P. W. van der Horst, 'Silent Prayer in Antiquity', *Numen*, 4 (1994), 1–25, at p. 12. A fine introduction to the Nag Hammadi material is J. D. Turner and A. McGuire (eds), *The Nag Hammadi Library after Fifty Years: Proceedings of the 1995 Society of Biblical Literature Commemoration* (Leiden, 1997), esp. pp. 4–8 for an account of the discovery.

15. *Tripartite Tractate* 54, in Robinson and Smith (eds), *The Nag Hammadi Library in English*, 62.

16. *Tripartite Tractate* 56, 63, 65, in Robinson and Smith (eds), *The Nag Hammadi Library in English*, 63, 66.

17. *Tripartite Tractate* 77, in Robinson and Smith (eds), *The Nag Hammadi Library in English*, 73; and cf. John 1.1.

18. *Allogenes* 53, in Robinson and Smith (eds), *The Nag Hammadi Library in English*, 495. For further examples of the importance of silence to the gnostics Basilides and Marcus, see Mortley, *From Word to Silence*, vol. 1, pp. 53, 57, 113, 122–3; vol. 2, p. 27. For a good treatment of one other particular theme of silence and naming, see P. Cox Miller, 'In Praise of Nonsense', in A. H. Armstrong (ed.), *Classical Mediterranean Spirituality: Egyptian, Greek, Roman* (London and New York, 1986), 481–504.

19. Parable of the Labourers in the Vineyard: Matt. 20.1–16. Teaching on the Marriage Feast: Luke 14.7–11. Parable of the Rich Man and Lazarus: Luke 16.1–31. On 'Son of Man', see B. Lindars, *Jesus, Son of Man* (London, 1983), esp. pp. 17–28 for discussion of the Aramaic *bar enasha*,

and pp. 97–100, 156–7; and G. Vermes, *Jesus the Jew* (London, 1973), 160–91, with comment at MacCulloch, *A History of Christianity*, 86.

20. *Second Treatise of the Great Seth* 53–4, in Robinson and Smith (eds), *The Nag Hammadi Library in English*, 364.

21. *Second Treatise of the Great Seth* 56, in Robinson and Smith (eds), *The Nag Hammadi Library in English*, 365.

22. G. Stroumsa, 'Christ's Laughter: Docetic Origins Reconsidered', *Journal of Early Christian Studies*, 12 (2004), 267–88, at p. 272.

23. This thesis is plausibly advanced by Stroumsa, ibid., 277–87.

24. Quoted in C. Baumer, *The Church of the East: An Illustrated History of Assyrian Christianity* (London and New York, 2006), 113. For further useful discussion, see Bruce, *Silence and Sign Language in Medieval Monasticism*, 32–3.

25. U. Eco, *The Name of the Rose* (London, 1983), 463–79 (Seventh Day: night). Cf. suggestive remarks about the all-pervasiveness and the suppression of laughter in the Renaissance and Reformation in M. A. Screech, *Laughter at the Foot of the Cross* (London, 1997), pp. xv and xxiii.

26. For accounts of the rise and relative atrophying of the 'Toronto Blessing' movement, see A. Anderson, *An Introduction to Pentecostalism: Global Charismatic Christianity* (Cambridge, 2004), 162–65, and M. Percy, *Engaging with Contemporary Culture: Christianity, Theology and the Concrete Church* (Aldershot and Burlington, Vt., 2005), ch. 7.

27. Mortley, *From Word to Silence*, vol. 2, pp. 33–5, and quotation at p. 34 from Justin, *Apology* 2.6.

28. See Justin's autobiography in A. Lukyn Williams (ed.), *Dialogue with Trypho the Jew* (London, 1930), 4–20 (chs 2–9).

29. Clement, *Stromateis* 5.11.67.3 and 7.7.40.1, quoted in Mortley, *From Word to Silence*, vol. 2, pp. 36–7. Clement was also extremely suspicious of visual representations of the sacred, thinking of their non-Christian use, going so far as to call the artist a deceiver: Clement, *Cohortatio ad gentes*, 4 (*PG* 8, cols 135, 136A).

30. Clement, *Stromateis* 6.15.132.1, quoted in Mortley, *From Word to Silence*, vol. 2, p. 39, and see preceding discussion there. For the Lord's Prayer, see Matt. 6.7–15 and Luke 11.1–4; Mark characteristically assumes that his audience knows the Lord's Prayer and merely alludes to it: Mark 11.25.

31. Jonah 2.1–9.

32. I draw in these two paragraphs on the excellent discussion by van der Horst, 'Silent Prayer in Antiquity', 17–20.

33. A fine guide to a vast literature is still W. H. C. Frend, *Martyrdom and Persecution in the Early Church: A Study of a Conflict from the Maccabees to Donatus* (Oxford, 1965).

34. Here I am aware of the case to the contrary eloquently argued by C. Moss, *The Other Christs: Imitating Jesus in Ancient Christian Ideologies of Martyrdom* (Oxford, 2010). I warm to her careful analysis of the way in which martyrologies rewrote Christ's Passion in Stoic terms, but the mass of evidence marshalled by Moss for martyrdom as an imitation of Christ needs to be balanced with an emphasis on the character of Stephen's martyrdom and his role as proto-martyr in the Christian tradition. Indeed, her presentation generously acknowledges that: see ibid., 12, 34, 53–6, 66–7, 174. For Luke's modification of the Passion narrative with Stephen in mind, see ibid., 56.

35. An interesting discussion of the tensions between martyrs and bishops is A. Brent, 'Cyprian's Reconstruction of the Martyr Tradition', *JEH* 53 (2002), 241–68.

36. *Testimony of Truth* 31, in Robinson and Smith (eds), *The Nag Hammadi Library in English*, 450. See discussion and further texts in E. Pagels and K. L. King, *Reading Judas: The Gospel of Judas and the Shaping of Christianity* (London, 2007), 59, 67–8, 71–4, 113.

37. On the rigorism of Novatianism and Donatism and their general context in the persecutions, see MacCulloch, *A History of Christianity*, 155–76, 211–12.

38. John 12.25; Matt. 10.23.

39. On the fourth-century appearance of the view that Peter had been the first Bishop of Rome, see H. Inglebert, *Les Romains chrétiens face à l'histoire de Rome: Histoire, christianisme et romanités en Occident dans l'Antiquité tardive (IIIe–Ve siècles)* (Paris, 1996), 197–9.

40. See excellent discussion in P. Zagorin, *Ways of Lying: Dissimulation, Persecution, and Conformity in Early Modern Europe* (Cambridge, Mass., and London, 1990), 15–25.

41. J. R. Curran, 'Jerome and the Sham Christians of Rome', *JEH* 48 (1997), 213–29, at p. 217.

42. J. R. Curran, *Pagan City and Christian Capital: Rome in the Fourth Century* (Oxford, 2000), 148–57.

43. For summary discussion, see MacCulloch, *A History of Christianity*, 193–5.

44. Moss, *The Other Christs*, 174

45. For early criticisms of pilgrimage, see P. Walker, *Holy City, Holy Places? Christian Attitudes to Jerusalem and the Holy Land in the Fourth*

Century (Oxford, 1990), and B. Bitton-Ashkelony, *Encountering the Sacred: The Debate on Christian Pilgrimage in Late Antiquity* (Berkeley and London, 2005).

46. Baumer, *Church of the East*, 66–71.

47. A very judicious account of monastic origins is to be found in Harmless, *Desert Christians*, 417–48.

48. S. Brock, 'Early Syrian Asceticism', *Numen*, 20 (1973), 1–19, at pp. 12–13.

49. T. Vivian and A. N. Athanassakis with R. A. Greer (eds), *The Life of Antony by Athanasius of Alexandria* (Kalamazoo, Mich., 2003), 161 [para. 47.1] (cf. the Coptic text's garbling or transformation of this point, ibid., 158, 160), and Harmless, *Desert Christians*, 66–7.

50. See e.g. P. Wood, 'The *Chorepiscopoi* in Sixth-century Mesopotamia', *JEH* 63 (2012), 446–57, esp. pp. 454–6, for the persistence of negative labelling of asceticism as 'Messalianism'.

51. For summary discussion of the place of Ethiopian monasticism in its Church's history, see MacCulloch, *A History of Christianity*, 242–3, 279–83. It is also worth remembering the significant phrase 'Silent rebellion', which has come to have a wider reference than the book title of which it forms a part: A. M. Allchin, *The Silent Rebellion: Anglican Religious Communities, 1845–1900* (London, 1958).

52. On the disappearance of Melitian monasticism from the record, see Harmless, *Desert Christians*, 422–4, 460–61; on Kellis, see I. Gardner *et al.* (eds), *Coptic Documentary Texts from Kellis I* (Oxford, 1999). A key discussion is G. Stroumsa, 'The Manichaean Challenge to Egyptian Christianity', in B. A. Pearson and J. E. Goehring (eds), *The Roots of Egyptian Christianity* (Philadelphia, 1986), 307–19; given the third-century origins of Manichaeism, it cannot be regarded as an originating force in Syrian monasticism – rather it was inspired in its monastic practice by the Syrians – but there is no reason to reject Stroumsa's suggestion that, once in place, Manichaeism maintained a real relationship to Christian monastic communities, especially in Egypt.

53. Harmless, *Desert Christians*, 160–63.

54. Acts 4.32–5.11; Cassian, *Conference* 18, quoted in Harmless, *Desert Christians*, 417.

55. The story is probably designed to illustrate the theological point that this community was the New Israel; in the old Israel, there had supposedly been a system of 'Jubilee', a year in which all land should go back to the family to which it had originally belonged, and during which all slaves should be released (Lev. 25).

56. Luke 12.33, 14.33.
57. G. Winkler, 'The Origins and Idiosyncrasies of the Earliest Forms of Asceticism', in W. Skudlarek (ed.), *The Continuing Quest for God: Monastic Spirituality in Tradition and Transition* (Collegeville, Minn., 1982), 9–43, may push the case for scriptural continuity with monasticism too far, but forcefully argues for the importance of Luke's Gospel to Syriac asceticism.
58. 1 Tim. 2.15.
59. Heb. 11.13; Brock, 'Early Syrian Asceticism', 9, translates it from Syriac versions to give the text as 'no more than strangers and passing travellers on earth'. See also Winkler, 'Origins and Idiosyncrasies', 21–3.
60. Aphrahat, *Demonstration* (*NPNF* ser. ii, XIII, vi, cols 241/16 f., 248.25), quoted in Brock, 'Early Syrian Asceticism', 10.
61. Luke 20.36; discussed ibid., 6–7.
62. Harmless, *Desert Christians*, 427: John 1.14, 18; 3.16, 18; 1 John 4.9. For some fertile observations on the contemporary relevance of this Syrian concept, see M. Ross, *Writing the Icon of the Heart: In Silence Beholding* (Oxford, 2011), 109–13.
63. A. Robertson (ed.), *Select Writings and Letters of Athanasius, Bishop of Alexandria* (*NPNF* ser. ii, IV), 329, and cf. 412–13 (*Four Discourses against the Arians*, 1.39, 3.34). For an earlier formulation by Irenaeus of Lyon, see A. Roberts and J. Donaldson (eds), *The Apostolic Fathers, Justin Martyr, Irenaeus* (*Ante-Nicene Fathers*, I, 1885), 526 (Irenaeus, *Against Heresies*, bk. 5, preface): 'our Lord Jesus Christ, who did, through His transcendent love, become what we are, that He might bring us to be even what He is Himself.'
64. S. A. Ivanov, *Holy Fools in Byzantium and Beyond* (Oxford, 2006). I draw together the connections between Diogenes, Simeon *Salus* and later holy fools in MacCulloch, *A History of Christianity*, 29–30, 40, 58–9, 207, 468, 509, 519, 528, 918.
65. Harmless, *Desert Christians*, 70–74, 78–81.
66. Ibid., 427, and Brock, 'Early Syrian Asceticism', 7, 10–11.
67. A. Hadjar, *The Church of St. Simeon the Stylite and Other Archaeological Sites in the Mountains of Simeon and Halaqa* (Damascus, [1995]), 16–17, 22–3, 26–7, 31, 49.
68. W. Dalrymple, *From the Holy Mountain* (London, 1997), 57–60.
69. For the desert/city aphorism, see Vivian and Athanassakis with Greer (eds), *Life of Antony by Athanasius*, 92–3 [para. 14.7]; cf. ibid., 78–9 [para. 8.2]. For Antony's boyhood, ibid., 60–63 [para. 3].

70. E. A. Judge, 'The Earliest Use of Monachos for "Monk" (P. Coll. Youtie 77) and the Origins of Monasticism', *Jahrbüch für Antike und Christentum*, 20 (1977), 72–89, at pp. 73–4.

71. Harmless, *Desert Christians*, 24, 443, and cf. pp. 420–21.

72. Ibid., 122.

73. Good discussion of Pachomius's initiatives is J. E. Goehring, 'Withdrawing from the Desert: Pachomius and the Development of Village Monasticism in Upper Egypt', *HTR* 89 (1996), 267–85, at pp. 275–7.

74. *Virtues of Abba Macarius the Great*, quoted in Harmless, *Desert Christians*, 220.

75. *Apophthegmata Patrum*, John Colobus 34, quoted in Harmless, *Desert Christians*, 199–200; on the role of tears, see Ross, *Writing the Icon of the Heart*, 108–21.

76. Zacharias of Sakhâ, *Encomium on the Life of John the Little* 56, quoted in Harmless, *Desert Christians*, 225.

77. Details of Pachomian daily life in the preceding paragraphs are from Harmless, *Desert Christians*, 125–30.

78. Bruce, *Silence and Sign Language in Medieval Monasticism*, 35, quoting *Vitae patrum* 5.4.7 on Agathon.

79. S. Brock, 'John the Solitary, *On Prayer*', *JTS* 30 (1979), 84–101, esp. pp. 84–6, 98.

80. Mortley, *From Word to Silence*, vol. 2, p. 122: see also ibid., vol. 1, pp. 110, 125; vol. 2, pp. 14, 98, 106, 119–23, 148, 253.

81. Ibid., vol. 2, p. 123.

82. Ibid., 128–70.

83. Gregory of Nazianzus, *Oration* 27.3: *Cyril of Jerusalem; Gregory of Nazianzen* (*NPNF* ser. ii, VII), 285 (*PG* 36, col. 13). See also J. Konstantinovsky, *Evagrius Ponticus: The Making of a Gnostic* (Farnham, 2009), 71.

84. L. Dysinger, *Psalmody and Prayer in the Writings of Evagrius Ponticus* (Oxford, 2005), 9–16.

85. Evagrius, ed. A. Guillaumont, *Les Six Centuries des 'Kephalaia Gnostica'* (Paris, 1958), 61–3 [II.4], quoted and tr. in Dysinger, *Psalmody and Prayer in the Writings of Evagrius Ponticus*, 41.

86. See extended discussion of *nous* in Konstantinovsky, *Evagrius Ponticus*, ch. 4, and B. Bitton-Ashkelony, 'The Limit of the Mind (ΝΟΥΣ): Pure Prayer according to Evagrius Ponticus and Isaac of Nineveh', *Zeitschrift für antikes Christentum/Journal of Ancient Christianity*, 15 (2011), 291–321.

87. Evagrius, ed. A. Guillaumont, *Kephalaia Gnostica*, 115 [III.42], quoted and tr. in Dysinger, *Psalmody and Prayer in the Writings of Evagrius Ponticus*, 37–8.
88. Evagrius, *Chapters on Prayer* 3, quoted in Bitton-Ashkelony, 'The Limit of the Mind', 298.
89. Dysinger, *Psalmody and Prayer in the Writings of Evagrius Ponticus*, 6, 193–5. On Evagrius's enthusiastic development of medical imagery, see ibid., 104–23.
90. A. M. Casiday (ed.), *Evagrius Ponticus* (London, 2006), 193 ['On Prayer', 67]. For a crisp dismissal of suggestions that Evagrius might have formed his mysticism in reference to Buddhism, see Bitton-Ashkelony, 'The Limit of the Mind', 292 n. 7.
91. The word 'meditation' was first regularly used only in the twelfth century: J.-F. Cottier, *Anima mea: prières privées et textes de dévotion du Moyen Âge latin. Autour des Prières ou Méditations attribuées à saint Anselme de Cantorbéry (XIe–XIIe siècle)* (Turnhout, 2001), pp. lvi–lvii.
92. F. de Sales, *Traité de l'amour de Dieu*, quoted in R. Parish, *Catholic Particularity in Seventeenth-century French Writing: 'Christianity is Strange'* (Oxford, 2011), 167; Parish has a fine exposition of the difference between meditation and contemplation here.

4. THE MONASTIC AGE IN EAST AND WEST: 451–1100

1. On the disputes which led to the Council of Chalcedon and on its consequences, see MacCulloch, *A History of Christianity*, chs 6–8, 13.
2. Isaac of Nineveh, *Centuries on Knowledge* 4.66, tr. S. Brock, *The Syriac Fathers on Prayer and the Spiritual Life* (Kalamazoo, Mich., 1987), 268–9 (slightly altered).
3. Isaac of Nineveh, *The First Part* 22, (169–70B), tr. Brock, *The Syriac Fathers on Prayer and the Spiritual Life*, 258, and discussion of this passage in B. Bitton-Ashkelony, 'The Limit of the Mind (ΝΟΥΣ): Pure Prayer according to Evagrius Ponticus and Isaac of Nineveh', *Zeitschrift für antikes Christentum/Journal of Ancient Christianity*, 15 (2011), 291–321, at pp. 312–13.
4. Isaac of Nineveh, *The First Part* 22 (174B), tr. Brock, *The Syriac Fathers on Prayer and the Spiritual Life*, 262, and cf. Bitton-Ashkelony, 'The Limit of the Mind', 314. She provides a translation of the original Greek of Evagrius, *Reflections* 27: 'Prayer is a state of the mind that arises under the influence

of the unique light of the Holy Trinity.' A fine if technical study of Isaac's thought is P. Hagman, *The Asceticism of Isaac of Nineveh* (Oxford, 2010).

5. R. Beulay, *L'Enseignement spirituel de Jean de Dalyatha: mystique syro-oriental du VIIIe siècle* (Paris, 1990), 62, 448 (quoting *Centuria* 1.17, letter 5.1; my English translations).

6. Acts 17.22–34; the reference to the 'real' Dionysius is at v. 34.

7. Mortley, *From Word to Silence*, vol. 2, p. 221, points to the early role of John, Bishop of Scythopolis, now Beit She'an in Israel (c. 536–50, also known as 'Scholasticus'). Excellent synoptic introductions to Pseudo-Dionysius are provided by S. Coakley and C. M. Stang (eds), *Re-thinking Dionysius the Areopagite* (Chichester, 2009), and also highly useful is W. J. Hankey, 'Augustinian Immediacy and Dionysian Mediation in John Colet, Edmund Spenser, Richard Hooker and the Cardinal de Bérulle', in K. Flasch and D. de Courcelles (eds), *Augustinus in der Neuzeit: colloque de la Herzog August Bibliothek de Wolfenbüttel, 14–17 octobre, 1996* (Turnhout, 1998), 125–60.

8. See discussion of Pseudo-Dionysius's engagement with the Sinai story in J. G. Finlayson, 'On Not Being Silent in the Darkness: Adorno's Singular Apophaticism', *HTR* 105 (2012), 1–32, at p. 11.

9. Quoted in Mortley, *From Word to Silence*, vol. 2, p. 230.

10. F. G. Mohamed, *In the Anteroom of Divinity: The Reformation of the Angels from Colet to Milton* (Toronto, 2008), 9. Mohamed's suggested etymology of the word 'hierarchy' there is eccentric – it simply means 'rule by a priest'.

11. On Colet's failings in practical reform, see the account of his ecclesiastical career in J. Arnold, *Dean Colet of St Paul's: Humanism and Reform in Early Tudor England* (London, 2007).

12. Mohamed, *In the Anteroom of Divinity*, ch. 1, and see at ibid., 21, his illustration of the scribal MS of Colet's commentary, British Library Additional MS 63853.

13. R. S. Pine-Coffin (ed.), *Saint Augustine: Confessions* (London, 1961), 196–9 [9.10]. On Augustine and language, see Mortley, *From Word to Silence*, vol. 2, pp. 192–210, and for summary discussion of Augustine's view of the use of human analogies to describe the divine, MacCulloch, *A History of Christianity*, 310–11.

14. An adventurous treatment of Augustine's attitude to reading and its afterlife is B. Stock, *After Augustine: The Meditative Reader and the Text* (Philadelphia, 2001).

15. Augustine, ed. R. P. H. Green, *De doctrina Christiana* (Oxford, 1995), 141 [III.v.9.21].

16. Ibid., 150–53 [III.xii.18.43]. This is a comment on Luke 7.36–50; there are parallels in John 12.1–8, Mark 14.3–9 and Matt. 26.6–13, in the latter two of which it is the Lord's head which is anointed.

17. Stock, *After Augustine*, esp. pp. 17–21.

18. C. Stewart, *Cassian the Monk* (Oxford, 1998).

19. On the relationship of Benedict's Rule to the slightly older *Regula Magistri*, see C. H. Lawrence, 'St Benedict and his Rule', *History*, 67 (1982), 185–94. There are many translations and attempted adaptations of the Benedictine Rule, relating to the original text to be found amid a vast volume of medieval commentary in *PL* 66, cols 215–930. An elegant English version, slightly adapted for monks and nuns alike, is P. Barry (tr.), *Saint Benedict's Rule: A New Translation for Today* (Ampleforth, 1997).

20. Basil of Caesarea, *Regula* 40 and 86, quoted in Bruce, *Silence and Sign Language in Medieval Monasticism*, 31.

21. Valerian of Cimiez, *Homilia* 5.7, quoted in Bruce, *Silence and Sign Language in Medieval Monasticism*, 36.

22. 'quamvis de bonis et sanctis et aedificationum eloquiis, perfectis discipulis propter taciturnitatis gravitatem, rara loquendi concedatur licentia . . . tacere et audire, discipulo convenit': *PL* 66, cols. 355–6.

23. On Jerome's spin-doctoring for scholarship, see MacCulloch, *A History of Christianity*, 295–6.

24. For a sceptical view of the universality of reading aloud in the ancient world, see M. Burnyeat, 'Postscript on Silent Reading', *Classical Quarterly*, 47 (1997), 74–6. Stock, *After Augustine*, esp. pp. 22–3, lays some stress on the shifts around silent reading and reading out loud.

25. Ambrose, *Enarrationes in XII Psalmos Davidicos*, prol.: 'Cum psalmus legitur, ipse sibi est effector silentii. Omnes loquuntur, et nullus obstrepit' (*PL* 14, col. 925b), quoted in Bruce, *Silence and Sign Language in Medieval Monasticism*, 40; my translation. It is possible that Ambrose had in the back of his mind Ps. 19, with its picture of the heavens engaged in silent music; he would not have been the first. Irenaeus mentions Marcus the Valentinian's use of that passage: Mortley, *From Word to Silence*, vol. 1, p. 56. The Hermetic tractate *The Discourse on the Eighth and the Ninth* 58 has Hermes Trismegistus instructing a pupil 'I have said, O my son, that I am Mind. I have seen! Language is not able to reveal this. For the entire eighth, O my son, and the souls that are in it, and the angels, sing a hymn in silence' (Robinson and Smith (eds), *The Nag Hammadi Library in English*, 325; quoted in Mortley, *From Word to Silence*, vol. 1, p. 91.

26. Bruce, *Silence and Sign Language in Medieval Monasticism*, 40, 44. A book which provides a remarkable overview of this subject is W. McNeill, *Keeping Together in Time: Dance and Drill in Human History* (Cambridge, Mass., 1995).

27. Bruce, *Silence and Sign Language in Medieval Monasticism*, 41.

28. M. A. Claussen, *The Reform of the Frankish Church: Chrodegang of Metz and the* Regula canonicorum *in the Eighth Century* (Cambridge, 2004).

29. Hildemar, *Expositio regulae sancti Benedicti* 65, ed. R. Mittermüller, in *Vita et Regula SS. P. Benedicti una cum Expositio Regulae a Hildemaro tradita* (Regensburg, New York and Cincinnati, 1880), 611–12, quoted in Bruce, *Silence and Sign Language in Medieval Monasticism*, 39.

30. That unquiet Trappist Thomas Merton (1915–68) was to call this turn of thought a 'Carolingian' moment, and in his radical reassessment of monastic life in the mid-1950s, he went so far as to say that 'Most of the problems of the Church start with Charlemagne': M. Furlong, *Merton: A Biography* (London, 1980), 220, 253, and see above, pp. 229–30.

31. Useful commentary on Eriugena is Hankey, 'Augustinian Immediacy and Dionysian Mediation', 125–9, and P. Rorem, 'The Early Latin Dionysius: Eriugena and Hugh of St Victor', in Coakley and Stang (eds), *Re-thinking Dionysius the Areopagite*, 71–84.

32. For an account of Cluny and its importance, see MacCulloch, *A History of Christianity*, 362–84.

33. Berno's will is *PL* 133, col. 857a, quoted in Bruce, *Silence and Sign Language in Medieval Monasticism*, 24.

34. Odo of Cluny, *Sermo* 3, *PL* 133, col. 722a, quoted in Bruce, *Silence and Sign Language in Medieval Monasticism*, 20.

35. Ibid., 3, 14, 20, 27–8, 69. For Gregory I's influence on Odo, see also C. A. Jones, 'Monastic Identity and Sodomitic Danger in the *Occupatio* by Odo of Cluny', *Speculum*, 82 (2007), 1–53, at p. 8.

36. Bruce, *Silence and Sign Language in Medieval Monasticism*, 11 n. 33. Bruce instances the signage developed in Canadian lumber-factories, but British readers may be more familiar with the signs once in use by workers in the cotton-mills of northern England, as evoked in the comedy of the late Les Dawson.

37. Ibid., 65–6, 71, 74–6, 79–88, 95, 123.

38. Ibid., 175–6, and see S. Plann, *A Silent Minority: Deaf Education in Spain, 1550–1835* (Berkeley, Los Angeles and London, 1997). For the uncomfortable reaction of *aggiornamento* Trappists in the twentieth century to Cistercian sign language, and Thomas Merton's ridicule of their efforts to reform it, see Furlong, *Merton: A Biography*, 276.

39. Bruce, *Silence and Sign Language in Medieval Monasticism*, 145.

40. Ibid., 116, 157–61. For another later simpler sign language among late-sixteenth-century Discalced Carmelites, see T. Johnson, 'Gardening for God: Carmelite Deserts and the Sacralisation of Natural Space in Counter-Reformation Spain', in W. Coster and A. Spicer (eds), *Sacred Space in Early Modern Europe* (Cambridge, 2005), 193–210, at p. 200.

41. On Scetis, see Harmless, *Desert Christians*, 173–83.

42. On Guigo and the complex analysis of meditation among his contemporaries, see Stock, *After Augustine*, 62–70.

43. J. Chryssavgis, *John Climacus: From the Egyptian Desert to the Sinaite Mountain* (Oxford, 2004), 161; on Climacus and Evagrius, see ibid., 183–7.

44. Guigo II, tr. E. Colledge and J. Walsh, *The Ladder of Monks* (London, 1978), xiv (p. 95); see also ix (ibid., p. 89).

45. On the growth of *lectio spiritualis* out of *lectio divina* and some of its consequences, see Stock, *After Augustine*, ch. 7.

46. Bruce, *Silence and Sign Language in Medieval Monasticism,* 161, quoting Peter of Celle, *Epistola 28*, ed. and tr. J. Haseldine, *The Letters of Peter of Celle* (Oxford, 2001), 98.

47. Bernard, Letter 89 (*c.* 1127); *PL* 182, cols. 220.1–221.2, tr. S. J. Eales (ed.), *Life and Works of Bernard of Clairvaux* (4 vols, London, 1888–97), vol. 1, pp. 318–20 (I have altered the presentation slightly). Isaiah 32.17 was a favourite eisegetical proof-text for monastic silence: cf. e.g. its use in relation to the monastic life by the Dominican Jordan of Saxony (tr. G. Deighan OSA), *The Life of the Brethren* (Villanova, Pa., 1993), 75.

48. J. Rubenstein (ed.) and J. McAlhany and J. Rubenstein (trs.), *Guibert of Nogent:* Monodies *and* On the Relics of Saints (New York and London, 2011), 15, and 293 n. 26: the reference is of course to Rev. 8.1.

5. FROM ICONOCLASM TO ERASMUS: 700–1500

1. For a summary account and discussion of the Iconoclastic Controversy, see MacCulloch, *A History of Christianity*, 442–56.

2. Excellent discussion is R. Cormack, 'The Arts during the Age of Iconoclasm', in A. Bryer and J. Herrin (eds), *Iconoclasm* (Birmingham, 1977), 35–44, although Cormack does not include Germigny in his survey.

3. J. R. Payton Jr, 'Calvin and the *Libri Carolini*', *SCJ* 28 (1997), 467–79.

4. P. Brown, 'A Dark Age Crisis: Aspects of the Iconoclastic Controversy', in Brown, *Society and the Holy in Late Antiquity* (London, 1982), 251–301, esp. at pp. 258–64, 272–4, 282–3.

5. S. Sabas Jerusalem MS 108, quoted in E. Kitzinger, 'The Cult of Images in the Age before Iconoclasm', *Dumbarton Oaks Papers*, 8 (1954), 83–150, at pp. 144–5.

6. Kitzinger, 'The Cult of Images in the Age before Iconoclasm', 135–6.

7. For major theologians of the Mediterranean Church *c.* 200 and their suspicion of visual images of the sacred, see ibid., 140–41, and n. 251.

8. Ibid., 138.

9. For useful discussion of the physicality of the Mass, see M. Milner, *The Senses and the English Reformation* (Farnham and Burlington, Vt., 2011), 156–61.

10. C. Barber, *Figure and Likeness: On the Limits of Representation in Byzantine Iconoclasm* (Princeton, 2002), particularly discussion at p. 138, and my further comments on the effect of icon-painting technique, MacCulloch, *A History of Christianity*, 453.

11. D. Trembinski, '[Pro]passio doloris: Early Dominican Conceptions of Christ's Physical Pain', *JEH* 59 (2008), 630–56, esp. pp. 651, 653–5.

12. J. Dillenberger, *Style and Content in Christian Art* (London, 1965), 57–60.

13. S. B. Meech and H. E. Allen (eds), *The Book of Margery Kempe* (Early English Text Society, 212 1939), 148, and discussion at R. Marks, *Image and Devotion in Late Medieval England* (Stroud, 2004), 124. One has to admit that it did not take much to trigger a good cry in Mistress Kempe.

14. Gregory Palamas, tr. N. Gendle, *The Triads* (Mahwah, NJ, 1983), 33 [I.iii.5].

15. Matt. 17.2: an addition to the versions in Mark 9.2–10 and Luke 9.28–36. See J. Lössl, 'Augustine in Byzantium', *JEH* 51 (2000), 267–95, at p. 277.

16. Introduction to the practice and history of the Jesus Prayer can be found in N. J. Chumley, *Mysteries of the Jesus Prayer: Experiencing the Presence of God and a Pilgrimage to the Heart of an Ancient Spirituality* (New York, 2010).

17. See fine discussion of this in Lössl, 'Augustine in Byzantium'.

18. J. Shepard, 'The Byzantine Commonwealth 1000–1550', in M. Angold (ed.), *The Cambridge History of Christianity 5: Eastern Christianity* (Cambridge, 2006), 3–52, at p. 39.

19. E. A. Zachariadou, 'Mount Athos and the Ottomans *c.* 1350–1550', in Angold (ed.), *Cambridge History of Christianity 5*, 154–68, at pp. 159–63.

20. J. R. Dupuche, 'Sufism and Hesychasm', in B. Neil, G. D. Dunn and L. Cross (eds), *Prayer and Spirituality in the Early Church III: Liturgy and Life* (Strathfield, NSW, 2003), 335–44.

21. On early Hesychast emphasis on navel-gazing by Nikephoros the Italian and later silence on the subject, e.g. in Gregory the Sinaite, see D. Krausmüller, 'The Rise of Hesychasm', in Angold (ed.), *The Cambridge History of Christianity 5*, 101–26, at pp. 103, 105–10.

22. See 2 Sam. 6.2–5, 14–23, for both royal and priestly dancing and for Yahweh's emphatic punishment of the queen who criticized it. On the Ethiopian Church's intense identification with Israel and its steadily expanding imitation of Jewish practice, see MacCulloch, *A History of Christianity*, 243–4, 280–83, 712.

23. Ibid., 317–18.

24. For further comment, ibid., 371–3.

25. The medieval story of the Carthusians' discountenancing of a pope who wished to ease their austerity when they sent him a delegation of astonishingly aged and healthy monks is probably *ben trovato*, but it can be found in C. E. Berseaux, *L'Ordre des chartreux et la chartreuse de Bosserville* (Nancy/Paris, 1868), 469–71, 504. A remarkable personal account of the last days of traditional Carthusian life in Parkminster, a twentieth-century English Charterhouse, is N. Klein Maguire, *An Infinity of Little Hours: Five Young Men and their Trial of Faith in the Western World's Most Austere Monastic Order* (New York, 2006).

26. J. Catto, 'The Burden and Conscience of Government in the Fifteenth Century', *TRHS*, 6th ser., 17 (2007), 83–100, at pp. 95–9. Carthusian architecture is sumptuously explored among the very extensive series of miscellanea edited by James Hogg, *Analecta Cartusiana*: more than 300 volumes published since 1970, which can be found listed at http://www.umilta.net/analectacartusiana.html.

27. D. Bachrach, 'Confession in the *Regnum Francorum* (742–900): The Sources Revisited', *JEH* 54 (2003), 3–22, esp. pp. 5–6.

28. An excellent introduction is A. Jotischky, *The Carmelites and Antiquity* (Oxford, 2002).

29. *Ignea Sagitta* xi, quoted in Jotischky, *The Carmelites and Antiquity*, 84.

30. T. Johnson, 'Gardening for God: Carmelite Deserts and the Sacralisation of Natural Space in Counter-Reformation Spain', in W. Coster and A. Spicer (eds), *Sacred Space in Early Modern Europe* (Cambridge, 2005), 193–210.

31. R. I. Moore, *The Formation of a Persecuting Society: Power and Deviance in Western Europe, 950–1250* (Oxford, 1987), and for a measure of the impact of his thesis, M. Frassetto (ed.), *Heresy and the Persecuting Society in the Middle Ages: Essays on the Work of R. I. Moore* (Leiden, 2006).

32. This word was first given currency in the 1120s by the Paris theologian Peter Abelard when he used it as title of a controversial discussion of Christian thought, his *Theologia Christiana*. For the Islamic origins of universities, see G. Makdisi, *The Rise of Colleges: Institutions of Learning in Islam and the West* (Edinburgh, 1981), esp. pp. 285–91.

33. A good recent study is L. H. McAvoy, *Medieval Anchoritisms: Gender, Space and the Solitary Life* (Woodbridge, 2011), esp. chs 4, 5. On the origins of the word 'anchorite', see above, p. 38.

34. For the truly extraordinary creative meditation of one thirteenth-century Viennese visionary in a work which long embarrassed less imaginative Catholics, see U. Wiethaus (ed.), *Agnes Blannbekin, Viennese Beguine: Life and Revelations* (Cambridge, 2002), esp. pp. 10, 30, 34–6, 157.

35. J. G. Finlayson, 'On Not Being Silent in the Darkness: Adorno's Singular Apophaticism', *HTR* 105 (2012), 1–32, at p. 27.

36. M. O'C. Walshe (ed.), *Meister Eckhart: Sermons and Treatises* (3 vols, Shaftesbury, 1987), vol. 2, p. 64 [Sermon 53]; vol. 2, p. 321 [Sermon 94]; vol. 2, p. 246 [Sermon 82].

37. C. Wolters (ed.), *The Cloud of Unknowing Translated into Modern English* (London, 1961), 137 [*Cloud*, ch. 70].

38. An excellent account is E. A. Jones and A. Walsham (eds), *Syon Abbey and its Books: Reading, Writing and Religion c. 1400–1700* (Woodbridge, 2009).

39. I am indebted to my sometime research student Kenneth Carveley for pointing me to these texts. See J. Boffey, '*The Charter of the Abbey of the Holy Ghost* and its Role in Manuscript Anthologies', *Yearbook of English Studies*, 33 (2003), 120–30. An excellent background survey is C. Whitehead, *Castles of the Mind: A Study of Medieval Architectural Allegory* (Cardiff, 2003).

40. Boffey, '*The Charter of the Abbey of the Holy Ghost* and its Role in Manuscript Anthologies', 121.

41. S. Noffke OP (tr.), *Catherine of Siena: The Dialogue* (Mahwah, NJ, 1980), 118 [*Dialogue*, 63].

42. N. Caciola, *Discerning Spirits: Divine and Demonic Possession in the Middle Ages* (Ithaca, NY, and London, 2003), 277–98.

43. M. Rubin, 'Europe Remade: Purity and Danger in Late Medieval Europe', *TRHS*, 6th ser., 11 (2001), 101–24, at p. 106.

44. MacCulloch, *Reformation: Europe's House Divided*, 98.

45. Erasmus, *Encomium matrimonii*, in J. K. Sowards (ed.), *Erasmus: Literary and Educational Writings* (*Collected Works of Erasmus*, vols 25–6, Toronto, 1985), 129–45, at pp. 130, 137. For the complicated history of

this work, see ibid., 528–9, and for further works, J. K. Sowards (ed.), *Erasmus: Controversies* (*Collected Works of Erasmus*, vol. 71, Toronto, 1993), 85–96, and G. Bedouelle (ed.), *Erasmus: Controversies* (*Collected Works of Erasmus*, vol. 83, Toronto, 1998), 115–48.

46. P. S. Allen, H. M. Allen and H. W. Garrod (eds), *Opus Epistolarum Des. Erasmi Roterodami* . . . (12 vols, Oxford 1906–58), vol. 3, no. 858, line 561, p. 376. Cf. a similar more extended passage in a letter to Servatius Rogerus in 1514, vol. 1, no. 296, lines 70–88, pp. 567–8, and for more extended comment, MacCulloch, *Reformation: Europe's House Divided*, 104.

47. On clerical anticlericalism, see ibid., 33–52. For mockery of Cluniac sign language by secular clergy from the twelfth century onwards, see Bruce, *Silence and Sign Language in Medieval Monasticism*, 144, 161, 167–8.

48. F. A. Yates, *Giordano Bruno and the Hermetic Tradition* (London, 1964), 164–6.

49. E. Rummel, *Desiderius Erasmus* (London and New York, 2004), 55–7.

6. THE PROTESTANT REFORMATION: 1500–1700

1. Innocent IV (pope 1243–54) founded the Hermits of Tuscany, united in 1256 by Innocent's successor Alexander VI (pope 1254–61) with two other very similar small Orders. I am very grateful to my sometime student Anik Laferrière for pointing out to me what should have been obvious to me.

2. V. Gillespie, 'Anonymous Devotional Writings', in A. S. G. Edwards (ed.), *A Companion to Middle English Prose* (Cambridge, 2004), 127–50, at pp. 131–2.

3. A convenient English edition of the original text from a MS of 1497 in Würzburg, rather longer than the text which Luther published, is the rather misleadingly titled S. Winkworth (ed.), *The Theologia Germanica of Martin Luther* (London, 1893); see also 'Preface to the Complete Edition of a German Theology, 1518', *Luther's Works*, vol. 31, pp. 71–7 (from *WA*, vol. 1, pp. 378–89). See also F. Posset, '"Deification" in the German Spirituality of the Late Middle Ages and in Luther: An Ecumenical Historical Perspective', *Archiv für Reformationsgeschichte*, 84 (1993), 103–26.

4. 'The Judgment of Martin Luther on Monastic Vows', *Luther's Works*, vol. 44, pp. 243–400, esp. pp. 317–25 (*WA*, vol. 8, pp. 573–669).

5. On clerical marriage, see MacCulloch, *Reformation: Europe's House Divided*, 130–31, 140, 145, 290, 363, 447, 619, 627, 634, 636–40, 647–54, 659. For examples of the influence of Luther's tract *Iudicium*, see

G. Dipple, *Antifraternalism and Anticlericalism in the German Reformation: Johann Eberlin von Günzburg and the Campaign against the Friars* (Aldershot, 1996), 134–48.

6. Examples of Lutheran survivals are given in O. Chadwick, *The Early Reformation on the Continent* (Oxford, 2001), 168–9.

7. For examples, see Dipple, *Antifraternalism and Anticlericalism in the German Reformation*, esp. pp. 212–15, and R. Rex, 'The Friars in the English Reformation', in P. Marshall and A. Ryrie (eds), *The Beginnings of English Protestantism* (Cambridge, 2002), 38–59.

8. On these, see MacCulloch, *A History of Christianity*, 738–55.

9. For a summary account of the central issues in the split between Lutheran and Reformed, see MacCulloch, *Reformation: Europe's House Divided*, 347–58. It is significant that the writing of Luther's which had most influence beyond the Lutheran world, when most of his oeuvre was ignored, was his commentary on Galatians, precisely the Pauline Epistle which provides the best platform for justification by faith. See J. Riches, *Galatians through the Centuries* (Oxford, 2008), 4, 8, 33, 56, 63, 98, and A. Ryrie, 'The After-life of Lutheran England', in D. Wendebourg (ed.), *Sister Reformations/ Schwesterreformationen* (Tübingen, 2010), 213–34, esp. pp. 216–17, 231.

10. V. Isaiasz, 'Early Modern Lutheran Churches: Redefining the Boundaries of the Holy and the Profane', in A. Spicer (ed.), *Lutheran Churches in Early Modern Europe* (Farnham, 2012), 17–38, at pp. 22–3.

11. So prominent and influential an Anglican interior as Christopher Wren's St James Piccadilly (London) had such an arrangement up to the nineteenth century. For surviving examples, see an eighteenth-century Anglican interior in England, King's Norton (Leicestershire), and a late eighteenth-century Methodist example derived from contemporary Anglican practice, Wesley's Chapel, City Road, London, which likewise had its imitators in Methodism.

12. For extended discussion of these themes, see MacCulloch, *Reformation: Europe's House Divided*, 142, 146–7, 155, 159, 172, 193–4, 210, 248–9, 307–8, 312, 324–5, 356–7, 424, 510, 551, 558–63, 583, 613, 623, 661.

13. P. Tudor-Craig, 'Henry VIII and King David', in D. Williams (ed.), *Early Tudor England: Proceedings of the 1987 Harlaxton Symposium* (Woodbridge, 1989), 183–206, esp. pp. 193–6 and appendix II.

14. The best treatment of the English Reformation's musical tradition beyond the cathedrals is C. Marsh, *Music and Society in Early Modern England* (Cambridge, 2010), esp. pp. 391–453.

15. Zwingli, 46th Conclusion (*Schlussrede*) of 1523, quoted in C. Garside Jr, *Zwingli and the Arts* (New Haven and London, 1966), 49.

16. The RSV interestingly departs from long anglophone tradition and avoids this meaning in its translation of Eph. 5.19, having 'singing and making melody to the Lord with all your heart'.
17. Garside, *Zwingli and the Arts*, 39–46.
18. G. R. Potter, *Zwingli* (Cambridge, 1976), 208–9; U. Gäbler, *Huldrych Zwingli: His Life and Work* (Edinburgh, 1987), 107–8.
19. Garside, *Zwingli and the Arts*, 61, 68–9, 182–3.
20. T. Harding (ed.), *The Decades of Henry Bullinger* (4 vols., Parker Society, 1849–52), vol. 4, 190–97, esp. pp. 191, 195.
21. K. H. Marcus, 'Hymnody and Hymnals in Basel, 1526–1606', *SCJ* 32 (2001), 723–42, esp. pp. 727–30; see also Garside, *Zwingli and the Arts*, 62, 182–3.
22. A. Spicer, *Calvinist Churches in Early Modern Europe* (Aldershot, 2007), 228.
23. J. Schofield, *St Paul's Cathedral before Wren* (Swindon, 2011), 185–6, 356; W. Longman, *A History of the Three Cathedrals Dedicated to St Paul in London* (London, 1873), 44–51, 54–6.
24. Spicer, *Calvinist Churches in Early Modern Europe*, 148–55.
25. A whole school of Lutheran theology, commonly termed in English the Finnish School because of its origins, has as its central preoccupation the attempt to prove the opposite contention, arguing that Luther has been misunderstood for five centuries. Ingenious and learned though its arguments are, it seems to me a misconceived enterprise inspired by modern ecumenical imperatives. For an introduction, see C. E. Braaten and R. W. Jenson (eds), *Union with Christ: The New Finnish Interpretation of Luther* (Grand Rapids, Mich., 1998); in particular, the first two essays by T. Mannermaa and the response by R. W. Jenson, pp. 1–41, reveal both the ecumenical dimension of the School and what the uncharitable might regard as wish-fulfilment on the subject of Luther's theology. The ecumenical motif in the title of one foundational anglophone introduction to the movement is significant: Posset, '"Deification" in the German Spirituality of the Late Middle Ages and in Luther: An Ecumenical Historical Perspective'. For a more sympathetic critique than mine of the Finnish School from an anglophone historian of the Reformation, see S. Hendrix, 'Martin Luther's Reformation of Spirituality', *Lutheran Quarterly*, 13 (1999), 249–70, at pp. 256–8.
26. M. Luther, 'The Babylonian Captivity of the Church', *Luther's Works*, vol. 36, p. 109 (*WA*, vol. 6, p. 562). P. J. Malysz, 'Luther and Dionysius: Beyond Mere Negations', in S. Coakley and C. M. Stang (eds), *Re-thinking Dionysius the Areopagite* (Chichester, 2009), 149–62, makes a brave

effort to rescue the relationship, but it is possible to admire the effort without being convinced.

27. J. Calvin, ed. J. T. McNeill and F. L. Battles, *Institutes of the Christian Religion*, Library of Christian Classics, 20, 21 (2 vols, Philadelphia 1960), vol. 1, pp. 164-5 [*Institutes* I.xiv.4].

28. D. MacCulloch, *Thomas Cranmer: A Life* (New Haven and London, 1996), 70-72; for a good assessment of Osiander and his theology, see D. Steinmetz, *Reformers in the Wings: from Geiler von Kaysersberg to Theodore Beza* (Oxford, 2001), 64-9.

29. A good account of Böhme is A. Weeks, *Boehme: An Intellectual Biography of the Seventeenth-century Philosopher and Mystic* (New York, 1991). On Kuhlmann and his death, see W. Schmidt-Biggemann, 'Salvation through Philology: The Poetical Messianism of Quirinus Kuhlmann (1651-1689)', in P. Schäfer and M. R. Cohen (eds), *Toward the Millennium: Messianic Expectations from the Bible to Waco* (Leiden, 1998), 259-98, esp. at p. 269.

30. A prime example of this opportunistic Protestant use of allegory was in relation to the perpetual virginity of the Virgin Mary: see D. MacCulloch, 'Mary and Sixteenth-century Protestants', in R. N. Swanson (ed.), *The Church and Mary* (SCH 39, 2004), 191-217.

31. E. Bunny, *A book of Christian exercise, appertaining to resolution* ... (Oxford, 1585; *RSTC* 19360.3), p. 5.

32. Ibid., prefaces, sigs. ( ) ii^r, iv^r, vii^r.

33. B. S. Gregory, 'The "True and Zealouse Seruice of God": Robert Parsons, Edmund Bunny, and *The First Booke of the Christian Exercise*', *JEH* 45 (1994), 238-68.

34. T. Schwanda, *Soul Recreation: The Contemplative-Mystical Piety of Puritanism* (Eugene, Ore., 2012) is a good study of Ambrose: ch. 4 discusses the meditation/contemplation distinction. Another prominent English Reformed Protestant divine of the previous generation, Bishop Joseph Hall (1574-1656), still awaits a full-length study of his writings on meditation and contemplation.

35. For consciousness of the differential abilities of poorer English Protestants in reading and writing, see J. Champion, ' "Directions for the Profitable Reading of the Holy Scriptures": Biblical Criticism, Clerical Learning and Lay Readers, *c.* 1650-1720', in A. Hessayon and N. Keene (eds), *Scripture and Scholarship in Early Modern England* (Aldershot, 2006), 208-30, at pp. 210-11.

36. On diary writing and its relevance to temporary faith, see MacCulloch, *Reformation: Europe's House Divided*, 390, 472; see also E. McKay,

'English Diarists: Gender, Geography and Occupation, 1500–1700', *History*, 90 (2005), 191–212. There is a fine literature on antinomianism now, two flagships of which are T. D. Bozeman, 'The Glory of the "Third Time": John Eaton as Contra-Puritan', *JEH* 47 (1996), 638–54, and D. Como, *Blown by the Spirit: Puritanism and the Emergence of an Antinomian Underground in Pre-Civil-War England* (Stanford, Calif., 2004).

37. On 'third way' rulers in mid-sixteenth-century Europe, see MacCulloch, *Reformation: Europe's House Divided*, 253–4, 317–18, 354.

38. J. A. Spohnholz, 'Multiconfessional Celebration of the Eucharist in Sixteenth-century Wesel', *SCJ* 39 (2008), 705–30; and see also J. A. Spohnholz, *The Tactics of Toleration: A Refugee Community in the Age of Religious Wars* (Newark, NJ, 2011).

39. J. F. G. Goeters (ed.), 'Zum Weseler Abendmahlstreit von 1561–1564', *Monatshefte für Evangelische Kirchengeschichte des Rheinlandes*, 2 (1953), 136, quoted in Spohnholz, 'Multiconfessional Celebration of the Eucharist', 711–12.

40. B. J. Kaplan, *Divided by Faith: Religious Conflict and the Practice of Toleration in Early Modern Europe* (Cambridge, Mass., and London, 2007), ch. 8, esp. pp. 200–204, 233.

41. For the effect of the Zwickau Prophets on Melanchthon, see W. G. Naphy (ed.), *Documents on the Continental Reformation* (Basingstoke, 1996), 30.

42. Como, *Blown by the Spirit*, 39.

43. A. Jelsma, 'A "Messiah for Women": Religious Commotion in the North-east of Switzerland, 1525–1526', in W. J. Sheils and D. Wood (eds), *Women in the Church* (SCH 27, 1990), 295–306. A fine survey of early female radical activism is C. A. Snyder and L. A. Huebert Hecht (eds), *Profiles of Anabaptist Women: Sixteenth-century Reforming Pioneers* (Waterloo, Ont., 1996).

44. Quoted in G. H. Williams, *The Radical Reformation* (3rd rev. edn, Sixteenth Century Essays and Studies, 15, 2000), 200. A fine account of Schwenckfeld's earlier career is R. E. McLaughlin, *Caspar Schwenckfeld, Reluctant Radical: His Life to 1540* (New Haven and London, 1986); on his deafness, ibid., 33–4, 55–6.

45. Williams, *The Radical Reformation*, 199–211, 624–8. For outline discussion of the issues at stake between Luther and Zwingli, see MacCulloch, *Reformation: Europe's House Divided*, 144–8, 171–9.

46. P. Brand, 'Standing Still or Running on? Reconsidering Rhetoric in the Strasbourg Anabaptist-Spiritualist Debates, 1530–31', *JEH* 62 (2011), 20–37, at p. 27.

47. On early Schwenckfeldian disputes with Anabaptists, see M. Rothkegel, 'Anabaptism in Moravia and Silesia', in J. D. Roth and J. M. Stayer (eds), *A Companion to Anabaptism and Spiritualism, 1521–1700* (Leiden, 2007), 163–216, at pp. 190–92, and W. Packull, *Hutterite Beginnings: Communitarian Experiments during the Reformation* (Baltimore and London, 1995), 144–6.

48. J. Lecler, *Toleration and the Reformation* (2 vols, New York and London, 1960), vol. 1, p. 168.

49. A fine analysis of the spectrum is G. Dipple, 'The Spiritualist Anabaptists', in Roth and Stayer (eds), *A Companion to Anabaptism and Spiritualism*, 257–98. For the break between Schwenckfeld and Franck, ibid., 278.

50. See Como, *Blown by the Spirit*, ch. 7, for discussion of Everard.

51. J. Everard, *The Gospel treasury opened . . . whereunto is added, the Mystical Divinity of Dionysius the Areopagite . . .* (2 pts in one, London, 1657; Wing E3531), vol. 2, pp. 315–16, and cf. Como, *Blown by the Spirit*, 264, for his quotation of a similar passage. For excellent discussion of the range of Everard's translations, and of a wider efflorescence of English translations of medieval and Reformation spiritual and radical literature from mainland Europe during the Interregnum, see N. Smith, *Perfection Proclaimed: Language and Literature in English Radical Religion 1640–60* (Oxford, 1989).

52. The controversy about the existence of the Ranters, sparked by J. C. Davis, *Fear, Myth and History: The Ranters and the Historians* (Cambridge, 1986), is judiciously surveyed in G. E. Aylmer, 'Did the Ranters Exist?', *Past and Present*, 117 (Nov. 1987), 208–20, with further useful comment in *Past and Present*, 140 (Aug. 1993), 155–210.

53. On Perrot, see B. Adams, 'The "Durty Spirit" at Hertford: A Falling out of Friends', *JEH* 52 (2001), 647–75, at p. 658; his challenge to George Fox's recommendation to remove their hats in worship might be seen as showing equal temerity. For more Quaker adventures involving the Maltese Inquisition and two Quaker ladies voyaging to Alexandria disguised as Franciscans, see C. F. Black, *The Italian Inquisition* (New Haven and London, 2009), 48; for English public reaction, see J. Miller, '"A Suffering People": English Quakers and their Neighbours *c.* 1650–*c.* 1700', *Past and Present*, 188 (Aug. 2005), 71–105.

54. H. Davies, *Worship and Theology in England II: From Andrewes to Baxter and Fox 1603–1690* (Princeton, 1975), 496–7.

55. Entries in J. L. Nickalls (ed.), *The Journal of George Fox* (rev. edn, London, 1975), 106, 419, reveal Fox as evasive about his relationship to the Seekers.

56. A. Bradstock, *Radical Religion in Cromwell's England* (London, 2011), 76–7, 96.
57. B. Young Kunze, *Margaret Fell and the Rise of Quakerism* (Basingstoke, 1994), 117, and Adams, 'The "Durty Spirit" at Hertford'.
58. G. Fox, *An epistle to all people on the earth* ... (London, 1657; Wing F.1805), 2–3.
59. Ibid., 5.
60. Ibid., 10; cf. Ezra 9.4.
61. W. Britten, *Silent meeting, a wonder to the world, yet practised by the Apostles and owned by the people of God, scornfully called Quakers* ... (London, 1660; Wing B.4825).
62. Davies, *Worship and Theology in England II*, 492.
63. W. Penn, *No Cross, No Crown. Part the first, containing a discourse, shewing the nature and discipline of the holy cross of Christ* ... (8th edn, Leeds, 1743), 57, 59. A work of Anglican piety from a Huguenot turned English clergyman, Luke de Beaulieu, published eight years after the first edition of Penn's work, took as its main theme this idea of the interior monastery, while going out of its way to be rude about the Quakers from whom de Beaulieu may have borrowed the idea ('the sullenness of Melancholy Fanaticks'). Beaulieu also made specific reference to Erasmus's ideas of 'the whole Commonwealth' as a large monastery: L. de Beaulieu, *Claustrum animae: The Reformed Monastery* ... (2 pts, London, 1676/7; Wing B.1571), preface, sigs. A6^r, A7^v, A8^r. I am grateful to Kenneth Carveley for pointing me towards de Beaulieu.
64. Young Kunze, *Margaret Fell and the Rise of Quakerism*, is an enthusiastic rehabilitation.
65. P. Crawford, *Women and Religion in England 1500–1720* (London, 1993), pt 3, is a judicious survey of the question. But note an important General Baptist recognition of women in the early nineteenth century which proved trail-blazing in English Nonconformity and its corresponding American churches: T. Larsen, '"How Many Sisters Make a Brotherhood?" A Case Study in Gender and Ecclesiology in Early Nineteenth-century English Dissent', *JEH* 49 (1998), 282–92.
66. For an account of this struggle and its outcome, see MacCulloch, *Reformation: Europe's House Divided*, 213–36, 270–315.
67. W. de Boer, *The Conquest of the Soul: Confession, Discipline and Public Order in Counter-Reformation Milan* (Leiden, 2000), and for the spread of the confessional into Lutheran North Germany and Scandinavia, see M. Range, 'The "Third Sacrament": Lutheran Confessionals in Schleswig (Northern Germany)', in C. King and D. Sayer (eds),

The Archaeology of Post-medieval Religion (Woodbridge, 2011), 53–66.

68. MacCulloch, *Reformation: Europe's House Divided*, 277 (where I note that Henry VIII had pioneered the idea in his schismatic England), 299, 406–7, 424, 687.

69. Black, *The Italian Inquisition*, 69.

70. H. J. Schroeder (ed.), *Canons and Decrees of the Council of Trent* (London, 1941), 182.

71. R. Bellarmine, *An ample declaration of the Christian doctrine. Composed in Italian by the renowned Cardinal: Card. Bellarmine. Translated into English by Richard Hadock D. of Diuinitie* (Rouen [*recte* England], c. 1604; *RSTC* 1834), 239. For other examples of the same sentiment, cf. D. S. Ellington, *From Sacred Body to Angelic Soul: Understanding Mary in Late Medieval and Early Modern Europe* (Washington, 2001), 168.

72. L. J. Lekai, *The Rise of the Cistercian Strict Observance in Seventeenth Century France* (Washington, 1968).

73. J. McManners, *Church and Society in Eighteenth-century France* (2 vols., Oxford, 1998), vol. 1, p. 595.

74. See MacCulloch, *Reformation: Europe's House Divided*, 218–25, 412, 644–6.

75. J. W. O'Malley, *The First Jesuits* (Cambridge, Mass., 1993), 37.

76. I am very grateful for discussions with Philip Endean SJ and Nicholas King SJ on this point.

77. J. Bergin, *Church, Society and Religious Change in France, 1580–1730* (New Haven and London, 2009), 316.

78. O'Malley, *The First Jesuits*, 162–4.

79. M. Laird, *A Sunlit Absence: Silence, Awareness and Contemplation* (Oxford, 2011), 96, 133–4.

80. Teresa of Avila, tr. M. Starr, *The Book of My Life* (Boston, 2007), 59–60 [ch. 9]; I have made minor alterations in the spelling of this and a subsequent extract.

81. Mortley, *From Word to Silence*, vol. 1, p. 125; vol. 2, pp. 221–2; L. Girón-Negrón, 'Dionysian Thought in Sixteenth-century Spanish Mystical Theology', in Coakley and Stang (eds), *Re-thinking Dionysius the Areopagite*, 163–76, esp. at pp. 170–73.

82. Teresa of Avila, tr. Starr, *The Book of My Life*, 104–5 [ch. 15].

83. For discussion of the resulting crypto-Judaism, see above, pp. 166–7.

84. E. K. Rowe, 'St. Teresa and Olivares: Patron Sainthood, Royal Favorites and the Politics of Plurality in Seventeenth-century Spain', *SCJ* 37 (2006), 721–38.

85. An excellent account of the Quietist movement in France is provided by R. Parish, *Catholic Particularity in Seventeenth-century French Writing: 'Christianity is Strange'* (Oxford, 2011), ch. 7; for a summary account, see also Bergin, *Church, Society and Religious Change in France*, 330–31.

86. W. J. Hankey, 'Augustinian Immediacy and Dionysian Mediation in John Colet, Edmund Spenser, Richard Hooker and the Cardinal de Bérulle', in K. Flasch and D. de Courcelles (eds), *Augustinus in der Neuzeit: colloque de la Herzog August Bibliothek de Wolfenbüttel, 14–17 octobre, 1996* (Turnhout, 1998), 125–160, at pp. 154–9. *L'Invasion mystique* was the title of vol. 2 of H. Brémond, *Histoire littéraire du sentiment religieux en France* (12 vols, Paris, 1916–36). For summary discussion of Bérulle in relation to early seventeenth-century religious movements in France, see MacCulloch, *Reformation: Europe's House Divided*, 474–80.

87. [J. de Guyon], *Moyen court et très-facile de faire oraison, que tous peuvent pratiquer très aisement, et arriver par là dans peu de tems à une haute perfection* (Lyon, 1686).

88. Ibid., 17–18: I have used the translation of Parish, *Catholic Particularity in Seventeenth-century French Writing*, 164.

89. *Moyen court*, 90–91: my translation. See Luke 10.38–42, and the echo of the story with a more Christological emphasis in John 12.1–3.

90. J. de Guyon, ed. C. Morali, *Les torrents et commentaire au Cantique des Cantiques de Salomon* (Grenoble, 1992).

7. SILENCES FOR SURVIVAL

1. P. Zagorin, *Ways of Lying: Dissimulation, Persecution, and Conformity in Early Modern Europe* (Cambridge, Mass., and London, 1990), 3–5.

2. M. Ruthven, 'Storm over Syria', *New York Review of Books* (9 June 2011), 16–20, at p. 18.

3. Acts 24.14; 1 Cor. 11.19; Gal. 5.20; Tit. 3.10; 2 Pet. 2.1.

4. For detailed documentation on religious persecution in various countries, of which Russia affords the most examples of Christians persecuting Christians, see the website of Forum 18: http://www.forum18.org/.

5. For Martin's reaction, see F. R. Hoare (ed.), *The Western Fathers: Being the Lives of SS. Martin of Tours, Ambrose, Augustine of Hippo, Honoratus of Arles and Germanus of Auxerre* (London, 1954), 137 [*Dialogue with Gallus* 13]; and for the Priscillianist affair, Stevenson (ed.), rev. Frend, *Creeds, Councils and Controversies*, 159–63.

6. For Diocletian's decree against the Manichees, see Stevenson (ed.), rev. Frend, *New Eusebius*, 267–8; ibid., 265–7 provides glimpses of Manichee texts.
7. R. I. Moore, *The War on Heresy: Faith and Power in Medieval Europe* (London, 2012), 272.
8. These arguments seriously proposed by inquisitors are presented in C. I. Black, *The Italian Inquisition* (New Haven and London, 2009), 69.
9. The standard study of the Waldensians is E. Cameron, *Waldenses: Rejections of Holy Church in Medieval Europe* (Oxford, 2000). For crisp rethinking on the chimera of Western dualism, see Moore, *The War on Heresy*.
10. One recalls the Zimbabwean President Robert Mugabe's speech on 'Heroes' Day' 1995 in which he described homosexuals as 'worse than dogs and pigs' (http://www.galz.co.zw/?page_id=300, accessed 31 March 2012).
11. Zagorin, *Ways of Lying*, 42 n.
12. N. Simms, 'Being Jewish in Colonial Brazil (1500–1822): Brushing History against the Grain', *JRH* 31 (2007), 421–50, at 437.
13. J. Cooper Burnett, 'The Pulse of God', *Reflections: A Magazine of Theological and Ethical Enquiry*, 98 (Spring 2011), 14–15.
14. This is an area of enquiry whose early history still requires investigation. There is much suggestive material in J. B. V. Tannous, 'Syria between Byzantium and Islam: Making Incommensurables Speak', Ph.D. dissertation, Princeton University (2010), especially ch. 11, 'The more things change, the more they stay the same'. I am indebted to Anna Chrysostomides for pointing me to this thesis: she proposes to make this question her particular concern in research.
15. On Cyprus, see P. Jenkins, *The Lost History of Christianity: The Thousand-year Golden Age of the Church in the Middle East, Africa and Asia* (New York, 2008), 177–8; on Asia Minor, see B. Clark, *Twice a Stranger: How Mass Expulsion Forged Modern Greece and Turkey* (London, 2006), 116–18.
16. A. Hamilton, *Heresy and Mysticism in Sixteenth-century Spain: The Alumbrados* (Cambridge, 1992).
17. MacCulloch, *A History of Christianity*, 655–67, and MacCulloch, *Reformation: Europe's House Divided*, 688–97. For parallel and startling long-term ramifications in both Jewish Eastern Europe and Middle Eastern Islam of the career of the Spanish-Jewish aspirant Messiah Sabbatai Sevi (1626–76), see R. Popkin, 'When It Is Advisable to Put on a Fez', *London Review of Books* (23 May 2002), 28–9.

18. This point was made to me by Professor Massimo Firpo, and I am most grateful for our conversations. For the early Jesuits and the *Spirituali*, see MacCulloch, *Reformation: Europe's House Divided*, 222.
19. Ibid., 188, 244-6, 259, 262, 678, 693, 734; J. Friedman, *Michael Servetus: A Case Study in Total Heresy* (Geneva, 1978).
20. W. McFadden, 'The Life and Works of Antonio del Corro, 1527-91', Ph.D. thesis, Queen's University Belfast (1953); I am indebted to Dr Ronald Trueman for access to this inexplicably unpublished work. For a treatment in print of del Corro, much indebted to McFadden's work, but with additional material, see C. M. Dent, *Protestant Reformers in Elizabethan Oxford* (Oxford, 1983), 119-22 (quotation at p. 122).
21. A useful discussion is Zagorin, *Ways of Lying*, ch. 11.
22. On gods of silence, see J. R. Snyder, *Dissimulation and the Culture of Secrecy in Early Modern Europe* (Berkeley, Los Angeles and London, 2009), 10-12. For Elyot, Cranmer and Harpocrates, see D. MacCulloch, *Thomas Cranmer: A Life* (New Haven and London, 1996), 79-82.
23. J[?ohn] F[?rench] (tr.), H. C. Agrippa, *Three Books of Occult Philosophy* (London, 1650; Wing A.789), 530 (bk iii, ch. 58); an English translation of Agrippa, *De occulta philosophia libri tres* (?Basel, 1533).
24. On classicism, atheism and sodomy, see MacCulloch, *Reformation: Europe's House Divided*, 621, 693-4. On Tacitism, Lipsius and disguised Machiavellianism, see Snyder, *Dissimulation and the Culture of Secrecy in Early Modern Europe*, 7, 15-16, 61, 121-38.
25. Ibid., 121-3.
26. The classic study is still B. B. Warfield, *Calvin and Augustine* (Philadelphia, 1956). For what follows, see G. H. Tavard, 'Calvin and the Nicodemites', in R. C. Zachman (ed.), *John Calvin and Roman Catholicism: Critique and Engagement, Then and Now* (Grand Rapids, Mich., 2008), 59-78, and Zagorin, *Ways of Lying*, ch. 4.
27. Ibid., 75-6. Calvin probably had in mind a previous writing by one of those friends, Gérard Roussel, who had made a rather more positive reference to Nicodemus in one of his treatises addressed to the reformist-minded sister of King François I of France.
28. M. MacDonald, '*The Fearefull Estate of Francis Spira*: Narrative, Identity and Emotion in Early Modern England', *Journal of British Studies*, 31 (1992), 32-61, and M. A. Overell, 'The Exploitation of Francesco Spiera', *SCJ* 26 (1995), 619-37. For support for Calvin's line from his fellow-French exile Pierre Viret and from the Italian exile Peter Martyr Vermigli, see Zagorin, *Ways of Lying*, 103-7, 109-11; on martyrology

across the Reformation divides, B. S. Gregory, *Salvation at Stake: Christian Martyrdom in Early Modern Europe* (Cambridge, Mass., 1999).

29. 'Cum enim hi causam separationis tuae ignorent, concitas tantum eos contra te et tuam causam, eoque alienores ab evangelio reddis; et praeterea sumis tibi privato quod publicum est, et ad publicos ecclesiae ministros tantum pertinent': P. Fraenkel (ed.), *Martini Buceri Opera Latina IV: Consilium Theologicum privatim conscriptum* (Leiden, 1988), 11 [ch. II, 44; my translation].

30. 'Quod officium pastorale hodie recte in ecclesiis papisticis posset agi': ibid., 34–5 [ch. X].

31. Ibid., pp. xvi–xx, xxxii.

32. For the complications of the issue which turned Elizabeth decisively against Knox, see J. Dawson, 'The Two John Knoxes: England, Scotland and the 1558 Tracts', *JEH* 42 (1991), 555–76, and S. Dolff, 'The Two John Knoxes and the Justification of Non-revolution: A Response to Dawson's Argument from Covenant', *JEH* 55 (2004), 58–74.

33. A. Walsham, *Church Papists: Catholicism, Conformity and Confessional Polemic in Early Modern England*, Royal Historical Society Studies in History, 68 (1993); Garnet's coinage is at H. Garnet, *A treatise of Christian renunciation* (London, 1593; RSTC 11617.8), 154, quoted in Walsham, *Church Papists*, 41.

34. P. Wiburn, *A checke or reproofe of M. Howlets vntimely shreeching in her Maiesties eares* (London, 1581; RSTC 25586), sig. Yy4r, quoted in Walsham, *Church Papists*, 37.

35. For what follows on Jesuits and Puritans, see Zagorin, *Ways of Lying*, chs 9–10, and E. Rose, *Cases of Conscience: Alternatives Open to Recusants and Puritans under Elizabeth I and James I* (Cambridge, 1975).

36. See P. Caraman (ed.), *John Gerard: The Autobiography of an Elizabethan* (London, 1951).

37. Thomas Cartwright, writing to Lord Burghley in 1590; see A. Peel and L. H. Carlson (eds), *Cartwrightiana* (London, 1951), 27. See also J. Gray, 'Conscience and the Word of God: Religious Arguments against the Ex Officio Oath', *JEH*, forthcoming.

38. Commentary on J. Throckmorton, *The Defence of Iob Throkmorton, against the Slaunders of Maister Sutcliffe . . .* (Middelburg, 1594; RSTC 24055), sig. Eiiᴿ, quoted in Zagorin, *Ways of Lying*, 233, and L. H. Carlson, *Martin Marprelate, Gentleman: Master Job Throkmorton Laid Open in his Colors* (San Marino, Calif., 1981), 124–5. P. Collinson, 'Ecclesiastical Vitriol: Religious Satire in the 1590s and the Invention of Puritanism', in J. Guy (ed.), *The Reign of Elizabeth I: Court and Culture*

in the Last Decade (Cambridge, 1995), 150–70, at pp. 157–8, made a brief challenge to Carlson's conclusions, in favour of Martinist authorship by George Carleton: even if that were to be followed up and proved, Throckmorton's involvement in the Martinist consortium remains undoubted, and his casuistry unmistakable.

39. Zagorin, *Ways of Lying*, 68–70, effectively demolishes Carlo Ginzburg's case for the importance of the radical humanist Otto Brunfels in pioneering the case for Nicodemism.

40. For Anabaptists and martyrdom, see Gregory, *Salvation at Stake*, ch. 6. On the boom in the cult of early Christian martyrs from the 1580s, see also MacCulloch, *Reformation: Europe's House Divided*, 401, 404, 454–5.

41. E. J. Furcha, 'Reform and Revolution among Sixteenth-century Radicals', *Renaissance and Reformation*, 9 (1972), 11–22.

42. F. H. Littell, *The Anabaptist View of the Church* (rev. edn, Boston, 1958), 25–26. For polemic about *Stillstand* among Spirituals themselves as an expression of their different interpretations of what Spiritualism might mean, see P. Brand, 'Standing Still or Running on? Reconsidering Rhetoric in the Strasbourg Anabaptist-Spiritualist debates, 1530–1531', *JEH* 62 (2011), 20–37, esp. pp. 26–9. Brand also points out (p. 33) a remarkable example of an activist Anabaptist, Melchior Hoffman, adopting the term *Stillstand* in calling for the suspension of adult baptism when faced with the execution of ten of his followers in December 1531.

43. A. Hamilton, *The Family of Love* (Cambridge, 1981); C. Marsh, *The Family of Love in English Society 1550–1630* (Cambridge, 1993).

44. E. Eisenstein, *The Printing Revolution in Early Modern Europe* (Cambridge, 1983), 82, 175–6; on Plantin, see also Hamilton, *Family of Love*, 43–8 and ch. 4, and Marsh, *The Family of Love in English Society*, 169.

45. On Perne and Whitgift, 'he ... that was somtime doctor Pernes boy, and carried his cloakbagg after him? Beleeve me he hath leapt lustily?': *Oh read ouer D. Iohn Bridges, for it is a worthy worke* (1588; *RSTC* 17453), 32; 'Doctor Perne, thou knowest was thy joy, and thou his darling ...': *The iust censure and reproofe of Martin Junior* ... (?Wolston, 1589; *RSTC* 17458), sig Cii[r]; for sustained outrageous double entendres about Whitgift, Perne and oral sex, 'Why every boy hath him in his mouth', etc., J. Throckmorton, *A dialogue. Wherein is plainely laid open, the tyrannical dealing of L. bishoppes against Gods children* (La Rochelle, 1589; *RSTC* 6805), sig. D2[v]. Perne spent his last years with Whitgift, living at Lambeth Palace. See P. Collinson, 'Andrew Perne and His Times', in P. Collinson *et al.*, *Andrew Perne: Quatercentenary Studies*, Cambridge Bibliographical Society, 11 (1991), 1–34, at pp. 1, 24, 34.

46. Cf. Marsh, *The Family of Love in English Society*, 88, 94–6, 162, 273, on the Revd Robert Sharpe of Essex, and note Sharpe's association with Perne's documentation on the Familists. For an even more exalted Familist clerical suspect, see D. Wootton, 'John Donne's Religion of Love', in J. Brooke and I. Maclean (eds), *Heterodoxy in Early Modern Science and Religion* (Oxford, 2005), 31–58.

47. C. W. Marsh, 'Nonconformists and their Neighbours in Early-modern England: A Tale of Two Thomases', in D. Chadd (ed.), *Religious Dissent in East Anglia III* (Norwich, 1996), 73–96. I am indebted to Dr Marsh for our enjoyable scrutiny of Balsham church in 2011.

48. I speculate irresponsibly on this matter and on Perne and his circle in D. MacCulloch, 'The Latitude of the Church of England', in K. Fincham and P. Lake (eds), *Religious Politics in Post-Reformation England: Essays in Honour of Nicholas Tyacke* (Woodbridge, 2006), 41–59, at pp. 49–52; I am ably abetted by D. Wootton, 'Deities, Devils, and Dams: Elizabeth I, Dover Harbour and the Family of Love', *Proceedings of the British Academy*, 162 (2009), 45–68.

49. Marsh, *The Family of Love in English Society*, 282–3.

50. D. Cawdrey, *Sathan discovered, or, The Jesuits last design to ruine religion* (London, 1657; Wing C.21), 22.

51. B. J. Kaplan, *Divided by Faith: Religious Conflict and the Practice of Toleration in Early Modern Europe* (Cambridge, Mass., and London, 2007), 144–9. For Lutheran and Reformed pettiness, see MacCulloch, *Reformation: Europe's House Divided*, 351–9.

52. On Lollardy, see A. Walsham, *Charitable Hatred: Tolerance and Intolerance in England, 1500–1700* (Manchester, 2006), 77; on churching and Catholics, ibid., 209, and on Baptist marriage, ibid., 210. For powerful arguments on these lines, see C. W. Marsh, *Popular Religion in Sixteenth Century England: Holding their Peace* (Basingstoke, 1998), particularly the summary at pp. 211–14.

53. D. Hilliard, 'UnEnglish and Unmanly: Anglo-Catholicism and Homosexuality', *Victorian Studies*, 25 (1982), 181–210.

54. The discussion of homosexuality has been bedevilled by the effects of M. Foucault, *The History of Sexuality 1: An Introduction* (New York, 1978), promoting the idea that in some sense it was 'invented' in the nineteenth century. For a more realistic perspective, see the survey of B. Reay, 'Writing the Modern Histories of Homosexual England', *Historical Journal*, 52 (2009), 213–33, and for the history of the word 'homosexuality', R. Beachy, 'The German Invention of Homosexuality', *Journal of Modern History*, 82 (2010), 801–38.

55. A fine study of this transformation is F. Dabhoiwala, *The Origins of Sex: A History of the First Sexual Revolution* (London, 2012); see also Mac-Culloch, *Reformation: Europe's House Divided*, 620–29.

56. R. Norton, *Mother Clap's Molly-house: The Gay Sub-culture in England 1700–1830* (rev. edn, London, 2006), chs 10, 15. Bishop Jocelyn ended his days as a butler under an assumed name in Scotland.

57. The definitive study of the older High Church movement is P. Nockles, *The Oxford Movement in Context: Anglican High Churchmanship, 1760–1857* (Cambridge, 1994), though see also useful discussion in F. R. Bolton, *The Caroline Tradition of the Church of Ireland: With Particular Reference to Bishop Jeremy Taylor* (London, 1958).

58. See my comments on the word 'Anglicanism' in MacCulloch, 'The Latitude of the Church of England', 41–2. The classic and pioneering statement of the association between the early Oxford Movement and homosexuality remains G. Faber, *Oxford Apostles: A Character Study of the Oxford Movement* (London, 1933), 215–32.

59. The best summary of the controversy around Newman is S. Skinner, 'History *versus* Hagiography: The Reception of Turner's *Newman*', *JEH* 61 (2010), 764–81, and subsequent debate between Skinner and E. Duffy, *JEH* 63 (2012), 534–67.

60. J. H. Newman to George Dudley Ryder, 22 July 1832: I. Ker and T. Gornall SJ (eds), *The Letters and Diaries of John Henry Newman, vol. 3: New Bearings (January 1832 to June 1833)* (Oxford, 1979), 70.

61. A modern description of an Anglo-Catholic theological college is to be found in A. N. Wilson, *Unguarded Hours* (London, 1978), a comic novel in the manner of Evelyn Waugh's *Decline and Fall*, whose *roman-à-clef* qualities, down to pen-portraits easily recognizable by cognoscenti, has probably ensured its regrettable lack of further reprints.

62. J. C. Waram (ed.), *The Tourist's Church Guide: Guide to Divine Service in Those Churches Wherein the Holy Communion is Celebrated Weekly* (London, 1874 and subsequent editions). Anglo-Catholics of more recent years will have used P. E. Blagdon-Gamlen, *The Church Travellers Directory* ... (2nd edn, London, 1973).

63. The Evangelical newspaper *The Rock* (June 1868), quoted in Hilliard, 'UnEnglish and Unmanly', 189.

64. C. Mackenzie, *Sinister Street* (2 vols, London, 1913), vol. 1, p. 226; the novel was dedicated to Darwell Stone (1859–1941), then principal of Pusey House Oxford, long a Mecca for discreet Anglo-Catholic homosexuals (perhaps it is more than coincidence that a particularly comic misunderstanding in Wilson, *Unguarded Hours*, 123–5, involves a

portrait of Darwell Stone). Mackenzie's later novel *Thin Ice* (London, 1956) was an even more frank portrait of the contemporary gay underworld.

65. Mackenzie, *Sinister Street*, vol. 1, pp. 229–30. A less sympathetic glimpse of the class-levelling effect of the movement from a decade or two later is provided by advice to an Oxford undergraduate in E. Waugh, *Brideshead Revisited* (London, 1967), 30: 'Beware of the Anglo-Catholics: they're all sodomites with unpleasant accents.'

66. S. Koven, *Slumming: Sexual and Social Politics in Victorian London* (Princeton, 2004), 255–81, is a useful analysis of sexual politics in the mainly Anglo-Catholic philanthropic settlements in the East End of London.

67. M. Stringer, 'Of Gin and Lace: Sexuality, Liturgy and Identity among Anglo-Catholics in the Mid-twentieth Century', *Theology and Sexuality*, 7 (2000), 35–54, repr. in S. Hunt (ed.), *Christianity* (Farnham and Burlington, Vt., 2010), 391–411, is a fine analysis, marred only by its fatal lack of engagement with Hilliard's work and its consequent assumption that the gay Anglo-Catholic sub-culture dates no further back than the 1920s.

68. A. Paton, *Apartheid and the Archbishop: The Life and Times of Geoffrey Clayton* (London, 1974), 11; see also ibid., 208.

69. See the review of Paton's book by H. Lindsell, *Church History*, 44 (1975), 277, which nevertheless fails to make the connection to Clayton's homosexuality in its indictment of his pusillanimity.

70. See comparisons in Beachy, 'The German Invention of Homosexuality', particularly pp. 825–7.

71. W. S. F. Pickering, *Anglo-Catholicism: A Study in Religious Ambiguity* (London and New York, 1989): ch. 8 is a particularly fine analysis of the gay male dimension in Anglo-Catholicism.

72. The impact of the LGCM is well chronicled in S. Gill (ed.), *The Lesbian and Gay Christian Movement: Campaigning for Justice, Truth and Love* (London and New York, 1998). Fr Kenneth Leech's now famous phrase began differently ordered, as 'lace, gin and backbiting', in a letter of his to the *Catholic Standard* (Nov. 1975), p. 3, and was reported in the *Church Times* (12 Dec. 1975), while popular usage gave it the more punchy formulation; see K. Leech, 'Beyond Gin and Lace: Homosexuality and the Anglo-Catholic Subculture', in A. Beck and R. Hunt (eds), *Speaking Love's Name: Homosexuality. Some Catholic and Socialist Reflections*, Jubilee Group Pamphlets (London, 1988), 16–27, at p. 16. I am indebted to Matthew Bemand-Qureshi for his assistance in ferreting out this intellectual genealogy.

73. My personal observation of these conversions concurs with the judgement of an anonymous Cambridge near-contemporary of mine, interviewed in a pioneering example of social observation of sexuality, in F. Musgrove with R. Middleton and P. Hawes, *Margins of the Mind* (London, 1977), 31: 'A very large percentage of Catholic converts are gay.' His observations of the Cambridge of the 1970s (ibid., 31–2) also corroborate my general picture of gay Anglo-Catholic Nicodemism.

8. THINGS NOT REMEMBERED

1. Among many poignant cases of institution versus people with which I will not deal further here is the long-hidden story of the stigmatization of German Lutherans in South Australia during two world wars, described in E. Koepping, 'Healing the Abscess: Pastoral Care in South Australia from the Perspective of Pulpit and Pew', in her *Food, Friends and Funerals* (Berlin, 2008), 36–56. The question of historical memory is usefully presented with many case studies in S. Radstone and B. Schwarz (eds), *Memory: Histories, Theories, Debates* (New York, 2010): the introduction by the editors (pp. 1–9) is a good orientation for what follows.
2. T. A. Fudge, review of J. Lössl, *The Early Church: History and Memory* (London and New York 2010), in *JRH* 35 (2011), 419. For an overview of the early phases of episcopacy, see MacCulloch, *A History of Christianity*, 130–36.
3. I. H. Garipzanov, 'Wandering Clerics and Mixed Rituals in the Early Christian North, *c.* 1000–*c.* 1150', *JEH* 63 (2012), 1–17, esp. p. 17, where Garipzanov *inter alia* notes the absence of any reference to Armenian bishops in O. Vésteinsson, *The Christianization of Iceland: Priests, Power and Social Change 1000–1300* (Oxford, 1999).
4. R. Vose, *Dominicans, Muslims and Jews in the Medieval Crown of Aragon* (Cambridge, 2009), 135.
5. For the background to this, see MacCulloch, *A History of Christianity*, 222–67, and for a near-contemporary Miaphysite Armenian commentary on the rise of Muhammad and the first Muslim expansion, which discusses Islam in cautiously sympathetic terms, see R. W. Thomson (tr.) with J. Howard-Johnston and T. Greenwood (eds), *The Armenian History Attributed to Sebeos* (2 vols, Liverpool, 1999), esp. vol. 2, pp. 134–77.
6. A. Hadjar, *The Church of St. Simeon the Stylite and Other Archaeological Sites in the Mountains of Simeon and Halaqa* (Damascus, [1995]), 24–6.

7. For Peter's emphatic anti-Chalcedonianism, see C. B. Horn, *Asceticism and Christological Controversy in Fifth-century Palestine: The Career of Peter the Iberian* (Oxford, 2006). The use of 'Iberia' for Georgia is confusing, since the same word was also used by the Romans (and still remains in use) for the western European peninsula which contains Spain and Portugal. On the Georgian Church's transition to Chalcedonian Christianity, see C. Baumer, *The Church of the East: An Illustrated History of Assyrian Christianity* (London and New York, 2006), 71.

8. G. A. Williamson (tr.), *Procopius: The Secret History* (London, 1966). There has been controversy as to whether the *Secret History* ought to be taken seriously, but there is no good reason to doubt the overall substance of what Procopius wrote.

9. M. Hunter, *Robert Boyle, 1627–1691: Scrupulosity and Science* (Woodbridge, 2000), ch. 10. T. Browne, *Religio Medici* (London, 1642; Wing B.5167), 82.

10. A. B. Worden (ed.), *A voyce from the watch tower. Part Five: 1660–1662*, Camden Society, 4th ser. (1978): see especially the introduction.

11. A. J. Schmidt, *Veiled and Silenced: How Culture Shaped Sexist Theology* (Macon, Ga., 1989), ch. 5.

12. R. Meens, 'Ritual Purity and Gregory the Great', in R. N. Swanson (ed.), *Unity and Diversity in the Church* (SCH 32, 1996), 31–43, at p. 35. Cf. L. Sherley-Price and R. E. Latham (eds), *Bede: A History of the English Church and People* (London, 1968), 76–83 [I.27–28], esp. p. 78.

13. Rom. 16.1–7.

14. M. Buhagiar, 'The Jewish Catacombs of Roman Melite', *Antiquaries Journal*, 91 (2011), 73–100, at pp. 83–4, adds one more reference from Malta (to Eulogia as *presbytera* and wife of the gerousiarch) to seven similar Diaspora texts gathered in B. J. Brooten, *Women Leaders in the Ancient Synagogue*, Brown Judaic Studies 36 (Chico, Calif., 1982); they use the title *presbytera*, *presbyterissa* or *presbytis* for women who served as elders in Hellenistic Jewish synagogues. Only three of these eight refer to a male relative as well, suggesting that their titles are not simply reflections of some male office-holder.

15. U. E. Eisen, *Women Officeholders in Early Christianity: Epigraphical and Literary Studies* (Collegeville, Minn., 2000), esp. on Junias, pp. 47–8, 54, 56, and on deacons, pp. 159–98. See also B. J. Brooten, '"Junia … Outstanding among the Apostles" (Romans 16.7)', in L. and A. Swidler (eds), *Women Priests: A Catholic Commentary on the Vatican Declaration* (New York, 1977), 141–4.

16. On these examples and others, see MacCulloch, *Reformation: Europe's House Divided*, 656–65.

17. N. Denzey, *The Bone Gatherers: The Lost Worlds of Early Christian Women* (Boston, 2007), ch. 7, esp. pp. 194–7.

18. M. J. Haemig, 'Elisabeth Cruciger (1500?–1535): The Case of the Disappearing Hymn Writer', *SCJ* 32 (2001), 21–44.

19. L. Scaraffia, 'A Woman's Intuition', 7 September 2011, http://www
.osservatoreromano.va/portal/dt?JSPTabContainer.setSelected=JSPTabC
ontainer%2FDetail&last=false=&path=/news/editoriali/2011/205q11-L-
intuizione-di-una-donna.html&title=%20%20%20A%20
woman's%20intuition%20%20%20&detailLanguage=en, accessed 4
April 2012.

20. D. MacCulloch, 'Mary and Sixteenth-century Protestants', in R. N. Swanson (ed.), *The Church and Mary* (SCH 39, 2004), 191–217.

21. C. Moyse, *A History of the Mothers' Union: Women, Anglicanism and Globalisation, 1876–2008* (Woodbridge, 2009), 46, 49–51, 97, 108.

22. J. Cruickshank and B. Curtis Clark, 'Converting Mrs Crouch: Women, Wonders and the Formation of English Methodism, 1738–1741', *JEH*, forthcoming (2014), citing R. P. Heitzenrater, 'The Second Rise of Methodism: Georgia', *Methodist History*, 28 (1990), 117–32, at p. 131.

23. C. Beardsley, *Unutterable Love: The Passionate Life and Preaching of F. W. Robertson* (Cambridge, 2009), and cf. her remarkably gracious reference to Fallows in relation to the Robertson MSS, ibid., pp. ix–x, xxx. For a portrait of Fallows, bringing out his many good qualities, see J. S. Peart-Binns, *Gordon Fallows of Sheffield* (Langley Park, 2007); he mentions the bishop's concealment at p. 89. For an artless account of the same events which did not pick up Bishop Fallows's manoeuvres, see M. Thomas, *The Diary: Sex, Death and God in the Affairs of a Victorian Cleric* (Bloomington, Ind., 2008). There are wise remarks about *de mortuis nil nisi bonum* in T. Beeson (ed.), *Priests and Prelates: The* Daily Telegraph *Clerical Obituaries* (London, 2002), pp. xi–xii.

24. D. MacKinnon, 'Tillich, Frege, Kittel: Some Reflections on a Dark Theme', in MacKinnon, *Explorations in Theology 5* (London, 1979), 129–37.

25. Karl Barth (1886–1968), whose formidably extensive work has remained more fashionable in theological circles than that of Paul Tillich, deserves similar scrutiny and assessment.

26. MacKinnon, 'Tillich, Frege, Kittel', 134–6.

27. A useful observation, which I first came across in M. Loudon, *Revelations: The Clergy Questioned* (London, 1994), 27.

28. K. Liebreich, *Fallen Order: A History* (London, 2004).
29. Ibid., 71, 13.
30. Ibid., 8, 49–50, 58, 69–71, 75–6, 78, 169–70, 213.
31. Ibid., 125, 169–74, 189, 192–3, 232, 257.
32. Ibid., 68; for a useful set of citations from early Egyptian monasticism, see Harmless, *Desert Christians*, 233–4.
33. For two local studies of this process, see J. Bottin, *Seigneurs et paysans dans l'ouest du pays de Caux, 1540–1650* (Paris, 1983), 269–71; R. Pörtner, *The Counter-Reformation in Central Europe: Styria 1580–1630* (Oxford, 2001), 4, 97–9, 182, 187.
34. W. Behringer, 'Witchcraft Studies in Austria, Germany and Switzerland', in J. Barry, M. Hester and G. Roberts (eds), *Witchcraft in Early Modern Europe: Studies in Culture and Belief* (Cambridge, 1996), 64–95, at pp. 86–8.
35. A similar observation might be made about the equally dismal efforts in various situations in the Protestant world to cover up wife-beating by the clergy. Such silences may be played out against a more general tolerance of marital abuse in some Christian communities. A useful discussion of both issues is E. Koepping, 'Silence, Collusion and Sin: Domestic Violence among Christians across Asia', *Madang*, 15 (July 2011), 49–74.
36. John 8.44.
37. Matt. 27.25.
38. Quoted in M. J. Salmon, *Preaching without Contempt: Overcoming Unintended Anti-Judaism* (Minneapolis, 2006), 132.
39. See J. D. G. Dunn, 'The Embarrassment of History: Reflections on the Problem of "Anti-Judaism" in the Fourth Gospel', in R. Bieringer, D. Pollefeyt and F. Vandecasteele-Vanneuville (eds), *Anti-Judaism and the Fourth Gospel* (Louisville, Ky., 2001), 41–60, esp. pp. 56–9. I am grateful to Prof. Dunn for our conversations about this.
40. On the origins of the blood-libel in Norwich, see S. Yarrow, *Saints and their Communities: Miracle Stories in Twelfth-century England* (Oxford, 2006), ch. 5, and on the blood-libel generally, see R. Po-chia Hsia, *The Myth of Ritual Murder: Jews and Magic in Reformation Germany* (New Haven and London, 1988).
41. For an unsparing indictment of one section of the Western Church in this respect which, despite its technicolor character, deserves to be taken seriously by those who would seek to refute it, see D. Goldhagen, *A Moral Reckoning: The Role of the Catholic Church in the Holocaust and its Unfulfilled Duty of Repair* (London, 2003). A wise approach to a corrective on such indictments is T. Kushner, '"Pissing in the Wind"? The

Search for Nuance in the Study of Holocaust "Bystanders"', in D. Cesarani and P. Levine (eds), *'Bystanders' to the Holocaust: A Re-evaluation* (London, 2002), 57–77, but see also a more measured and still sobering survey, F. Buscher and M. Phayer, 'German Catholic Bishops and the Holocaust, 1940–1952', *German Studies Review*, 11 (1988), 463–85.

42. For Barth's regret at being inhibited by his political realism in the 1934 discussions on drafting the declaration, see M. D. Hockenos, *A Church Divided: German Protestants Confront the Nazi Past* (Bloomington, Ind., 2004), 172–3. For the text of the Barmen Declaration, and related documents, see A. C. Cochrane, *The Church's Confession under Hitler* (Philadelphia, 1962), esp. pp. 238–42.

43. *Church Assembly Report of Proceedings*, 16 (1935), 464, quoted in T. Lawson, *The Church of England and the Holocaust: Christianity, Memory and Nazism* (Woodbridge, 2006), 35.

44. There is now a considerable literature on Parkes, based on his archive at Southampton University: see T. Kushner, 'James Parkes, the Jews and Conversionism: A Model for Multi-cultural Britain?', in D. Wood (ed.), *Christianity and Judaism* (SCH 29, 1992), 451–61, R. Everett, *Christianity without Antisemitism: James Parkes and the Jewish-Christian Encounter* (Oxford, 1993), and H. Chertok, *He Also Spoke as a Jew: The Life of the Reverend James Parkes* (London and Portland, Ore., 2006). *Crockford's Clerical Directory* during Parkes's lifetime records him as having one curacy in Hampstead (1925–8) and no subsequent parish; he was Public Preacher in the dioceses of St Albans and Rochester from 1935.

45. Lawson, *The Church of England and the Holocaust*, 102–5; quotation (ibid., 105) from Lambeth Palace, Temple Papers 31, fo. 397, William Temple to Louis Sherman, 6 April 1944, and cf. Temple Papers 31, fos. 282–96.

46. Lawson, *The Church of England and the Holocaust*, 6, 22, 66–7, 92–5, 107–11; on Bell and de-Nazification, ibid., 153–5. For the German Churches' involvement with Nazism, and their chequered record in de-Nazification after 1945, see E. Klee, *Persilscheine und falsche Pässe: wie die Kirchen den Nazis halfen* (Frankfurt am Main, 1991).

47. Text given at V. Barnett, *For the Soul of the People: Protestant Protest against Hitler* (Oxford, 1998), 209. N. Railton, 'Escaping from Sodom: A Christian Jew Encounters German Antisemitism', *JEH* (forthcoming, 2013), a sobering indictment of the general German Protestant record before and after 1945, makes the point that only four out of twenty-seven

provincial Churches adopted the Declaration in 1945. It must be said that the most frank Vatican discussion of the Holocaust, *We Remember: A Reflection on the Shoah* (Holy See: Commission for Religious Relations with the Jews, 1998), also just stops short of speaking of sins of commission on the part of Catholics during the Holocaust.

48. M. S. Mayer, *They Thought They Were Free: The Germans, 1933–45* (2nd edn, Chicago, 1966), 168–9, probably records the earliest version, from soon after 1945. For Harold Marcuse's fascinating chronicle and analysis of the origins and afterlife of the quotation, see http://www.history.ucsb.edu/faculty/marcuse/niem.htm, accessed 7 April 2012.

49. F. J. Coppa, *The Policies and Politics of Pope Pius XII: Between Diplomacy and Morality* (New York, 2011), 13, 72–3, 101–14. Besides Coppa's short study (which is judicious and has a useful bibliography but is marred by extremely incompetent presentation), recent summaries of the results of a vast field of research are N. Atkin and F. Tallett, *Priests, Prelates and People: A History of European Catholicism since 1750* (London, 2003), 244–7, and E. Duffy, *Saints and Sinners: A History of the Popes* (3rd edn, New Haven and London, 2006), 345–50.

50. The title of J. Cornwell, *Hitler's Pope: The Secret History of Pius XII* (London, 1999).

51. A full-length study of this is E. Fattorini, *Pio XI, Hitler e Mussolini: la solitudine di un papa* (Turin, 2007), now published in English translation by C. Ipsen as *Hitler, Mussolini and the Vatican: Pope Pius XI and the Speech That Was Never Made* (Cambridge, Mass., 2011).

52. Duffy, *Saints and Sinners*, 348.

53. F. J. Coppa, *The Papacy, the Jews and the Holocaust* (Washington, 2006), 212–14.

54. J. R. Oldfield, *'Chords of Freedom': Commemoration, Ritual and British Transatlantic Slavery* (Manchester, 2007), summed up at pp. 172–4.

55. M. Jackson, *Let This Voice Be Heard: Anthony Benezet, Father of Atlantic Abolitionism* (Philadelphia, 2009).

56. MacCulloch, *A History of Christianity*, 782–83, and N. Keene, '"A Two-edged Sword": Biblical Criticism and the New Testament Canon in Early Modern England', in A. Hessayon and N. Keene (eds), *Scripture and Scholarship in Early Modern England* (Aldershot, 2006), 94–115.

57. For that contradictory point of view, see M. Barton, 'Was Paul an Arch-advocate of Slavery or a Liberator?', in A. G. Reddie (ed.), *Black Theology, Slavery and Contemporary Christianity* (Farnham, 2010), 47–58, but compare, J. A. Harrill, *Slaves in the New Testament: Literary,*

Social and Moral Dimensions (Minneapolis, 2006), 6–16, 177–8. A tradition about the letter has Onesimus stealing money from Philemon and then running away from his master to meet Paul, for reasons unknown (cf. ibid., 6–7). This has no basis in the text and probably arose from a desire to make sense of the letter's peculiar content. The survival of the tradition unchallenged in much contemporary biblical commentary is significant, and probably results from modern embarrassment at Paul's obvious acceptance that Onesimus could be useful to him as a slave. See also MacCulloch, *A History of Christianity*, 114–16, 866–73.

58. A crisp discussion is G. M. E. de Ste Croix, 'Early Christian Attitudes to Property and Slavery', *SCH* 12 (1971), 1–38, esp. pp. 19–24.

59. For what follows, see H. R. Davis, 'The Negro a Beast: *Nachash* Theology and the Nineteenth-century Re-making of Negro Origins', Ph.D. dissertation, St Louis University (2012), esp. pp. 32–41, 65, 67–8, 82–100, 108–41, 155–70, 186–92, 201–14. I am extremely grateful to Dr Davis for making his thesis available to me.

60. A. Clarke, *The Holy Bible: Containing the Old and New Testaments* (4 vols, London, 1810), vol. 1, p. 115. I feel a particular poignancy in Clarke's posthumous predicament, having been custodian of his personal papers for twelve years as librarian and archivist of Wesley College, Bristol. For Hamitic theories about blacks and slavery, see MacCulloch, *A History of Christianity*, 867–8.

61. T. Glasson, *Mastering Christianity: Missionary Anglicanism and Slavery in the Atlantic World* (Oxford, 2012); USPG website, http://www.uspg.org.uk/article.php?article_id=130, accessed 4 April 2012. In April 2007 I found a full page dealing with the Codrington Plantation on the website, of which a record remains (http://web.archive.org/web/20070405173142/http://www.uspg.org.uk/, accessed 17 April 2012); the page itself has since disappeared. Excellently frank by contrast is an essay in the official commemorative volume published for the USPG: N. Titus, 'Concurrence without Compliance: SPG and the Barbadian Plantations, 1710–1834', in D. O'Connor, *Three Centuries of Mission: The United Society for the Propagation of the Gospel 1701–2000* (London, 2000), 249–61.

62. *Guardian* (27 March 2007): http://www.guardian.co.uk/uk/2007/mar/27/race.world1, accessed 27 Jan. 2012. For an honourably complex reflection on the event by the brother of its organizer, see A. G. Reddie's introduction to Reddie (ed.), *Black Theology, Slavery and Contemporary Christianity*, 1–30.

9. SILENCE IN PRESENT AND FUTURE
CHRISTIANITIES

1. I must record my gratitude to Fr Christophe Lazowski and the Abbot and community of Saint-Wandrille for their warm welcome and hospitality during our visit in July 2007.
2. M. Laird, *A Sunlit Absence: Silence, Awareness and Contemplation* (Oxford, 2011), 6. For further wise words on silence from a secular composer of modern times, see the e-essays of Michael Pisaro, http://www.timescraper.de/pisaro/MPTexte_e.html, accessed 17 April 2012.
3. E. Hynes, *Knock: The Virgin's Apparition in Nineteenth-century Ireland* (Cork, 2008), 1, 178.
4. D. Blackbourn, *Marpingen: Apparitions of the Virgin Mary in Bismarckian Germany* (Oxford, 1993), 2. On Lourdes, see R. Harris, *Lourdes: Body and Spirit in the Secular Age* (London, 1999).
5. Hynes, *Knock*, 31–2, 132–4, 148–54, 163–71, 211–14, 221–34, 255–6.
6. See ch. 1 above.
7. See pp. 61–4 above.
8. See pp. 80–83 above.
9. See ch. 4 above.
10. See pp. 105–24 above.
11. For a sympathetic commentary, see D. N. Maltz, 'Joyful Noise and Reverent Silence: The Significance of Noise in Pentecostal Worship', in D. Tannen and M. Saville-Troike, *Perspectives on Silence* (Norwood, NJ, 1985), 113–37.
12. P. Jenkins, *The Lost History of Christianity: The Thousand-year Golden Age of the Church in the Middle East, Africa and Asia* (New York, 2008), 37.
13. See pp. 142–4 above.
14. Quoted in obituary by R. Eyre, in the *Guardian* (26 Jan. 2009). Fenton would have appreciated a further recent development of this theme at the centre of R. Muers, *Keeping God's Silence: Towards a Theological Ethics of Communication* (London, 2008).
15. This quotation is often attributed as original to Vanstone, e.g. in his obituary by T. Beeson, *Daily Telegraph* (15 March 1999), repr. T. Beeson (ed.), *Priests and Prelates: The* Daily Telegraph *Clerical Obituaries* (London, 2002), 214–16, or alternatively to Vanstone's close friend Archbishop Robert Runcie, but I am indebted to Prof. Jane Dawson for her Methodist insight in sourcing Gordon Rupp's Presidential Address to the 1968 British Methodist Conference, reported in the *Methodist*

Recorder (20 June 1968), with reference specifically to some younger ordained Methodist ministers, whom Rupp likened to 'a swimming bath where all the noise, the shouting and the splashing is coming from the shallow end'. His subsequent exchange on the subject with Dr John Vincent, *Methodist Recorder* (25 July 1968), is worth savouring as a vintage no-holds-barred intra-Methodist conversation: both anthologized in J. A. Vickers, *Wisdom and Wit: An Anthology from the Writings of Gordon Rupp* (London, 1993), 90 and n.

16. G. Steiner, *Errata: An Examined Life* (New Haven and London, 1997), 152, quoted in D. F. Ford, 'Apophasis and the Shoah: Where Was Jesus Christ at Auschwitz?', in O. Davies and D. Turner (eds), *Silence and the Word: Negative Theology and Incarnation* (Cambridge, 2002), 185–200, at p. 185.

17. E. Berkovits, *Faith after the Holocaust* (New York, 1973); R. Harries, *After the Evil: Christianity and Judaism in the Shadow of the Holocaust* (Oxford, 2003), 30–37, 57–9. On Qoheleth, see above, p. 23.

18. Parkes's awkwardness is put into especially effective counterpoint with his career by H. Chertok, *He Also Spoke as a Jew: The Life of the Reverend James Parkes* (London and Portland, Ore., 2006). A glance at the excellent article on Bishop Herbert Hensley Henson in the *Oxford Dictionary of National Biography*, s.v. Henson, Herbert Hensley, will reveal the same character traits: cf. p. 209 above. W. James, *Varieties of Religious Experience: A Study in Human Nature*, Centenary Edition (London and New York, 2002), 23–5, has wise remarks on the paradox.

19. R. Wagner, *Secrecy, Sophistry and Gay Sex in the Catholic Church: The Systematic Destruction of an Oblate Priest* (Las Vegas, Nev., 2011). His doctoral thesis is reprinted as pp. 137–245. It was presented to the Institute for Advanced Study of Human Sexuality, San Francisco, a non-accredited degree-granting institution, founded in 1976 with backing from the United Methodist Church, United Church of Christ, two Presbyterian Churches and an American Baptist Church, and still in existence. The Institute's own current homepage (as at 23 January 2013) is http://www.humansexualityeducation.com.

20. Wagner, *Secrecy, Sophistry and Gay Sex in the Catholic Church*, 62.

21. A book containing both autobiography and reflection on the future of the Church of England is M. Hampson, *Last Rites: The End of the Church of England* (London, 2006). Like Fr Wagner's book, it is extremely, if understandably, angry. A moving parallel account, with a positive message, from one gay Catholic Irish-American priest is

B. J. Lynch, *If It Wasn't Love: A Journal about Sex, Death and God* (Alresford, 2011), especially ch. 1, 'Journal Entry Number 1.

22. A. Patrick, 'Contextualising Recent Tensions in Seventh-Day Adventism: "A Constant Process of Struggle and Rebirth"?', *JRH* 34 (2010), 272–88. The textbook was R. W. Schwarz, *Light Bearers to the Remnant: Denominational History Textbook for Seventh-Day Adventist College Classes* (Mountain View, Calif., 1979).

23. F. M. Brodie, *No Man Knows My History: The Life of Joseph Smith* (New York, 1945).

24. P. Lindholm (ed.), *Latter-day Dissent: At the Crossroads of Intellectual Inquiry and Ecclesiastical Authority* (Salt Lake City, 2011), pp. xx–xxi. An interesting intra-Mormon confrontation is building in 2012 over the production of a YouTube coming-out video produced by USGA (Understanding Same-Gender Attraction), 'an unofficial group of Brigham Young University students, faculty, and friends': http://www.youtube.com/watch?v=YmojXg-hKCI, accessed 30 June 2012.

25. One able recent exposition and expansion of the 'Axial Age' theory has been K. Armstrong, *The Great Transformation: The World in the Time of Buddha, Socrates, Confucius and Jeremiah* (London, 2006). I reviewed this irreverently in the *Guardian* (18 March 2006), and, while I remain sceptical about the coherence of the 'Axial Age' thesis, I must concede that my own analysis of changing attitudes in the Tanakh to silence (above, Ch. 1), might be seen as one illustration of the Axial Age argument.

26. T. Schwanda, *Soul Recreation: The Contemplative-Mystical Piety of Puritanism* (Eugene, Ore., 2012), and on Barth's resistance to mysticism, ibid., 202–16.

27. M. Furlong, *Merton: A Biography* (London, 1980), 220, 253, and see especially ibid., chs 16–17.

28. N. Mayhew-Smith, *Britain's Holiest Places: The All-new Guide to 500 Sacred Sites* (Richmond, 2011). For a brilliant analysis of the fate of sacred places after the British Reformations, a more complex picture than might be expected, see A. Walsham, *The Reformation of the Landscape: Religion, Identity and Memory in Early Modern Britain and Ireland* (Oxford, 2011).

29. L. Baron, 'Noise and Degeneration: Theodor Lessing's Crusade for Quiet', *Journal of Contemporary History*, 17 (1982), 165–78, at p. 166.

30. A. Topham, *Chronicles of the Prussian Court* (London, 1926), 245, recalling her conversation about the Canadian remembrance with Kaiser Wilhelm II, who unsurprisingly was unenthusiastic about corporate

silence. G. Prochnik, *In Pursuit of Silence: Listening for Meaning in a World of Noise* (New York, 2010), 39, is probably misplaced in his scepticism about that story, but otherwise has a useful account of the origins of the Remembrance Silence.

31. M. Pisaro, 'Time's Underground', http://www.timescraper.de/pisaro/MPTexte_e.html, accessed 17 April 2012. A good study of a now iconic exercise in musical silence is K. Gann, *No Such Thing as Silence: John Cage's 4´33˝* (New Haven and London, 2010), and there is an interesting short discussion in C. Kenny, *The Power of Silence: Silent Communication in Daily Life* (London, 2011), ch. 5: 'Film, TV, and Music'.

32. G. L. Prestige, *The Life of Charles Gore* (London, 1935), 428–9.

33. A. Lingas, 'Medieval Byzantine Chant and the Sound of Orthodoxy', in A. Louth and A. Casiday (eds), *Byzantine Orthodoxies* (Aldershot, 2006), 131–50, esp. pp. 144, 146.

34. Useful discussion of Erasmian humanism and musical reform is found in S. M. Holmes, 'The Title of Article 27(26): Cranmer, Durandus and Pope Innocent III', *JEH* 64 (2013), forthcoming.

35. A particularly egregious example is the Agnus Dei of Mozart's *Missa Brevis* in D major, K. 194. NB James, *Varieties of Religious Experience*, 35: 'There must be something solemn, serious and tender about any attitude which we denominate religious. If glad, it must not grin or snicker; if sad, it must not scream or curse.' I have to say that the really rather noisy final *Dona nobis pacem* of Bach's B minor Mass manages to square the circle in a fashion of which James would approve.

36. On Tippett's agnostic and Jungian transcendentalism and the *Vision*, see I. Kemp, *Tippett: The Composer and His Music* (Oxford and New York, 1987), 12, 36–7, 39, 400–401. During my youth in Wetherden (Suffolk), I liked to imagine the young Michael Tippett half a century before, occupying the proprietory pew of his home, Martin's Farm, immediately behind the Rectory pew in which I sat in the chancel of the parish church, but I fear that those appearances are likely to have been very occasional.

37. 'Dicebamus ergo: si cui sileat tumultus carnis, sileant phantasiae terrae et aquarum et aeris . . .' Augustine, *Confessions*, 9.10.25: PL 32, col. 774.

38. Isaac the Syrian, 'On Silence', in *The Ascetical Homilies of Saint Isaac the Syrian* (Boston, 1984), 33, quoted in Laird, *A Sunlit Absence*, 80.

39. S. L. Greenslade (ed.), *The Cambridge History of the Bible: The West from the Reformation to the Present Day* (Cambridge, 1963), 7, 20–21, 25, 100; G. Rupp and B. Drewery (eds), *Martin Luther* (London, 1970),

87–91. For (perhaps evangelically indulgent) treatment of examples of the ways in which Luther pushed the Bible's meaning towards his own priorities, see M. D. Thompson, *A Sure Ground on Which to Stand: The Relation of Authority and Interpretive Method in Luther's Approach to Scripture* (Carlisle, 2004), esp. pp. 112–46, 235–9.

40. For one exception to prove the rule, see J. Lössl, 'Augustine in Byzantium', *JEH* 51 (2000), 267–95.

41. 'orationes . . . raptim quodammodo iaculatas': Augustine to Anicia Faltonia Proba, letter 130.20 (*PL* 33, col. 501); I have adapted and altered the translation from W. Parsons (ed.), *The Writings of St Augustine, vol. 10: Letters II* (New York, 1953), 391.

42. Evagrius, *Talking Back: A Monastic Handbook for Combating Demons. Prologue* (Collegeville, Minn., 1993), quoted in Laird, *A Sunlit Absence*, 13.

43. T. A. Fudge, review of J. Lössl, *The Early Church: History and Memory* (London and New York, 2010), *JRH* 35 (2011), 419.

44. M. Ross, *Writing the Icon of the Heart: In Silence Beholding* (Oxford, 2011), 89–98, speaks interestingly of a parallel process of 'practical adoration', moving from 'apophatic' silence to 'logophatic' adoration into a deeper silence.

45. Luke 4.9–12; note the different positioning in Matt. 4.5–7.

46. D. MacKinnon, 'Tillich, Frege, Kittel: Some Reflections on a Dark Theme', in MacKinnon, *Explorations in Theology 5* (London, 1979), 129–37, at pp. 136–7.

47. See above, p. 2; M. Atwood, *The Blind Assassin* (London, 2000), 395.

Index

All dates are CE unless stated as BCE. Popes are cross-referenced from their entry under their birth-name to their papal name, s.v. Rome; monarchs are gathered under their principal territory, and Archbishops of Canterbury under Canterbury. Members of European nobility are indexed under their surnames. Those who have been declared saints by one or other Christian Church are indexed either under their first names or their surnames, not at 'Saint'.

Ghislieri, Michele: *see* Rome,
Church of, Popes: Pius V
Gibson, Mel 208
Gifford Lectures 4–5, 202, 228, 238
gilds/guilds (confraternities; mysteries) 154
Giles of Rome 197
Gilgamesh, Epic of 20
Ginzburg, Carlo 289
'Glorious Revolution' (1688) 176
glossolalia 42, 44–5, 233
gnosticism and *gnosis* 56–62,
70–71, 73, 78, 81, 88, 121,
145, 220, 229; and martyrdom
65–6, 68, 180, 203, 220, 223
see also apocryphal writings;
Basilides; Judaism; Nag
Hammadi; Valentinus and
Valentinianism
God 4, 43, 45, 63, 121, 131–2, 148,
158; anger 12–13, 18–19;
divine grace 135; as Father 79;
in gnosticism 57–63; in
Judaism Ch. 1, 58; hidden 18,
122; judgement 29; as *Kyrios*
26; nature of 46–7, 220–21;
and Plato 25–6, 57–61, 220;
representations of 105–6;
silence of 18–19, 33–5, 78–9,
122, 223–4; sufferings 224;
'that yonder' 78–9; universal
20–22; unknowable 79, 122;
vision of 86, 89
see also Arius and Arianism;
gnosticism and *gnosis*; Holy
Spirit; Iconoclastic Controversy; Jesus Christ; negative
theology; soteriology; *Tetragrammaton*; *theosis*; Trinity,
Holy; Unitarianism; Yahweh

Goethe, Johann Wolfgang von 259
Golgotha 224, 238–9
see also Jesus Christ: crucifixion
and death
Goodman, Gabriel 175
Gore, Charles 232
Gorze Abbey 94
Gospels 31–42, 72, 154, 219–20 *see
also* Bible; Synoptic Gospels
Goya, Francisco 205
grace of God 111
see also Augustine of Hippo; God;
soteriology
Grande Chartreuse 99
Great Britain (United Kingdom)
213, 230
Queens:
Elizabeth II 216
Victoria (Queen-Empress) 200
see also Atlantic Isles; British
Empire; England; Ireland;
Scotland
Greece, ancient 90, 228; and
Judaism 24–9; philosophy in
24–9, 57–62, 219
Greek language 11, 18, 24–7,
30–31, 236; theological terms
26–7, 57–9, 73, 75–6, 81, 100,
107, 109, 111, 120, 135, 145,
180, 197, 221
see also Septuagint
Greek Orthodoxy: *see* Byzantine
Empire; Constantinople;
Orthodox Christianity
Gregorian Reform 105, 114–16,
160, 165, 197
see also Rome, Church of, Popes:
Gregory VII
Gregory of Nazianzus 79
Gregory of Nyssa 79

Quakers: *see* Friends, later Society
  of Friends
Quietism 157–60
Qumran community 258
Qur'an (Koran) 42

racism 202, 211
  see also anti-Semitism; apartheid;
  Nazi Party and Nazis
radical Reformation 140–50,
  178–84, 223, 245; in England
  144–50, 198–9
  see also Amish; Anabaptists;
  Family of Love; Friends, later
  Society of Friends; Libertines;
  Melchiorites; Mennonites;
  Ranters; Spirituals, radical;
  Unitarianism; Valdés, Juan de
radios and radio technology 211,
  217
Ranters 146–7, 168, 202
Raphael (Raffaello Sanzio da
  Urbino) 200
Ratisbon: *see* Regensburg, Colloquy
  of
Ratti, Achille: *see* Rome, Church of,
  Popes: Pius XI
reading aloud 93
reason of state 172
recusancy (Catholic) 175–8, 183–4,
  198–9
Red Sea 20
redemption: *see* soteriology
Reeves, Ambrose 189
Reformation, Protestant 68, 105–6,
  124–6, Ch. 6, 170–84, 198,
  222–3, 245, 264; and Anglicanism 232; character 128–44;
  magisterial Reformation 129,
  140–41, 148, 150, 179

see also Protestantism; radical
  Reformation; Reformed
  Protestantism
Reformations, three Ch. 5
Reformed Protestantism 129–40,
  178, 183, 195; *defined* 129; in
  England 136–9, 145, 177; in
  Germany 140, 208; in Hun-
  gary/Transylvania 133; and
  images 106–7
  see also Bucer, Martin; Bullinger,
  Heinrich; Calvin, John; Dutch
  Reformed Church; England:
  Church of; Geneva; Germany;
  Huguenots; iconoclasm and
  iconophobia; metrical psalms;
  Presbyterian Churches; Puritan-
  ism; Scotland; Strassburg;
  Switzerland; Vermigli, Pier-
  martire; Zürich
Regensburg (Ratisbon), Colloquy of
  174
Regula Magistri 271
regular clergy: *see* monks, monasteries and monasticism
relics 179
  see also Jesus Christ; shrines
Remembrance Day silence 231
Renaissance (14th-16th cents) 89,
  125–6, 264
  see also Carolingian Renaissance;
  humanism, Renaissance
reunion of Churches 174
  see also Regensburg, Colloquy of
Richelieu, *see* du Plessis, Armand
  Jean, Cardinal-duc de Richelieu
Riga 199
Robertson, Frederick William
  201, 203
Rollius, Nicholas 139–40